T0330827

Social Choice

First published in 1971, *Social Choice* is both a text and reference containing the proceedings of a conference dealing with contemporary work on the normative and descriptive aspects of the social choice problem. This reissue will be of interest to advanced undergraduate and graduate courses on group decision making and social choice. Economists, social psychologists, political scientists and sociologists will welcome this valuable work.

Social Choice

Edited by
Bernhardt Lieberman

First published in 1971
by Gordon and Breach, Science Publishers, Inc.

This edition first published in 2011 by Routledge
2 Park Square, Milton Park, Abingdon, Oxon, OX14 4RN

Simultaneously published in the USA and Canada
by Routledge
270 Madison Avenue, New York, NY 10016

Routledge is an imprint of the Taylor & Francis Group, an informa business

© 1971 Gordon and Breach, Science Publishers, Inc

All rights reserved. No part of this book may be reprinted or reproduced or utilised in
any form or by any electronic, mechanical, or other means, now known or hereafter
invented, including photocopying and recording, or in any information storage or
retrieval system, without permission in writing from the publishers.

Publisher's Note
The publisher has gone to great lengths to ensure the quality of this reprint but points
out that some imperfections in the original copies may be apparent.

Disclaimer
The publisher has made every effort to trace copyright holders and welcomes
correspondence from those they have been unable to contact.

A Library of Congress record exists under ISBN: 0677147708

ISBN 13: 978-0-415-61576-1 (hbk)
ISBN 13: 978-0-203-82954-7 (ebk)

SOCIAL CHOICE

Edited by

BERNHARDT LIEBERMAN

Professor of Social Psychology
in the Departments of Sociology and Psychology
University of Pittsburgh

GORDON AND BREACH   SCIENCE PUBLISHERS

New York   *London*   *Paris*

Copyright © *1971 by*
    Gordon and Breach, Science Publishers, Inc.
    440 Park Avenue South
    New York, N.Y. 10016

Editorial office for the United Kingdom
    Gordon and Breach, Science Publishers Ltd.
    12 Bloomsbury Way
    London W.C.1

Editorial office for France
    Gordon & Breach
    7–9 rue Emile Dubois
    Paris 14ᵉ

Library of Congress catalog card number 75–132954. ISBN 0 677 14770 8 (*cloth*)
0 677 14775 9 (*paper*). All rights reserved. No part of this book may be reproduced or
utilized in any form or by any means, electronic or mechanical, including photocopying,
recording, or by any information storage and retrieval system, without permission in
writing from the publishers. Printed in east Germany.

MONOGRAPHS AND TEXTS
IN THE BEHAVIORAL SCIENCES

This series consists of monographs, textbooks, and collections of papers each designed to contribute to interdisciplinary behavioral science. The monographs will report the results of research efforts; the textbooks will summarize the findings of some meaningful area of study in the behavioral sciences; and the collections of papers will bring together previously unpublished papers, or papers that have been published previously, but which need to be brought together in a single volume.

BERNHARDT LIEBERMAN

v

PREFACE

This volume presents the proceedings of a Conference on the Descriptive and Normative Aspects of Social Choice held at the University of Pittsburgh from September 9 through 13, 1968. The conference was held to bring together a number of investigators who were doing work designed to increase our understanding of collective decision processes. It was also designed to summarize the current state of work dealing with the descriptive aspects of the social choice problem, and to present some representative work currently being done on the normative aspect to the problem.

All but four of the papers in this volume were presented at the conference. James Coleman's paper (3.3) and my own (3.2) were included because they served to define the descriptive problems involved in making collective decisions; one of the purposes of this volume is to serve as an introduction to the descriptive aspects of the social choice problem and these two papers both serve that purpose. Donald Harnett's paper (4.7) was also published prior to the conference and was included because it is one of the earliest experimental studies that explicitly considers a collective decision situation. The paper by Richard and Lynne Ofshe (4.8) was not presented at the conference but was included because it presents a particularly interesting approach to the collective decision problem; one that combines somewhat diverse coalition and utility approaches.

The conference was supported by the National Institute of Mental Health (Grant Number MH 13942), The Office of Naval Research (Grant Number NONRG 00006-68), and the University of Pittsburgh; and we are indebted to these organizations for making the conference possible.

It is a pleasure to thank many people for help in the planning and conduct of the conference. R. Duncan Luce served as co-chairman of the conference and contributed to its planning, giving many excellent suggestions. His lucid and critical comments at the presentations of the papers served to stimulate the sessions. Lorraine Torres, Executive Secretary of the Behavioral Sciences Study Section of the National Institute of Mental Health and Dorwin Cartwright, a member of the Study Section, offered especially sympathetic understanding of the travails of a conference chairman, as did Luigi Petrullo, Bert King, and John Nagay of the Office of Naval Research. I am especially indebted to Susan Brown who served as conference administrator and who attended to the many details of the planning and the conduct of the conference.

I would also like to acknowledge the permission of *The American Journal of Sociology* to reprint James Coleman's article, "Foundations for a Theory of Collective Decisions"; the American Psychological Association publisher of the *Journal of Personality and Social Psychology* for permission to reprint Donald Harnett's article, "A Level of Aspiration Model of Group Decision Making"; and the University of Pittsburgh Press for permission to reprint my own article, "Combining Individual Preferences into a Social Choice" which appeared in *Game Theory and the Behavioral Sciences*, edited by Ira Buchler and Hugo Nutini.

BERNHARDT LIEBERMAN

INTRODUCTION

This volume is designed to serve a dual purpose; to present the proceedings of a Conference on the Descriptive and Normative Aspects of Social Choice, and also to serve as an introduction to work that has been done dealing with the problem of collective decisions. When a collection of two or more individuals must select one alternative from among two or more alternatives we have a social choice or collective decision situation. Individuals normally have preferences among alternatives; one person would like the group to select one alternative, while another person would like the group to select a different one. In some way the preferences must be combined or amalgamated to produce the group or social choice. In any group of people, in any society, social choices are constantly being made. Examples include the selection of the President of the United States, the selection of an automobile or a house by a husband and a wife, the election of a chairman of a university department, and the adoption of one of a number of resolutions in the Security Council of the United Nations—innumerable other examples could be offered.

The problem is so significant that it could not have escaped study by philosophers and economists, and indeed, by members of other disciplines. One of the earliest considerations of the problem—but probably not the earliest consideration, for certainly intellectual traditions other than western learning must have dealt with the topic—was by Aristotle in his discussion of distributive justice. Modern consideration of the problem started in the eighteenth century with the work of Condorcet and Borda. Work continued through the nineteenth century and one line of work culminated in the efforts of welfare economists to find a social welfare function—some method of producing a convincing or satisfactory aggregation mechanism, one that would produce a satisfactory selection of an alternative no matter how contradictory are the preference patterns of the participants.

Until very recently almost all work that was done dealt with this normative task, that of finding a satisfactory mechanism of amalgamation. A question just as significant was neglected: how do people actually resolve these questions—how do people actually amalgamate their preferences and produce a social choice? The literature dealing with the normative question, is much larger than that dealing with the descriptive question, hence the conference was held to stimulate the descriptive work, and this volume was produced.

Section 3 contains two papers that have already been published, one by James Coleman and a second by Bernhardt Lieberman. Both of these papers serve to define more clearly what the social choice problem is—or more accurately what the many problems are. Both the Coleman and Lieberman papers emphasize the descriptive aspects of the problem.

Section 4 contains papers that report the results of very recent research dealing with the various descriptive questions, while section 5 reports the results of studies of normative questions.

CONTENTS

SECTION 1

DEFINING THE PROBLEM

INTRODUCTORY DISCUSSION

The two papers of this section, which were written independently, serve as introductions to social choice problems. They are similar in certain ways, but are also somewhat different. Both briefly review the history of the normative social choice work, both contain discussions of the various descriptive problems involved in making collective decisions, and finally both offer some theoretical notions designed to describe how decisions are made. They contain discussions of power, utility, and interpersonal comparisons of utility. Coleman's paper offers an hypothesis about the interaction of power and utility, while Lieberman's paper hypothesizes that individuals maximize some joint welfare total; members of a group select the alternative that yields the highest payoff to the group.

COMBINING INDIVIDUAL PREFERENCES INTO A SOCIAL CHOICE

BERNHARDT LIEBERMAN

University of Pittsburgh

How persons in interaction combine their individual preference patterns into a social choice is a fundamental question about which there has been much speculation, and an amount of mathematical work; but there have been few, if any, empirical studies dealing directly with the question.[1] The problem is ubiquitous; examples abound. The eleven members of the Security Council of the United Nations must decide to take or not take some action; a president of the United States must be selected from the millions of eligible citizens, but particularly from the dozen or so likely possibilities; a university research institute must plan a research program that will interest its members who have diverse preferences and satisfy its sources of support; consumer goods must be produced and distributed to satisfy the preferences of millions of consumers; Congress must apportion the $ 50 billion defense budget among the Army, Navy, Air Force, and Marines; and a family must decide whether it is to live in the city or a suburb. All of these diverse decisions have something in common: In some way the preferences of different individuals or groups must be summed up or amalgamated into a social or group choice.

Societies, groups, and organizations have produced a variety of decision-making procedures: the majority vote with veto power; the majority vote without veto power; the economic market mechanism; the dictatorial father who decides unilaterally where the family shall live; bargaining and persuasion among the Joint Chiefs of Staff; the advisers to the Secretary of Defense who use techniques of modern mathematical economics; the executive committee or governing board that reaches a consensus and imposes its decisions on a larger group; and the system of primary elections and conventions for the selection of the presidential candidates. Group decisions are made in these and many other ways.[2]

SOME BRIEF HISTORICAL REMARKS

Mathematical work dealing with these election and social choice problems appears to have had its origin in the second half of the eighteenth century in the work of Borda and Condorcet. An anomalous situation, which has been termed variously the paradox of voting or the Condorcet effect, has intrigued thinkers for almost two hundred years. Its fascination stems from the fact that it illustrates that the very structure of a social choice situation can produce a perplexing or disturbing result. Consider the following situation.[3]

Let 1, 2, 3 be three alternatives; let A, B, C be three individuals and let (A, B, C) be the community. Let $1 > 2$ mean 1 is preferred to 2. If for A, $1 > 2, 2 > 3$, and we assume transitivity, then $1 > 3$. Similarly for B, if $2 > 3, 3 > 1$ then $2 > 1$. For C, if $3 > 1, 1 > 2$ then $3 > 2$. Since a majority, A and C, prefer 1 to 2, and a majority, A and B, prefer 2 to 3, we would hope that a majority also prefers 1 to 3. But this is not the case, since B and C prefer 3 to 1.

This perplexing situation becomes more vivid if we consider an analogue of it, the following game, where side payments, payoffs among players, are not allowed. The game is described by the following payoff matrix.

Alternative	Payoff to		
	A	B	C
1	30	10	20
2	20	30	10
3	10	20	30

In this situation, the three players, A, B, and C must select a single alternative from among 1, 2, and 3. If they choose 1, A receives 30 dollars (or jobs if the payoff is patronage in a political situation), B receives 10, and C receives 20. If alternative 2 is chosen, A receives 20, B receives 30, and C receives 10. If they choose 3, A receives 10, B receives 20, and C receives 30. Examining this situation, we can see that A prefers 1, B prefers 2, and C prefers 3. Since side-payments are not allowed, there is nothing in the structure of the situation that will enable the three participants to come to some agreement about the selection of the alternative. If side-payments were permitted, the three could agree on alternative 1, for example, and A could give B a payment of 10; there would then be an equal division of the rewards, one possible and common outcome. The situation is indeed perplexing, and nothing in its structure gives a clue to its solution. As we have defined the situation, even the decision-rule is not specified; we have not said whether a majority vote or a unanimous choice is required to select the alternative.

Another possible way of obtaining a group choice in this situation would be to present two of the three alternatives, have the three players choose the one they prefer, and then have them compare the third alternative with the alternative they preferred from the first pair. However, if this is done, the order of presentation of alternatives will effect the outcome. For example, if 2 and 3 are compared first, 2 will be preferred by a majority. Then, if 2 is compared to 1, 1 will be preferred by the majority and will be the group choice. If, however, the first pair considered is 1 and 3, and then 2 is compared with the survivor, the group choice will be 2. For theorists seeking a rational, universal social choice procedure, the fact that the order of presentation of alternatives effects the outcome is highly unsatisfactory.

Situations such as this and similar aberrant situations helped to stimulate mathematicians to investigate the formal properties of election processes. The general problem the theorists attempted to solve can be stated as," How can we design an election procedure that will produce a result consistent with the preference patterns of the participants? How can we design an election procedure so that the order of the presentation of alternatives does not spuriously determine the outcome? How can we assure ourselves that the 'wrong' candidate is not selected?" Borda, Condorcet, Laplace, Francis Galton, C. L. Dodgson (Lewis Carroll) and others have considered the problem.[4]

In the late nineteenth century, and in this century, economists set themselves the task of discovering a social welfare function, a general rule or process by which any given set of individual preference patterns could be merged into a social choice. For the purpose of this discussion, the social welfare function can be defined as follows.[5]

Social welfare function—a rule or process which produces a group or social choice from the individual orderings of alternatives or from the preferences of the individuals involved. The rule must produce a satisfactory social choice, in every case, not matter how contradictory the preferences of the individuals involved.

In a work that has since become classic, Arrow (1963) demonstrated that given a number of reasonable conditions about the choice structure, where there are at least two persons involved and three or more alternatives to choose from, it is not possible to construct a general social welfare function. He also demonstrated that where the alternatives are limited to two, no matter how many persons are involved, the majority decision rule is a satisfactory social welfare function. Arrow's work served as a stimulus to a variety of theoretical studies of the normative question.

THE NORMATIVE AND THE DESCRIPTIVE PROBLEMS

The problem of combining individual preferences into a social choice has both normative and descriptive aspects. The normative question is, briefly, how *should* we combine individual preferences to obtain sensible, consistent, or rational results? The descriptive question is, essentially, how *do* individuals, groups, and economists actually amalgamate their preferences?

For two reasons it seems appropriate to raise the descriptive question. First, Arrow has shown that, if we allow only ordinal measurement or ranking, it is not possible to obtain a general social welfare function. But the fact that Arrow has demonstrated the impossibility of the abstract task does not prevent individuals from actually merging their preferences. Each day innumerable decisions of this kind are arrived at. In fact, attempts to circumvent the Arrow paradox raise behavioral or descriptive questions. Luce and Raiffa (1957) discuss a number of ways of overcoming the difficulties presented by Arrow. These include obtaining more data about the values or preferences of the participants. This process involves utilizing behavioral scaling methods, and also gives some information about the strengths of preferences of the participants. Where we can obtain measures of the strengths of preferences by utilizing risky alternatives, lotteries, and well-established behavioral scaling techniques, we can often obtain a satisfactory resolution of difficult social decision questions (Luce and Raiffa 1957:ch. 14).

Consider the following example of two persons, A and B, and two alternatives, 1 and 2. A ranks the alternatives 1, 2; B ranks the alternatives 2, 1. If we assume that neither party has sufficient power to determine the outcome, the preference structures lead to a stalemate, an irreconcilable conflict. However, if we can take into consideration the strengths of preferences of the participants, the following example makes it clear how trivial the case can be. Consider the case of a husband and wife who are considering going to a movie (1) or a concert (2). The husband prefers 2, the wife prefers 1. If the husband's preference of 2 over 1 is only slight, but the wife's preference is very great—she actively dislikes the music being performed on that night—in all likelihood, the conflict will be resolved in favor of going to the movie, and with relatively little effort and ill-feeling.

Even this example reveals that people in actual social decision situations have a variety of techniques for resolving difficult problems of social choice. The resolutions may or may not be optimal or particularly rational, but it is of considerable interest to examine the techniques carefully.

RELATIONSHIP TO PSYCHOLOGY AND ANTHROPOLOGY

For some time now, psychologists have seen the realtionship of the issues raised here to their attempts to describe and explain human behavior. Anthropologists, however, have been slow to see the relevance of such problems to their own work, and so it is worthwhile to make that relevance explicit. These problems undoubtedly have bearing on the intellectual activity of anthropologists, both to those doing what may be called traditional anthropology—qualitative, holistic studies of social groups or societies—and to those anthropologists who are doing more behavioral, quantitative studies.

The point has certainly been made before that the traditions and customs of any social group or society serve, among other functions, that of conflict resolution. Most conflicts in a social group contain some element of conflict of interest or, in the terms of this analysis, conflicting preference patterns. The traditions and customs of both Western and non-Western societies prevent conflicts from arising that stem from contradictory preference patterns, and are, therefore, conflict resolution mechanisms. These conflicts may exist in many domains of behavior: the economic domain, the family-personal domain, the domain of permissible sexual behavior, and the domain of political behavior.

Incest taboos may be interpreted as quite successful attempts to prevent family members from expressing their sexual preferences for each other. The assignment of certain economic activities to certain families or subgroups of a particular society serves to prevent other members of the society from expressing their preferences for desirable occupations, with the resultant economic conflict. Established matrilocal or patrilocal residence patterns avoid the conflicts that might arise among newlyweds about where they are to reside, should they have conflicting personal preferences about the matter. Many of our traditions or customs could have arisen out of a need to resolve conflicts that are seen to be either inevitable or very likely.

The research that could be done using the methods of analysis employed here should be of interest to anthropologists. Indeed, they have been doing this kind of research for quite some time, without the benefits that quantitative analysis yields. Some cross-cultural research on methods of conflict resolution has been done by social psychologists working, generally, with literate Western societies. It would be of considerable value to look at the conflict resolution mechanisms of non-Western societies and national groups.[6]

The notion of maximization provides us with an important, provocative problem, one that may stimulate an amount of interesting cross-cultural research. The theory of games and the literature dealing with social choice involve the assumption that individuals behave in such a way as to maximize some value, either monetary payoff or a utility of some kind. The decision-making literature indicates that this assumption is not wholly realistic or descriptive of behavior in our Western culture, but at the same time the evidence is such that we cannot deny that some notion of maximization, or action in one's interest, is characteristic of much human behavior. Thus the degree to to which the maximization notion is an adequate descriptive or explanatory principle is an unanswered question. An even more provocative and stimulating question is the degree to which a maximization notion is descriptive of nonliterate groups. Cross-cultural research using situations such as the Condorcet paradox, two-person games, and three-person games involving coalitions should yield fascinating results.

HOW DECISIONS ARE ACTUALLY MADE

In the discussion above we saw that Arrow demonstrated that given certain reasonable conditions, it is not possible to obtain a general social welfare function; but we also saw an example of a husband and wife who, with little effort, were able to make a satisfactory social choice, although they had contradictory preference patterns, by taking into account each other's strengths of preference.

Difficulties arise when preference patterns are contradictory. Often but not always, persons involved in making a choice have consistent preference patterns that enable them to make a large number of group choices with little difficulty. In addition, persons who cluster together often have similar preference patterns over a wide range of choice domains prior to their interaction in a group. As they function together and interact, their prefer- ence patterns become more similar, resulting in a large number of social choices that are made with little difficulty.[7] However, many situations yield a constellation of preference patterns that lead to disagreement about social choice, and it is these perplexing situations that present the intellectual and practical challenges.

The conduct of international affairs provides us with situations in which numerous anomalous and paradoxical preference patterns exist. It is often difficult in international affairs to make side-payments. Husbands and wives, political leaders in a legislature, faculty members in a university department, and the employees of complex organizations often have many ways in which they can bargain, negotiate, and effect side-payments—ways that enable them to effect satisfactory social choices in difficult situations. But in the conduct of international affairs the fundamental interests of the participants are often in intractable conflict, and internal constraints— national politics—may operate on the leaders to prevent them from striking what might be desirable bargains.

If we examine just how group decisions are arrived at, we may note that a variety of behavioral processes or factors influence the outcome. These vary from the power of the various members—for a single member of the group may have sufficient power to determine the group choice—to the strength of preferences of the participants and the personality and intellectual characteristics of those involved. We will discuss the various determining behavioral processes under the following headings.

1. The distribution of power
2. The joint welfare function
3. Bargaining and coalition processes
4. Individual differences and characteristics of the participants
5. Group processes and phenomena
6. Previous experiences and commitments of the group members, and the possibility of future interaction

The distribution of power

In many situations the social choice is effected rather simply and directly. A single person has the power to determine the decision, and where the preference patterns of those involved are contradictory or anomalous, he exercises that power. The dictatorial father who decides where the family shall live; the president of a small college who makes an appointment when his deans and faculty cannot agree; the president of a small company who holds 51 per cent of the stock of the company and who makes a decision by himself when his employees are in hopeless disagreement—all these are examples of the exercise of dictatorial power.[8]

At the opposite extreme from the situation of dictatorial power is a situation in which power is equally distributed among all participants involved in the decision process. Perhaps the most vivid and detailed example of such a situation is the election described in C. P. Snow's novel, *The Master*. Snow describes in detail the bargaining, personal preferences, unconscious processes, and other considerations that exist when a group of eleven men, all with equal power and the desire to exercise it, produce a social choice.

However, in most decision situations the power is not so simply distributed among the participants in the decision; in the large number of social choice situations power is neither equally divided among all participants nor does a single person hold sufficient power to determine the decision. More often power is diffused among participants, with some having a great deal, others having very little, and some having a moderate amount. Often the exact distribution of power among those involved is not known even to the participants. Each has some approximate estimation of the power distribution, but the distribution of power may be only imprecisely defined, and judgments about relative power may differ.

To obtain an understanding of how social choices are made, it is necessary to clarify the role of power in the decision process. Although there have been many interesting speculative analyses of power in the sociological literature, little of it sheds useful light on the social choice problem.[9] Recently, however, the literature of game theory has produced some insightful notions that bear directly on the processes of social choice. Subsequent sections of this paper will deal with the distribution and role of power among a group of persons who must effect a social choice. Shapley's ideas (Shapley 1953), as well as those of Shapley and Shubik (1952), will be discussed; their notion of power is termed σ-power here. A notion of power, termed δ-power will be introduced which will emphasize the participants' perception of their own power to influence the decision process.

σ-Power Shapley and Shubik have offered a method for evaluating the distribution of power in social choice situations where a specific decision must be made and the voting power of each participant is known. A committee in which each member has a single vote, the Security Council of the United Nations where the major powers have a veto, and a corporation

where the power is distributed according to the ownership of stock are examples of bodies in which such situations occur.

The notion of power, which is termed σ-power here, attempts to solve the problem that is raised by the fact that power is not always distributed exactly as votes are distributed. When one man holds 51 per cent of the stock in a corporation, for many purposes he holds complete power, and the decision processes of such a group usually reflect this reality. The persons involved usually defer to the power-holder. They attempt to influence decisions by influencing the majority stockholder. In the situation in which each person has a single vote the σ-power distribution is identical to the distribution of votes. In a group of four persons, where the votes are distributed 10-5-5-1, the person holding the ten has more than 50 per cent of the power, though his votes total less than 50 per cent of the total.

Shapley and Shubik offer a definition of power in which the power of each member of a decision-making group depends on the chance he has of being crucial to the success of a winning coalition; the chance he has of effecting a winning coalition. Hence, where one man is a winning coalition he has complete power; where each person has a single vote, each has equal σ-power. In situations between these extremes, the power distribution is not so clear, and the calculation of σ-power is more subtle.

The Shapley and Shubik definition of power does not take into consideration the many personal, political, and sociological factors that affect any analysis of power in an actual social choice but, as they point out, their scheme is a very useful first approximation of the actual power distribution in a committee or group situation. They explain the general rationale for their definitions of power as follows:

Consider a group of individuals all voting on some issue. They vote in order and, as soon as a majority has voted for a resolution, it is declared passed. The voting order of the members is chosen randomly and it is possible to compute the frequency with which an individual belongs to the group whose votes are used to effect the decisions; and more importantly, it is possible to compute how often the person's vote is pivotal. The number of times the person is pivotal, yields the index of σ-power. This index yields a measure of the number of times the action of an individual affects the decision, changing the state of affairs of the group. The Shapley and Shubik scheme credits an individual with $1/n$th power where there are n persons, each holding one vote. If votes are weighted unequally, the resulting power distribution is complicated. Generally more votes mean more power, but σ-power does not increase in direct proportion to an increase in votes.

Considering the passage of a bill in our executive-congressional system, the σ-power of the House of Representatives, the Senate, and the President are in the proportion of $5:5:2$; and the σ-power indices for a single congressman, single senator, and the President are in the proportion $2:9:350$. In the U. N. Security Council, which consists of eleven members, five of whom have vetoes, the σ-power measure gives 98.7 per cent to the Big Five and 1.3 per cent to the six small powers. Each major nation has a power ratio greater than 90 to 1 over a single smaller nation. A share owner in a corporation, who holds 40 per cent of the stock with the remaining 60 per cent distributed equally among 600 small share owners has a power index of 66.6 per cent. The $400:1$ ratio in share holdings yields a power advantage greater than 1,000 to 1.[10]

It is quite clear that this very precise measure of power in a committee system is only an approximation of the realities of the decision process in social choice situations. As a result, it is necessary to introduce another concept, δ-power, which is designed to describe the power distribution the participants in a decision process actually act upon.

δ-*Power*   In some committees or social decision situations, where the decision-rules and voting weights are explicitly formulated, the σ-power index can serve as an excellent first approximation of the actual distribution of power among the participants. When the appropriate historical, sociological, and psychological analysis is done, it is possible to obtain a realistic picture of the role power plays in effecting the social choice. However, in a large number of social choice situations decision mechanisms are not explicitly defined, and the participants behave on the basis of their own beliefs about, or their own perceptions of, their power. Understanding these phenomena is essentially the understanding of a set of beliefs, a social-psychological process. Any analysis of a complex social choice process, where the power mechanisms are not explicitly defined, requires this analysis of the δ-power distribution—an analysis of the participants' beliefs about their own power to influence the decision.

The σ-power and δ-power analyses are not unrelated, for in the dictatorship situation and in the situation of equal or nearly equal distribution of power, the participants ordinarily have reasonably accurate perceptions of their power. In the former situation the persons involved usually attempt to effect the decision by influencing the powerful person; in the latter situation the persons involved are usually aware that their power is $1/n$th of the total. In the situations between these two extremes, where it takes some effort to compute the σ-power distribution even when we know the Shapley formula, the most confusion occurs, and the participants may be confused or uncertain about their power.

In complex organizations, this complex and indefinite power situation is often present. Two, three, ten, or even more people may share the power to determine a decision. A detailed analysis of the facts of the situation and the perceptions and beliefs of the participants is necessary to untangle the threads of the power relations.

The joint welfare function

In the example of the husband and wife who had contradictory preference patterns, we saw that the conflict was solved simply and directly. This resolution was made possible because the husband perceived that his wife had a strong distaste for alternative 2 and a strong preference for alternative 1, while he had only a slight preference for 2 over 1. Difficult social choices may be resolved by taking into account the strengths of preferences of the participants. A decision process that allows a single group member to veto a proposal makes explicit use of the belief that a single, strong negative preference should be allowed to outweigh all other positive preferences. The veto provisions of the U. N. Security Council voting procedures and the ability to veto entrance into membership into college fraternities and adult social clubs are examples of this process.

When this technique is used and persons involved in the social choice process take into account the strength of preferences of other participants, it becomes clear that some intuitive process involving interpersonal comparisons of utility is involved. We may hypothesize that the decision process is one in which some *Joint Welfare Total* is maximized. Where a difficult social choice decision is made, we hypothesize that intuitive interpersonal comparisons of utilities are made.[11]

If we examine the husband-wife decision to go to the movie in these terms, the following analysis may shed light on the decision. We assign the following utilities to the situation.

Alternative	Payoff to		Joint Payoff
	H	W	Sum
1	8	10	18
2	10	−30	−20

If the couple goes to the movie—alternative 1 is selected—the payoff to the group is 18 whereas if they go to the concert—select alternative 2—the payoff to the group is -20.

It is possible to develop a more sophisticated line of reasoning using a simple algebraic model suggested by Sawyer.[12] We have hypothesized that a group tends to select the outcome that offers the highest joint welfare total (JWT). The JWT may be computed as follows:

Let individuals be designated A, B, ..., Z.
The payoffs to the individuals are P_a, P_b, ..., P_z.
The alternatives to be chosen from are designated 1, 2, ..., n.
The payoff to the set of individuals for the various alternatives are designated P_{a1}, P_{a2}, ..., P_{zn}.

A payoff to another person may not have the same value to oneself as an equal payment to oneself. This may be expressed in the model by assuming that a payoff to another person is some fraction or multiple of the payoff to oneself. Then the parameters that reduce a payment to another to a payment to oneself may be designated:

$$x_{ab}, x_{ac}, \ldots, x_{ba}, x_{bc}, \ldots, x_{zx}, x_{zy}$$

where x_{ab} is the fraction that transforms a payment to B into a payment to A.

The members of a group that is faced with a decision communicate among themselves, and in this process they are able to communicate to each other— in some intuitive or perhaps explicit way—the utilities of the various alternatives to each other. Once these communications are possessed by the members of the group, some intuitive multi-person, interpersonal comparison of utilities process occurs. Discussions, bargaining, clarifications, and the like occur, and then the group choice is made.

We are now in a position to examine how a group of individuals may determine the JWT of the various alternatives from which they must select a group choice. Consider the example of the payoff matrix presented on page 96. The JWT's may be computed once the parameters are hypothesized.[13] If, for person A, a payoff to another person is worth one half of a payment to himself, then $x_{ab} = x_{ac} = 0.5$; and if for person B, a payoff to another is worth just as much as a payoff to himself, then $x_{ba} = x_{bc} = 1$; and if for C, a payoff to another is worth only one-one hundredth of a payment to himself, then $x_{ca} = x_{cb} = 0.01$. The JWT's can be computed using the following formulas:

$$\text{JWT (Alt. 1)} = P_{a1} + (x_{ab}P_{b1} + x_{ac}P_{c1}) + P_{b1} + (x_{ba}P_{a1} + x_{bc}P_{c1})$$
$$+ P_{c1} + (x_{ca}P_{a1} + x_{cb}P_{b1})$$
$$\text{JWT (Alt. 2)} = P_{a2} + (x_{ab}P_{b2} + x_{ac}P_{c2}) + P_{b2} + (x_{ba}P_{a2} + x_{bc}P_{c2})$$
$$+ P_{c2} + (x_{ca}P_{a2} + x_{cb}P_{b2})$$
$$\text{JWT (Alt. 3)} = P_{a3} + (x_{ab}P_{b3} + x_{ac}P_{c3}) + P_{b3} + (x_{ba}P_{a3} + x_{bc}P_{c3})$$
$$+ P_{c3} + (x_{ca}P_{a3} + x_{cb}P_{b3})$$

Substituting the values of the first payoff matrix and the values of $x_{ab}, x_{ac}, \ldots, x_{cb}$ we can compute the value of JWT (Alt. 1):

$$\text{JWT (Alt. 1)} = 30 + [0.5(10 + 20)] + 10$$
$$+ [1(30 + 20)] + 20 + [0.01(30 + 10)] = 125.4$$

Similarly:

$$\text{JWT (Alt. 2)} = 110.5 \quad \text{and} \quad \text{JWT (Alt. 3)} = 125.3$$

Since the Joint Welfare Totals of Alt. 1 and Alt. 3 are approximately equal and larger than the Total of Alt. 2, we hypothesize that it is unlikely that Alt. 2 will be chosen. The probabilities of choosing Alt. 1 and Alt. 3 are approximately equal. However, the arguments concerning the JWT's are but one factor of the many that determine a social choice. For the simple example of the husband and wife who had to choose between the concert and the movie, the maximization of JWT appears to be an adequate hypothesis. In other more complex decision situations, the many factors dealt with in this paper may modify the decision. For example, where one person has the power to determine the decision, he may select the alternative that maximizes the payoff to himself, though another alternative might have a higher JWT. Some other relevant factors will be discussed below.

Bargaining and coalition formation

When persons must combine contradictory preferences into a social choice in situations in which the power distribution does not permit a single individual to determine the outcome, the process is successfully completed usually because the participants are able to bargain, negotiate, form coalitions, compromise, and make side-payments among themselves. The social choice situation in a realistic setting is ordinarily complex enough so that the persons involved may effect a satisfactory social choice by producing an outcome that yields some rewards to each participant who holds some power. This procedure of dividing the rewards of the social choice situation is analogous to the payoff function—and the phenomenon of making side-payments—of game theory. In fact, in the earlier explication of the Condorcet effect, the ordinal statements of the original paradox were transformed into a game-like statement, assuming cardinal measures of the utilities.

Thus, the theory of games of strategy may be seen to be a theory for the production of social choices among individuals with different preference patterns. Payoff functions are the ways of expressing the preference patterns of the persons involved; the person prefers the outcome with the largest payoff to himself, or in the case of the non-zero-sum game, the alternative with the highest Joint Welfare Total.

Game theory has both descriptive and normative aspects. The entire corpus of solution theory may be considered prescriptions for the production of reasonable social choices. Two-person, zero-sum theory prescribes a reasonable value of a game when the parties involved are in direct conflict. In two-person, non-zero-sum, and *n*-person theory, solutions—to the extent that they are successful—prescribe the social choices the parties should make when elements of conflict and cooperation are both present.

In a series of papers, Thomas Schelling has offered some hypotheses concerning bargaining processes and has related them to choices, decisions, and strategies in the conduct of international affairs. Schelling is primarily responsible for an entire reorientation of game theory, from the zero-sum, non-zero-sum orientation to one in which social choices are viewed as being on a continuum, from pure coordination through mixed motive games to pure conflict games. Schelling has offered a variety of provocative hypotheses about the role of communication, bargaining, threats, promises, and a variety of other behavioral phenomena. Schelling's work can also be interpreted as offering hypotheses concerning certain social choice problems (Schelling 1960).

Since most social choices can be effected only if coalitions are formed, processes of coalition formation must be understood if an understanding of social choice mechanisms is to be obtained. Gamson (1964: 81 – 110) recently reviewed experimental studies of coalition formation and found "an encouraging convergence of theoretical explanations of coalition formation." He discusses four "theories" of coalition formation: a minimum resource theory, a minimum power theory, an anticompetitive theory, and an utter confusion theory.

The minimum resource theory "emphasizes the initial resources to effect a decision which the players bring to the situation, rather than their strategic bargaining position." The central hypothesis states that a coalition will form in which the total resources (weights or votes) are as small as possible, while still being sufficient to effect a decision favorable to the coalition that has formed (Gamson 1964 : 86).

The minimum power theory is a modification of the minimum resource theory. It makes use of the Shapley value and states that all participants will demand a share of the payoff proportional to their pivotal power (σ-power). This pivotal power hypothesis is again a minimum resource hypothesis, but in this case the power of the winning coalition is defined by the Shapley value, σ-power (Gamson 1964 : 88).

Gamson (1964:90) describes a hypothesis about the formation of coalitions derived from the work of Vinacke and his associates. Players whose behavior supports the anticompetitive hypothesis are focused on maintaining the social relationships in the group. An anticompetitive norm exists against efforts to strike the most advantageous deal possible. Coalitions will form along the lines of least resistance.

The fourth hypothesis is an "utter confusion theory" (Gamson 1964:92):

"Many coalition situations are conducted under conditions which are not at all conducive to rational calculation and analysis. It is well known that political conventions, for example, are frequently scenes of bedlam. Thus, according to this theory, coalition formation is best understood as an essentially random choice process. The coalition which forms will be the result of such fortuitous events as a chance encounter or a missed telephone call."

Individual differences

When individuals actually are attempting to merge their preferences into a social choice, the characteristics of the individuals undoubtedly play some role. It is possible to hypothesize that certain cognitive-intellective factors such as intelligence, bargaining ability, and persuasiveness do have an effect. Some people may be particularly skillful bargainers, or particularly skillful in the task of persuasion, and they may effect a social choice in their favor. Also, certain personality factors may affect outcomes: a more aggressive person may be more effective in causing the outcome to be favorable to himself. Even though at this time it is not possible to specify what particular factors or individual characteristics do affect outcomes, there is every reason to believe, a priori, that individual characteristics do affect outcomes.

2*

The few studies that have been done that have attempted to examine the effect of individual differences on bargaining and negotiation behavior have been rather disappointing.[14] Undoubtedly, individual differences do affect the outcomes of bargaining processes; however, until now it has been diffi-cult to specify precisely what individual characteristics affect outcomes in a particular way. This is probably because our studies of individual differences, though there are many of them, have not isolated significant factors that affect bargaining behavior. It may also be that the part played by individual differences may be small and may be masked by the formal, structural pro-perties of the bargaining situations.[15]

Group processes

The extensive literature of the field of small groups bears upon the present analysis, which deals with the summation of individual preferences of mem-bers of a small group. Although the literature is uncoordinated and contains few, if any, general principles that further our understanding of the processes of social choice, numerous studies yield isolated results that are relevant to the present problem. Vinacke and Arkoff (1957: 406–14) and Liebermann (1962: 203–20) found that in cases of three-person interaction two indivi-duals may unite and form a coalition against a third whom they perceive as stronger in order to gain rewards from the stronger-appearing person. Schel-ling, too, has argued that in a bargaining situation the weaker member may gain concessions from the stronger because the two have coordinate interests and the stronger must yield concessions to the weaker (Schelling 1960).

Careful review of the small group literature would undoubtedly reveal other studies that describe phenomena and characteristics of individuals functioning in a group situation which will shed light on social choice pro-cesses. These many phenomena considered together may detail a picture that is not particularly elegant or simple, but then it is likely that an under-standing of the processes of social choice, when we obtain it, will not be simple or elegant either.

Past and future commitments

One set of processes that undoubtedly have great influence on the social choice problem, but have been virtually unstudied, are the processes involv-ing the effect of past commitments and decisions, and anticipations of the effect of future social choice situations and commitments on the present problem. Difficult social choice situations, where preference patterns are hopelessly contradictory, may be resolved because of the past experience of the group, or because those members of the group who have their preferences satisfied can make commitments about future social choices, making concessions or promises in advance.[16]

The group in an actual social choice situation is usually one with a significant past history and with the prospect of a continued lengthy existence. This feature often enables the participants to make a difficult social choice but is particularly difficult to study experimentally and even empirically. However, a thorough treatment of the question of social choice must deal with such questions.

CONCLUSION

The general problem raised in this paper, that of understanding the processes involved when a group of individuals must amalgamate their preferences to produce a social choice, has been seen to be a very general and complex one. It will be very difficult to study all its aspects in a single empirical or experimental study; actually the problem reduces to a number of subproblems, about which some evidence and knowledge already exists. This evidence comes from studies of bargaining and coalition processes, theoretical discussions of the interpersonal comparison of utilities, and theoretical and empirical studies of the role of power in decision processes.

The particular way this paper analyzes the general problem is, of course, not the only way it can be conceptualized. The rubrics under which the various discussions were organized were used primarily because they were convenient and, to some extent, convincing. Further analyses and study may very well yield another, equally convincing, but somewhat different organization. For example, the entire discussion of the interpersonal comparison of utility might very well have been subsumed under the discussion of individual differences. The parameters hypothesized may account for much of the variance involved in social choice processes, and these parameters may reflect stable characteristics of individuals and differ significantly among individuals.

At any rate, when our understanding of social choice processes is deepened and organized, it is likely that a complex picture of many factors operating, and operating with interactions among them, will emerge. As already stated, it does not matter how some persons value a payoff to others in a group if the others have the power to determine the group decision. To understand such a social choice it is necessary to understand the preference patterns of the powerful members of the group and how the less powerful members influence the decision-makers. Carefully done experimental and empirical studies are necessary to develop an understanding of social choice processes.

NOTES

1 Before preparing the initial draft of this paper, I was not able to find any theoretical discussions of the descriptive questions involved, and only one empirical study. After I had distributed copies of the draft, Professor Harrison White told me of Professor James Coleman's current work on the problem. Coleman's ideas can be found in his "Collective Decisions," *Sociological Inquiry* (Spring 1964), pp. 166–81; "Foundations for a Theory of Collective Decisions," *Amer. Journal of Sociology*, 71 (May 1966), pp. 615–27. "The Possibility of a Social Welfare Function", mimeo., Johns Hopkins University, November 1964. There are some similarities between Professor Coleman's and my own work, though he has taken a somewhat different—more normative—approach. The one empirical study is Clyde Coombs, "Social Choice and Strength of Preference," in R. M. Thrall, C. H. Coombs, and R. L. Davis, eds., *Decision Processes*, New York: Wiley, 1954. This paper offers the thesis that a considerable body of work done in other contexts can be interpreted to be related to the social choice question.

2 Two different problems have been mixed together in this introductory discussion: social choices in large groups such as national elections, and social choices in small groups or committees. The ideas presented in this paper are relevant to decision-making by small groups and committees. Since the literature, until now, has dealt with the normative question, it was really not necessary to make this distinction. However, the empirical processes involved in elections, where *n* is large, and in decisions by small groups are obviously quite different.

3 For a discussion of the history of the general problem and the Condorcet effect see: Arrow (1963); Luce and Raiffa (1957:ch. 14); Duncan Black, *The Theory of Committees and Elections*, Cambridge: Cambridge U. Press, 1958; and William H. Riker, "Voting and the Summation of Preferences," *Amer. Political Science Rev.*, 55 (December 1961), pp. 900–11.

4 See the references in note 3, especially Black, for discussion of the contribution of each of these men.

5 This definition is not rigorous but will serve for the present discussion. For a rigorous definition see Arrow (1963 : 23). p. 23.

6 I am aware of two articles in the anthropology literature that make use of the notions discussed here. They are: Frederik Barth, "Segmentary Opposition and the Theory of Games: A Study of Pathan Organization," *J. of the Royal Anthropological Inst.*,

89: 5–21; and William Davenport, "Jamaican Fishing, A Game Theory Analysis," in *Papers on Caribbean Anthropology* (Yale U. Publications in Anthropology Nos. 57–64) 59, pp. 3–4.

7 It seems worthwhile to make this obvious point because the social choice literature seems to concern itself only with preference patterns leading to conflict. Of course, these are the provocative situations.

8 The terms dictatorship and dictatorial power are used here, as they are in the social choice literature, with no opprobrium or other value judgement attached.

9 For other discussions of power see: Robert Bierstedt, "An Analysis of Social Power," *Amer. Sociological Rev.*, 15 (December 1950), pp. 730–36; Amitai Etzioni, *Modern Organizations*, Englewood Cliffs: Prentice-Hall, 1964; Herbert Goldhamer and Edward Shils, "Types of Power and Status," *Amer. Sociological Rev*, 45 (September 1939), pp. 171–82; John R. P. French, Jr., "A Formal Theory of Social Power," *Psychological Rev.*, 63 (May 1956), pp. 181–94; Harold D. Lasswell and Abraham Kaplan, *Power and Society*, New Haven: Yale U. Press, 1950; John C. Harsanyi, "Measurement of Social Power in *n*-Person Reciprocal Power Situations," *Behavioral Science* 7 (January 1962), pp. 81–91. The empirical work most directly related to the ideas expressed here has been done by Edgar Vinacke and his students and colleagues. A number of studies have been done dealing with power and coalition formation in three-person groups. References can be found in George Psathas and Sheldon Stryker, "Bargaining Behavior and Orientations in Coalition Formation," *Sociometry*, 28 (June 1965), pp. 124–44.

10 This discussion follows the Shapley and Shubik presentation very closely. For further discussion of these ideas see Shapley and Shubik (1952: 787–91).

11 A word seems to be in order about the frank use here of interpersonal comparisons of cardinal utilities. It is generally agreed that we have no satisfactory formal treatment of cardinal utilities that will enable us to make rigorous statements about interpersonal comparisons of the utilities. However, this paper contends that it is profitable to hypothesize that individuals do make intuitive, interpersonal comparisons of the various alternatives facing them, and that these comparisons serve as one determinant of many social choices. Specifically the hypothesis offered is that a joint welfare total is maximized. It is also possible, I believe, that this hypothesis can, with a bit of effort, be confirmed or refuted by experimental and empirical work. Discussion of the problem can be found in Luce and Raiffa (1957: 33, 131, 345); John C. Harsanyi, "Cardinal Welfare, Individualistic Ethics and Interpersonal Comparisons of Utility," *Jl. Political Economy*, 63 (1955), pp. 309–21; Clifford Hildreth, "Alternative Conditions for Social Orderings," *Econometrica*, 21 (1953), pp. 81–94; and John C. Harsanyi, "Cardinal Utility in Welfare Economics and in the Theory of Risk-Taking" *Jl. Political Economy* 61 (1953), pp. 434–35.
Discussions of the problem of interpersonal comparisons of utility are complex and contradictory. To compound the confusion, a group of statisticians identified as "Bayesian Statisticians" have recently advanced arguments that imply—if they do not explicitly state—that individuals are able or can be taught to make interpersonal comparisons of cardinal utilities. The root of the difficulty lies in the fact that our rigorous knowledge of the measurement of behavioral phenomena is inadequate and

fragmentary. For a description of the Bayesian position, see Robert Schlaifer, *Probability and Statistics for Business Decisions*, New York: McGraw-Hill, 1959. For a discussion of the current state of measurement theory, see Patrick Suppes and Joseph L. Zinnes, "Basic Measurement Theory," in R. Duncan Luce, Robert Bush, and Eugene Galanter, eds., *Handbook of Mathematical Psychology*, V. I, New York: Wiley, 1963, pp. 1–76.

It is also possible, I believe, to demonstrate rigorously the possibility of making sensible interpersonal comparisons of utility. For the present, we assume that where payoffs are made using money, utility and money are equal.

12 I am indebted to Professor Jack Sawyer of the University of Chicago for suggesting this approach. He developed an Altruism Scale which is a measure "for assessing directly the value one places upon the welfare of another in relation to his own." Sawyer's method involved two people, Person and Other. The current treatment is a generalization of Sawyer's method. See: Jack Sawyer, "The Altruism Scale: A Measure of Cooperative, Individualistic, and Competitive Inter-personal Orientation," *Amer. Jl. of Sociology*, 71 (January 1966), pp. 407–16.

13 In actual analyses of specific social choices these parameters can be obtained using any one of many available scaling procedures. Sawyer has used ranking and direct scale estimation procedures. See Sawyer, pp. 3–9.

14 For a review of this literature see Philip S. Gallo, Jr. and Charles G. McClintock, "Cooperative and Competitive Behavior in Mixed-Motive Games," *Jl. of Conflict Resolution*, 9 (March 1965), pp. 68–78. Also, Fouraker and Siegel hypothesize that three bargaining types exist: The simple maximizer (M), the rivalist (R), and the cooperator (C). The maximizer is concerned solely with his own profit; the rivalist may reduce his opponent's profit in his desire to surpass his rival; the cooperator derives some satisfaction from the prosperity of his opponent. See Lawrence Fouraker and Sidney Siegel, *Bargaining Behavior*, New York: McGraw-Hill, 1963.

15 Technical information and special competence can be considered individual characteristics that may be influential in some committee decisions. Often the person having such competence may have very little power, yet he may be most influential in effecting a decision.

16 Professor Coleman has treated this problem at greater length in his work cited above. In addition, he has discussed certain "alternatives to consent," such as crime and revolutionary activity. One could also consider withdrawal from the group and the use of violence as social choice mechanisms. However, these processes, though they often do produce a social choice, are beyond the scope of the present discussion.

17 The work reported in this paper was performed under a contract with the United States Office of Education, Department of Health, Education and Welfare, under the provisions of the Cooperative Research Program. Additional support came from the University of Pittsburgh's International Dimension Program supported by the Ford Foundation and the University. I am grateful to Robert Glaser, J. Steele Gow, Jr., James Kehl, and Richard Park for their encouragement and support of this work, and to M. Hinich, L. Brownstein, J. Sawyer, J. Coleman, W. E. Vinacke, and M. Mandelker for ideas and comments.

Portions of this paper were presented orally at the meetings of the Psychonomic Society in Chicago in October 1965; at the meetings of the Eastern Sociological Society in Philadelphia in April 1966; and at the Sixth World Congress of Sociology in Evian, France in September 1966.

REFERENCES

Arrow, K. J. *Social Choice and Individual Values.* (2nd ed.) New York: Wiley, 1963.

Gamson, W. Experimental Studies of Coalition Formation. In Leonard Berkowitz (Ed.), *Experimental Social Psychology.* Vol. 1. New York: Academic Press, 1964.

Lieberman, B. Experimental Studies of Conflict in Two-Person and Three-Person games. In J. Criswell, H. Solomon, and P. Suppes (Ed.), *Mathematical Methods in Small Group Processes.* Stanford: Stanford University Press, 1962.

Luce, R. D., and Raiffa, H. *Games and Decisions.* New York: Wiley, 1957.

Schelling, T. C. *The Strategy of Conflict.* Cambridge: Harvard University Press, 1960.

Shapley, L. S. A Value for n-Person Games. In H. W. Kuhn, and A. W. Tucker (Ed.), *Contributions to the Theory of Games.* Vol 2. Princeton: Princeton University Press, 1953.

Shapely, L. S., and Shubik, M. A Method for Evaluating the Distribution of Power in a Committee System. *American Political Science Rev.* 1952, **48**, 787–792.

Vinacke, W. E., and Arkoff, A. An Experimental Study of Coalitions in the Triad. *American Sociological Rev.* 1957, **22**, 406–414.

FOUNDATIONS FOR A THEORY
OF COLLECTIVE DECISIONS

JAMES S. COLEMAN

Johns Hopkins University

There is one general approach to theory that has been used most widely in both common-sense and formal approaches to the society. This is the approach that threats the acting individual as a purposive agent acting with some goals or purposes in mind.

I do not want here to argue the merits of this purposive approach versus other approaches to theory, though I hope the paper itself will aid that argument. I want merely to make clear that this approach will be the starting point for my discussion of collective action. As a starting point, it will illustrate the fundamental problems in devising a theory of collective action.

THE PROBLEM OF COLLECTIVE ACTION

From the point of view of purposive action theory, an *action* by an actor is easily explained. The one governing principle of the theory serves to explain it: the actor is striving to maximize his utility.

There is no such principle, however, to explain joint or collective action. For the principle is posed at the level of the individual actor and not at the level of a pair or collectivity. The utility of the collectivity is a meaningless quantity. Is it to be the sum of the utilities of the individual actors? If so, what weights are to be applied to the individual actors' utilities?

The lack of such a principle of behavior for "collective actors" does not prevent explanation of many types of social interaction by use of the individual calculus of purposive behavior. Recent books by Homans, Thibaut and Kelley, and Blau use that calculus to explain many types of behavior in social situations.[1] Even more broadly, economic theory uses this calculus as the basis for explaining the functioning of economic systems, and economic systems involve much interaction between actors. The calculus of individual purposive behavior explains the functioning of economic systems in a way illustrated by Adam Smith's famous statement in *The Wealth of Nations*. "It is not by the benevolence of the butcher, the brewer, or the baker that we expect our dinner, but from their regard to their own interest."[2]

Yet there is a whole set of social phenomena that this calculus will not explain. It is best illustrated by examining somewhat more fundamentally the economic interactions to which it is so well suited. Why is it that an economic exchange involving two actors is carried out? Clearly, in terms of this theoretical approach, it will be carried out only if both actors find it to their individual advantage to do so. It involves the voluntary action of two actors, A and B, and, consequently, four possibilities exist: neither A nor B finds the action beneficial; A finds it beneficial, but B does not; B finds it beneficial, but A does not; or both A and B find it beneficial.

An economic exchange occurs, or a social interaction occurs, when the last of these conditions holds. This is spontaneous action, for it is willed by both actors involved. But does this means that no action will take place except when the last condition holds? If such were the case, almost any action on the part of a large collectivity would be impossible, because as the actors increase to A, B, C, then A,B,C,D, A,B,C,D,E, and so on, the number of no-action conditions increases to 7, 15, 31, and so on, in powers of 2, while there remains only one condition for action: the condition in which the same action alternative is preferred by all.

This is one of the two fundamental problems of collective action. Only under the most extreme condition of consensus does action spring spontaneously from the actors' individual goals. Under any other condition, there is no spontaneous action, for at least one actor prefers a different course of action.

The second fundamental problem of collective action may be called the problem of "contingency." The action may be beneficial to all parties but only if other parties participate in it (and thus pay the cost of participation). That is, there may be complete consensus on the action, contingent on the participation of others. (Even in an exchange, the problem of contingency arises. The exchange is to the mutual advantage of both actors only if both carry out their half of the exchange.) But it is even more to the advantage of each not to participate, if all others do. This problem arises in the economics of public finance, and is known as the "free-rider" problem. Recently, Mancur Olson has treated such action problems more generally, in the context of voluntary associations such as trade unions. He has developed from it a theory of interest-group formation and strength at some variance with existing interest-group theory.[3]

This problem of contingency ordinarily arises only for those collective actions that are implemented by acts of members of the collectivity, such as payment of taxes, and even more for those actions that involve no collective decision at all, but only individual decisions, such as contributions to a voluntary fire association. For other collective actions, such as declaration of war or the decision to build a new courthouse, the decision is truly collective, and the action is implemented by an agency of the collectivity. Even for those collective actions that entail actions of members of the collectivity, it is often the case that a collective decision includes a provision for enforcement designed to remove the problem of contingency. Though the problem is never fully solved, it will not be treated in this paper. It will be assumed that any collective decision includes some provision for enforcement or is implemented by an agency of the collectivity.

Returning to the problem of consensus, societies and organizations have evolved numerous devices by which the problem may be partly circumvented and collective action carried out. One of the most fully formalized of these is the institution of voting, together with the voting rule. A majority rule is a simple and pervasive rule, but one in which nearly half the actors may prefer another action. A plurality rule (when there are several alternatives) is even weaker, for a majority may prefer actions other than the one selected by the rule. Other rules are more stringent than a majority rule, for example, a two-thirds majority. And in some instances one finds, even in a large and diverse society, the most stringent rule; a requirement that the action be unanimous.

These are the rules made in a society that partially solve the practical problem of collective action. But they neither wholly solve the practical problem nor in any way solve the theoretical problem. For what is to prevent those who disagree from simply withdrawing from the collectivity or refusing to accept the action and rebelling against it? There are many examples of small but violently opposed minorities that refuse to accept a collective action. Civil rights activity has been the scene of many such examples, both by certain segregationists and by certain integrationists who refuse to obey laws they disagree with. This in fact is a curious case, for minorities on each side have refused to accept the collective actions of the society as a whole.

There are many other examples of refusal to accept the collective action under a given set of decision rules in an organization or a society. The physical barriers to exodus from Iron Curtain countries stand as reminders that many persons would withdraw from these societies rather than accept the collection actions if they were not physically constrained. The splitting of sects from a parent church exemplifies the same unwillingness to accept the actions of the collectivity as a whole. The revolutions and coups d'état in many developing countries and the extreme instability of governments throughout the world are sufficient indication that mere construction of a decision rule does not begin to solve the problem.

Another way of putting the issue is that the construction of a constitution is nothing more than putting words on paper and can be done by a dolt, but the construction of a constitution that will allow collective action to proceed without splitting the society apart is nearly equivalent to devising a complete theory of collective action.

To summarize again the problem of collective decisions when one starts with purposive action theory:

a) In actions of individual actors, where each alternative action produces an outcome that has associated with it a utility for that actor, he will by definition spontaneously carry out the action with highest utility.

b) When the outcome depends upon the action of two or more actors (including actions ordinarily referred to as exchange), there may be an alternative preferred by all (assuming that any problems of contingency are solved), in which case the action can be labeled spontaneous, since it spontaneously proceeds from individual utilities. But more often, there will be no action preferred by all, and the theory breaks down. Because of such cases, modifications and additions must be made for collective action must be added to the basic theory of purposive action, if that theory is to be useful in the analysis of collective action. Without such addition, theories of purposive action can only be used to treat those areas of social life, such as exchange in economic markets, which are spontaneous in that the same action alternative is preferred by all parties (usually only two) to the action.

APPROACHES TO THE PROBLEM OF COLLECTIVE ACTION

Sociologists have not been numerous among those who have made attempts to solve this fundamental problem. I do not know the reason for sociologists' neglect, except for the relative absence throughout sociology of systematic theory and the tendency in sociological theory to take social structures as given and thus to accept coercion, authority, and constitutions without raising theoretical questions about why the actors themselves accept them or refuse to accept them.

Political scientists and economists have shown the greatest concern over this problem of consensus in collective action. The classical political philosophers, such as Thomas Hobbes, John Locke, and John Stuart Mill, took this as a central problem. Among economists, those concerned with public finance and, in general, welfare economists have had to face it. This is most obvious in taxation, for one is forced to ask such questions as what is a "just" distribution of taxes and public services? Or less normatively, what is a distribution of taxes and services that the society will accept?

One of the best known contributions to this theory is a negative one, by an economist, Kenneth Arrow, who showed that no voting decision rule could give a socially "reasonable" outcome under all distributions of individual preferences.[4] But this does not help much, for several reasons. First, the correct task is not to find socially reasonable outcomes but, rather, to link together individual preferences and collective action in the way they are in fact linked in social organization. Second, the theory, to be at all useful, should indicate the conditions under which collective action can be taken by a social organization and the conditions under which it will lead to withdrawal, revolt, or disobedience.

It should first be recognized that there are many kinds of social organizations and many kinds of collective actions. The religious rites of a sect or a primitive tribe are collective actions apparently spontaneously entered into by all members, directed toward a common goal desired by all members. At the other extreme, the actions of a bureaucracy are directed toward a goal held only by a very few at the top of the bureaucracy, and there is no expectation that the goal will be shared by all members of the organization. The collective actions of a feudal estate, a medieval household, or a slave-holding plantation are designed to benefit the actor at the top of the authority pyramid, yet many contribute to these actions.

The actions of a trade union and other mass-based collectivities are not always toward goals collectively held, but the very existence of the collectiv-

ity is based upon action toward collective goals. The government of a
large, diverse nation carries out many collective actions as the acting agency
of the nation as a whole, yet it is obvious that none of these is directed
toward goals held by every member of the nation.

As a consequence of this diversity of kinds of social organizations, the
theory of collective action must be a diverse one indeed. It is clear that in
some of these organizations the principal process is a stable pattern of
exchange and can perhaps be treated as a branch of the general theory of
exchange. For example, in a rational bureaucracy the employee explicitly
exchanges autonomy over his actions in return for money or similar resources that make the exchange a profitable one for him. In this way an entrepreneur who begins with enough such resources can organize a collective
action involving the interdependence of many individual actors. In such a
circumstance no confrontation of diverse preferences is necessary, since
the entrepreneur has "bought" the action of his employees and can so
organize it to carry out his own goals. It thus appears, at least on the surface,
that the explanation of collective action in such organizations requires no
new theoretical principles.[5]

It is quite different, however, for social organizations in which the power
over collective action is distributed over more than one person. It is in such
organizations that some device such as a voting rule is established for
bringing this dispersed power to bear on questions of collective action.
And it is clear that such procedures exist at some point in most social
organizations, so that the problem of collective action arises somewhere in
the organization.

I will take as the focus of inquiry, then, social organizations in which
there is a genuine collective decision, where power over the outcome is
distributed over more than one person. This means also that I will not ask
how that distribution of power arose. I will not examine the question of a
"constitution," either informal or formal, but will take the constitution,
which establishes the decision-making procedure, as given.

Perhaps the best way to see the difficulties that arise in moving from
individual rationality to collective decisions is to study the contradictions
that arise in voting rules. Consider a simple decision involving a collectivity
of these actors with a choice among three alternatives. Each actor has a
preference ordering for the three alternatives; a possible preference ordering
is shown in Table 1.

The situation shown in Table 1 produces curious results. For suppose
the alternatives are presented to the voters in a pairwise fashion, first A

and B, and then the winner versus C. In the A versus B vote, A wins with two votes. In the A versus C vote, C wins with two votes. But now suppose we start with a different pair in the first vote, say B versus C. In the B versus C vote, B wins; and then in the B versus A vote, A wins. Thus merely by

Table 1   Preferences of Actors X, Y, and Z
for alternatives A, B, and C

Rank	X	Y	Z
1	A	B	C
2	B	C	A
3	C	A	B

shifting the order of voting, the over-all outcome shifts from C to A. If the third order were used, starting with A versus C, this would result in still a different winner, B.

This decision rule appears to violate one's sense of what is a reasonable outcome, for the outcome should not change merely by changing the order of voting. This is the general direction of the argument Kenneth Arrow made. He laid down several conditions that any decision rule should meet if it were to give "reasonable" social outcomes, and then showed that such a decision rule was logically impossible.

Such a result, however, flies in the face of reality. Social organizations do establish decision rules, decisions are made, and the organizations persist. Are we reduced to saying that their actions are as grossly unreasonable as the example above suggests?

As numerous students of this problem have pointed out, there would be no difficulty if we had some measure of intensity of feeling. For example, in Table 1, suppose there were a number expressing the amount of utility that X, Y, and Z each associate with alternatives A, B, and C, as indicated in Table 2. In this example, alternative A clearly has the highest total amount of utility. A decision rule that merely determined the outcome by the highest aggregate utility would always give the decision to alternative A, independent of the order of comparison, and no "unreasonable" outcomes would result.

The fatal flaw in this solution is that there is no meaning to the notion of "amount of utility" or "intensity of feeling" unless it is expressible in the behavior under consideration. Voting certainly allows no such expression, but only registering a preference. Looking at the matter naively, we might then say that we could merely ask each actor to write down the amount of utility each alternative held for him. Then we would have the data for Table 2 and could merely aggregate the amounts and arrive at a winner.

Table 2 Amounts of utility of alternatives A, B, and C for Actors X, Y, and Z

	X	Y	Z	Total
u_a	10	8	9	27
u_b	5	10	8	23
u_c	1	9	10	20

But, in truth, this is merely chasing after a chimera. The matter is not solved so easily, for such a procedure invites strategic behavior, writing down whatever utilities will be most likely to give the outcome one wants. For example, Z has merely to inflate the quantity he writes down for C, and C will win—unless, of course, X and Y do the same for their favorites. In effect, asking an actor to write down utilities for each alternative, subject to an over-all maximum, say, of thirty, is nothing other than asking him to cast thirty votes rather than one. Since his goal is to maximize his expected utility, he will cast these votes in a way he hopes will do that, rather than to express the "relative utility" each has for him. However, if there were some way, in the decision process itself, for each actor in his behavior to express his intensity of preference, then this would give a start toward the solution.

BEHAVIOR IN A SYSTEM OF COLLECTIVE DECISIONS

An examination of empirical voting systems immediately yields a wealth of such behavior. First, suppose we put back this single decision into the context from which it was abstracted—taking for simplicity a legislature as the context, with a whole sequence of collective decisions on which to act. In such a situation, is it possible to express intensity of preference? The answer is that legislators do so by using the resources at their disposal. These resources consist of a number things, depending on their positions within the legislature. But the most simple case, and a relatively frequent one, is an exchange of resources: legislator X agrees to vote as Y wishes on one action in return for Y's agreement to vote as X wishes on another action. They do so because each sees a gain. Each loses his vote on an action where the outcome makes little difference to him but gains a vote on an action where the outcome matters more. Each has in that exchange expressed something about his intensity of preference. Each has given up a vote on an issue in which the utility difference between alternatives is *less* than the utility difference between alternatives on the vote he has gained.[6] This can be stated more precisely by means of algebra, but the substantive point is most important. By this action, there has been introduced into the system the first step in transforming ordinal preferences into cardinal utility differences that can be aggregated to arrive at a collective decision.

It is not true, however, that any procedure for arriving at cardinal utility differences will be sufficient for use in collective decisions. It would not be correct, for example, merely to use a von Neumann-Morgenstern lottery ticket procedure for arriving at cardinal utility differences and then aggregate them to arrive at a collective decision.[7] It is crucial to the establishment of a measure of utility that the behavior carried out by the actors involve resources they control within the system under consideration. The reasons for this are evident below.

It does not require much stretch of the imagination to see how this first step can be followed by others, so that each actor, through the vote exchanges or agreements he makes, expresses in minute gradation the interest he has in a given outcome, that is, the difference in utilities that the different possible outcomes would have for him. However, for each step toward a fine expression of intensity of interest in an action, another action is needed. Each actor needs a large set of votes on actions of varying interest to him to be able to express precisely his interest in any one. Each of these votes has the same function as goods in an economic system with barter exchange: it has certain direct utility for him if he uses it to satisfy his own interests; but it also has a certain value to others, so that its use in exchange might bring him resources more relevant to his interests. The precise statement of the conditions under which an actor in such a system will be willing to carry out an exchange is given in Appendix 1.

The necessity for replacing the single action back in its context of a whole set of collective actions should now be obvious. Without these other actions, each actor has no resources he can use to express how strongly he feels about this one. With only the single action, it is of supreme importance to all, for there is nothing to measure it against. The only measuring instruments are provided by the costs of the alternatives to accepting an unfavorable collective decision. Withdrawal, rebellion, and disobedience, together with their many variations, are the alternatives; and some measure of the intensity of his interest in the outcome is given by his willingness to resort to one of these alternatives.

3*

POWER IN THE SYSTEM

The case of refusal to accept the decision will be examined later at somewhat more length. However, it is useful first to consider more carefully the question of power and the comparison between utilities of different persons. We can approach the matter very heuristically by reflecting on what does in fact constitute power in such a system. Quite simply, we think of power of an actor in a system of collective decisions as the ability to obtain the outcomes that will give him highest utility. He is given by the constitution or rules a certain amount of direct control over various collective decisions—for example, in a legislature, each member ordinarily has one vote on each action. In the general case, he will have differing amounts of control over different actions. He may have a large amount of control over a number of actions. Does this mean he has a great amount of power in the system? It is easy to see that it does not, for it could be that no one is interested in the outcomes of the actions over which he has a great amount of control.

It is clear, then, that his power, or ability to get what he wants in the system, depends both upon his formal control of various collective actions and on the interest of others in those actions. If he has a large amount of control over only one action, but that action has much interest to many other actors, then this is a very valuable resource for him, and he can use it to get his way on those actions of interest to him.

For an ideal system, comparable to a market with pure competition, there are a great many collective actions of widely varying interest to the actors. For such a system, in which exchanges can be carried out to express minute differences in interest, the precise expression for the power of an actor can be given. This is given algebraically in Appendix 2. In words, it can be stated this way:

The value of control over an action is equal to the sum of the interests of each actor in that action times the total power of that actor. In turn, the total power of an actor is equal to his constitutional control over each action times the value of that action, summed over all actions in the system.

The basis for this definition of the value of control over an event can be seen as follows: Suppose an actor has some interest in an action. The effect of this interest is to make him willing to employ a portion of his resources, that is, his partial control of other actions. But **his** resources depend on the value of the actions that he has some control over, that is, on the amount of interest that those with power have in the actions he has control over.

On the other hand, suppose another actor has some control over this action which interests the first actor. He will want to exact the highest price he can get for giving up this control. He will hold out for the most power he can get, either in control of actions of interest to him or control of actions that he can further exchange for control that interests him.

Thus the definition of value is one in which there is a simultaneous calibration of the value of different actions and the power of different actors. Actions are valuable when powerful actors have a great deal of interest in them. Actors are powerful when the actions they control have high value. A consequence of this definition is that the value of an action is the cost of obtaining complete control over it (in this perfect market). Thus, with a probabilistic decision rule, an actor can fully control an action only if he has total power greater than the value of the action and is willing to employ all his resources toward gaining control of it.[8]

There are numerous examples which illustrate the way this principle operates in a social system. The classical example is that of the king who has control over nearly all actions but suddenly becomes entranced with a poor but beautiful girl who has nothing but her own autonomy. His interests are now focused on the actions he does not have control over, the actions of this girl. Thus, her power in the society jumps from near zero to the greatest of all, for she has control over the only actions that interest the king, who controls everything that interests anyone else. Obviously, for such a system to work, the girl must be in no way beholden to the king, a matter which in such tales is usually contrived by her being the daughter of a poor but independent woodchopper living off the forest at the edge of the kingdom.

INTERPERSONAL COMPARISON OF UTILITY

This examination of power allows us to return to the question of interpersonal comparison of utility. As an earlier point in the paper, it was evident that one could not naïvely ask people to give their intensity of feeling, and then merely add up these utilities to arrive at a collective decision that "maximized utility." But now, with somewhat more sophistication, we can come back to the question of interpersonal comparison of utility, having defined the value of an action and the power of an actor, as indicated above. The exchanges themselves provide a comparison of different actors' utilities or interests.

As a result of the exchanges, each actor has a certain power. Thus, just as the value of an action is the sum over all actors of their power times their interest in that action, the value of one actor's interest in an action is his power times his interest in it. That is, if two actors have identical interests in an action (i.e., action occupies the same proportion of their total interests), then actor A's interests are more valuable than B's if his total power is greater than B's. This difference in power results, of course, from the fact that A has control over more valuable resources than does B and thus has more power to see his interests realized.

Thus an interpersonal comparison of utility automatically occurs in exchange, weighting an actor's interests by his total power. But such a comparison raises questions about interpersonal comparison in the usual sense. Are we not assuming that individuals communicate with others the precise size of their interests in arriving at a value? The answer to this is "No." The only communication assumed here is that assumed in any market: what exchanges an actor will make and what ones he will not. The perfect functioning of the market assumes that he has complete knowledge of what exchanges others will make and can thus assess the value-in-exchange of any power he gains in an exchange. It does not assume, however, that he makes his interest known in any way beyond stating which exchanges he will agree to and which ones he will refuse. It is worthwhile to note the sense in which the actor's power provides a scale by which his utilities may be compared to others. His wants are exactly as important as is his ability to realize them. If A has twice the power of B, his wants or interests are worth twice B's. This is no value judgment of ours as analysts but a description of the value judgment implicit in the distribution of control over actions in the system.

A question can be raised in this context concerning the maximization of social welfare. In a perfect exchange system, as described above, do the exchanges result in a maximization of social welfare? This is a reasonable question because each exchange will benefit at least both parties to it; and in a perfect exchange system, when the state has been reached in which no other exchanges are possible, is this not a maximization of social welfare?

It becomes clear that this question can only be answered relative to a given framework of constitutional control. The situation is exactly analogous to a perfect market of private goods. Utility for each trader is maximized, but relative to the goods he brought to the market, that is, the resources he began with. Similarly in collective actions. The perfect exchange system maximizes social welfare, but only when each person's welfare is weighted according to his power that derives from his constitutional control of actions. The scientific question becomes: Given the distribution among actors of constitutional control over collective actions, what procedures will insure that each actor's interests will be realized to the extent provided by his power? The answer lies in making the system most closely approximate a perfect market in which resources may be exchanged. But the utilmate question of what degree of constitutional control each actor should have is outside the system and becomes truly an ethical question or else one that is answered in terms of the ultimate recourse, the physical force that can be used by each actor in fixing his constitutional control.

ALTERNATIVES TO CONSENT

The outcome of a collective decision will ordinarily benefit some actors in the system and harm others. If it benefited all, then the action would be spontaneous, just as in ordinary economic exchanges which benefit both parties. If it benefited none, it would not be taken, since there would be no actor favoring that outcome.

In such a situation, the question must arise: Under what condition will those who see themselves as hurt by the action consent to be hurt by it? To answer such a question, one must first have some idea of the possible alternatives to consent. At the most general level, there seem to be two kinds of alternatives to consent. One is not to consent to the specific action, and the other is not to consent to the totality of actions of which the system is composed. The former refusal to consent can be implemented only for certain kinds of collective decisions. These are decisions that involve some action on the part of the actors themselves, such as a law against stealing, or a compulsory military draft, or a law against excluding persons from a place of public business. In all those cases, and others like them, civil disobedience is an alternative to consent. Breaking the law by stealing, or by failing to register for the draft, or by arbitrarily refusing to serve customers, is a refusal to consent.

In other kinds of collective decisions, such refusal to consent is less easy. Passage of a foreign aid bill, declaration of war, decision to carry out nuclear testing, all are implemented by government authorities and require no implementation of each actor in the system. Even in many of these cases, however, there can often be refusal to consent by actively impeding the action. Some citizens have protested nuclear testing by placing themselves in an exposed position at the time of the test. Some citizens have protested declaration of war by refusing to work in war-related industries or pay taxes. These protests ordinarily cannot halt the action, however, but only apply pressure toward its reconsideration.

In considering disobedience of a collective decision which results in an outcome unfavorable to him, the actor has two sets of utilities to compare. One is the utility of his disobedience (considering both the costs and the benefits, and, if necessary, estimating probabilities of punishment, etc.), and the other is the utility of consenting to the unfavorable outcome. If he expects to lose more by disobeying than he loses by consent to the unfavorable action, he will consent. If he expects to lose more by consent to the action, he will disobey.

We may for a moment take the perspective of those whom the outcome favors, to examine the role of police. They also must make a calculation. Recognizing that the calculations of those who see themselves as hurt by the action will sometimes lead to disobedience, they can affect that calculation. They can do so by increasing the costs of disobedience through apprehension and punishment of the disobedient. Their calculations then must involve the cost to them of policing the decision versus the cost of allowing disobedience. The police activity will be supported up to the point that the costs of further policing surpass the benefits from reduction in disobedience they would bring about.

Different governments (and at a microcosmic level, different heads of households) employ quite different strategies in demanding consent. In a "police state," the number of actors who are hurt by a collective decision is quite high, and a large amount of police activity is necessary to reduce disobedience to levels that will not be costly to the government. In a more open society where police activity is minimal, the costs of disobedience to the citizen remain low, so that the threshold of disobedience is much lower.

The strategy of high police activity, however, is a dangerous one for the state. If policing makes costs of disobedience very high, the number of actors dissatisfied with any action, though consenting to it, may be very high. Thus the state has no good way of knowing the level of dissatisfaction in the society, and may invite a more general refusal to consent.

It is to this more general refusal to consent that I now turn. This is the refusal to consent to the whole set of collective decisions. Parenthetically, it may be noted that any delimitation of a set of collective decisions from the stream of events that occur in a social system is an arbitrary one. However, in this as in other things, people engage in a discounting of future events; consequently, the present theory, which consists of an arbitrary set of actions, is a first approximation to a theory that would delimit the set through the time-discounting that occurs.

Considering this set of actions, each actor can estimate, as the system proceeds, the expected utility to him over the whole set of actions. This may be difficult to do until some exchanges have taken place, and at best, there may be a high degree of error in such estimations. Nevertheless, each actor will be motivated to make such an estimation for comparison with the utility to him of alternatives to consenting. These alternatives are many and varied, but they can be roughly grouped into two classes: withdrawal from the system, and revolt. Withdrawal can take two forms: either emigration, leaving the system alone, or secession, a splitting off of an organized subset of actors. The calculations for the first on the part of the actor are much like those for disobedience, in that he weighs the costs and benefits of leaving the system versus the expected utility over the whole set of actions in the system. The difference is that the comparison in the case of disobedience was over only the single action; here it is over the whole set.

From the point of view of those who remain, the frequency of such emigration can be greatly reduced by increasing its costs. The question of whether to introduce police measures to increase these costs, as in the case of the Berlin Wall, or to keep the costs of emigration low, as in nineteenth-century Ireland, depends on two considerations: the cost of the police and the value to the system of the potential emigrants. The police cost is relatively small. However, in those systems where wealthy, skilled, and educated classes have lost power, such as Communist countries, the potential emigrees are the upper and middle classes. They are of high value to the system, in contrast to the poor, who are the potential emigrants under circumstances of poverty in the society. Thus the value to Ireland of those who left in the nineteenth century was quite low and perhaps negative, given its overpopulation. The value to East Germany of those who would have left if possible, however, is quite high.

Secession, as the other form of withdrawal, is complex indeed, for it involves three levels of decision-making: by the system as a whole, by the subsystem that is a potential seceder, and by the individuals in that subsystem. This complexity puts the problem beyond this paper.

Revolt against the system is also complex, for it can never be carried out by a single actor, except in the case of a very small collectivity. Thus the development of a revolutionary organization, collective decisions within it, and its very membership, are all problematic. It too is beyond the scope of this paper, except for a single point. The special character of revolutionary activity is that it is designed to change the constitutional distribution of control of decisions. Thus we come full circle to this constitutional distribution which we took as given at the outset. Revolutionary activity can change this distribution; and revolutionary activity is itself a function of the degree to which different actors can realize their interests within the existing system. Pending careful analysis, it would appear that revolutionary activity will be carried out only by groups with control of resources that lie outside the system of collective decisions (i.e., the government), such as actors with newly gained economic power, or those with military force but little governmental power, or those with access to resources supplied by another social system. As is evident, this paper can do no more than locate the conditions of revolution within the general context of a theory of collective decisions.

CONCLUSION

I have embarked upon a task here that is both difficult and rewarding: how to describe and account for collective decisions in terms of the rational behavior of individual actors. The problem arises because of the fact that a collective decision ordinarily is disadvantageous to some of those who participate in it, yet they consent to it. Under such conditions, how can a collectivity continue intact, how do collective decisions get made, and when will there be a refusal to consent? These are the major questions to which this paper has addressed itself. My intent has been to present a starting point for a theoretical treatment of those phenomena central to the functioning of social systems: collective decisions and collective action.

APPENDIX 1

Conditions for an exchange in a system of collective decisions

Consider a system of actors $j = 1, ..., n$, with a series of two-outcome collective decisions to be carried out, $i = 1, ..., m$. The system is defined by the set of actors, the set of decisions, and the decision rule for each decision.

Each outcome of each action has consequences for each actor to which he attaches a given amount of utility, say u_{1ij} and u_{2ij}, the utilities for actor j of outcomes 1 and 2 on action i.

His *interest* in this action is $|u_{1ij} - u_{2ij}| = x_{ij}$. His subjective probability of a favorable outcome on action i with the present status is p_{is}.

Postulate

He will be willing to make an exchange, moving the system from status s to status s' if and only if his expected utility under status s' exceeds that under status s, that is, if and only if

$$x_{ij}p_{is'} + x_{kj}p_{ks'} > x_{ij}p_{is} + x_{kj}p_{ks}. \tag{1}$$

Equation (1) can be restated as

$$x_{ij}(p_{is'} - p_{is}) > x_{kj}(p_{ks} - p_{ks'}). \tag{2}$$

Ordinarily, the change in status is one in which one probability increases (through power gained) while the other decreases (through power given up).

Suppose status s' is a status with less power over action k and more power over action i. Suppose we consider also the special case in which the increase in perceived power (i.e., subjective probability of a favorable outcome) over i equals the decrease in perceived power over k. Then $p_{is'} - p_{is} = p_{ks} - p_{ks'}$, and the exchange will be carried out if and only if

$$x_{ij} > x_{kj}. \tag{3}$$

The condition for an exchange between individuals j and j' is that the individual condition stated above for statuses s and s' hold for both individuals j and j'. Under the condition given above, s' will be a status in which j' has more power over action k and less over i. In the special case where the increase in perceived power of j' over k equals the decrease in perceived power over i, this applies, analogously to (3), that j' will be willing to make an exchange if and only if

$$x_{kj'} > x_{ij'}. \tag{4}$$

Note — A structural situation in which the above conditions can be realized is one in which each actor has one vote on each decision, all exchanges are made before any decisions are voted on, and the decision rule is probabilistic, with the probability of outcome 1 given by the proportion of votes for outcome 1. It still may be the case that subjective probabilities may not correspond to objective ones, but in this case, the objective probabilities do give the special case of equation (3) and (4).

APPENDIX 2

Power of an actor and value of a collective action in an ideal system of collective decisions

An ideal system of collective decisions is one in which there is perfect competition for each resource (e.g., each vote of each actor), and a price (e.g., in terms of other votes) becomes established. Such a system can be approximated by a system with the following conditions:

a)   The number of actors is very great;
b)   The constitutional control of any actor is small relative to the total;
c)   The distribution of interests for different actors is highly varied;
d)   There are a large number of collective decisions;
e)   Full communication exists;
f)   The decision rule is probabilistic.

Given   1. A matrix C of constitutional control, showing the amount of direct control that each actor has over each action. The element c_{ij} is the direct control of actor j over action i. The sum of c_{ij} over i equals 1.0 or less (less than 1.0 if the outcome is partly determined by unknown and uncontrolled factors outside this system).

2)   A matrix X of interest, showing the relative amount of interest of each actor in each action. The element x_{ij} $(= |u_{1ij} - u_{2ij}|)$ is actor j's interest in action i. The sum of x_{ij} over actions i must equal 1.0. Then the fundamental equation from which the value of each action can be calculated is based on the following identity:

The value of control over action i *is equal to the sum of interests of* i *of each actor times the total power of that actor. In turn, the total power of actor* j *is equal to the power of* j *over each action* k *times the value of action* k, *summed over all actions* k.

This definition of value of an action is only relative to the values of the other $m - 1$ actions in the system. In a system with m actions, we will let the sum of the values of these actions be equal to m.

In algebraic expression, the identity is:

$$v_i = \sum_j x_{ij} \sum_k c_{kj} v_k,$$

or in matrix notation,

$$V = XC'V.$$

The value of an action and the power of an individual is given by solution of the above equations. This may be carried out as follows, in non-matrix form. Transposing v_i, we have a set of m equations, one for each action,

$$0 = \sum_{j=1}^{n} \sum_{k=1}^{m} x_{ij} c_{kj} v_k + v_i.$$

There are $m - 1$ independent v_i's and $m - 1$ independent equations. If we rescale v_i such that $v_i^* = v_i/v$, than $v_m^* = 1$. Solution of the first $m - 1$ equations for v_i^* by successive elimination will give the values of v_i^*. Then, using the fact that

$$\left(\sum_{i=1}^{m-1} v_i^* + 1 \right) v_m = m,$$

it is possible to solve for v_m and then for v_i by $v_i = v_i^* v_m$. The real power of actor j in the system, say r_j, is the sum of his constitutional control, c_{ij}, over action i times the value of event $_i$:

$$r_j = \sum_{i=1}^{m} c_{ij} v_i.$$

In matrix operations, the above solution is obtained by defining a vector V^* with $m - 1$ elements v_i^* defined as above, a matrix $W = CX'$, a matrix W^* which is W reduced by deleting the last row and column, and a vector Y, consisting of the first $m - 1$ elements of the last column of W, $(w_{1m}, w_{2m}, \ldots, w_{m-1,m})$.
Then

$$V = WV,$$

$$0 = (W - I) V,$$

$$0 = (W^* - I) V^* + Y,$$

$$-Y = (W^* - I) V^*.$$

Since $(W^* - I)$ is a non-singular square matrix, it has an inverse, and we can solve for V^*: $V^* = (W^* - I)^{-1}(- Y)$. Then as above v_i may be found from v_i^*, and r_j from c_{ij} and v_i.

NOTES

1   George C. Homans, *Social Behavior: Its Elementary Forms* (New York: Harcourt, Brace, and World, 1961); John W. Thibaut and Harold H. Kelley, *The Social Psychology of Groups* (New York: John Wiley & Sons, 1959); Peter M. Blau, *Exchange and Power in Social Life* (New York: John Wiley & Sons, 1964).

2   Adam Smith, *The Wealth of Nations* (New York: Modern Library, 1937), p. liv.

3   Mancur Olson, *The Logic of Collective Action* (Cambridge: Harvard University Press, 1965); also see Richard Musgrave, *The Theory of Public Finance* (New York: McGraw-Hill Book Co., 1959), for the general problem in economic theory.

4   Kenneth J. Arrow, *Social Choice and Individual Values* (New York: John Wiley & Sons, 1951).

5   A deeper analysis of such organizations would show much more complexity, for many such organizations appear to depend greatly on the fact that employees do become imbued with the goals of the organization and contribute to it in ways not at all covered by the exchange agreement they made in selling their labor. In addition, there appear to be processes by which employees over time gain rights to participate in the organization's decision-making processes, thus bringing about a dispersal of power over the organization's collective actions.

6   This is slightly oversimplified, since his action depends also on the change in probability of a favorable outcome that the vote given up or gained will make. However, it will serve as a first approximation, to be modified later.

7   Patrick Suppes and Muriel Winet, "An Axiomatization of Utility Based on the Notion of Utility Differences," *Management Science*, I (1955), 259, describe such a procedure.

8   A probabilistic decision rule, in which the probability of a positive outcome is proportional to the proportion of positive votes, is the only one in which the actual control of an actor over an action is equal to his constitutional control and not contingent on the particular coalition.

SECTION 2

DESCRIPTIVE STUDIES

INTRODUCTORY DISCUSSION

The ten papers included in this section offer a representative picture of the work currently being done dealing with descriptive aspects of the collective decision problem. The first four papers by Vinacke, Lieberman, Riker, and Willis all deal with problems of coalition formation, which is a central process of collective decision making. Vinacke's paper deals with the effect of the size of the group on coalition behavior. Lieberman's paper describes the first study in which coalitions were manipulated experimentally; coalitions were formed and broken by varying the payoff function, or rewards, to the subjects. Riker examines coalition formation in a three-person, non-zero-sum game, but concentrates his analysis on the effect of informal rules on behavior. "Informal rules are those which describe the game as it is brought out of the eternal world of mathematics into the temporal world of actual play. In general, informal rules are those necessay for play but not necessary to calculate the solution." (Riker p. 116). Willis examines coalition formation in inessential games, situations where the total payment to the set of players is exactly the same as the sum of the payments to all the individual players, and so there is little incentive for the players to form coalitions. Such situations are then interesting because they offer situations in which a number of behavioral or "social man" hypotheses may be tested.

The work by Harnett and Cummings also examines behavior in three-person groups, but it stems from a different tradition—studies of bargaining using a situation similar to the one employed by Siegel and Fouraker in their well known work. Harnett and Cummings examine the effect of information, communication, and risk-taking propensity on bargaining behavior.

The paper by Harnett was published previously in the *Journal of Personality and Social Psychology* in 1967 and is included in this volume because it is the first experimental study (that the editor is aware of) that deals explicity with a social choice problem. Harnett offers the hypothesis that the subject's level of aspiration is a very significant factor in determining which alternative is chosen and offers data that give some support to that hypothesis.

The paper by Richard and Lynne Ofshe, which was not delivered at the conference, is included here because it presents a novel approach to the collective decision problem. The Ofshes study a three-person coalition situation using a type of model first developed by Siegel which employs utility and marginal utility notions together with a stochastic model. The work presents a very interesting convergence of a number of lines of work.

The paper by Birnberg and Pondy reports work that explicity studies social choice processes. It considers the effects of three different voting rules on collective decision behavior.

The paper by Lawrence Messé comes from a rather different line of work, one that can be characterized as a more traditional social psychological approach; Messé has obtained detailed information about conceptions of fairness.

In his paper Coleman contributes to the literature designed to give us an understanding of power. He offers a measure of power different than that of Shapley and Shubik and then proceeds to show how this measure tells us something about the ability of a collectivity to act.

CHAPTER 2.1

NEGOTIATIONS AND DECISIONS IN A POLITICS GAME[1]

W. EDGAR VINACKE

State University of New York at Buffalo

The experimental study of small groups has had a relatively brief, but extraordinarily active, history. The research area dates primarily from the work of Sherif and of Lewin and his collaborators in the 'thirties. Currently, studies of gaming have moved to the center of the stage. Some investigators have concerned themselves primarily with the exploration of specific variables, such as variations in payoff, instructions, and personality variables (see Vinacke, 1969, for a review of this area). Others have been oriented more toward theory. Finally, unlike in many of the subfields of social psychology, experts in gaming have displayed a pervasive interest in the possible relations between laboratory findings and real life problems, including economic and political decision making and international conflict. Therefore, simulation techniques have been quite prominent.

A curious feature of all this research is its concentration on extremely limited situations. The great preponderance of experiments have dealt with just three different games: the Prisoner's Dilemma (Rapoport and Chammah, 1965), the Deutsch and Krauss (1960) trucking game, and the board game used in my own experiments (Vinacke and Arkoff, 1957). There are, of course, merits in seeking to understand particular situations before launching off in other directions, but there are also clear limitations to the generalization of findings. Not only have situations been defined narrowly, but the properties of the group have also been extraordinarily specialized. Most of the work has dealt with dyads, with a secondary attention to triads. Sizes beyond three have virtually been ignored. The importance of the size variable is

4*   51

recognized (Simmel, 1902–03; Bales and Borgatta, 1965; Thomas and Fink, 1963), but very few investigators have tried to assess interaction processes across variations in size.

There is, first of all, the general question about the degree to which behavior alters as a function of size. Usually, this issue is investigated by comparing a couple of sizes, such as two and four, with the aim of assessing either group efficiency or member satisfaction. In general, such studies show that efficiency is sometimes related to size, depending on the task, and that members usually feel more satisfied in smaller groups, because of greater opportunities to participate. In addition, Bales and Borgatta (1965) have examined changes in the interaction profile in discussion groups ranging from size 2 to size 7, but with little systematic relation.

From the outset of our research on triads, we have recognized that we were dealing with only one size, and that the phenomena of coalition formation must be examined in other sizes, as well. Both Shears (1967) and Willis (1962) have conducted experiments with tetrads, and I propose, here, to describe in detail research with groups ranging in size from triads to enneads.

First, however, let us look at some of the issues which prompt an interest in size variation.

Simmel (1902–03) pointed to a basic discontinuity between dyads and triads. If conflict arises when two persons compose the group, a division destroys the group, leaving two isolated persons. In the triad, however, a division in the group at least leaves a dyad, so that the group is not destroyed. It is for this reason that the triad has an inherent interest. Taking the step from the dyad to the triad, therefore, initiates attention to the fundamental fact of *coalitions*. Clearly, if coalitions can occur in the triad, then they can occur even more importantly in still larger groups. But at this point there appears another possible discontinuity. In triads, any coalition less than the whole—and we must not overlook a consensus of all members—must be composed of only two members. In the tetrad and larger sizes, however, we move to coalitions of three or more members and to more than one coalition, or competing blocs of members. We cannot achieve full understanding of coalition behavior by confining ourselves to triads. Simmel appears to suggest that increases in size beyond three are not as significant as the increase from two to three, except for the fact that various problems of social structure and organization become more important. It is clearly interesting, however, to explore systematically just what changes take place as additional members are added.

A second problem arises when we consider the two broadly contrasting strategies that we have found in comparing male with female triads. Exploitative strategy, typical of male groups, is characterized by intense orientation toward winning, accompanied by ruthless bargaining and behavior reflecting the maximizing of individual gain. Accommodative strategy, typical of female groups, is featured by an orientation to the social interaction aspects of the situation, accompanied by an avoidance of invidious actions, and a concern for fair outcomes. These differences may be treated as attitudinal variables which occur in both sexes, although in different degree. In one experiment (Vinacke, Cherulnik, and Lichtman, 1968), we pre-selected Ss of both sexes by means of a special Test of Strategy, composing groups consisting of three players high, moderate, or low in accommodative tendencies. Groups of both sexes were generally similar at each level, thus indicating that both strategies occur in both sexes, but in different degrees.

Clearly, these differences exist in triads, but would they continue to be present in larger groups? More explicitly, is there a systematic relation between exploitative and accommodative forms of behavior and size of group? We can, in fact, hypothesize with equal plausibility three opposing effects. (1) The two sexes may differ regardless of size of group. (2) As the size of the group increases, the two sexes become increasingly different, with males becoming more exploitative and female groups becoming more accommodative. (3) As the size of the group increases, the two sexes become more alike, with differences becoming attenuated, perhaps because of factors inherent in the greater diversity of the social situation itself. In undertaking this experiment, we did not have any preference among these three hypotheses, since arguments in favor of one could readily be balanced against those in favor of another.

It should be observed, in passing, that the concepts of exploitative and accommodative strategy offer interesting possibilities for a broad view of socio-cultural adaptation. They represent, in fact, deeply contrasting approaches to social problems in a variety of contexts. The exploitative, or male, strategy rests on the exercise of power, control of resources, and the solution of problems through confrontation and effective aggression. The accommodative, or female, strategy stresses the exercise of feeling and sensitivity to the needs of others, the pooling of resources, and the solution of problems through mutual agreement. I refrain from the temptation to see local, national, or international affairs from either perspective. Nor am I inclined to suggest that one strategy is necessarily better than the other. The point, here, is simply the fascinating fact that the *same* problem can be viewed in very different ways, with very different outcomes. Perhaps it is this fact that makes the female sex so puzzling: they have the aggravating faculty for treating a situation in a female way. Our experiments suggest, however, that their way is equally as meaningful as the male way, if only we could understand (or accept)it.

I have avoided using the terms competition and cooperation in this discussion, even though there is obviously a generally similar implication in the concepts of exploitative and accommodative strategy. One reason for preferring the latter terms is that competition and cooperation refer especially to the general conditions of social interaction, such as the character of the task, the rules that determine behavior in it, and whether there is differential payoff to the participants. From this standpoint, the games we have used should be characterized as competitive for both sexes. However, one may be competitive in different ways, a fact that the distinction between exploitative and accommodative strategy is intended to convey. Thus, it is not so much that females are not acting competitively, as that they act to handle a competitive situation in their own fashion. In a similar manner, we might expect to see differences in managing a cooperative situation, in which, also, exploitative and accommodative tendencies may appear.

Finally, this research was prompted, also, by some specific theoretical issues. In accounting for the particular coalitions that occur in the triad, three different theories have been advanced, based on derivations from the theory of games, from analyses by Caplow (1956) and Vinacke and Arkoff (1957), and from Gamson's theory (1961). We may call these positions, respectively, strictly rational theory, perception of strength theory, and cheapest winning theory.

Consider the type of power pattern which we may call "all different," as shown in Table 1. Here we have three players, A, B, and C, with weights of 4, 3, and 2. Let us assume that a single prize is to be gained by winning, and that players may form coalitions if they choose. Evidently, any pair can win by establishing an alliance, and the question is, which one is most likely. The three kinds of predictions, illustrated in the table, may be formulated, as follows:

1 Strictly rational theory

The three assumptions of the theory of games are, first, that players will seek, obtain, and process accurately all available information; second, that players will act exactly on that information; and, third, that players will act to maximize their gains and minimize their losses (the utility assumption). In the All Different pattern, it is apparent that full understanding of the situation involves two points, (a) that a coalition is necessary to win, and (b) that whichever coalition is reached will obtain all of the reward. Thus, differences in weights are wholly irrelevant, and, therefore, any coalition is just as good as any other coalition. We would predict that no pair should occur any more often than any other pair, and that every coalition should be based on a 50/50 split of the reward. The same point can be made by analyzing what must happen, given our assumptions, in a bargaining sequence, as demonstrated in the table. No matter whether a player seeks to obtain a share commensurate with his relative weight, the other two players can always reach a better mutual agreemeet, until the limit of an equal split is reached. In our experiments, we find that such results do not occur. Instead, the pair BC is most frequent and deals are frequently made in disproportionate terms. Thus, we are led to a second interpretation.

2 Perception of strength theory

The assumptions of this theory are that players will act in accordance with apparent relative power, regardless of whether it is real or not, and will act to overcome the seeming advantage of another player. That is, coalitions will be formed to enhance the partners' ability to achieve superior power. In addition, they will see their joint interests as arising from their weakness relative to a stronger player. Thus, B and C will join forces to defeat A. As illustrated in the table, B and C together have a strength of 5, compared to A's weight of 4. From this standpoint, we predict that BC will be the most frequent coalition. Our experiments have borne out this prediction.

3 Cheapest winning coalition theory

The assumptions of this theory are similar to those in the preceding theory, except that it allows more fully for the relative weights of the players. Gamson (1961) first assumes that minimal winning coalitions will occur (i.e. the smallest number of members required to produce a combined weight in excess of the weight(s) of the remaining player(s). Gamson (1961) also assumes that each player "will expect others to demand from a coalition a share of the payoff proportional to the amount of resources which they contribute to a coalition." From this standpoint, a minimal winning coalition will occur in which each member can expect to receive the greatest possible proportion of the prize. As shown in the table, this coalition would be BC, since together they have a weight of five and B gains 14% compared to an alliance with A, and C gains 7% compared to an alliance with A.

Now, it is curious to see that Gamson's theory cannot be readily tested, if at all, in triads, because the BC coalition is predicted equally well by the perception of strength theory.[2] We require a situation in which the "cheapest winning" coalition is different from the "weakest winning" coalition. Such situations are found in tetrads, or larger groups, as shown in Table 1.

Table 1   Weights in the All-Different Power Pattern,
and Coalitions Predicted by Three Theories

In Triads: A = 4, B = 3, C = 2

Coalitions	Proportional Deals
AB (43)	57/43
AC (42)	67/33
BC (32)	60/40

1   Strictly rational theory. Predicts Any on 50/50 basis, since if A offers B 43, C an offer B more than 43, then A can offer more to B than C does, converging on 50/50. Similarly, for A to C, B to C, etc.
2   Perception of strength theory. Predicts BC, since (3 + 2) > 4.
3   Cheapest winning theory. Predicts BC, since B = 60, vs 43 with A, and C = 40, vs 33 with A).

In Tetrads: A = 4, B = 3, C = 2, D = 1

Coalitions	Proportional Deals
AB (43)	57/43
AC (42)	67/33
BCD (321)	50/33/17

1   Strictly rational theory. Probably predicts AB, AC, ABC, ABD, BCD all equally likely, since internal adjustments in deal can approximate what any member can obtain from a different coalition.
2   Perception of strength theory. Predicts BCD, since (3 + 2 + 1) > 4 or (3 + 2).
3   Cheapest winning theory. Predicts AC, since A gains more and C does not lose. However, note that in this pattern C has no preference between AC and BCD.

Here it can be seen that A can win with either B or C, and that C gains nothing by preferring an alliance with B and D to an alliance with A. Therefore, the cheapest winning alliance should be AC. The weakest winning alliance is the triple BCD. Taken purely in literal terms, therefore, Gamson's theory should predict that AC will occur most often; the perception of strength theory should predict that BCD will occur most often. By using larger groups than triads, some light should be cast on the factors that actually determine coalitions.

Experiments by Willis (1962) and Shears (1967) are equivocal in their results. In the two types of power pattern used by Willis, either certain pairs or certain triples can be defined as cheapest winning coalitions. Both occurred frequently. In one type, two of the weak players fared equally well in pairs or triples, and in this case the weak winning coalition occurred most often. Shears cites the Gamson theory in analyzing her results. In one power pattern—a tie situation, in which the three weak players can prevent the strong player from winning, but cannot win themselves—the winning pairs occurred most often, although the weak triple also achieved significance. In the other type, the cheapest winning coalition (a pair) far exceeded weak triples.

These studies do not clearly support either theory. One reason lies in the fact that the cheapest winning and weak winning coalitions are not entirely distinct. Other reasons, as Shears points out, stem from the special characteristics of larger groups. In such cases, weak winning coalitions require a large number of members. As a consequence, one must trust more people than in smaller coalitions, and, aside from that, negotiations become more complex and the difficulty of establishing coalitions increases. In the triad, these problems are no greater for strong pairs than for weak pairs. Thus we see highlighted a significant discontinuity between triads and larger groups, namely, there must be larger coalitions to counteract strong members and these subdivisions demand a greater or at least more complex degree of mutual trust. We may suppose that numerous aspects of negotiation, mediation, and interpersonal activity vastly increase in importance as we move from the triad into larger groups.

Our concern, then, in this experiment was to investigate negotiation, coalition formation, and decisions, as the size of the group increases. We hoped to contribute to an understanding of the three problems just described: how does size affect the kind and frequency of coalitions? how are exploitative and accommodative tendencies influenced by increases in size? how do factors of perception of strength and of cheapest winning deals determine coalition formation as size increases?

METHOD

In planning this experiment, we had to face some difficult problems. We required a situation which could incorporate essential features of the board game employed in previous studies, especially variations in power pattern. It is not hard to see that differences in voting power could serve this purpose. In addition, however, we required a game that would be identical in its specifications for groups of any size. The board game would be much too cumbersome for more than four or five players. Finally, we wished to devise a game with a minimum of equipment and a maximum of interest. The former consideration stemmed from the uncertainty of fixed laboratory accommodations in a university undergoing exceedingly rapid growth within very limited space. The latter consideration represents a desire to maximize the motivation of the subjects.

The upshot is the Politics Game, which I shall now describe.

The politics game

A certain amount of direct involvement in the national pastime of politics guided the development of the game. It consists of a series of steps which can best be taken up in order.

The situation was introduced, once the group was assembled, as a "politics game." These persons, we said, were politicians meeting in a typical "smoke-filled room" to settle things among themselves. The group was seated around a table, with a large card mounted before each member. Each card contained a letter, representing the player's name (for triads, A, B, and C; for pentads, A, B, C, D, and E; etc.). The purpose of the meeting was explained to be to decide on a candidate for the party chairman. Each person present was a politician representing a segment of the voting population. Each, therefore, had a certain number of votes in his pocket, and could cast them for any candidate he wished. We explained that, for our purposes, we would assume that one of the persons present would be the candidate.[3] These votes would be assigned before the game began, we explained. At that time the weights were announced publicly, and it was pointed out that the number stood symbolically for a certain number of 100s or 1000s of votes.

We also explained to the group that in this kind of situation, special advantages, or "spoils," were available, such as patronage, offices, financial gain, etc. It would be necessary, therefore, not only to choose a candidate but also to decide how the spoils should be divided. For this purpose, the number of "100" was used to represent the spoils, and it was requested that deals be cast as proportions of 100.

1 Preliminary communication

In everyday politics, the participants often have paved the way for meetings by telephone conversations, letters, luncheon sessions and various informal contacts. We did not want the players to begin their negotiations with no preparation. Therefore, we permitted them to write messages. Any player could write a message to any other player (to as many as he wished), but did not need to write to anyone unless he wished. This step was Round 1. Then in Round 2, replies could be sent, once more as many as the player wished, or none.[4] There was another reason, also, for the messages: we knew that the two sexes might well differ in the game, and we believed that negotiation might differ under written and direct communication. By providing for both we might hope to avoid favoring one sex. It turned out, however, as will be seen, that each sex behaved similarly in both communication conditions.

2 Conferences

It was announced that anyone who wished to do so could confer with anyone else—as many or as few as desired. An offer to confercould be refused. Conferees were sent out into the corridor. Usually, especially in the larger groups, conferences of the whole were held in the experimental room. There were no restrictions in time, nor in number of conferences, except that uninvited members could not join a conference. The E did not attempt to monitor conferences, except to maintain a record of who the members were. This stage continued until no more conferences could be arranged.

3 Vote

Before the actual election, a vote was taken on the issue of whether or not to call for the election. For this purpose, each player had *one* vote, and a majority determined the outcome.[5] Abstentions were permitted. If the vote failed, Ss were permitted to hold additional conferences. Usually, they did. After that, a second vote was taken. In the rare cases when this vote also failed, we announced that although the vote had failed, we would hold the election anyway, just for the record.

4 Election

Polling consisted of running alphabetically through the letters, asking for a show of hands. The sum of the weights for each candidate was determined, and the winner announced. Thereafter, the members of the winning coalition were asked to explain whatever deal might have been reached. E permitted secret ballots, if asked for, and permitted the group to record the deal privately, if they wished. Both these requests were rare.

Upon completion of the election, all messages were collected and placed into labeled envelopes. Then, if time permitted, the game was repeated with a different power pattern. A second or third session was scheduled when necessary to complete all five power patterns. These sessions were run, regardless of the number of members who appeared (except, of course, if only two showed up). Above size 3, more than half the male groups and about a third of the female groups lost members in subsequent sessions. Many more female than male groups completed the experiment in a single session.

Questionnaires

Prior to the play of each game, Ss were asked to fill out a three-item questionnaire. The same items were administered as a post-test, with tense altered, immediately following the election. The three items were, as follows:[6] 1. How much do you think you will like the game you are about to play? (5-point scale); 2. How much do you think you will like the other players in the game? (3-point scale); 3. Regardless of your feeling about the game or the other players, how would you describe your attitude about winning the competition? (5-point scale).

Power patterns

As the group becomes larger, the variety of possible power types increases rapidly. We decided to use five basic types, each of which could readily be adapted to the size of the group. These five types were All-Equal (AE), Tie (T), All-Powerful (AP), All-Different (AD), and One Stronger-One Weaker (OSW). In the All-Powerful type one player can determine the outcome of the election by his own vote alone. In the Tie and OSW types, two players can decide the election. In the AE and AD types, coalitions must be larger and/or more complex as size increases. Incidentally, it is clear that the necessity to receive a majority vote imposes severe constraints on the ability of the strongest player to arrange a minimal coalition. Oddly enough, this obstacle was not as great as might be expected. The weights may be reconstructed by the following specification, with examples for the triad and hexad: AE, one vote each (111; 111111); T, one player as many votes as the sum of the others, each with one vote (211; 511111); AP, one player with one vote more than the sum of the others (311; 611111); AD, each player holding one vote more than the next weakest (432;[7] 654321); and OSW, one player less than any other, one player holding votes equal to the sum of intermediate players (322;[7] 822221).

Before beginning the experiment, we planned to obtain at least five groups of each sex at each of the seven sizes, 3 through 9. Recruitment problems— especially the failure of scheduled Ss to appear, soon made it impossible to follow a systematic plan. Instead, we prepared 10 different orders for the power patterns and simply assigned each successive group of the same size to a new order. Thus, power patterns were rotated from group to group. Members of groups were randomly assigned weights.

Subjects

A total of 275 males served in 49 groups, and 320 females served in 56 groups.[8] The number of groups beginning in Session 1 and completing the experiment at each size was, as follows: Male—Size 3, 11 (11); Size 4, 7 (3); Size 5, 7 (3); Size 6, 6 (6); Size 7, 6 (0); Size 8, 7 (2); Size 9, 5 (2); Female —Size 3, 11 (10); Size 4, 9 (8); Size 5, 7 (6); Size 6, 7 (5); Size 7, 8 (3); Size 8, 8 (6); Size 9, 6 (2). In subsequent sessions, the number of groups at the several sizes varied because of attrition. At each size, from 5 to 16 groups were available for each power pattern, except for size 9, with two exceptions (both male, for which only three heptads played OSW and only three octads played T). Among enneads, from 3 to 5 groups played each power pattern, save for only 2 male groups with T. All Ss were SUNY/B undergraduates, recruited from introductory psychology, and awarded laboratory credits. In later tables, we shall not always present the N's represented in particular analyses. Reference to the figures above will provide approximate information.

RESULTS

Our account of the procedure followed in this experiment suggests the kinds of variables available for analysis. In reporting the data, we shall look at sex differences, as evidence for exploitative and accommodative tendencies, at differences between power patterns, and at trends as a function of size. Aspects of performance to be examined include the characteristics of messages, the number and size of conferences, the results of the vote on holding an election, the character of the election coalition and who was elected, and the character of deals reached. In addition, responses to the questionnaire will be presented.[9]

Messages

After considering the great number and variety of messages, we finally devised a set of categories into which frequencies of occurrence could readily be cast.[10] These categories were, as follows:

Definite offers to ally, with specific reference to the spoils, such as, "If you join with me, you can have 60%."

Definite offers to ally, with general reference to the spoils, such as "Let's ally and share the spoils." Or "Let's ally with F, and make a deal."

Definite offers to ally, with specific reference to other considerations, such as, "We can join with E, and make him chairman." Or, "I'll join with you, if you vote for me."

Definite offers to ally, with general reference to other considerations, such as, "Let's get A and B to join with us, and we can control the election."

Indefinite offers to ally, such as, "How about holding a conference with me?"

Game-winning remarks, such as, "Between us, we have enough votes to win."

Other remarks, such as, "I don't like this game."

Irrelevant, such as, "Did you go to class this morning?", or "I like your dress."

For the most part, messages were similar in both Round 1 and Round 2 (replies). In general, as might be anticipated, messages served to initiate coalitions, and to open the way to negotiation for deals. However, males were much more specific in these respects than females. Furthermore, female messages typically contained statements peripheral or irrelevant to the negotiation situation. With respect to differences between patterns, males were especially active in initiating definite offers in types AE and OSW, females initiated indefinite offers in all types, except AP. Both sexes were generally least active in the AP game, reflecting, probably, the fact that only one member appeared to have any importance.

With respect to size, perhaps the most interesting result, similar for both sexes, was the tendency for definite offers to decline and for indefinite offers to increase, with increasing size. In line with earlier comments, we may suppose that the larger the group the more difficult it is to determine where one's interests lie and also the more necessary it becomes to establish working relationships with other members.

In any case, it appears that the messages served to set the stage for the conferences, albeit in somewhat different ways for the two sexes. The males have already made some progress toward forming coalitions, but the females have apparently engaged in less definite social interaction.

Conferences

It might follow from the foregoing interpretation that fewer conferences would be needed by the males to arrive at coalitions—unless the messages merely stimulated their exploitative inclinations. In point of fact, the males consistently held a greater number of conferences (t-tests conducted only for pattern and size totals). Males held significantly more conferences in the T, AD, and OSW than in the AE and AP types; sex differences were significant only in sizes 4 and 7. For both sexes, the AP pattern elicited fewer conferences than other types, and the AD pattern elicited more conferences. It is of interest to note that the T and OSW types produced levels of conferring no higher than AP, in the case of the females, whereas the males made a much sharper distinction.

Variations by size were not systematic, and further research will be necessary to determine whether the significant differences found represent size-specific characteristics. Certainly, mere increase in size by itself is not accompanied by a necessity to hold more conferences.

The picture is quite different for the number of members in conferences, as shown in Figure 1. There is a highly consistent increase in the average size of conferences as the size of the group increases, quite similar for both sexes. The only exception is size 9, but this difference must be interpreted with caution because of the small number of cases. Pattern differences are also rather slight, except that male groups tend to hold larger conferences in the OSW pattern (significant at sizes 5 and 6). This finding is a little surprising, because perceived power differences are greatest in this type, and any pair involving the strong member can win. At the same time, the cheapest winning coalition for all the weak players is distinctly more favorable than a coalition with the strongest player, especially at larger sizes. Thus, larger conferences may reflect an effort to organize the minority. Here, of course, the weakest winning and cheapest winning coalitions are identical. Since the ability of the minority to overcome the strongest member is most readily perceived in the OSW type, we might expect this factor to be especially important.

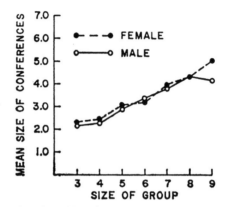

Figure 1   Mean Size of Conference by Size of Group.

Another point of distinct interest emerges from these data. The ratio of mean size of conference to size of group is remarkably constant, for groups larger than three. The value of this ratio is somewhat more than 0.50, or approximates a majority. I do not know if there is a possible law of negotiation here, but that was the characteristic of these groups. We had expected the females to hold larger conferences than males, but clearly they obey in this respect the same general principle that governs male behavior.

Voting

It will be recalled that a simple vote was held, after the conferences, to decide whether or not to proceed with the actual election. The measure that seems best to portray the outcomes is the percentage of groups in which the vote was unanimously "Yes." Only the first vote is considered here. There was no systematic trend either by power pattern or size. Thus, this characteristic appears to be a property of the group itself. There may be some tendency for male groups to display less unanimity at large sizes, as indicated by the octads and enneads, but larger samples would be necessary to establish the point. Such an interpretation, however, fits the general picture of male groups, as we shall see. In any case, sex differences are certainly far more striking than differences in size or differences in power pattern, with the females consistently reaching consensus more often. The lack of difference between types of game is especially noteworthy, since the problem of holding an election is quite different in patterns such as AP and OSW, compared to the others. That is, it requires a majority vote to permit the election to be held, yet a single player or a pair can control the election in AP, OSW, and T. For this reason, we might expect significantly more opposition in the vote in these latter cases. There is a tendency in this direction for AP, but in the opposite direction for OSW. We may suppose that establishment of a coalition usually takes the vote into account, so that enough members are recruited to constitute a majority.

The sex difference means that, regardless of the actual coalition, females tend to vote "Yes." The males, on the other hand, in agreement with the concept of exploitative behavior, very often oppose the coalitions perceived to have formed, and by making the vote fail, bring about additional negotiation. Usually, this tactic led to sufficient concession to produce a majority vote.

Election

Turning now to the actual election, we find generally similar results for the two sexes. First, we can look at the number of votes received by the winning candidate. As shown in Table 2 there is a regular increase as the size of the group increases. Such a result is not surprising. More interesting is the relation of this outcome to the minimum vote required to elect a candidate. Here we find that the actual vote quite consistently exceeds this minimum, and that this difference tends to become greater the larger the group, except for the AE type, in which both sexes tend to approximate the minimum. Especially in the T and AP types, female groups increasingly exceed the minimum. There are several possible reasons for exceeding the minimum, which can only be clarified by future research. One potent reason lies in the requirement for a majority vote that preceded the election. The size of this majority in part determines how many votes will be cast for the winning candidate. Simple calculations, however, reveal that this factor does not wholly account for the trend. In addition, other considerations must influence the coalition process, of which three seem worthy of mention. By establishing a larger coalition than would strictly be necessary, the winning bloc protects itself against defection. Aside from this, the negotiation process no doubt creates various commitments and obligations, which act against wholly free choice of coalition members. Finally, a kind of bandwagon

Table 2 Mean Number of Votes Cast for Winning candidate in the Election, by Size of Group and Power Pattern

	AE		T		AP		AD		OSW	
Size	M	SD	M	SD	M	SD	M	SD	M	SD
Male groups										
3	2.31	0.46	3.43	0.73	4.15	0.95	6.58	1.61	5.56	1.32
4	3.17	0.69	5.20	0.75	6.00	1.07	8.50	1.94	7.40	2.06
5	3.40	0.80	4.50[a]	0.50	7.83	1.46	11.40	3.04	9.67	2.56
6	5.00	1.07	7.25	1.63	9.17	1.07	13.25	2.73	13.00	3.05
7	4.86	1.36	9.80	1.47	11.29	0.88	20.14	3.68	14.75	4.21
8	5.40	0.49	9.75	2.68	10.33	2.13	22.00	2.45	19.00	4.75
9	5.00	0.00	9.40	1.96	10.75	1.47	31.00	9.93	18.13	2.87
Female groups										
3	2.33	0.75	3.18	0.94	3.83	1.34	6.33	1.43	6.08	1.11
4	3.00	0.77	4.89	0.87	5.89	1.20	7.67	1.83	5.43	1.50
5	3.57	0.49	6.63	0.99	7.75	1.20	11.44	3.59	10.67	2.36
6	4.43	1.18	7.63	1.41	9.22	1.99	13.78	4.66	12.75	3.23
7	4.44	1.42	9.86	1.96	10.14	1.55	18.86	5.74	17.00	3.95
8	6.13	1.36	11.78	2.17	10.56	3.44	26.13	4.94	20.38	5.26
9	5.33	0.47	14.00	1.63	13.75	2.77	28.50	7.65	21.60	4.50

[a]vs. Female, $t = 4.95$, $n - 14$, $p < 0.01$.

effect sometimes occurs, with non-members of the coalition deciding to go along with the seeming winner, even without promises of benefit. All these conditions must surely become increasingly important as the size of the group increases. I believe that overshooting in establishing coalitions may well be the rule where power differences exist, even without the antecedent vote requirement. It is also probable, in line with the concept of accommodative strategy, that these factors influence females more than males.

The question now arises concerning the number of persons who compose the election coalition (the same number, of course, as the number of votes in the AE type). These data show that the size of the coalitions increases with size of group, as expected. Contrary to our anticipation, however, there were no significant differences among the power patterns for either sex. Here, again, the most interesting point is the tendency to overshoot the minimum number of persons required in the types where power differences exist, increasing with the size of the group, and considerably more pronounced in female groups.

Table 3 Who Was Elected by Size of Group (in per cent)

Size	T		AP			AD									Mean	OSW		
	Wk*	Str*	None	Wk	Str	1	2	3	4	5	6	7	8	9	Wt	1	2	Str
Male Groups																		
3	0	86	14	0	100	—	17	33	50							3.3	—	62	38
4	20	80	—	0	100	0	0	50	50							3.5	0	20	80
5	50	50	—	0	100	0	0	20	20	60						4.4	17	50	33
6	33†	56	11	29†	71	0	22	0	11	33	33					4.3	10†	20	70
7	20	80	—	0	100	0	0	14	14	14	29	29				5.4	0	25	75
8	0	100	—	33	67	0	0	0	0	0	20	40	40			7.1	14	0	86
9	0	60	40	0	100	0	33	0	0	0	0	67	0	0		5.0	0	0	100
Female Groups																		
3	36	45	18	58	42	—	64	27	9							2.7	—	67	33
4	55	45	—	20	80	11	0	33	56							3.3	29	29	43
5	50	50	—	62	38	11	0	0	56	33						4.0	0	22	78
6	26	63	13	33	67	0	22	0	0	57	11					4.0	0†	13	75
7	29	57	14	43	57	0	0	0	14	46	29	0				5.1	60	0	40
8	38	63	—	33	67	13	13	13	13	13	0	25	13			4.6	13	75	13
9	67	33		25	75	0	17	17	0	17	17	0	17	17		5.5	0	60	14

M vs F:

X^2 10.36 ($n = 1$)   16.87 ($n = 1$) Strongest: 4.87 ($n = 1$)   2.82 ($n = 1$)

P <0.01 <0.01 <0.05 <0.10

Inter-Pattern Comparison (Strong vs Other): X^2 ($n = 1$)

	Male			Female		
	AP	AD	OSW	AP	AD	OSW
T	4.29[a]	8.72[b]	1.63	1.03	9.96[b]	0.33
AP		29.33[b]	13.64[b]		17.11[b]	2.51
AD			4.00[a]			6.55[a]

[a] $p < 0.05$ [b] $p < 0.01$

* Wk = Weak; Str = Strong

† One male group elected an external figurehead; one female group elected no one.

Next we can ask who was actually elected, when potential candidates differ in their strength. In three of the types, we can easily subdivide the players into two or three categories, as shown in Table 3. In the case of the

T and AP situations, it is quite apparent that in male groups the strong player is consistently much more successful in getting elected than occurs in female groups. Indeed, in the AP type, a female with the strong weight is quite willing to cast her votes for one of the weak players. This result is in line with previous findings, and fits the accommodative concept. In the OSW pattern, however, this difference is not significant. Rather, the weakest member tends to give way to one of those with a higher weight. In male groups, the strongest player appears to have an increasing advantage as size of group increases, with an opposite trend for female groups.

The AD type is clearly more complex than the others. Nevertheless, even here male groups significantly more often than female groups elect the strongest player. In fact they never elected the weakest player in sizes above the triad. Females distribute their choices more widely, with, apparently, less regard for the power of the candidate. This tendency, also, accords with accommodative strategy.

Comparison of power types reveals that for groups of both sexes, election of the strongest player was especially typical of the AP pattern, least for the AD pattern.

Deals

As in the real game of politics, so in this Politics Game election is only one kind of payoff. Players also engaged in settling on agreements concerning the spoils—at least the males did. The females evidently had other interests, suggesting that the clearly mixed-motive game of the males was for the females a mixed-up-motive game. The deals represent coalitions as much as do the elections; they were not always the same. In the case of the males, there were many instances when members of the group included in deals that involved the winning candidate did not receive a share of the spoils. Sometimes this outcome surely reflected little more than the bandwagon effect; at other times, however, we noted conspicuous instances of outright treachery. This latter phenomenon was never observed in female groups.[11] The opposite was, in fact, typical of female groups. Members of the group who did *not* vote for the winning candidate were often included in deals. On occasion, there must have been informal understandings which could only be understood by complete records of the conferences. For example, a girl might recognize that the election was settled and decide to vote for an excluded member of the coalition, with the rest of the group understanding this outcome.

For deals, we have the kinds of agreement reached and the division of the spoils. On the first of these points, it turned out that there were actually four categories of deals, namely, (1) equal sharing by members of the coalition, (2) unequal sharing of the spoils, (3) agreements only on potential resources other than spoils, and (4) no deal at all. In the third of these categories—which we shall call "Other Deals"—members agreed only on various governmental or party positions, or on rewards outside the spoils, such as new cars, vacation trips, or public services like building new roads or hospitals. A breakdown of deals into the four categories just mentioned is shown in Table 4. It can be seen that the overwhelming difference lies between the two sexes. Males in all types of power pattern, except for AE. arrive at unequal division of the spoils. Female groups decide not to have any deals at all, or secondarily, agree on various terms other than spoils. Both sexes more often arrive at equal deals in the AE pattern, as would be expected. Furthermore, the males respond more selectively to variations in power, for example, significantly less often reaching equal deals in the AP pattern. Females tend to treat alike all situations in which there is one clearly powerful person, here the T, AP, and OSW types.

The foregoing results greatly reduce, for the females, the number of quantitatively-stated deals available for analysis. For subsequent treatment, we have included only deals involving the spoils, rather than trying to re-cast other deals in these terms.

These results can be summarized without presenting tables.

There is a general tendency, in both sexes, for the weaker players to receive greater than their proportional share, and for the strongest players to receive less than a proportional share. This result agrees with previous findings (Willis, 1962; Shears, 1967).

The analysis can be carried a little farther by looking at the number of groups in which weak and strong players exceeded the proportional amounts in the T, AP, and OSW types. In female groups, the strong player has a disadvantage in all three types. However, in the AP type, male groups do not significantly assign lower shares to the strong player than would be expected from his relative weight.

The AD pattern is considerably more complex. In general, weaker players, when they are members of coalitions, receive more than expected, strong players less than expected. The lowest weights generally receive greater than a proportional share, with the highest weights receiving less than a

Table 4   Characteristic Deals Made, by Size of Group and Power Pattern (in per cent)

Size	AE			T			AP			AD			OSW		
	$=$[a]	Dis[a]	None or P[a]	$=$[a]	Dis	None or P	$=$	Dis	None or P	$=$	Dis	None or P	$=$	Dis	None or P
Male groups															
3	8	75	17 (17)	31	54	15 (0)	0	50	50 (17)	54	31	15 (15)	40	40	20 (13)
4	43	43	14 (14)	17	83	0	13	63	25 (13)	0	88	13 (0)	17	83	0
5	80	20	0	33	33	33 (0)	0	67	33 (0)	20	80	0	33	50	17 (0)
6	22	44	33 (11)	10	40	50 (0)	13	63	25 (0)	20	50	30 (10)	27	45	27 (9)
7	43	57	0	17	83	0	20	80	0	29	57	14 (14)	20	80	0
8	100	0	0	50	25	25 (0)	17	67	17 (0)	40	40	20 (0)	29	43	29 (0)
9	33	67	0	0	20	80 (0)	0	25	75 (0)	33	67	0	0	100	0
Mean	46	44	9	23	48	29	9	59	32	28	59	13	24	63	13
Female groups															
3	25	25	50 (8)	9	36	54 (9)	9	45	45 (0)	18	27	55 (9)	0	45	55 (9)
4	0	40	60 (10)	0	30	70 (10)	0	40	60 (30)	11	33	56 (0)	14	14	71 (0)
5	14	29	57 (14)	0	29	71 (0)	13	13	75 (13)	22	22	56 (11)	0	22	78 (56)
6	43	0	57 (0)	22	33	44 (22)	13	38	50 (25)	33	33	33 (11)	13	50	38 (13)
7	44	0	56 (11)	14	29	57 (14)	29	14	57 (0)	14	43	43 (0)	0	20	80 (20)
8	0	38	63 (13)	11	33	56 (0)	11	22	67 (0)	0	17	75 (13)	13	0	88 (0)
9	25	25	50 (0)	0	0	100 (0)	0	25	75 (0)	0	17	83 (17)	20	20	60 (20)
Mean	22	22	56	8	27	65	11	28	61	14	29	59	9	24	67
M vs F ($n = 1$)															
X^2	3.7*	8.2†	22.6†	3.6b	4.3*	11.3†	—	9.2†	7.7†	3.4b	7.1†	18.4†	7.8†	8.8†	26.3†

Inter-pattern comparisons (X^2) $(n = 1)$

	Male				Female			
	T	AP	AD	OSW	T	AP	AD	OSW
Equal vs Other								
AE	—	12.2†	—	— (More)	—	—	—	4.01* (More)
T		3.63*	—	6.73* (Less)		—	—	—
AP			7.60*	6.73* (Less)			—	—
AD				—				—
Unequal vs Other	No significant differences				No significant differences			
None + P vs Other								
AE		8.50*		— (Less)	No significant differences			
	No other difference is significant							

P* < 0.05   † P < 0.01.

ᵃ = refers to equal deals, Dis refers to unequal deals, P refers to agreements on positions, etc. The figures in parentheses show the per cent of "P".

ᵇP > 0.05.

proportional share. This cross-over phenomenon is shown for the male enneads in Figure 2. In female groups, although the same trends occur, differences are not significant, again indicating a tendency to disregard power relationships. However, it should be noted that very few female

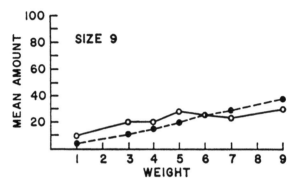

Figure 2 Amount Received in Deals versus Proportional Amount:
Type AD, Male Groups.

groups formed deals on the spoils. The fact that sex differences are not significant suggests that females at least establish deals similarly to males when spoils are involved.

Cheapest winning vs. weakest winning coalitions

Unfortunately, the power patterns used in this experiment do not yield an unequivocal distinction between cheapest coalitions and weakest winning coalitions. In each case, at least one of the players has the same proportional share in both deals. However, several sorts of evidence can be cited on this point. In general, the strongest player would always be included in the cheapest deal, the weakest player in the weakest deal. We have examined membership of individual players in deals in several different ways. There is some tendency for male groups more frequently to establish coalitions that include the strongest player, compared to those that include the weakest player, but it fails to achieve statistical significance. Indeed, in type AD, coalitions at all sizes include members of all weights with high frequency (see Table 5). As we have pointed out, the necessity to produce a majority in the antecedent vote could act against negotiating the cheapest deal. Therefore, we can examine the incidence of deals that involve more than a majority and less than a majority of the players. These data show that in

Table 5 Per cent of Inclusion in Deals, All Different Pattern*

Size	Weight:	1	2	3	4	5	6	7	8	9
					Male Groups					
3		—	77	92	62					
4		100	100	100	63					
5		80	60	100	60	80				
6		55	36	36	55	64	82			
7		57	57	71	57	29	100	81		
8		20	60	60	80	40	80	80	40	
9		67	33	67	67	67	100	100	33	67
	Mean	63	60	75	63	56	91	87	37	67
					Female Groups					
3		—	73	82	64					
4		67	67	67	89					
5		44	44	78	78	89				
6		50	70	60	60	80	80			
7		71	71	71	57	71	86	71		
8		25	63	75	25	63	83	100	75	
9		50	67	83	50	67	83	50	83	50
	Mean	51	65	74	60	74	83	74	79	50

* Including coalitions on bases other than spoils.

OSW, the greater occurrence of majority or smaller deals is not significant, but in AD the difference is significant. In OSW, for both sexes, the smaller coalitions include significantly more often the strongest player, but this difference is not significant for the AD pattern. These results provide some evidence for the cheapest winning coalition theory, but it is tenuous. Certainly, the overshooting of minimum coalitions, together with the marked advantage of the weak player previously mentioned, are equally striking.

Index to accommodative strategy

In previous experiments with triads, we have endeavored to combine several kinds of difference between the sexes into a general index. Expressed in the accommodative direction, this measure has included six components, namely, (1) not establishing coalitions, (2) forming triple alliances, (3) low level of bargaining in patterns when any two can win, (4) forming coalitions in the All-Powerful pattern, (4) reaching 50/50 deals, and (6) altruistic offers, in which one player suggests that the other two ally to her own disadvantage.

It appeared that we might be able to develop a similar index for the Politics Game. Accordingly, we sought for measures in this situation that can be regarded as the counterparts of those in the Board Game. A considerable number of possible variables were tested for sex differences. Some of them were not statistically significant, such as coalitions of all members (comparable to triple alliances in triads). Others were based on the special conditions of the Politics Game, such as the election. Finally, we settled on seven components, stated in the accommodative direction, as follows:

1. Number of Conferences: less than 2 in particular games, or with the mean less than two when games are pooled.
2. Rejection of Offers to Confer: none.
3. Vote to Hold Election: 100% "Yes" for individual games, or 100% "Yes" in three or more games for pooled analysis.
4. Elected a Weak Member: In T, AP, AD, or OSW, or two or more times for pooled games.
5. Size of Deal Coalition: above the minimum required, or four or five above the minimum for pooled games.
6. Kind of Deal: none, equal, or on a basis other than spoils, with such outcomes in 4 or 5 games for pooled data.
7. Altruistic Outcomes: Any instance in which someone is elected by the other players, with the member in question voting for one of them, or abstaining.[12] For example, the all-powerful player might cast her votes for one of the others, or in a pentad OSW, where the weights are A6, B2, C2, D2, and E1, the result might be 12 votes for E, or a coalition of ABCD, with E voting for one of the others.

Each of these seven measures differentiates between the sexes to a high degree of significance, with Chi Square ranging from 5.79 (Sign 5, $n = 1$, $p < 0.02$) to 22.86 (Sign 4, $n = 1$, $P < 0.001$). Furthermore, differences are consistent across the seven sizes. Therefore, we need consider the data only for the total Index (Figure 3). It can be seen that the two sexes differ significantly at each size. The trends for the two sexes are in opposite directions, albeit slight, with the males showing a decrease in accommodativeness with increasing size, the females an increase. (When the index was computed only for the groups that remained the same size in all sessions, the results were quite similar.) The two even sizes, tetrads and hexads, display a distinct reversal for the females. The other even size, octads, does not appear to be a reversal, but we must allow for the very small sample of enneads. Thus, it appears that small even-numbered sizes somehow influence females differently from odd-numbered sizes. The obvious reason, no doubt, lies in the greater difficulty in achieving decisions by majority action in even-numbered sizes. We cannot confirm this notion from the data of this experiment, nor explain why the males did not manifest the same phenomenon.

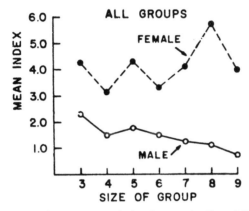

Figure 3   Index to Accomodative Strategy by Size of Group.

Questionnaire

We turn, finally, to our measures of attitudes, using data from Session 1. The results are closely similar to those obtained in previous experiments. With respect to interest in the game (Question 1), the males initially antici-pate significantly more enjoyment but by the end of the session the differ-ence is not significant. Both sexes express significantly greater enjoyment at the end of the session. The opposite effect occurs for liking of the other players. The males express less liking, and, although both sexes indicate more liking after the session, the sex difference continues to be significant. With regard to winning, males indicate a significantly greater desire to win, with females indifferent to winning. The actual play has little effect, with this difference about the same after as before the game was played. There may be some trends in these attitudes as a function of size, but they are slight.

These results mirror our distinction between exploitative and accommoda-tive strategy. It is clearly in line with exploitativeness to withhold too great liking for one's opponents, if one is to engage in behavior that may injure him. Similarly, a strong desire to win lies at the heart of exploitativeness. The fact that the game was enjoyed equally by both sexes also fits our concepts. The two strategies are simply contrasting ways to deal with the same situation.[13]

DISCUSSION

We have waded through a mass of data as best we could. In view of the numerous dimensions of the experiment, it may be well briefly to summarize the outstanding points.

We can organize the findings under the headings of *sex differences*, *comparison of power patterns*, and *variations in size of group*.

Sex Differences

Females send many more messages than males, with a higher incidence of general, peripheral, and irrelevant content. Males hold more conferences, especially in power patterns in which internal differences are important in determining the winner. Females hold fewer conferences, with less regard for the power situation. This difference is interesting because the written messages do not appear to serve for the females the function of arriving at outcomes. In spite of this antecedent opportunity to negotiate, the females were no farther toward establishing coalitions than the males—less, in fact, judging by the content of the messages. Both sexes were alike in the size of the conferences held. When the issue was raised of voting on the holding of an election, the females typically voted unanimously in favor, the male groups typically contained dissident or abstaining members. In their composition, election coalitions were much alike in the two sexes. However, the males typically elected the strongest member of the group, the females typically did not discriminate on the basis of strength. In both sexes, the coalitions typically exceeded the minimum required, partly, at least, because of the requirement for a majority vote on the election. With respect to deals, male coalitions were characterized by orientation to the spoils and by disproportionate allocations to the members. Female coalitions typically ignored the spoils, divided equally, or refused to make a deal. Males responded to variations in power pattern; females did not distinguish so clearly between patterns. Finally, the two sexes displayed highly significant differences on seven general characteristics, which we cast in the form of an Index to Accommodative Strategy.

Power patterns

Aside from sex differences in reacting to the several patterns, it is remarkable that in general behavior was quite similar on all the patterns. Those differences that do occur are much as would be expected. The AP pattern elicited fewer conferences and placed the strongest player in a more favorable position, compared to other patterns.

It was not expected that behavior would be so similar in the several patterns, judging from triad studies. A possible reason lies in the vote requirement, as previously mentioned. The ability of the minority to counteract the powerful member is clearly apparent. Under these circumstances we might even be surprised that the strong member, in male groups, does as well as he does. An important factor here is the ability of the strong man to pit one member against another, especially in the AP pattern, when no one can win without him.

Another factor that may tend to vitiate differences in power pattern is the basic character of the game itself. It was introduced and described as a game of politics. This simulation generally served to mobilize attitudes that are probably not salient, if they operate at all, in most experimental games. Thus, players commented on voting to preserve party loyalty, individuals elected indicated the importance of obtaining widespread support in order to carry out policy, etc. Thus, sheer power was far from the major consideration in the actions of either weak or strong players. Thus, as we have pointed out elsewhere (Vinacke, 1969), studies of experimental games require the investigation of diverse situations. Certainly coalition formation in our simulated politics game is not wholly the same phenomenon as in the board game.

Size of group

Judging by the written messages, negotiation, at least in its early stages, has a less specific character as size increases. Within the range of three to nine, direct conferences do not increase in number, as size increases. That is, enneads did not require appreciably, if any, more conferences to arrive at decisions than triads. Our policy of not monitoring the conferences means that we do not know whether they may have varied in character in larger groups. It is probable, for example, that they may more often have involved blocs and/or their representatives. Thus, larger groups may use conferences to arrange blocs and then to consolidate interests—a two- or three-stage process—whereas smaller groups may proceed directly to the terms of agreement—a one-stage process. In any case, the actual episodes themselves are apparently similar in number. The size of conferences increases, as would expected from the increased size of the majority required. In the election, the significant point is the phenomenon of "overshooting" the minimum needed to win, in the patterns with internal power variations (except for AP). This overshooting appears to become increasingly greater as size increases, especially in female groups. As size increases, male groups increasingly elect the strongest member of the group, with the reverse effect for females. Finally, males appear to become increasingly exploitative as size increases, females to become increasingly accommodative, save for the possibility that even-numbered groups pose special difficulties for females.

Thus, we have considerable evidence about how small groups act in this kind of negotiation situation. In answer to the first problem raised at the beginning, it is evident that group size is an important factor influencing the formation of coalitions. For one thing, the tendency for the weaker players to unite against the stronger member is drastically reduced, and the chance for the weakest person to be elected becomes very slight in male groups. However, the weak member of coalitions is very likely to have an increasing advantage in deals as size increases, relative to his contribution in power. We can see, then, important differences between triads and larger groups. Finally, the overshooting phenomenon appears to increase with size. Future research can explore this phenomenon farther, particularly to ascertain the factors responsible. Certainly, the problems of putting together a sufficient coalition become noticeably greater in larger groups. We might posit an uncertainty principle. In small groups, commitments and expectations are no doubt clearer and more dependable. In larger groups, these relationships are less dependable.

The second issue concerns the characteristics of strategy, as reflected in sex differences. It was sharply evident that the two sexes play the game of politics quite differently, as summarized above. We see exploitative strategy manifested in intensive bargaining, in adapting to variations in power relationships, in the success of the strong member in winning election, and in orientation to the division of spoils. Accommodative strategy, on the other hand, pays less attention to power relationships, leads to more unanimity in decisions, more equal allocation of resources, and less concern for the spoils of victory.

The important point, here, is that both strategies are fully effective in solving the central problem: electing a member of the group. Accommodative persons choose one of their number to be party chairman, too, but the basis on which they do so is different. Decisions are less influenced by power relationships and personal gain. The implications of this difference are well worth considering. Our society follows primarily an exploitative model, at least on the surface. Would we be better off with an accommodative orientation? We would have a different society, but whether it would be better or worse is a matter of speculation. Some part of the answer might be provided by research in which these two kinds of strategy are deliberately manipulated and allowed to operate in a variety of problem situations.

Finally, we raised the theoretical issue of whether coalitions are based on perception that solidarity can overcome power or on cheapest winning deals. Although our data do not permit a clear test, the available evidence strongly suggests that neither theory is correct. The overshooting phenomenon, especially, indicates that the problem of establishing an effective coalition supersedes in importance the particular terms of winning. On the other hand, in this experiment, at least, the weak minority seldom succeeded in forming a winning coalition. Rather, in groups larger than triads, the strong player is the key member, and the coalition forms around him, especially in male groups. It is safe to say that no single factor, nor any simple theory, can by itself explain coalition formation. We require, instead, a field theory that allows for the interaction of all relevant variables (Vinacke, 1969).

One final comment. Have we successfully simulated politics in this Politics Game? It was not our primary intention to do so, but rather to investigate a number of variables in small groups of varying size. Therefore, the most we can say is that we were concerned with smallgroup politics. There are, of course, many natural settings like this, including the "smoke-filled rooms" to which we oriented our subjects. It is to be hoped that our findings contribute something to understanding such situations. Beyond that, we can suppose that by clarifying factors in coalition phenomena we may contribute to an understanding of politics at any level. Finally, the concepts of exploitative and accommodative strategy appear to have important implications for the real world of politics.

NOTES

1 The research on which this article is based was supported by contract with the Office of Naval Research [Nonr 4374(00)].

2 The latter theory is stated, here, in the way we have consistently interpreted it. In Caplow's (1956) original formulation, he suggested that AC is also likely, because of the attractiveness of C for A. Gamson's theory predicts BC, not BC *or* AC.

3 All groups, except one, treated those present as potential candidates. One male group regularly elected a figure-head from outside the group, thus aiming to control the party.

4 Instructions were given to identify on each message the letter of the sender with an arrow indicating the recipient. Sheets were numbered "1" and "2" to identify messages and replies.

5   In a few cases, we allowed a plurality to settle the matter, in the interests of proceeding with the election. In actual politics failure to achieve a majority would no doubt always lead to further negotiation.

6   These questions were retained without change from previous experiments, despite some ambiguity, here, in what constituted "winning". This bothered some Ss, but most of them filled out the blank without comment.

7   Retained from previous studies for comparison and to avoid ties.

8   Two male groups were eliminated, both of size 6, because they stated that they had treated the experiment as a joke. There was plenty of evidence to sustain this assertion. This left 6 hexads.

9   Space limitations prevent tabular presentation of all data. These materials may be found in Vinacke (1968).

10 My thanks go to Stuart Katz for ably conducting this tedious tabulation.

11 We must, of course, allow for the fact that the experimenter was a male of high status. Even so, it is doubtful that the characteristics of the experimenter can wholly account for this difference. Rather, we attribute it primarily to the difference between exploitative and accommodative strategy.

12 In some cases, this phenomenon might reflect some attitude other than altruism, such as rejection of responsibility.

13 Our policy has always been to avoid direct influence on participants in the game. Both sexes are allowed, insofar as possible, to construe the game in their own fashion. We would expect to see the females expressing less enjoyment if they were required to act exploitatively, and probably vice versa. I say "probably" because we have found through administering the Test of Strategy (Vinacke, Cherulnik, and Lichtman, 1968) that there are relatively more accommodative males than there are exploitative females.

REFERENCES

Bales, R. F., and Borgatta, E. F. Size of Group as a Factor in the Interaction Profile. In A. P. Hare, E. F. Borgatta, and R. F. Bales (Eds.), *Small Groups: Studies in Social Interaction*. (Rev. Ed.) New York: Knopf, 1965. Pp. 495–512.

Caplow, T. A theory of coalitions in the triad. *American Sociological Review* 1965, **21**, 489–493.

Deutsch, M., and Krauss, R. M. The effect of threat upon interpersonal bargaining. *Journal of Abnormal and Social Psychology*, 1960, **61**, 181–189.

Gamson, W. A. A theory of coalition formation. *American Sociological Review*, 1961, **26**, 373–382.

Rapoport, A., and Chammah, A. M. *Prisoner's Dilemma; A Study in Conflict and Cooperation*. Ann Arbor, Michigan: University of Michigan Press, 1965.

Shears, L. M. Patterns of coalition formation in two games played by male tetrads. *Behavioral Science*, 1967, **12**, 130–137.

Simmel, G. The number of members as determining the sociological form of the group. *American Journal of Sociology*, 1902–03, **8**, 1–46; 158–196.

Thomas, E. J., and Fink, C. F. Effects of group size. *Psychological Bulletin*, 1963, 60, 371–384.

Vinacke, W. E. Negotiations and decisions in a politics game. Technical Report No. 13, 1968, State University of New York at Buffalo, Contract Nonr 4374(00).

Vinacke, W. E. Variables in experimental games: toward a field theory. *Psychological Bulletin*, 1969, **71**, 293–318.

Vinacke, W. E., and Arkoff, A. An experimental study of coalitions in the triad. *American Sociological Review*, 1957, **22**, 406–414.

Vinacke, W. E., Cherulnik, P. D., and Lichtman, C. M. Strategy in Intra-Triad and Inter-Triad Interaction. Technical Report No. 12, 1968, Nonr 4374(00). Buffalo, N. Y.: State University of New York at Buffalo.

Willis, R. H. Coalitions in the triad. *Sociometry*, 1962, **25**, 358–376.

COALITION FORMATION AND CHANGE[1]

BERNHARDT LIEBERMAN

University of Pittsburgh

Three persons who interact may find themselves in situations in which they must communicate, negotiate, and make a decision which produces some outcome; this outcome may yield some quantifiable reward or payoff to the group of three, and the members of the group must then divide this payoff. Many situations of this kind exist: three business concerns may collude to limit their production and divide a particular market; three partners in a business firm may divide the work load, income, and profits; and three nations may divide the costs of a military facility.

This general situation is both fascinating and complex and the understanding of it may be advanced in a number of ways. In recent years investigators, stimulated by modern notions of decision theory and game theory, have focussed their attention on the processes involved when three persons form coalitions.[2] Analysis of the three-person coalition situation indicates that it is one in which both cooperation and conflict are present simultaneously. The three persons involved in the group usually stand in some relationship to one or more other persons; and it is in the interest of each one to maximize the payoff of the group. But once the payoff to the group is specified the three no longer have completely coordinate interests; it is then in each person's interest to either maximize the return to himself, or strike a bargain he considers favorable or satisfactory. In this situation if two of the three persons form a coalition against the third to advance their interests they can often obtain an advantage over the third person. Of course, the two must not so disadvantage the third so that he withdraws from the group.[3]

6*

Lieberman (1969) has argued that understanding coalition processes is essential to the understanding of the resolution of difficult social choice problems. If one person has the power to resolve a difficult social choice, and if there is disagreement among the participants in the decision, the powerful person will, in all likelihood, make the decision himself. However, in most difficult collective decision situations one person usually does not have sufficient power to effect the decision; he must secure the agreement of the others involved—coalitions must be formed. Hence, understanding coalition processes is essential to the understanding of the social choice problem.

This paper reports the results of two studies; the first was designed to discover whether cohesive coalitions could be produced in an experimental game situation. When the results of this first study showed this was possible a second study was done in which three-person coalitions were manipulated. After stable coalitions were formed the rewards or payoffs to the players were altered so that the cohesive coalitions were broken.

These games raise a number of interesting questions. The first question, which is an empirical one, is whether it is possible to form stable cohesive coalitions and then break them in experimental situations.

The second set of questions raised by the studies are questions traditional in science. They are descriptive questions of the following order: how do people behave when they are in a three-person bargaining situation? What are the factors or forces that explain the observed behavior?

A third set of questions raised by the studies, normative questions, pose a number of provocative questions. These questions raise the ancient problem of what is right and wrong, what is fair and unfair—the question of how people *should* behave. For many years most behavioral scientists believed, and some still do, that science should not concern itself with questions of value, morality, and fairness—the normative questions.[4] Recent work has shown, however, that the two sets of questions, the normative and descriptive, are related (Lieberman, 1960, 1962, 1964); and that both the normative and descriptive aspects of behavior may be treated objectively and rigorously, utilizing mathematical notions of considerable depth, and also empirical techniques (Luce and Raiffa, 1957; Rapoport, 1962). It is interesting to note that we have again raised the older philosophical questions of right and wrong, of fairness and unfairness. But these classical problems have been raised somewhat differently; they have been posed in other, behavioral contexts, in the context of multi-person interaction, in situations in which people are in conflict or in situations of joint conflict and cooperation. The older, general unanswerable questions have been replaced by more sophisticated, manageable questions. Instead of raising the general questions: what is right, how should people behave, we raise a more specific question. Given an explicit value system or purpose, how should people behave to satisfy that value system? Thus, we have divided the gross, normative question into two questions: what goals or values shall people have, and given these goals or values how shall they behave to obtain these goals? The work to be reported here deals only cursorily, if at all, with the first question, but it deals more fully with the second question. This work assumes that individuals wish to obtain some maximum or satisfactory amount of reward or payoff. The analysis then proceeds to an examination of how they should behave to obtain this reward, and also how they actually do behave. The particular three-person, non-zero-sum games our Ss played do not have any precise, rational solution in a conventional game-theoretic sense. Previous work has shown that when Ss play games with precise solutions many of them do adopt these solutions, and some behave as the normative model prescribes. But in games that have no precise solutions, Ss exhibit a variety of behaviors[5] (Lieberman, 1960, 1962).

The study reported here was of this latter type; the normative, mathematical theory offered no prescription that would yield a stable, convincing resolution of the conflict. The Ss had to find ways of resolving the conflict situation they found themselves in to receive the rewards that were available. Careful examination of the Ss' behavior will enable us to examine the characteristics of the exhibited behavior which will enable us to consider the adequacy of a notion—*behavioral solutions* of games.

In its most general meaning a solution of an *n*-person game is a prescription to the participants that dictates to each exactly how he should behave. These prescriptions are not arbitrary, random, or capricious. The prescriptions are said to have certain properties; they offer the participants a "stable," "rational," or "fair" outcome to the conflict they are engaged in. Formal game theory (the mathematical developments) has failed to offer satisfying and convincing solutions to *n*-person games. Von Neumann and Morgenstern in commenting on the limitations of the normative theory indicate that behavioral considerations have a bearing on solution notions. Normative theory may provide a set of imputations or possible outcomes, but behavioral considerations determine which of these outcomes are chosen.

The study to be reported here yields information about which of the possible outcomes are selected. We can examine our Ss' behavior to see whether they produce *behavioral solutions*, resolutions of the conflicts that have the properties of solutions—properties of "stability," "rationality," and "fairness."

Study 1

Method

The Game   The Ss played repetitions of a three-person, non-zero-sum majority game described by the following payoff function.

If players one and two formed a coalition they received $ 0.20 from *E*; player three received nothing.

It players one and three formed a coalition they received $ 0.20 from *E*; player two received nothing.

If players two and three formed a coalition they received $ 0.20 from *E*; player one received nothing.

If no pair or coalition formed no payoff was made.

It was possible for the players to receive bonus payments. If, for 10 consecutive choices, two players chose each other, they received a bonus payment. For the first 10 mutual choices the two players made they received an additional $ 0.50. If, without interruption, they proceeded to choose each other for another 10 choices, they received an additional $ 1.00. If they again chose each other for a third consecutive 10 choices, they received a bonus of $ 1.50. If they continued to choose each other for a fourth consecutive 10 choices, they received a bonus of $ 2.00.

If two players chose each other 10, 20, or 30 times consecutively and there were fewer than 10 choices remaining, the appropriate bonus was paid for consecutive choices fewer than 10 that concluded the game. For example, if two players chose each other on trials 23–32 they received the normal payment of $ 0.20 per trial plus the bonus of $ 0.50. If they continued to choose each other on trials 33–40 they received the $ 1.00 bonus in addition to the normal payments.

If a particular coalition held together for 20 consecutive choices they first received the 50-cent bonus and then the $ 1.00 bonus. If the coalition split after 20 choices and a different coalition formed for 10 choices, that coalition received the initial bonus of $ 0.50.

Subjects   The Ss were 33 men, undergraduate students of the State University of New York at Stony Brook in residence during the academic year 1962–1963. Eleven groups of three Ss took part in the experiment.

Materials   The materials used consisted of the following items: (1) written instructions to the Ss; (2) red, white, and blue chips; (3) red, white and blue choice cards that the Ss used to indicate who they wished to form a coalition with; (4) red, white, and blue message cards that the Ss used to communicate with; (5) pencils and scrap paper which were available to the Ss.

Procedure   The Ss were blindfolded and brought to the experimental room so that they could not see who the two other players were. They were seated at three tables which were separated from each other by two screens, so that all through the experimental session the Ss could not see the other two players.

The Ss had copies of written instructions in front of them throughout the play of the game; prior to play these instructions were presented to them orally by means of a tape recorder. The Ss listened to the instructions and were instructed to follow the instructions on the written instruction sheets in front of them. The instructions described the three-person, non-zero-sum majority game—what the Ss were to do to receive payoffs. The game was played 40 times; on each play of the game the Ss placed in front of them one of the three choice cards available to them. Each S could choose a zero, which indicated that he did not wish to form a coalition with either one of the other players, or he could choose the number of one of the two other players. After the three choices were made the *E* collected the cards and informed the Ss which coalition had formed. Payoffs were made with chips immediately after each play of the game. When a bonus was due to a coalition, chips were given immediately. Before and after each play of the games the players were permitted to communicate using written messages. The cards were used to communicate, make suggestions, offer bargains, accept bargains, reject bargains, and divide the winnings. The Ss had to divide the payments, since each payment was to the coalition. The Ss wrote messages to make these divisions.

Each S was given $ 2.00 worth of chips at the start of the game; this was a base pay which the Ss received whether or not they earned any additional money during the course of play.

Questionnaires   The Ss completed a questionnaire at the conclusion of the play of the game. The questionnaire was a simple one which asked the Ss how they played the game, what determined their choices, and how they divided the winnings.

Solutions

To some extent the minimax theorem offers an adequate solution of the two-person, zero-sum game; although the solution is convincing, it does have some weaknesses. The minimax solution does not enable the person following its prescription to take advantage of any weakness in his opponent's play. The minimax solution assumes that an opponent is both rational and clever. Should an opponent apparently be playing non-rationally in a series of plays of the game, the player who uses the minimax solution must consider the possibility that his opponent is attempting to trick him and so the player adopting the minimax solution must adopt the conservative prescription of the theory, even when he is playing against a weak opponent.

When we consider n-person, zero-sum and n-person, non-zero-sum games we see that the solution notions offered are even less adequate than minimax theory. The solution notions offered do not yield precise prescriptions of behavior to each player. Since the very essence of a convincing solution is the requirement that it unambiguously direct the behavior of the players so that they accomplish their goals, current solution theory of n-person games is admittedly inadequate. The von Neumann and Morgenstern solution of n-person games yields a set of imputations, a plethora of possible outcomes, and from these the players must somehow choose a stable outcome.

Luce and Raiffa (1957) point out that the von Neumann and Morgenstern, and other solutions, include no psychological or sociological assumptions about behavior which will enable those in conflict to find a stable solution of the game they are playing. This fact is a major weakness of current n-person solution theory. The solution notions also contain no treatment of communication and coalition formation processes, both of which must be considered to obtain a convincing solution of n-person games. The research described here deals with just these questions, communication and coalition formation, in an attempt to deepen our understanding of these processes.

If the mathematical theory does not yield convincing solutions of the n-person game we may raise the question, what can descriptive studies do to illuminate solution processes? One tack is possible. We can analyze what general properties solutions have, what the characteristics of a convincing solution are. We can then examine the actual behaviors, the resolutions of the conflict that our Ss adopt, and see whether the exhibited behavior has some of these properties or characteristics.

Analysis of the properties or characteristics of a solution indicate that there are a series of related but somewhat ambiguous notions involved in the concept of a solution. *One usually thinks that a solution should prescribe rational, optimal behavior to the participants, behavior that will enable the participants to find an equitable, stable, and possibly a unique resolution of their conflict.*

A convincing solution should prescribe, rather precisely, what the participants in a game should do, exactly how they should behave. The minimax solution of a two-person, zero-sum game does this quite adequately. In a strictly-determined game the solution tells each player to choose one of his available strategies on a single play, or repeatedly if repetitions of the game are played. In a game requiring the use of mixed strategies the minimax prescription is also adequate; it tells the players with what probability to choose each of his available strategies, and gives him instructions how to make his choices on each play of the game—a random device should be used. The minimax solution also dictates how the reward being contested for should be divided; the *value* of the game determines this most important consideration. But in most *n*-person games, both zero-sum and non-zero-sum, the solutions we have fail to specify precisely how the players should behave; the solutions fail to prescribe precisely which coalitions should form and how the available rewards should be divided among the members of the successful coalition. A convincing solution of an *n*-person game should do just these things: it should prescribe precisely how each player should behave on each play of a game; it should prescribe which coalitions should form, and which should not; and it should prescribe how the rewards being contested for should be divided among the participants.

A solution should prescribe "rational" behavior to the players. But the term rational is a vague one, and one of the contributions of minimax theory has been to make specific, for the two-person, zero-sum game, one definition of rationality. The notion of rationality usually refers to some maximization process, a procedure by which the players receive some maximum amount of a reward. The maximization notion is quite specific for the two-person, zero-sum game. Since it is assumed that each player wishes to maximize the payoff to himself, and since the game is one of pure conflict, where whatever one person gains the other loses, each player is attempting to inflict a maximum loss on the other. What emerges is a very specific notion of maximization, that of minimizing maximum loss. The player who adopts a minimax strategy is aware of the wishes of his opponent and is willing to settle for maximizing his minimum gain.

In the n-person game we do not have a comparable, sophisticated, convincing notion of maximization. What we have are a number of different maximizing notions (e.g. maximize the product of the payoffs as in a Nash solution) or just the primitive, undefined notion that something should be maximized.

The notion that the outcome of the game, the division of the payoffs, should be fair or equitable in some sense contradicts another element of the idea of a solution—that each player should maximize the return to himself. Minimax theory resolves this contradiction by employing the concept of the value of the game. If a player is willing to adopt the conservative, minimax strategy he is assured of getting at least the value of the game. The outcome is fair or equitable in that sense. The various solution notions offered for n-person games yield different "values"; the various solution notions do not yield a value that is as convincingly fair as the value of the minimax solution. A convincing solution of the n-person game, be it normative or behavioral, will have to deal with the problem of fairness.

Discussions of solutions state that a solution should be stable or in equilibrium; that is, once the players adopt the behavior prescribed by the solution there should be no force (or the forces should be negligible) acting upon them to change their behavior. Again the minimax solution satisfies this requirement, for if a player deviates from the prescribed strategy he usually runs the risk of losing more (or winning less) than the value of the game. N-person solution theory offers us no such assurance of stability. In the von Neumann and Morgenstern solution players may move from one set of imputations to another without violating the solution notion.

The final property which a solution should, hopefully, have is that of uniqueness or optimality. In some way the solution should prescribe behavior that is best, and hopefully a *single* prescription of behavior should have this characteristic of "bestness." The minimax solution satisfies this requirement partially, for the *value* of the game is unique. However, one or both players may obtain this value by adopting a number of different strategies, although in some games the prescribed strategies are unique. In n-person games we normally have a surfeit of possible solutions and neither the strategies to be adopted nor the payoffs to the players have the optimality-uniqueness characteristic.

Results

Table 1.1 presents the percentages of outcomes—the coalitions that formed—for the 11 groups of Ss in blocks of five trials (plays of the game). No coalition formed 1.4% of the time; coalition (1, 2) formed 17.0% of the time; coalition (1, 3) formed 36.1% of the time; and coalition (2, 3) formed 45.5% of the time. The (2, 3) coalition occurred with the greatest frequency.

Table 1.1 Percentage of outcome in blocks of five trials

Trial Block	Percent of Outcome			
	0	1	2	3
1– 5	5.5	20.0	18.2	56.3
6–10	0	9.1	18.2	72.7
11–15	1.8	21.8	18.2	58.2
16–20	0	27.3	25.5	47.3
21–25	1.8	18.2	43.6	36.4
26–30	0	10.9	61.8	27.3
31–35	0	14.5	49.1	36.4
Mean	1.4	17.0	36.1	45.5

0 indicates no coalition formed; 1 indicates coalition (1, 2) formed; 2 indicates coalition (1, 3) formed; 3 indicates coalition (2, 3) formed.

The data of Table 1.1 describe the coalition formation processes, over the 440 plays of the game, but they are not the most interesting results. Since all coalitions received the same payoff we would expect to find no differences in the frequency of the formation of the different coalitions. The observed differences are most likely the result of the lack of independence among the choices.[6]

Table 1.2 contains data describing the stability of the coalitions that formed. Column 2 presents the number of coalition changes that occurred; these varied from 0–7—when the number of changes was 0 the Ss formed a coalition on the first play of the game and continued to make the same choices throughout the entire 40 plays of the game. The modal number of coalition changes was 0, the mean 2.64, the median 3. Column 5 indicates the number of runs, the number of times successive, identical coalitions formed; there is always one more run than coalition change.

Table 1.2 Stability of Coalitions

1	2	3	4	5	6
Game No.	No Coalition Changes	Length of Last Run and Outcome		No Runs	Length of Runs
1	4	26 (1, 2)		5	2 1 1 10 26
2	7	2 (1, 3)		8	1 10 1 10 10 3 3 2
3	3	24 (1, 3)		4	10 5 1 24
4	2	38 (1, 3)		3	1 1 38
5	3	14 (1, 3)		4	4 21 1 14
6	0	40 (1, 3)		1	40
7	0	40 (2, 3)		1	40
8	0	40 (2, 3)		1	40
9	6	6 (1, 2)		7	10 10 10 3 3 3 1 0
10	4	16 (1, 3)		5	2 10 11 1 16
11	0	40 (2, 3)		1	40

Number of Coalition Changes		*Length of Runs*	
Mean	2.64	Mean	11
Median	3	Median	5
Mode	0	Mode	1

Columns 3 and 4 indicate the length of the last run and the coalition that formed on that last run. In games 6, 7, 8, and 11 where there were no coalition changes at all, there was but one run. In games 7, 8, and 11 the (2, 3) coalition occurred on all trials; in game 6 coalition (1, 3) occurred on all trials. These data make clear why there were a larger number of (1, 3) and (2, 3) coalitions. Once Ss formed a stable coalition, either (1, 3) or (2, 3), there was considerable pressure—the bonus payments—to keep the coalition intact. Hence, we find the largest number of (2, 3) coalitions, a lesser number of (1, 3) coalitions, and the smallest number of (1, 2) coalitions.

Column 6 of Table 1.2 contains the lengths of the various runs that occurred. Four of the games had runs of 40; the other games had runs of varying sizes. The modal length of runs was 1, with a median of 5 and a mean of 11.

Division of payoffs   Most of the 20c payoffs, 87.8% of them, were divided evenly by the pair that received them. The only other division of earnings that occurred with any appreciable frequency (11.3% of the time) was the 15–5 division. And even some of these were, in reality, an even division, for the Ss alternated 15–5, 5–15 divisions to produce an even split of the earnings. Where the 15–5 split did occur it often came about after one player—the one who accepted the 5c payoff—was left out of a long series of coalitions and he was willing to accept the smaller payoff in order to obtain some payoff. Forty-one of the 42 bonus payments were equal divisions.

Analysis of messages and questionnaires   The messages that the Ss wrote and their answers to the questionnaires indicate that two very different strategies were adopted which led to stable outcomes (or perhaps solutions) of the games. If neither of these over-all strategies were adopted instability characterized all 40 plays of the games.

Five of the 11 groups adopted what has been termed an exploitative or competitive strategy (Gamson, 1964). These Ss simply formed a coalition on the first play of the game (or in one game on the third play) and that coalition remained stable through to the termination of the game. This strategy was accompanied by an even split of the payoffs and the bonuses. The Ss were quite aware of the instabilities and chaos that could result from attempting to change coalition partners or trying to get more than 50% of the payoffs and bonuses. The third player, the one left out of the coalition, usually tried to break the coalition by making attractive offers of uneven divisions of payoffs to one or both players in the coalition. In these five games those offers failed; indeed, the threat to the cohesiveness of the coalition served to fortify it. The members of the coalition in these situations would send reassuring notes to each other, imploring each other to be faithful to their mutual interest.

The members of two of the groups adopted what Gamson (1964) has termed an anti-competitive (or cooperative) strategy. Prior to the first trial the Ss communicated in some detail forming a plan of alternating coalitions or series of 10 coalitions. This plan enabled them to divide the earnings approximately equally, still managing to earn some bonus money.

If the Ss did not adopt one of the two strategies described above there was little stability or order present in their behavior. Coalitions would form and be maintained for 20, 10, or fewer plays. The 40 trials would conclude with bargaining and instability still present.

Study 2

The results of study 1 demonstrated that it was possible, in some cases, to produce cohesive, stable coalitions in a three-person, non-zero-sum game, by offering bonus payments to players who repeatedly formed the same coalition. In study 2 an attempt was made to manipulate coalition formation; stable coalitions were induced as in study 1, and then payoffs were changed so that players in the stable coalition were induced to break that coalition.

The study employed a complex design; Ss played a three-phase, three-person, non-zero-sum game. In phase 1 the Ss became familiar with the complex bargaining processes that can occur in such games. In phase 2 the Ss played a game very similar to that of study 1 which led to stable coalitions. In phase 3 the groups that formed stable coalitions were offered payoffs that tended to break the coalitions.

The study design provided, in phase 3, greater and lesser incentives to maintain the stable coalitions that formed in phase 2, in an attempt to assess the relative effects of present reward and past bargaining experience on the stability of coalitions. There were two experimental groups and one control group. For the players in one of the experimental groups the stable coalition that formed in phase 2 received a very small payoff if it continued into the third phase. The second experimental group received a larger payoff (than the first group) if the coalition remained stable, but there was still an incentive to dissolve the stable coalition that formed in phase 2. The details are discussed below.

Method

The methods of study 2 were identical to those of study 1 with the exceptions necessary to conduct the three-phase game. The Ss were 75 male, undergraduate students of the State University of New York at Stony Brook in residence during the academic year 1963–64. Seventy-five men, randomly selected from the entire male undergraduate student population, participated in the study. The materials, procedures, and questionnaires were similar to those in study 1 but were adapted for the three-phase game.

The game   The Ss played a three-phase, three-person, non-zero-sum game; payoffs varied in each phase. The study design is summarized in Table 2.1.

The Ss were divided into three experimental groups or conditions (A, B, C). There were nine triads in condition A, eight in condition B, and eight in condition C. The payoffs for all conditions were identical in the eight trials of phase 1. If the (1, 2) coalition formed it received 20 ¢ from the experimenter; player 3 received nothing and lost nothing. The (1, 3) coalition received 16 ¢ and the (2, 3) coalition received 12 ¢; the excluded player in each case lost nothing.

Table 2.1 Design of study 2

Phase	Group A	Group B	Group C
Phase 1 8 Trials	(1, 2) R + 20 (1, 3) R + 16 (2, 3) R + 12	(1, 2) R + 20 (1, 3) R + 16 (2, 3) R + 12	(1, 2) R + 20 (1, 3) R + 16 (2, 3) R + 12
Phase 2 40 Trials	(1, 2), (1, 3), (2, 3) R + 20 Bonus $ 0.50, 1.00 1.50, 2.00	(1, 2), (1, 3), (2, 3) R + 20 Bonus $ 0.50, 1.00 1.50, 2.00	(1, 2), (1, 3), (2, 3),R + 20 Bonus $ 0.50, 1.00 1.50, 2.00
Phase 3 20 Trials	*(1, 2) R + 4 (1, 3) R + 28 (2, 3) R + 28	*(1, 2) R + 16 (1, 3) R + 24 (2, 3) R + 24	(1, 2), (1, 3), (2, 3) R + 20

*Assumes (1, 2) stable coalition in Phase 2

(1, 2) R + 20 indicates that this coalition received 20 ¢.

In phase 2, which lasted 40 trials in all conditions, all three coalitions received 20 ¢ and bonus payments of 50 ¢, $ 1.00, $ 1.50, and $ 2.00, as in study 1.

The payoffs of phase 3 were designed to break the stable coalitions that formed in phase 2. In condition C, the control condition, the Ss continued to receive 20 ¢ for each coalition that formed, but no bonus payments were offered. For condition A, if we assume that the coalition (1, 2) formed and was stable in phase 2, in phase 3 that coalition received 4 ¢ and the other two coalitions: [(1, 3) and (2, 3)] received 28 ¢. For the Ss of condition B the stable coalition that formed in phase 2 received a payoff of 16 ¢ on each trial while the other two coalitions received 24 ¢. Thus we see that for the players of condition A the incentive to break the coalition was considerable—24 ¢ on each play of the game—while it was much less for the players of condition B—8 ¢ on each play of the game.

Results

Table 2.2 reports the outcomes of the coalitions formed by all the triads in conditions A, B, and C in phases 1 and 2 of the study. The Ss of all three conditions received the same treatment, the same payoffs, and so all triads have been combined in this analysis. The number of no coalition outcomes was 10.5% in the first phase and decreased to 0.5% in phase 2, where bonus payments were offered. In phase 1 coalition (1, 2) formed most frequently, 39.5% of the time; coalition (1, 3) formed 30.5% of the time; and coalition

Table 2.2   Percentage of outcomes in phases 1 and 2

	Coalition Formed	Per cent in Phase	
		1	2
Outcome	0	10.5	0.5
	1	39.5	39.1
	2	30.5	37.0
	3	19.5	23.4
	Total	100	100

Outcome   0 = no coalition formed
          1 = (1, 2) coalition
          2 = (1, 3) coalition
          3 = (2, 3) coalition formed

(2, 3) formed least frequently, 19.5% of the time. Thus, the coalition that formed most frequently was the one that received the highest payoff (20 ¢), and the coalition that received the lowest payoff (12 ¢) formed least frequently.[7] In phase 2, where all coalitions received the same payoff—20 ¢ and bonuses—the differences are smaller; coalition (1, 2) formed 39.1% of the time, coalition (1, 3) formed 37.0% of the time, and coalition (2, 3) formed 23.4% of the time.

Examination of data of phase 1 not presented here demonstrates quite clearly that there was little stability in the coalition formation. In only four of the 25 triads did a coalition form on the first trial and remain stable throughout the eight plays of phase 1; in one other triad a coalition remained stable for seven plays, and in another a coalition remained stable for six plays. In 12 of the 25 triads the last coalition formed on the last trial and it was preceded, on the next to the last trial, by a different coalition. The next to the last coalition that was formed lasted only one or two trials. This confirms the finding of a previous study which used a similar game (Lieberman, 1962).

The results of phase 2 are quite different. The Ss responded to the possibility of obtaining bonus payments by forming more stable coalitions, as shown in table 2.3. This table shows which coalition was the last to be formed, the number of consecutive trials it occurred on, the next to last coalition that was formed, and the number of consecutive trials it occurred on. In 13 of the 25 triads stable coalitions were formed.[8] In condition A, six of the triads formed stable coalitions; in condition B there were five stable coalitions; and in condition C, two stable coalitions formed. Thus we see that in about half of the triads, stable coalitions, in the sense of this study, were formed.

The data describing the next to last coalition that formed indicate that if the Ss did not remain together for the 40 trials there was an amount of instability, but the Ss did tend to remain together for blocks of 10 or 20 trials to earn the bonus money. In six of the 12 triads that did not form stable coalitions, the final run lasted either 10 or 20 trials.

The corresponding stability data for phase 3, not presented here, indicates that six of the 25 triads formed stable coalitions in phase 3.[9] Of these six, five had formed stable coalitions in phase 2. And of these five stable coalitions that formed in phase 2, the stable coalition that formed in phase 3 was the same as the one in phase 2. Thus, in three of the 25 triads a coalition formed at the beginning of phase 2 and remained stable through the end of phase 3.

7   Lieberman (1477)

Table 2.3 Summary of the last two coalition changes

			Phase 2			
Group	Last Coalition Formed	Number of Trials	Next to Last Coalition Formed	Number of Trials	Stability of Coalitions	
A1 (2)	2	19	1	14	NS	6
A2 (2)	2	40			S	Stable
A3 (3)	3	40			S	
A4 (1)	1	40			S	3 Not
A5 (1)	1	40			S	Stable
A6 (1)	1	20	2	20	NS	
A7 (2)	1	1	2	1	NS	
A8 (2)	2	40			S	
A9 (3)	3	40			S	
B1 (1)	1	40			S	5
B2 (1)	3	2	2	1	NS	Stable
B3 (2)	3	20	1	20	NS	
B4 (1)	1	40			S	3 Not
B5 (1)	1	40			S	Stable
B6 (2)	2	40			S	
B7 (2)	2	40			S	
B8 (3)	2	10	1	10	NS	
C1	1	1	3	1	NS	2
C2	3	11	1	1	NS	Stable
C3	3	10	2	10	NS	
C4	2	40			S	
C5	1	2	2	1	NS	
C6	2	40			S	
C7	1	11	2	10	NS	
C8	3	20	1	20	NS	13 S
						12 NS

S = Stable Coalition
NS = Coalition Not Stable

Transition from phase 2 to phase 3 The transition from phase 2 to phase 3 was a critical point in the study. The payoffs of phase 3 were designed to have an effect on the stable coalitions that formed in phase 2; the payoffs were varied to determine the effects of differing payoffs on coalition behavior. Table 2.4 describes the transition from phase 2 to phase 3, showing

Table 2.4 Coalitions formed on last trial
of phase 2 and first trial of phase 3

Game	Coalition Formed	
	Phase 2	Phase 3
A1	2	0
A2	2*	1
A3	3*	3†
A4	1*	2
A5	1*	3
A6	1	2
A7	1	1
A8	2*	1
A9	3*	2
B1	1*	2
B2	3	1
B3	3	1
B4	1*	0
B5	1*	1†
B6	2*	1
B7	2*	3
B8	2	1
C1	1	2
C2	3	3†
C3	3	1
C4	2*	1
C5	1	2
C6	2*	3
C7	1	2
C8	3	2

* Indicates stable coalition formed on phase 2.

† Indicates coalition that formed on last trial of phase 2 also formed on first trial of phase 3.

the coalition that formed on the last trial of phase 2 and the one that formed on the first trial of phase 3. There is no evidence that either the stability of the coalition in phase 2 or the size of the payoff in phase 3 affected which coalition formed on the first trial of phase 3. In only three of the 25 games did the coalition that formed on the 40th trial of phase 2 also form on the first trial of phase 3, and these 3 games were distributed over the three conditions, one each in conditions A, B, and C. Two of these three continu-

7*

ing coalitions occurred in triads that had formed a stable coalition in phase 2; the third occurred in a triad that did not have a stable coalition in phase 2. Thus, when the Ss moved from phase 2 to phase 3 a new coalition usually formed on the first trial of the new phase. Those coalitions which had been unstable in phase 2 remained so, and those which had been stable in that phase dissolved on the first trial of the third phase.[10]

Results in phase 3 The payoffs of phase 3 were designed to determine the effects of payoffs of differing size on the stability of coalitions. For the Ss of condition A, when a stable coalition formed in phase 2, that coalition received only a 4 ¢ payoff in phase 3. The other two possible coalitions received a 28 ¢ payoff. For the Ss of condition B the stable coalition of phase 2 received a 16 ¢ payoff, the other two coalitions received a payoff of 24 ¢, in phase 3. Thus, the difference in payoffs to the Ss of condition B

Table 2.5 Percentage of outcomes—phase 3, group A

Trials	Percent Outcome				
	0	4¢ Payoff	28¢ Payoff	28¢ Payoff	Total
1–5	2.2	11.1	40.0	46.7	100%
6–10	0	11.1	48.9	40.0	100%
11–15	0	11.1	28.9	60.0	100%
16–20	0	13.3	35.6	51.1	100%
Percent over 20 Trials	0.6	11.7	38.3	49.4	100%

N = 9 Games

between continuing the stable coalition in phase 3 was relatively small (8 ¢ per trial) when compared to the difference for the Ss of condition A, where it was 24 ¢ per trial. The Ss of condition C received a 20 ¢ payoff per trial in phase 3, no matter which coalition formed.

The percentages of the various outcomes for the three conditions are presented in tables 2.5, 2.6, and 2.7.[11] The differing payoffs did, obviously, have an effect on the coalitions that formed in phase 3. In condition A the stable coalition of phase 2 (the one that received the 4 ¢ payoff) formed only 11.7% of the time while for condition B the stable coalition (the one that received the 16 ¢ payoff) formed 30% of the time. Thus, the Ss of condition A were quite ready to abandon the stable coalition of phase 2 when that coalition proved to be unprofitable. This is by no means an obvious result for the Ss were in a very difficult and unstable situation and previous findings (Lieberman, 1964) had shown that many Ss do, in an inherently unstable situation, prefer a smaller payoff to a stable coalition, to a larger payoff in an unstable situation.

The data of tables 2.6 and 2.7, condition B and condition C, appear to be quite similar. Thus it appears that the Ss avoided the low payoffs they received in condition A but were indifferent to the differences present in conditions B and C.

Table 2.6 Percentage of outcomes—phase 3, group B

Trials	Percent Outcome				
	0	16¢ Payoff	24¢ Payoff	24¢ Payoff	Total
1–5	2.5	27.5	32.5	37.5	100%
6–10	2.5	30.0	25.0	42.5	100%
11–15	2.5	27.5	27.5	42.5	100%
16–20	2.5	35.0	22.5	40.0	100%
Percent over 20 Trials	2.5	30.0	26.9	40.6	100%

N = 8 Games

Table 2.7 Percentage of outcomes—phase 3, group C

Trials	Percent Outcome				
	0	1	2	3	Total
1–5	0	32.5	42.5	25.0	100%
6–10	0	40.0	37.5	22.5	100%
11–15	0	10.0	45.0	45.0	100%
16–20	7.5	30.0	25.0	37.5	100%
Percent over 20 Trials	1.9	28.1	37.5	32.5	100%

N = 8 Games

Transition probabilities[12]   The transition probabilities for the Ss in the three conditions in phase 3 yield additional information about the Ss behavior. These transition probabilities are presented in tables 2.8 and 2.9, for conditions A and B, respectively. Six stable coalitions formed among the triads of condition A in phase 2. In only one of these six triads was there a

Table 2.8   Transition probabilities—phase 3, group A

$n+1$ n	0	$0.04 payoff	$0.28x payoff	$0.28y payoff
0	0.00	0.00	1.00	0.000
$0.04 Payoff	0.00	1.00	0.00	0.000
$0.28x Payoff	0.00	0.02	0.17	0.821
$0.28y Payoff	0.00	0.00	0.65	0.35

Table 2.9   Transition probabilities—phase 3, group B

$n+1$ n	0	$0.16 Payoff	$0.24x Payoff	$0.24y Payoff
0	0.00	0.20	0.40	0.40
$0.16 Payoff	0.02	0.88	0.10	0.00
$0.24x Payoff	0.01	0.02	0.77	0.14
$0.24y Payoff	0.00	0.10	0.03	0.87

continuation of the coalition in phase 3 and for this group the same coalition remained stable for all 20 trials of phase 3. This is reflected in table 2.7 where the probability of moving from a 4 ¢ payoff on trial n to a 4 ¢ payoff on trial $n + 1 = 1.0$. The larger number of choices were of one of the two 28 ¢ payoffs (we have designated one of the payoffs 28x, the other 28y). The probability of remaining in a 28x payoff was 0.16 and remaining in a 28y payoff was 0.35. The probability of alternation, moving from a 28x payoff to a 28y payoff was 0.82, while the probability of alternating from a 28y payoff to a 28x payoff 0.65. These probabilities reflect the Ss behavior of alternating between these two coalitions to divide the earnings equally or nearly equally. The probability of moving from either 28 ¢ payoff state to the 4 c payoff state was negligible—0.0 and 0.02.

The Ss of group B tended to remain in a state once they were in it, as evidenced by the transition probabilities in table 2.8. The probability of remaining in the 16 ¢ payoff state was 0.88; of remaining in the 24x payoff state was 0.77; and remaining in the 24y state was 0.87. The other probabilities are quite small. In condition A we found a reversal; Ss in the 28x state tended to move into the 28y state while in condition B the Ss tended to remain in the same payoff state. Both of these reflected, to some extent, a similar, underlying behavioral mechanism—equal division of the payoffs. In condition A it took the form of alternating trials while in condition B it took the form of alternating series of trials; hence the different results as expressed in the tables of transition probabilities. This phenomenon will be discussed in greater detail below.

The Ss of condition C received a 20 ¢ payoff no matter which coalition formed. The transition probabilities not presented here reflected stability from trial to trial. The probability of remaining in a (1, 2) coalition state was 0.56; of remaining in a (1, 3) state was 0.78; and remaining in a (2, 3) state was 0.58.

Division of the payoffs   The most frequent division of the payoffs was an even split, which confirms the findings of earlier studies (Lieberman, 1962). In phase 1, 51.3% of the payoffs were divided evenly; in phase 2, 88% of the 20 ¢ payoffs were divided evenly and 96.7% of the bonus payments were divided evenly. In phase 3, the Ss of condition A divided 75% of the payoffs evenly—all the 4 ¢ payoffs were divided evenly and 71.7% of the 28 ¢ payoffs were divided evenly. In phase 3 the Ss of condition B divided 73.7% of the payoffs evenly—100% of the 16 ¢ payoffs were evenly divided. The Ss of condition C divided 78.1% of the 20 ¢ payoffs evenly.

Some of the divisions of payoffs that were not an equal split of the payoff of a single play were still, at times, attempts to create an even division of earnings over the three phases of the game or within one phase. Table 2.10 shows the total payoffs to each S in each game, for all three conditions. These data indicate that there were a number of games in which there was an obvious attempt to equalize the payoffs among three players, or in some cases between two players. Games A2, A3, A4, A7, A8, A9, B2, B3, B4, B5, B8, C1, C5, C6, C7, and C8 indicate that two, or three players earned approximately equal amounts.

Social Choice

Table 2.10 Total payoff to each subject*

Game Player		Condition		
		A	B	C
1	1	6.08	6.64	5.11
	2	4.91	5.84	4.57
	3	3.69	4.16	4.78
2	1	8.10	4.54	2.94
	2	3.58	4.88	6.43
	3	8.12	4.64	5.23
3	1	0	5.81	5.88
	2	7.38	5.82	5.94
	3	7.38	5.53	4.08
4	1	8.72	8.62	8.70
	2	8.60	8.46	1.82
	3	2.84	0.24	7.80
5	1	7.30	8.92	4.74
	2	8.10	8.88	4.78
	3	4.80	0	4.66
6	1	7.15	9.69	7.48
	2	5.05	2.96	3.00
	3	5.76	6.67	7.48
7	1	5.00	8.60	5.28
	2	5.24	2.50	5.32
	3	4.82	8.02	5.10
8	1	8.42	5.14	5.02
	2	2.66	5.21	5.82
	3	8.56	5.91	5.20
9	1	3.34		
	2	8.28		
	3	8.22		

* In addition to these amounts each subject received $ 2.00 base pay.

Description of Ss strategies   The Ss of this second study exhibited behavior quite similar to that of the Ss of the first study, though the behavior had to be adapted to the requirements of the more complex, multi-phase game. As in the first study, Ss adopted what might be called an exploitative or competitive strategies and also what Gamson has termed an anti-competitive strategy.

One way of resolving the situation would have been for two of the Ss to have formed a coalition on the first play of the first phase of the game and continue that coalition through all three phases. This would have assured those two players of considerable earnings. In only one of the 25 triads did this happen. There are obvious reasons for this not happening. The first phase was one in which the Ss learned the complexity of the situation they were in. Also, for conditions A and B—and particularly for the players of condition A—a considerable amount was lost in phase 3 if the stable coalitions of phase 2 continued in phase 3. However, in three triads the same coalition formed on all trials of phase 2 and phase 3. A more common outcome which allowed the Ss to earn more money was the following: the two Ss who had formed a stable coalition in phase 2 would realize that if they continued their coalition in phase 3 they would be forced to accept lower payoffs, though they would be certain of some continued earnings. However, if the Ss who had formed the stable coalition of phase 2 suggested to the third player, the one who was not included in the coalitions of phase 2, that he alternate in forming coalitions (or form an equal number) with the two, then all could earn more money. The third player usually agreed; when he didn't he could be compelled to by the two. If he did not he would receive nothing. At times the third player attempted to get more than one-half of the payoff, but the two were usually able to enforce a 50–50 split.

With some frequency other Ss attempted to divide the earnings equally (or approximately equally) among the three players over all three phases. In phase 2 the Ss might alternate the formation of coalitions in runs of 10 to obtain the bonus payments, or they might sacrifice the bonus and alternate choices on each trial to produce an equitable outcome. In some games, where a single coalition remained stable in phase 2, the third player who earned no money in phase 2 would be allowed to earn a larger share of the payoffs in phase 3. Thus, some of the unequal divisions of payoffs in phase 3 were part of a larger attempt at an equal division of payoffs over the entire game.

Discussion

The results presented in Table 1.2 show that in study 1 the coalition that formed on the first play of the game often remained stable; the most frequent resolution of the conflict the Ss found themselves in was a relatively simple one—they remained in the coalition they formed first. This was one reasonable way to resolve the conflict and many of the Ss adopted this resolution, despite the efforts, pleadings, and expressions of hostility of the excluded player. These results demonstrated quite clearly that stable, cohesive coalitions could be formed by rewarding, providing incentives to, the Ss. With this information it was possible to conduct study 2 which enabled us to manipulate coalition structure.

By far the most frequent division of payoffs in study 1, and study 2, was the even division of the reward, a result found previously. Riker (1967) has termed this result an artifact; in a study utilizing a three-person, non-zero-sum game Riker found that Ss divided payoffs in a way predicted by Aumann and Maschler (1964) which was not an even division. Riker's experimental procedure was somewhat unconventional; he allowed Ss to bargain outside of the experimental sessions.

The data of table 2.3 which describe the stability of the coalition formation indicate that it was possible, in about half the triads of study 2, to manipulate coalition stability by manipulating rewards, but it was not possible to get uniform reactions to the experimental manipulation. Half of the triads responded to the incentives by forming the stable coalitions. But in any complex game situation the Ss analyses of the situation differ and they may perceive it to be more rewarding not to form stable coalitions. In those triads in which the Ss responded to the possibility of bonus payments by forming a stable coalition, it was more rewarding to the two players who successfully negotiated the stable coalition. But it was quite unrewarding to the third, the excluded player. By the time the Ss began phase 2 of study 2, where the bonus payments were made, they had the experience of negotiating in phase 1 where they were introduced to the complexities and uncertainties of the situation. The rewards available to the Ss were not certainties, rather they were very elusive quantities, and a player who attempted to obtain the maximum possible payoff might very well receive nothing in phase 2. It occurred, and solution notions tell us, that it certainly is not unreasonable for Ss to perceive as most rewarding an equal, or approximately equal, division of the payoffs. Thus, Ss who were aware of the risks involved would believe the equal division outcome to be safer and have a higher reward value.

Actually the instability that occurred in phase 2 served as a rewarding tendency. As long as no stable coalition formed each S was assured of some reward, though by not forming a stable coalition he was running the risk of being excluded from payoffs if the other two players did form a stable coalition. In this situation one must not take a simple view of what is rewarding. Unstable coalitions could also be considered rewarding.

The data of table 2.4 are somewhat surprising—one might have expected more continuity in the transition from phase 2 to phase 3, not necessarily from the Ss of condition A, but certainly from the Ss of condition B. The results of an earlier study (Lieberman, 1964) indicated that in an unstable situation players were often willing to accept smaller payoffs if these payoffs were certain, rather than risk the complexities and uncertainties of the unstable bargaining situation. It is, therefore, somewhat surprising that the Ss of condition B did not continue the coalitions that were stable in phase 2 into phase 3. Only one of the five stable coalitions that formed in phase 2, in group B, continued on the first trial of phase 3. The Ss of condition A were in a somewhat different situation. The payoff in phase 3 to the stable coalition of phase 2 was so small (4 ¢ vs. 28 ¢) that it is easy to understand why there was little continuity from phase 2 to phase 3. The Ss of condition C continued to receive the same 20 ¢ payoff in phase 3, but since only two of the eight triads formed stable coalitions in phase 2, it is difficult to make any statement.

Two mechanisms may help us understand the behavior of the Ss in phases 2 and 3. The Ss who formed stable coalitions in phase 2 were earning reasonably significant amounts of money. In addition to their base pay of $ 2.00 they were earning 4, 5, or 6 dollars for approximately two hours of participation in an interesting and challenging task. In the third phase, the Ss who had formed a stable coalition in phase 2 were often, but not always, satisfied with their earnings and willing to allow the third person some payoff. For the players of condition A, this generosity was not only the result of altruistic motives, it was also profitable, because where the partners in the stable coalition could arrange alternating coalitions in phase 3, they could both maximize the payoffs to themselves and divide the earnings with the third, the excluded player. Similar considerations were present for the players of condition B.

The differences between groups A and B in the percentages of choice of the stable coalition in phase 3 is not surprising since the players of condition A were so slightly rewarded if they continued the stable coalition. But one might have expected a larger percentage of the lower payoff outcomes from groups B and C. The analyses of tables 2.5, 2.6, and 2.7 tend to underestimate the effect of the stability of coalitions. The data of these tables report the behavior of all triads; those that did form stable coalitions in phase 2 and those that did not. Analyses, not presented here, show that for only the Ss of group B who were in stable coalitions, 40 % of the choices in phase 3 were of the 16 ¢ payoff; the corresponding percentage of choice of the Ss of group A was 17%. In both conditions the Ss who were members of stable coalitions were more likely to choose the lower payoff than were the Ss in triads who were not part of a stable coalition in phase 2.

The transition probability data of table 2.7 for group A reveal a number of interesting things about the Ss behavior. The single group of Ss who selected the 4 ¢ alternative never left that state—their coalition remained absolutely stable, in phase 3. They accepted the smaller payoff and did not change their choices. Two other entries of the cells reveal the alternation that existed; Ss alternated between the two, 24 ¢ states. In group B the alternations were less frequent; when they did occur the alternations were in blocks of 10.

Behavioral solutions   The analyses of the questionnaires the Ss completed indicated that it is possible to characterize their behavior by describing two strategies—a competitive, exploitative strategy and a cooperative strategy. When Ss did not behave in either of these two ways bargaining continued throughout the games and no resolution of the conflict no stability, appeared.

We can term each of these two ways of resolving the conflict a *behavioral solution* to the complex game the Ss played. They are not solutions in the mathematical sense; where axioms are stated and given these axioms certain precise statements about a satisfactory resolution of the conflict are derived. However, mathematical solution theory has not satisfied its own standards, that a solution prescribe to a player precisely how he should behave in a conflict situation. Since mathematical solution theory has failed to produce convincing resolutions of conflict situations it seems appropriate to ask whether empirical work can tell us something about the normative questions. Mathematical statements about rationality, fairness, stability, and uniqueness are only one class of statements about these matters. Some Ss who play *n*-person games appear to resolve the conflict situation they are in, they produce some stability by adopting some discernible strategy.

Then we may ask how well do the competitive and cooperative strategies resolve the conflict? These strategies, which have been termed *behavioral solutions* here, have certain properties or characteristics. How similar are these characteristics to the characteristics of a solution—optimality, fairness, stability, etc.? In this discussion optimality, fairness, stability and uniqueness will not be defined with the precision characteristic of mathematical discourse. Rather these terms will be left undefined for it appears that the requirement that we precisely define these terms prevents us from obtaining a convincing solution. Optimality, uniqueness, and fairness will be discussed relying on the intuitive meanings of the terms.

The competitive or exploitative strategy In the three-person games played the competitive strategy resulted in an outcome that was rational or optimal (in a maximizing sense) for two of the three participants, but it certainly was not optimal for the third player. If we require of a strategy, for it to be a convincing behavioral solution, that it correctly advise the player who uses it how to maximize his payoff, then the competitive strategy is *not* rational in such a sense. For if a player proposes such a strategy, and it is not accepted, he has probably increased the likelihood that he will be excluded from a stable coalition; the other two players might be more likely to form such a coalition. A player who was perceived as "greedy" by the two other players was sometimes excluded from coalitions. However, it might be advisable to direct a player to accept such an offer if one is made to him, or to tentatively try and learn whether one of the other two players might be willing to accept such a proposal. Thus, the competitive strategy can be seen to be an optimal or rational strategy if one is included, but disastrous if excluded—and as a result must be offered as a prescription only with severe limitations.

The competitive strategy can certainly not be said to be fair. In game theory fairness is not necessarily equivalent to an equal distribution of payoffs, or some other intuitively appealing outcome. For example, in certain two-person zero-sum games an outcome or prescription may be considered fair even though it might yield a generous payoff to one player and an equivalent negative payoff to the second player. It is fair in the sense that given the particular payoff matrix under consideration each player is doing as well as he could expect to do. The competitive strategy is not fair in this sense, nor is it fair in the intuitive, common sense meaning—as equitable. The Ss who adopt this strategy are aware that they are violating the custom of equity, and sometimes, they may relent and include the excluded player, if the situation allows as in phase 3 of study 2, where the changes in payoffs signified a change in the situation. The excluded player often feels that he has been treated unjustly and frequently says so and protests such treatment.

In many *n*-person game situations there is a great deal of instability. Phase 1 of study 2 is such a situation. The bonus payments of phase 2 tended to reduce the instability by offering premium payments for stable behavior. It is just this, the threat of instability in the situation, that often produces stability. When the Ss become aware of the instability and chaos possible in the situation they would sometimes develop some resolution of the conflict and cling to it. The competitive strategy does have the property of stability. As long as players do not defect, they are assured of some satisfactory payoff, and often they verbalize this. Stability seems to be increased when the players divide the rewards evenly. When there is an unequal division of the earnings the stability of the coalition seems threatened. Although such an analysis has not been done, one could examine the transition probabilities of remaining in the same coalition state following an equal split of a payoff and compare these probabilities to the transition probabilities of remaining in the same coalition state following an unequal split of the payoff. Observations of the behavior of the Ss indicate that the former probabilities would be higher than the latter ones.

The competitive strategy does not offer a unique prescription. In many *n*-person games, both zero-sum and non-zero sum, conventional solution theory offers a value for each player but does not offer a unique and precise prescription. The competitive strategy, similarly, does not offer a unique and precise prescription to each of the players. In the three-person game, three different coalitions can form; the competitive solution does not prescribe which of these three should form. However, it does rather precisely prescribe that once a coalition has formed it should be permanent, and in this limited sense is unique and precise.

The cooperative or anti-competitive strategy   The cooperative strategy is rational or optimal in one sense, and is not a rational-maximizing strategy in another sense. The S who accepts the cooperative strategy is giving up the possibility of earning the maximum amount that he would obtain if he successfully used the competitive strategy. If the payoffs are biased in his favor, and he accepts the notion of the equal division, as most Ss who adopted the cooperative strategy did in most cases, he is also then giving up any premium payoff that one might believe is due him. The Shapley value and the payoff distribution recommended by the von Neumann and Morgenstern solution of the three-person game often suggest, as rational, divisions of payoffs other than the equal split. Thus, in a sense, the player is not maximizing.

But if we draw an analogy to the minimax solution—where the rational-maximizing player who adopts the minimax strategy gives up the possibility of his maximum gain—then the cooperative strategy may be thought to be a rational-maximizing strategy. Like the minimax strategy it is a conservative strategy. But unlike the minimax strategy adoption of the cooperative strategy does not *guarantee* the S any specific amount, for the other two players may still adopt the competitive strategy against him. Thus we see a difference between a prescription to one player and a prescription to the group. The cooperative strategy may be said to be—*behaviorally rational*, in the sense of this discussion—if adopted by the group, but it is hardly a rational prescription if it is suggested by one player and rejected by the other two players, and this rejection is followed by the adoption of the competitive strategy by the other two.

If the cooperative strategy is adopted by the group of players, it can be said to be fair. The Ss often perceive an equal occurrence of coalitions, together with the equal distribution of the payoffs, as fair, and hence we can call this situation *behaviorally equitable*. Mathematical solution notions are somewhat different from these behavioral notions. If payoffs to the various coalitions differ then most mathematical solution notions attempt to reflect these differences in their prescriptions. Our Ss were often indifferent to the subtleties that lead solution notions to prescribe unequal divisions of payoffs and, in most cases, considered the equal split the fair outcome. We would certainly, in constructing a behavioral prescription, direct the player to suggest even splits. Attempting to obtain any premium payment above the equal split, even where this seems justified by the notions of solution theory, is often disadvantageous and dangerous.

The cooperative strategy, particularly where it includes an equal division of the payoffs, was stable. The players who adopted it did not defect and try to obtain more money by abandoning the strategy once it was agreed upon. In fact, in phase 2 adoption of the strategy was particularly risky for the one player who was left out of the first set of 10 plays, where alternation in sets of 10 plays was agreed upon. The player excluded from the first set of 10 plays had to believe that after these 10 plays were concluded the other two players would honor their commitments, the coalition would change, and he would begin to receive his payoffs. The players did keep their agreements in all situations where the three Ss agreed to adopt the cooperative strategy. Thus, the cooperative strategy can be said to be *behaviorally stable*.

The cooperative strategy is, in a sense, unique. It prescribes that all three coalitions form equally often, and that the players should receive equal amounts of money. In this sense it offers a relatively precise prescription of how to play to each of the players. But there are a number of different ways of producing the equal distribution of the rewards. Coalitions can alternate in series of 1, 2, 5, or 10; this did occur in phase 2 of study 2. Also all coalitions do not have to form exactly the same number of times—the payoff divisions can be adjusted, as they sometimes were—to get the equal division the players wanted. Thus, we may say the cooperative strategy was *behaviorally unique*, and was relatively a *behaviorally precise prescription.*

Relative propriety and morality   During the course of their communications the Ss revealed that they held different ideas about what was proper and moral. When a S's behavior violated the "principles" of the other two players he might be excluded from future coalitions. Or, one player might point out that another player violated what was "obviously proper." For example, some Ss thought it improper and "wrong" to want more than 50 per cent of a payoff, while other Ss accepted the desire to "get as much as you can." Some Ss proceeded to make simultaneous offers to each of the other two players, believing that such behavior was quite proper in the game situation. Other players saw this as "greediness" and evidence of an exploitative nature. Beliefs about what was proper behavior could determine which coalition formed. Such differences in beliefs about propriety were sometimes used by one player to influence a second player into excluding the third player from coalitions. These results appear to have implications for the experimental study of beliefs about propriety and morality.

CONCLUSIONS

Two studies were conducted in an attempt to manipulate coalition formation experimentally—to produce stable, cohesive coalitions and then break those coalitions. The first study demonstrated that it was possible to manipulate coalition formation. In the second study Ss played three variations of a three-phase, three-person, non-zero sum game. The results indicated that cohesive coalitions could again be formed in some, but not all, cases. The stable coalitions that formed were usually, but not always, broken when it was no longer profitable to remain in such coalitions. The immediate prospect of reward appeared to be a more potent determinant of the Ss behavior than the previous experience of being in a stable, cohesive coalition.

    Ss adopted two strategies which have been called a competitive-exploitative strategy, and a cooperative strategy. Each of these strategies allowed the Ss to resolve the difficult, unstable conflict situations facing them. Each of these strategies, which have been called behavioral solutions have some of the properties that we expect of a solution of a game—stability, rationality, uniqueness, etc.,—but neither satisfies the requirements of a rigorous solution of a game.

NOTES

1 This work was supported by a grant (MH-0766) from the National Institute of Mental Health. Additional support came from the International Dimension Program of the University of Pittsburgh. The funds of this program were supplied by the Ford Foundation and the University.

2 For a review of this literature see an article by William Gamson in Berkowitz, 1964·

3 Situations similar to this one have been studied before; see Liebermann: 1962, 1964. In these studies coalitions were formed, but the stability and continuity of the coalitions were not manipulated.

4 Psychologists, by and large, have rejected the normative questions, and have concerned themselves with descriptive problems. Sociologists, whose discipline has a history of advocacy of social reform and a concern for normative questions, have debated rather vigorously the appropriateness of a concern with normative questions. The more rigorous sociologists have been less concerned with normative questions. Many economists, particularly the welfare economists, have been quite concerned with normative questions. Although no discipline has completely rejected normative questions, the approach of this (and similar) work is different because the normative and descriptive questions are intimately intei wined and it is almost inevitable that a behavioral scientist doing this work concern himself with, or at least be aware of, the two sets of questions.

5 The term game used here refers to a situation of interaction among intelligent individuals. Persons are assumed to be in conflict for some quantifiable good or commodity, and a cooperative aspect is also present in the situation.

6 See footnote 7 for a more detailed discussion of the statistical questions involved in this analysis.

7 The observed differences appear to be large enough to be statistically significant, but a statistical test may be misleading for the choices of the Ss were not independent. A two-tailed chi-square test yields a chi-square value of 13.39 which is certainly significant with $\alpha = 0.05$, and d.f. $= 2$. This test was done using the frequencies of coalitions formed, excluding the no coalition outcomes, and assuming the probability of each coalition forming $= 1/3$. However, the entries in the cells of observed frequencies are not independent, and so a very important assumption of the chi-square test is violated. The Ss were paid a bonus to form stable coalitions; a situation that rewards dependencies in the choices.

8 A stable coalition was defined, prior to the data collection, as a situation in which Ss would select each other repeatedly, and not defect from the coalition for a higher offer from the third player. The stable coalition would be said to exist if (1) the same coalition formed on all 40 plays of the game, (2) the same coalition formed for more than 20 trials on the concluding run. As it turned out, in 13 triads the same coalition formed for 40 trials and in no games did a coalition form for more than 20 trials but less than 40 trials. If a game did not have a single run of 40 trials it did not have a concluding run of greater than 20 trials. Careful examination of the messages the Ss sent in the 3 games that had concluding runs of 20 indicated that the coalitions that formed were

not stable in the sense that this study requires—cohesive, and resistant to breaking by offers from the third player. Thus the definition of a stable coalition in this study is rather simple and unequivocal: that the coalition form of the first trial and remain in effect throughout the 40 plays of phase 2. However, it should be kept in mind that a stable coalition, in the sense meant here, could occur if the same coalition formed for 25–30 in 35 trials of the concluding run.

9   Five of the six formed the same coalition on all 20 trials; one formed the same coalition on the concluding 19 trials.

10   It should be pointed out, however, that the samples on which these statements are made are quite small. There were only six stable coalitions in group A, five in group B, and two in group C.

11   In table 2.5 the 4c payoff in phase 3 was assigned to the coalition that was stable in phase 2. For example, if the (1,2) coalition was stable in phase 2 that coalition received a payoff of 4c each time it formed in phase 3. The first 28c payoff column then signifies the (1,3), and the last 28c column signifies the (2,3) coalition. Similarly, for condition B if the (1,3) coalition was stable in phase 2 the 16c payoff was assigned to that coalition in phase 3 and the 24c payoffs were assigned to the (2,3) and (1,2) coalitions. In these triads in which no stable coalition formed, the 4c and 16c payoffs were assigned, at random, to one of the three coalitions.

12   The findings presented in this section should be treated as speculations or hypotheses about behavior since the statements are based on a very small number of observations. The results can, at best, be considered suggestive.

REFERENCES

Aumann, R. J. and Maschler, M. The bargaining set for cooperative games. In Dresher, M., Shapley, L. S., and Tucker (Eds.), A. W., *Advances in Game Theory*. Princeton: Princeton, 1964.

Gamson, W. Experimental studies of coalition formation. In Berkowitz, L. (Ed.), *Advances in Experimental Social Psychology*, Vol 1. New York: Academic Press, 1964.

Lieberman, B. Human behavior in a 3 × 3 matrix game. *Behavioral Science*, 1960, **5**, 317–322.

Lieberman, B. Experimental studies of conflict in some two-person and three-person games. In Criswell, J. H., Solomon, H., and Suppes, P. (Eds.), *Mathematical Methods in Small Group Processes*. Stanford: Stanford U. Press, 1962.

Lieberman, B. *i*-Trust: A notion of trust in three-person games and international affairs. *Journal of Conflict Resolution*, 1964, **7**, 271–280.

Lieberman, B. Combining individual preferences into a social choice. In Buchler, I. and Nutini, H. (Eds.), *Game Theory in the Behavioral Sciences*. Pittsburgh: University of Pittsburgh Press, 1969.

Luce, R. D. and Raiffa, H. *Games and Decisions*. New York: Wiley, 1957.

Rapoport, A. and Orwant, C. Experimental games: A review. *Behavioral Science*, 1962, **7**, 1–37.

Riker, W. Bargaining in a three-person game. *The American Political Science Review*, 1967, **61**, 642–656.

AN EXPERIMENTAL EXAMINATION OF FORMAL AND INFORMAL RULES OF A THREE-PERSON GAME*

WILLIAM H. RIKER

University of Rochester

The mathematical enterprise of the theory of games is to derive a solution of particular games and classes of games. A game, say von Neumann and Morgenstern, "is simply the totality of the rules that describe it." (Von Neumann and Morgenstern, 1953, 6.1, p. 49). A solution, in turn, is a "characterization of 'rational behavior'" (4.1.4, p. 33). Hence, the content of the mathematical enterprise is to analyze the rules in order to derive an optimal expectation.

One would expect that, in such an enterprise, the derived solution would reflect the influence of all of the rules. Presumably if a specific rule contributes nothing to the expectations of rational players so that the solution would be the same even if the rule did not exist, then a compact statement of the rules could omit it as unnecessary. On the other hand, if all the rules are necessary in the sense that each influences expectation of outcomes, then to omit one from consideration in deriving the solution would mean that the solution offered did not truly state rational expectations.

As it turns out, however, the von Neumann–Morgenstern solution of *n*-person games does not take *all* the rules into consideration. One can distinguish two classes of rules: (1) *Formal* rules are those which describe a game as it exists in the imaginary and external world of mathematics. In general, the formal rules are those necessary to calculate the von Neumann–Morgenstern solution. Examples of formal rules are the payoffs to

---

* See note (*) on page 137.

participants, the choices available at moves, and, typically, all the rules which appear in a description of a game in a rule book. (2) *Informal* (or *temporal*) rules are those which describe the game as it is brought out of the eternal world of mathematics into the temporal world of actual play. In general, informal rules are those necessary for play but not necessary to calculate the solution. Examples of informal rules are the sequence in which players of an n-person game negotiate with each other prior to a move (and in general the physical circumstances of the negotiation), the information they possess in such negotiations, and, typically, all those rules that players have to make up for their local needs when they play a match under the set of rules drawn from a rule book. In the more familiar terms of organizations, the formal rules may be thought of as analogous to constitutions, while the informal rules may be thought of as analogous to by-laws. The von Neumann–Morgenstern solution is based entirely on formal rules or constitution and does not attempt to take the by-laws or informal rules into account in deriving solutions.

It may well be, however, that the informal rules do influence outcomes in nature (where, if any place, temporal rules are relevant) so that actual outcomes among rational players will differ from solutions mathematically derived from the formal rules. And if actual outcomes do differ, then a complete theory of games should include the effect of both kinds of rules.

The projects of this essay are, therefore, to examine some evidence about whether or not informal rules are significant for outcomes and rational expectations of n-person games and then to begin the task of weaving together the implications for rational behavior of both kinds of rules.[1]

1

As a preliminary, it seems desirable to show in some detail that the von Neumann–Morgenstern solution of an n-person game is based on only a part of the rules.

The outcome of an n-person game is, of course, a division of the stakes of the game to particular players, which for n players is expressed as a vector, $x = (x_1, x_2, \ldots x_n)$. While the rules, as they appear in a rule-book or a constitution, may place no constraints on the vector x, still some intuitively defensible constraints can be placed on x immediately. Since one is seeking "rational expectations," one such constraint is individual rationality: Assuming that the worst that can happen to an individual player is to stand alone and that the worst payoff in such circumstance is an amount $v(\{i\})$, then $x_i \geqq v(\{i\})$. This is to say that no, matter how the players distribute themselves into coalitions, no player will accept a share of the stakes which is worse than he could do by himself. Similarly, the entire set of players can also be expected to behave rationally in the sense that they will achieve as much as the stakes allow, which can be denoted as the value. v, of the set of all the players, I. So $\Sigma_i = v(I)$. All divisions of the stakes that satisfy these two elementary constraints, von Neumann and Morgenstern call *imputations*.

A solution, as *I* indicated earlier, is a statement of rational expectations for the players. Of course it takes the form of imputations. What one is looking for as a solution, then, is imputations that are stable because they are what rational players can expect to get.

In their search for a solution, von Neumann and Morgenstern interject an intermediate step, the characteristic function, $v(S)$. This function is the value of a two-person game derived from the n-person game by allowing the n players to form two subsets, S and its complement $-S$. Since S (and hence $-S$) can be formed in a variety of ways, naturally $v(S)$ can have different real values as S varies. Hence $v(S)$ is a numerical set function. In extensive form, $v(S)$ is a table of the values for all sets, S, where S is a subset of the set, I, of all players. As such, $v(S)$ is then a statement of what all possible coalitions in a game are worth, assuming of course that $-S$ forms.

When introducing the notion of the characteristic function von Neumann and Morgenstern remark: "... we expect to base the entire theory of the zero-sum, n-person game on this function." (25.2.1, p. 240). And in somewhat revised form it is the base of the theory of general n-person games as well. "...we expect to find," they say, "that the characteristic function determines everything, including the 'imputation'" [i.e. the elements of the solution]. (25.2.2, p. 240.)

And this is in fact the case. Since one is looking for a solution composed of imputations that are in some sense better for rational players than others, one needs a notion of "better." Von Neumann and Morgenstern provide the notion of *domination*. One imputation, x, is said to dominate an imputation, y, with respect to a set, S, if

1   S is not empty;

2   $\sum_{i \epsilon S} x_i \leqq v(S)$; and

3   $x_i > y_i$, for all $i \epsilon S$.

The characteristic function thus enters fundamentally into the definition of „better" or domination. Since the notion of a solution is in turn based on the notion of domination, the characteristic function can be truly said to imply the solution. A solution, V, is said to be a set of imputations such that:

1 For any imputation, y, not in V, some imputation, x, in V dominates y; and

2 No x in V dominates y in V.

Of course, in the actual calculation of imputations in V, the fundamental constraint is the characteristic function. The imputations in V are simply appropriate divisions of $v(S)$. Hence the characteristic function as a statement of what coalitions can expect to get thus determines—along with the notions of domination and solution—what individual players can expect to get. And in terms of actual values, the solution is derived from the characteristic function and the definition of a solution and nothing else.

Many writers have criticized the von Neumann-Morgenstern notion of a solution because it is based on the characteristic function with its behaviorally dubious assumption that, if S forms, its complement -S forms. (See, for example Luce and Raiffa, 1957, p. 190 and 204). Alternative solutions have been offered to avoid this dependence, though they too are based on some notion of the value of a coalition. The criticism offered here, however, is fundamentally different. On the basis of my work with three person games I have no quarrel with the assumption that, if S forms, -S forms. In three person games, it can hardly be otherwise if S has two or three members. And indeed I find that in some circumstances the solution based on the characteristic function is both *a priori* reasonable and behaviorally descriptive. Rather my criticism is that the characteristic function is an insufficient basis to advise rational people what to expect or to describe what in fact they do receive. The von Neumann–Morgenstern solution is inadequate, not because of what it assumes, but because of what it omits.

2

It is impossible to investigate mathematically the charge that a solution based only on the characteristic function is an inadequate statement of rational expectations. A mathematical investigation can involve only inferences drawn from manipulations of the formal rules. Yet the substance of the charge is that knowledge of the formal rules is itself insufficient to establish rational expectations. To break out of this circle it is necessary to examine the game with the temporal rules included, which means that one must investigate the outcome of actual plays of the game among rational players in the natural world.

Yet such an investigation itself involves serious conceptual problems. Suppose one observes, in a number of natural plays of a game, a significant difference between the imputations generated in them and the imputations in the *a priori* solution. Is this observation then sufficient evidence that the solution is inadequate by reason of a failure to consider the informal rules? Not at all, for there may be several quite reasonable explanations of the discrepancy, that do not in the least call into question the adequacy of the solution. For example, it may be said that the players vary in bargaining ability, perception of reality, etc., so that the explanation of the discrepancy is simply the differences in the players' skills. Von Neumann and Morgenstern themselves pointed out that such discrepancies in actual behavior are to be expected. For another example, it may be said that the players share an ethical standard different from that embodied in the solution. For the games to be considered in this essay, the solution embodies a moral principle equivalent to what Aristotle called proportionate equality, that is rational players are expected to share out the stakes somewhat in proportion to the bargaining advantage or disadvantage they have under the formal rules. But, if players in the real world are strongly attached to the moral principle that Aristotle called numerical equality, or share and share alike, then it can hardly be expected that they reach agreement on imputations in the solution. Again von Neumann and Morgenstern anticipated such discrepancies.

What one needs, therefore, in order to observe whether or not the informal rules are necessary for a complete solution is a set of observations arrived at in such a way that neither of these two explanations of any discrepancy are appropriate.

In the next section, therefore, *I* describe some experiments that reveal a discrepancy which cannot easily be explained in these ways and which must, *I* think, be explained as a derivative from the informal rules.

3

The game under consideration here is a non-zero-sum, three–person game with the following payoff rule:

$$v(1) = v(2) = v(3) = 0;$$
$$v(1, 2) = \$\,4.00;$$
$$v(1, 3) = \$\,5.00;$$
$$v(2, 3) = \$\,6.00;$$
$$v(1, 2, 3) = 0.$$

If the foregoing rule is restated as in note 2, or "...$v(1, 2, 3) = \$\,6.00$," then this rule is the characteristic function of the game. The von Neumann–Morgenstern solutions derived from this characteristic function are:

$$
V = \begin{cases}
(1.50,\ 2.50,\ 0) \\
(1.50,\ 0,\ 3.50) \\
(0,\ 2.50,\ 3.50) \\
\text{and an infinity of imputations having the properties} \\
\text{either} \left\{ \begin{array}{l} 1.50 \leqq x_1 < 3.50 \\ 2.50 \leqq x_2 < 4.50 \\ 0 \quad < x_3 \leqq 2.00 \\ \text{and} \sum_{i=1}^{3} x_i = 6.00 \end{array} \right\} \quad \text{or} \quad \left\{ \begin{array}{l} 1.50 \leqq x_1 < 2.50 \\ 0 \quad < x_2 \leqq 1.00 \\ 3.50 \leqq x_3 < 4.50 \\ \text{and} \sum_{i=1}^{3} x_i = 6.00 \end{array} \right\}
\end{cases}
$$

Normalizing this solution into the $(-1, 0)$ normalization used by von Neumann and Morgenstern according to this formula, where x'_i is the payment in the normalized score:

$$
x'_i = \begin{cases}
\dfrac{x_i - 2}{2}, & \text{if} \quad x_i \neq 0 \\[2ex]
\dfrac{4 - x_j - x_k}{2}, & \text{if} \quad x_i = 0
\end{cases}
$$

results in the following statement of the solutions:

$$
V = \begin{cases}
(-0.25,\ 0.25,\ 0) \\
(-0.25,\ -0.50,\ 0.75) \\
(-1.00,\ 0.25,\ 0.75) \\
\text{and an infinity of imputations having the properties} \\
\text{either} \left\{ \begin{array}{l} -0.25 \leqq x_1 < 0.75 \\ 0.25 \leqq x_2 < 1.25 \\ 0 < x_3 \leqq -1.00 \\ \text{and} \sum_{i=1}^{3} x_i = 0 \end{array} \right\} \quad \text{or} \quad \left\{ \begin{array}{l} -0.25 \leqq x_1 < 0.25 \\ -1.00 < x_2 \leqq -0.50 \\ 0.75 \leqq x_3 < 1.25 \\ \text{and} \sum_{i=1}^{3} x_i = 0 \end{array} \right\}
\end{cases}
$$

These solutions may be visualized in a two dimensional space as in Figure 1. The space is divided by three ordinates into 60° sextants with each ordinate representing, for some one i, $x_i = 0$. As von Neumann and Morgenstern showed, all imputations possible in the game lie in the fundamental triangle (i.e. the big triangle in Fig. 1) formed by the intersection of lines representing $x_i = -1$. The points of a particular solution consist of the three principal points lying at the vertices of the dotted triangle inside the fundamental triangle in Figure 1 and of all points on any pair of lines moving with no greater than 30° turns through the smaller shaded triangles

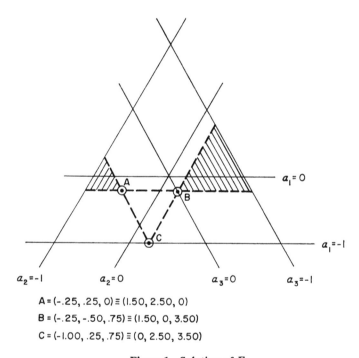

A = (-.25, .25, 0) ≡ (1.50, 2.50, 0)
B = (-.25, -.50, .75) ≡ (1.50, 0, 3.50)
C = (-1.00, .25, .75) ≡ (0, 2.50, 3.50)

Figure 1 Solution of Γ

in Figure 1 from the vertices at a principal point to $x_2 = -1$ or $x_3 = -1$. Each solution therefore contains an infinity of points. Since an infinity of lines can be drawn through the shaded triangles, naturally there are an infinity of solutions, all of which, however, have the principal points in common.

So much for the formal rules. The informal rules include the following:[3]

1   Selection of subjects

In all cases subjects were males chosen from the student body of the University of Rochester. Of the seven groups, Group 1 were 28 businessmen chosen from students in summer school night courses at the school of business administration (see Riker, 1967(a) (b), for a fuller description of this group.) All other groups were chosen from the undergraduate body (with an occasional graduate student), which is mostly upper middle class in social and economic back ground and contains one barely distinctive large ethnic group, Jews, who constitute about 35%. Group 2 (25 sophomores) was chosen at random from the students in the class. Group 3 (47 sophomores and juniors), Group 4 (16 sophomores to seniors) and Group 5 (14 sophomores to seniors), were chosen in response to advertisements. Group 6 (13 sophomores to seniors) were students in the experimenter's undergraduate class on positive political theory. Group 7 (six sophomores and juniors) were chosen in response to advertisements.

Consistent attempts were made to match subjects who were initially unacquainted or only slightly acquainted, although in a few instances subjects discovered, when actually face to face that they had some previous acquaintanceship. In Group 1 to 4 subjects were never matched together twice so that while a subject might play as many as nine games he never saw previous opponents again (except socially). But in Groups 5 and 6 subjects were usually matched twice and occasionally thrice, while in Group 7 players were all matched together four times. In no case, however, did subjects ever repeat the same set of three players. Thus in Groups 1 to 4 players could be certain that once they played together they would not meet again in a match, while in Groups 5 to 7 they could not be certain.

2   Procedure of negotiation

In all groups, players negotiated in pairs for six to nine conversations of three to five minutes, thus in groups 1 to 5, subbjects were assured of exactly nine conversations. In Groups 6–7, subjects were assured of only six conversations and the match was abruptly halted at some point in Round 3 chosen at random from the following times: before conversation 7, after 2 minutes into conversation 7, after 4 minutes into 7, end of 7, after 2 minutes into 8, after 4 minutes into 8, end of 8, after 2 minutes into 9, after 4 minutes into 9, end of 9. The conversations were carefully timed; subjects were informed of the time remaining (except in uncertain third rounds) at one minute, one-half minute, and fifteen seconds before the end; and conversations were halted promptly at the end.

Round	Conversation	Players	Duration
1	1	(i, j)	5 minutes, Groups 1–4
1	2	(i, k)	3 minutes, Groups 5–7
1	3	(j, k)	
2	4	(i, j)	
2	5	(i, k)	5 minutes, all Groups
2	6	(j, k)	
3	7	(i, j)	5 minutes for all Groups
3	8	(i, k)	except those for which Round 3
3	9	(j, k)	was uncertain

3 Setting of negotiations

Pairs of subjects negotiated in a large well-lighted office, sitting across a table from each other so that they were face to face about three feet apart. A microphone was placed off center between them and at the other end of the table (about six feet away) sat an assistant operating a tape recorder. The experimenter, usually another assistant and sometimes other observers sat around the edge of the room six to ten feet from the subjects. Most groups played in the evenings, but Groups 4 and 7 played in the afternoon. Nothing prohibited the players from taking notes and in Group 7 all players regularly did so; in other groups, however, note-taking seemed to be regarded as evidence of untrustworthiness (on the assumption that it is harder for most people to remember lies than the truth) and so occurred only infrequently.

Considerable care was taken to assure that subjects in a particular match did not converse with each other except at the times when the tape recorder was operating for a conversation. They were informed of an appointment for the match by a post card timed to arrive the day before. Given their relative lack of acquaintance, it seems unlikely that they were able to seek each other out before arriving at the negotiation office at the time of a match. On arrival before the time set for the match, subjects were asked to wait alone in the "storage" room until the match started. Sometimes, owing to simultaneous arrival, subjects saw and greeted each other and on a few occasions conversed, although never, we are told, about the forthcoming match except in occasional wisecracks. The subject not involved in a particular conversation was "stored" in a neighboring office which was, for all groups except Group 1, a different one for each player. Subjects were individually escorted from the playing room to storage room and vice versa by the experimenter. Of course, they were asked not to talk to each other except in the negotiation room when the tape recorder was in operation. By all these precautions, we hoped to insure that no bargains were made without our knowledge. I think we succeeded, although occasionally after matches were over shamefaced winners proposed to buy abashed losers a beer, presumably thereby redistributing the stakes somewhat.

4 Procedure of voting

At the end of negotiations, players were placed in isolated storage until individually escorted back to the negotiation room. In Groups 5 to 7, while in storage, they filled out a questionnaire after each round, including the last, which forced them to think seriously about the way each player would vote. After the final conversation (and questionnaire) they were individually escorted to the negotiation room and asked to state the name of the player with whom they had formed a coalition and the division of the stake. When all had voted, they were all brought back to the negotiation room and, if two had named each other and the same division of the stake, the assistant paid them. They knew that if they named different amounts, no one would be paid. Their memories for divisions were invariably good in spite of the typical reluctance to take notes.

5 Sophistication of subjects

In most groups none of the subjects had heard of the game prior to initial instructions, which consisted of an explanation of the characteristic function, the procedure of negotiation, and the procedure of voting. Consequently, they did not initially know the solution. In Groups 5 and 6, however, some subjects knew persons who had participated in previous groups and hence perhaps had some idea of the solution initially. In Group 3 at least one player calculated the solution (by solving the simultaneous equations) after instructions were given but before the matches began. Even, however, in Groups 3, 5, and 6 very few of the subjects were initially sophisticated.

In Group 1, we did nothing to instruct the subjects, so that the solution remained for them as much as a mystery at the end as at the beginning. After the work with Group 1 was concluded however, I realized that I was interested not in learning theory, but in sophisticated play. So in Groups 2 to 7, I attempted to instruct the players without revealing the solution by showing them a brief protocol after each match. From this each one learned what had happened in the conversations from which he had been absent and the losers, especially, could in a four-way conversation question the winners about what they (the losers) had done wrong. As a consequence of this kind of instruction and frequent private discussions in the dormitories all players in Groups 2 to 7 came to recognize (usually after one match) some special significance in $ 1.50, $ 2.50, and $ 3.50 as divisions of the stake. Since the matches for each group were spread out over several weeks or months and subjects played at most twelve matches, they had plenty of time to think and talk about the complexities of the game and some invented especially ingenious bargains.

Despite their ultimate recognition (except in Group 1) of the special significance of $ 1.50, $ 2.50, and $ 3.50, only the very few who were mathematically oriented conceptualized the principal points of the solution as a coherent whole. None recognized the existence of other points in the solution besides the principal points, even though they discovered in Group 6 a way to reach them. The vagueness of their notions of the solution is indicated by the fact that, even in the most sophisticated groups, considerable distaste was expressed for "average" or "median" divisions which were the kind of names they invented for $ 1.50, $ 2.50, and $ 3.50. One can say, therefore, that, while they learned through experience something about the solution, none ever became sophisticated in a game theory sense, although for Groups 5 and 6 the theory was explained in some detail after the matches were over.

6 Assignment of subjects to positions

Subjects were assigned to positions in two ways: In groups in which there were a large number of subjects, so that no subject played more than four or five times, a conscious effort was made to see that each subject played in each position (1, 2, and 3) approximately the same number of times. In smaller groups, where subjects played eight to twelve times, they were assigned to position either on the plan just described or by a random number assignment. In any event, subjects typically played each position with about equal frequency. While this procedure had the desirable effect of permitting us to abstract the roles 1, 2, and 3, from the real persons occupying them, the main reason for the procedure of assignment was simply to retain the cooperation of the subjects. I suppose very few subjects would stay with the experiment if they were permanently assigned to position 1 with its expected value of only $ 1.50.

7   Order of negotiations

One of the main differences in the informal rules among the seven groups was the rule for order of negotiations. In Group 1, 2, 3, 5, and 6, the order for each round was [(1, 2), (1, 3), (2, 3)] so that player 1 was excluded from the last conversation. In Group 4, the order for each round was [(2, 3), (1, 3), (1, 2)] so that player 3 was excluded from the last conversation. In Group 7, the order was [(2, 3), (1, 2), (1, 3)] so that player 2 was excluded from the last conversation. In Groups 6 and 7, the end was, as previously noted, uncertain and in fact the excluded player might be in the last conversation, but he did not know this until just before the voting, so 2 and 3 respectively were excluded from the last guaranteed conversation.

4

The most notable fact about these seven experiments is the degree to which they confirm the von Neumann–Morgenstern theory. If one adopts as the null hypothesis the proposition that the actual outcomes are not significantly different from the principal points in the von Neumann–Morgenstern solution, it appears to be impossible to reject this hypothesis in six of the seven cases. Indeed, for $6\frac{2}{3}$ of the 7.

The data for a test of the hypothesis is set forth in Table 1 which includes, for each coalition (i, j) in each group, the mean amount actually won by i and by j, along with the standard deviations of the mean.

The t statistic was calculated for each mean and Table 1 then includes, for each t, the probability that a t of that absolute value might be achieved by chance.

As is apparent from the table, only in the case of Group 4, coalition (2, 3), is the probability of a t of the given value so low as to render the null hypothesis doubtful $P[|t| > 2.03] \simeq 0.06$. All other probabilities are so high as to give considerable confidence in the null hypothesis.

Table 1 Summary of Outcomes of Matches by Groups*

	Coalition (1, 2)		Coalition (1, 3)		Coalition (2, 3)	
	1	2	1	3	2	3
Group 1						
n	9		10		13	
μ	1.69	2.31	1.42	3.58	2.52	3.48
σ	0.349	0.349	0.307	0.307	0.360	0.360
t		0.54		0.25		0.05
$Pr[t]$	$P[\lvert t\rvert > 0.54] \simeq 0.60$		$P[\lvert t\rvert > 0.25] \simeq 0.80$		$[P\lvert t\rvert > 0.05] \simeq 0.96$	
Group 2						
n	4		3		12	
μ	1.56	2.44	1.62	3.38	2.47	3.53
σ	0.658	0.658	0.262	0.262	0.589	0.589
t		0.09		0.46		0.05
$Pr[t]$	$P[\lvert t\rvert > 0.09] \simeq 0.90$		$P[\lvert t\rvert > 0.46] \simeq 0.60$		$P[\lvert t\rvert > 0.05] \simeq 0.95$	
Group 3						
n	5		15		18	
μ	1.46	2.54	1.41	3.59	2.47	3.53
σ	0.055	0.055	0.222	0.222	0.214	0.214
t		0.73		0.41		0.14
$Pr[t]$	$P[\lvert t\rvert > 0.73] \simeq 0.50$		$P[\lvert t\rvert > 0.41] \simeq 0.60$		$P[\lvert t\rvert > 0.14] \simeq 0.85$	
Group 4						
n	9		5		14	
μ	1.44	2.56	1.77	3.23	2.88	3.12
σ	0.556	0.556	0.365	0.365	0.187	0.187
t		0.10		0.74		2.03
$Pr[t]$	$P[\lvert t\rvert > 0.10] \simeq 0.90$		$P[\lvert t\rvert > 0.74] \simeq 0.50$		$P[\lvert t\rvert > 2.03] \simeq 0.06$	
Group 5						
n	8		11		16	
μ	1.39	2.61	1.48	3.52	2.55	3.45
σ	0.306	0.306	0.265	0.265	0.295	0.295
t		0.35		0.07		0.17
$Pr[t]$	$P[\lvert t\rvert > 0.35] \simeq 0.75$		$P[\lvert t\rvert > 0.07] \simeq 0.95$		$P[\lvert t\rvert > 0.17] \simeq 0.80$	
Group 6†						
n	11		7		15	
μ	1.55	2.45	1.66	3.34	2.53	3.47
σ	0.151	0.151	0.374	0.374	0.142	0.142
t		0.33		0.43		0.21
$Pr[t]$	$P[\lvert t\rvert > 0.33] \simeq 0.75$		$P[\lvert t\rvert > 0.43] \simeq 0.65$		$P[\lvert t\rvert > 0.21] \simeq 0.80$	

* Matches resulting in single member coalitions omitted.

† Matches resulting in grand coalitions omitted.

Table: 1   (con't)

| | Coalition (1, 2) | | Coalition (1, 3) | | Coalition (2, 3) | |
	1	2	1	3	2	3
Group 7						
n	4		10		6	
μ	1.41	2.59	1.50	3.50	2.52	3.48
σ	0.086	0.086	0.161	0.161	0.249	0.249
t	1.05		0.00		0.08	
$Pr[t]$	$P[|t| > 1.05] \simeq 0.35$		$P[|t| > 0.00] \simeq 1.00$		$P[|t| > 0.08] \simeq 0.90$	

It has often been remarked, especially by partisans of alternative solutions, that the von Neumann–Morgenstern solution is not very useful. It appears from these experiments, however, that, given the informal rules here used, the von Neumann–Morgenstern solution predicts behavior fairly well. Science could hardly ask for more utility.

The closeness of the experimental outcomes to the von Neumann–Morgenstern solution is indicated on Figure 2, where the range of averages for two-person coalitions are depicted as lying on lines parallel to the sides of the fundamental triangle between points (A, B), (C, D), and (E, F). Point F represents the one average outcome that may not satisfy the null hypothesis (Group 4, coalition (2, 3). Even considering it, however, it is apparent that these outcomes are quite close to the principal points of the solution. In Figure 2, the points (labelled G, H, I, J, K) in the solution in the right hand shaded triangle are the five individual (not average) outcomes from Group 6 in which grand coalitions were formed. The present interest in these points is that they too fall within the solution. The main defect of the solution from an experimental point of view is that it does not account for the outcome at (0, 0, 0) when only one-person coalitions formed.[4]

Doubtless the main reason that there is such close agreement between the theory and experimental results is the fact that the theory captures the essence of the conflict and cooperation in this social situation. But a part of the reason, at least, for the close agreement is that the informal rules of the game in this experiment were designed to encourage it. My intention was to obtain some results close to the theory so that deviations might stand out for investigation and examination. With this in mind the informal rules were designed to make it easy for subjects to reach the principal points of the solution. Thus, the subjects were given a substantial amount of time for negotiation (25 to 45 minutes), an amount that proved adequate for all except the most loquacious. Furthermore, there were two or three rounds

of bargaining so that subjects could make offers, counteroffers, and coun-
ter-counter-offers. Consequently, subjects had time and interchange enough
to go beyond initial greed, initial confessions of weakness, and conventionally fair "fifty-fifty" divisions to seek imputations appropriate for the formal

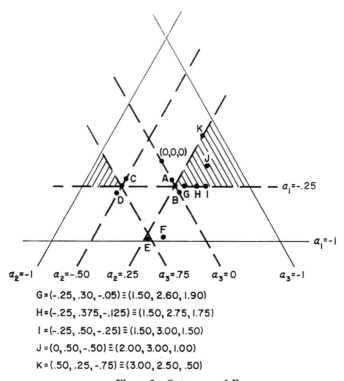

G = (-.25, .30, -.05) ≡ (1.50, 2.60, 1.90)
H = (-.25, .375, -.125) ≡ (1.50, 2.75, 1.75)
I = (-.25, .50, -.25) ≡ (1.50, 3.00, 1.50)
J = (0, .50, -.50) ≡ (2.00, 3.00, 1.00)
K = (.50, .25, -.75) ≡ (3.00, 2.50, .50)

Figure 2 Outcomes of Γ

rules. For another thing, they were scheduled to play over a period of
several weeks or months so that they had full opportunity to reflect on the
nature of the game and appropriate strategies. Not all may have done so,
but we know many did. Consequently they became somewhat sophisticated
during the course of each experiment as evidenced by the fact that in all
groups they had by the end abandoned their initial conviction that coalition
(2, 3) was preferable for players 2 and 3 simply because it had the largest
payoff. Again, the subjects were mostly selected and matched so that they
were initially unacquainted. Consequently, their bargaining was fairly
impersonal and self-interested and the game was played in relative isolation
from considerations in the larger world outside the laboratory.

9   Lieberman (1477)

Assume the solution does in fact embody some of the fundamental features of conflict and cooperation. Then, given all this built-in bias toward extensive, sophisticated and self-interested play, it is not surprising that the subjects came close to the solution most of the time. The only informal rule I can think of that *might*—and I emphasize might—have brought them even closer to the solution is to require bargaining in triads rather than dyads. (I tried this with one group, but with me in the room as a target, they insisted on transforming the game into a four-person zero-sum conflict, often arriving at the imputation (2.00, 2.00, 2.00, −6.00). Since this was an experiment on three-person games, I used the happenstance of a broken ankle as a graceful way to cancel the series.) Even without results on triadic negotiation, however, I am satisfied by the evidence that the subjects delivered strong verification of the theory of the solution.

I am therefore led to inquire why in one case they did not. In Group 4 for coalition (2, 3), they produced results which appear to be markedly different from outcomes in all other groups and even from outcomes in the same group for other coalitions. Of course, from one point of view the Group 4 results are not significantly different from the others. There are, in all seven experiments, twenty-one distinct calculations of t. At the 0.05 level of significance it is to be expected that approximately one (i.e. five per cent) of the these t values be such that it would be achieved by chance less than five per cent of the time. And in fact exactly one such value is close to that amount. Hence the one high value for t in twenty-one cases can be interpreted as precisely what one would expect at the five per cent level of significance. To interpret the statistic in this way, however, is to assume that the seven experiments are substantially identical, which they were not in terms of persons, rules, etc. It seems more reasonable to interpret each experiment as wholly independent, in which case the t statistic can be taken as indicating the truth of the null hypothesis in all cases but Group 4, coalition (2, 3). So the question recurs: Why in this one case did the subjects produce markedly different results?[5]

As mentioned earlier, obvious explanations of this deviation are that the subjects varied in skill or that the subjects held to moral standards different from those embodied in the solution. But in this case, owing to the fact that we have six other similar experiments, we can, I believe reject these explanations easily.

The subjects in Group 4 who formed (2, 3) coalitions significantly different from the comparable point in the solution were of course precisely the same subjects who formed (1, 2) coalitions quite similar to the comparable point in the solution. That is, the subjects alternated among the positions so that each subject played each position about the same number of times. It is hard to imagine them skillful in position I and unskillful in position 3, especially when subjects in six other groups (chosen in a similar way from the same population) were equally skillful in all three positions. We cannot, I think, attribute the deviation to variations in skill, which are a normal part of the situation in all seven experiments but which would then be said to affect the average outcome only in Group 4.

Nor can we attribute the deviation to variations in moral standards. If we had only the results from coalition (2, 3) for Group 4, with its average of $ 2.88 for 2 and $ 3.12 for 3, and its large (6 of 14) proportion of imputations at or near (0, 3.00, 3.00), we might conclude that the players chose a fifty-fifty split as an expression of the moral standard of numerical equality between them. But we have the additional evidence that, in six other groups, the imputation (0, 3.00, 3.00) occurred very rarely and that the average payment to player 3 is very close to $ 3.50. In no other groups did the subjects, when playing position 3, show much interest in numerical equality when proportional equality gave them 50 ¢ more. And these very same subjects, when playing position 1, agreed to imputations close to the appropriate point in the solution, even though that proportional equality gave them 50 ¢ less than numerical equality. Again, it seems highly unlikely that the subjects in position 3 in Group 4 chose to deviate for moral reasons.

If we are to find an explanation for their behavior, it must be in the informal rules. And such an explanation is readily at hand. The main difference in the informal rules for Group 4 as against other groups is the order of negotiations. As previously noted, five of the seven groups negotiated in the order: [(1, 2), (1, 3), (2, 3)] and in Group 4 the order was [(2, 3), (1, 3), (1, 2)]. The notable difference between Group 4 and all the others is that player 3 is excluded from the last conversation. In all groups, players frequently remarked that it was advantageous to be in the last conversation, whether that was known prior to the play as in Groups 1–5 or known only after the play as in Groups 6–7. And they were quite correct, for in Groups 1–3 and 5, the coalition (2, 3), which had the last conversation for certain, formed 57 times as against 39 times for (1, 3) and 26 times for (1, 2). In Group 7, on the other hand, where (1, 3) had the last certain conversation, (1, 3) formed 10 times as against 4 for (1, 2) and 6 for (2, 3). Even in the first match subjects played in, they often recognized the advantage of the last conversation; and as they progressed in experience they sometimes devised elaborate strategies of negotiation that exploited this advantage.

9*

Knowing the disadvantage involved in missing the last conversation, many subjects in the 3 position offered to pay heavily to secure at least some money. I offer some excerpts from the conversations of a player 3 (Group 4, match 13, conversation 1), where player 1 is called A, 2 is B, and 3 is C:

3   ...I suppose we could just go down the middle with a, ah, three-three split and see how things to in...

2   Yeah, thats...

3   ...the second round. Our main problem with B and C [i.e. 2 and 3] is that, ah, there's two more conversations after we meet.

2   (laugh). Yeah.

3   And from what I've seen so far, B and C combinations have been pretty hard to form because of that. Because...

2   Yeah, well that's...

3   ...either one or the other panics, you know, even though it's worth the most money, the six bucks, either one or the other panics because he gets the feeling he's going to get screwed by the other guy and he ends up making a deal for less total money. — So you'd think that these — coalitions would be the easiest to form, but so far as, as far as I can see, they've been by far the hardest to form.

2   Well, the first several coalitions [i.e. in the first several matches of the series] were B C coalitions.

3   Yeah, those first, the first couple of times; but I don't... well... but this is my fourth time at it.

Conversation 2

3   Um, I'll be perfectly honest. C's been getting screwed in these things, pretty much so at least...

1   C has?

3   C has. I don't know when...

1   Well, I did the other day, but, um ...

3   I was screwed as C the first time [i.e. which resulted in an imputation of (0, 0, 0)] and, ah, from what, from the one that I played in and the ones I've heard about, C has been, ah, taking a, has been losing, um, the majority of the time. And from what I think this is — because he never has the last conversation. — So, ah, for, ah, I'm perfectly willing right now just to start off, well, since this is our first conversation, why not take a two-fifty split [i.e. of $ 5.00].

1   Well, I, I wasn't expecting as much. Now, this is the...

3   Yeah, ok.

1   Thing...

3   O.K., I know what you mean. I mean, you think, you know, o.k., B and C are, let's say we go three, three right down the middle. Then you figure right, that I, that I, that I'd take that [i.e. $ 3.00] over, let's say, three, two.

1   Yes.

3   O.K. Well, o.k., if you wanted to go to something just a bit higher then that. See, 'cause I also got a problem here, you know. I make a deal that's too advantageous for me with you; and then you and B get together the last time. You say, "Look, ah, C's trying to screw both of us. C's going to take most of the money. So why don't the two of us make a deal and screw C, you know, maybe, you know, one of us is going to end up...

1   Yeah.

3   "with less money."

1   Yeah.

3   "But, you know, we're going to screw C out there and you know he's been trying to get the most money from us." Anyway, I think that's unconscious, I believe. So when C comes in here, C's got the most valuable coalition, there's always the feeling, you know,

1   Yeah.

3   you know, get-together-and-screw-the-big-boy, you know. That's that's see that's, what I'm sort of trying to fight this time, if at all possible.

Ultimately in this match, player 3, calling himself a coward, negotiated an imputation (0, 3.25, 2.75) with 2. Player 3 stuck to it, spurning even the offer from 1 of an imputation (1.25, 0, 3.75). Not surprisingly 2 kept this highly advantageous bargain so the final imputation was (0, 3.25, 2.75). An observer might think 3 gave up too much; but it is hard to argue with winning.

If one untangles the expressed motives for 3's behavior, he was influenced to ask for a relatively small amount by the facts that (1) he was to be absent from the last conversation and (2) he feared an animosity by 1 and 2 toward the "big boy", himself.

There can be no doubt that this second consideration is pervasive, for it was frequently referred to by subjects in all positions and in all groups. I think, however, that the subject just quoted states it somewhat incorrectly. It seems less an irrational animosity of poor toward rich and more a simple self-interest of the poor to get some of the rich's money.

The solution concept embodies this motive and provides for its effective operation under other circumstances, namely the shaded areas in Figure 1.[6] In Group 6 my subjects found a way to enter the shaded area thus:

1   In conversation 1, player 1 proposed to 2 that 2 give 1 $ 1.50, in return for which 1 would vote for an imputation (0, 4.00, 0), would tell 3 of the bargain and refuse to negotiate with 3, and would give 2 his (1's) partly used meal ticket as surety of his (1's) vote with the understanding 2 would return it when the vote was cast as agreed.
2   Player 2 accepted and in the 3rd conversation proposed to 3 an imputation (0, 4.50, 1.50). Since 3 already knew (from conversation 2 with player 1) that his choice was either to accept the proffered $ 1.50 or to receive nothing, he too accepted.
3   Thus the final imputation was (1.50, 3.00, 1.50).

While this imaginative and clever way to combine against player 3 was always available, especially when the order of negotiation was [(1, 2), (1, 3), (2, 3)] as in Groups 1–3 and 5–6, still very few players discovered it. So in the absence of such knowledge, most of the time in most groups, player 3 took home the largest payoff. But in Group 4, the informal rules kept player 3 out of the last conversation. This is the first consideration our quoted subject referred to and he seems to be correct in believing that it hurt the 3 position.

I am suggesting here a distinction, inherent in the remarks of the subject, between the consideration of ganging up on the big-boy and the consideration of the last conversation. Ganging up is inherent in the formal rules and can occur under any order of negotiations. But the presence or absence of a player from the last conversation is a matter of the informal rules. What I have wanted to show is that for Group 4 the informal rules forced player 3 to accept less than he did in other groups. And both the statistical and observational evidence suggests strongly that they did work that way. It seems reasonable to conclude that the informal rules occasioned a significant deviation from the solution.

One might ask, however, why omission from the last conversation had this effect on player 3, but not on players 1 and 2? The answer is that it did, but in another way. Although the theory says nothing about the expected frequency of occurrence of the three coalitions around the principal points, it is reasonable to suppose in the abstract that (1.2), (1, 3), and (2, 3) each happen about 1/3 of the time. But this is clearly not the case. In Groups 1–3 and 5–6, where player 1 was excluded from the last conversation, the frequency of the several coalitions was:

(1, 2) 37 times or 24%
(1, 3) 46 times or 29%
(2, 3) 74 times or 47%

Thus, while player 1 might be expected to win 2/3 of the time, subjects in that position won only slightly over 1/2 the time. Similarly, in Group 7, where player 2 was excluded from the last conversation, the outcomes were:

(1, 2) 4 times or 20%
(1, 3) 10 times or 50%
(2, 3) 6 times or 30%

So player 2, who might be expected to win 2/3 of the time, won only 1/2 of the time. In Group 4, where player 3 was excluded from the last conversation, this effect did not occur. Instead, we have:

(1, 2) 9 times or 32%
(1, 3) 5 times or 18%
(2, 3) 14 times or 50%

where 3 wins the expected 2/3 of the time.

We can explain the situation thus: Exclusion from the last conversation had the effect on 1 and 2 of permitting them to win with less than the expected frequency. Exclusion of player 3, however, had the effect of permitting him to win with the expected frequency but of forcing him to accept less money when he did win.

Post hoc, there seems a perfectly reasonable explanation of this fact. For player 3, with his large expected winning, it seemed reasonable to guarantee winning something (less than the expected) by a sacrifice. Hence, when excluded, he won about as often, but less total money. For players 1 and 2, however, significant sacrifices when deducted from their smaller expected winnings took them down to the range where the then expected take-home did not itself seem significant. Most of our subjects rejected offers of less than $ 1.00 as beneath their dignity, often expressing a preference for losing as against taking home so little. And subjects in the 2 position often stated $ 2.00 as their minimally acceptable offer. Hence 1 and 2, when excluded from the last conversation, simply did not win very often.

5

This essay began with the assertion that the informal rules contribute something to the rational expectations of players. I have shown, I believe, that, in a series of experiments in which the informal rules were devised to encourage outcomes consonant with a solution derived exclusively from the formal rules, it is nevertheless true that one informal rule, viz. the order of negotiation, has itself a significant and consistent effect on the outcome and hence presumably on the expectations of rational players. At least, I am myself certain that, were I to play in the position excluded from the last conversation, I would lower my expectations from what the solution prescribes.

Other experiments suggest the same thing, In Professor Lieberman's experiments with a similar game and a similar solution, subjects concentrated on fifty-fifty divisions quite outside the solution. (Lieberman, 1962). Though his experiments were not extensive enough to explain this outcome for certain, it appears to me that the rule providing for brief and attenuated negotiations was what occasioned the concentration. Jumping quite far afield, Professor Rappaport's experiments with prisoners' dilemma games suggest that a variety of variations of the informal rules alter rational expectations. (Rappaport and Chammah, 1965).

If informal rules do then contribute to rational expectations, their effect should certainly be comprehended in solutions which are "characterizations of rational behavior." The question is: How to do so? I have nothing profound or revolutionary to offer in response. But the following remarks summarize my present opinions on the subject:

One might restate the principal points of the solution of the game played by Group 4 as follows:

$$(1.50 - \varepsilon < x_1 < 1.50 + \varepsilon, 2.50 - \varepsilon < x_2 < 2.50 + \varepsilon, 0)$$
$$(1.50 + \varepsilon, 0, 3.50 - \varepsilon)$$
$$(0, 2.50 + \varepsilon, 3.50 - \varepsilon)$$

Clearly this restatement lacks the inner stability of the von Neumann–Morgenstern (and other) solutions and certainly cannot satisfy the geometric rationale of Figures 1 and 2. Yet it does express what happened in Group 4, even to the point of accounting for the relatively large standard deviation in the outcomes for coalition (1, 2) and the excessively large proportion of (0, 0, 0) imputations.

Unsatisfactory as this restatement is, however, it may nevertheless suggest the general effect of the informal rules, when they force deviations from the mathematical solution. This particular rule generates instability, whereas other comparable rules generate a preference for the coalition (2, 3) over others. Extrapolating, the general case may be that any informal rule directing the behavior of rational subjects away from the mathematical solution introduces either instability or a preference for some particular coalition.

Unfortunately, if this is the general effect of informal rules, then it is probably not possible to incorporate their effects in *a priori* solutions. Once instability is introduced, anything can happen and what does in face happen must be discovered case by case. The situation with this rule is instructive. Most sophisticated social scientists would, I am sure, predict *a priori* that the order of dyadic negotiations would, affect the income of the player in the position excluded from the last conversation. But I think it highly unlikely that even the most sophisticated would predict that the exclusion of 1 and 2 would affect primarily their frequency of winning, while the exclusion of 3 would affect primarily the amount won per match.

And so I conclude with some remarks on what is apparently one main purpose of this conference, namely, the consideration of what social scientists can learn from and contribute to game theory. If informal rules introduce instabilities into the expectations from formal rules, then one of the main contributions social scientists can make to game theory is to specify precisely what these instabilities are in important cases. This is, of course, what they have been doing all along as, for example, in the study of oligopoly or in the study of voting rules. But, to study a particular instability against a known solution is vastly more instructive than to study an instability in isolation. And this is what the social scientist can learn from game theory.

NOTES

* Six of the experiments reported here were done with the assistance of a grant from the National Science Foundation. One was done with the assistance of a grant from the Center of Naval Analysis. In neither case is the grantor responsible for the opinions expressed. I thank very much the grantors for the financial assistance; and my research associates, William Zavoina and Robert Samberg, for tireless labor.

1 This enterprise is, of course, analogous in the field of n-person games to the work of Schelling on two person, non-zero-sum games (Schelling, 1960). When compared to the unique imputation in the von Neumann-Morgenstern solution to the two-person,

zero-sum game, the infinity of imputations in their solution to the two-person, non-zero sum game is less than satisfactory for a social theory. So Schelling attempted to render solutions somewhat more specific by introducing many considerations from the temporal context. As is appropriate, considering the complexity of n-person zero-sum and non-zero-sum games, the number of von Neumann-Morgenstern solutions is infinite and in many cases each of these infinity of solutions contains an infinity of imputations. It seems reasonable to suppose that, by introducing considerations from the informal rules, one might illuminate n-person, non zero-sum games as much as Schelling illuminated two-person, non-zero-sum games.

2　The sentence "$v(1, 2, 3) = 0$" means that the instructions to the players were that the experimenter would pay nothing to the grand coalition. While this rule was strictly adhered to, it does not prohibit the formation of a grand coalition by reason of private agreements among the three players, although, given the temporal rules of the matches, considerable ingenuity was required to construct the coalition of three. A few subjects were sufficiently ingenious to do so. Properly, therefore, this should read: "$v(1, 2, 3) = 0$, if the coalition (1, 2, 3) is reported as a three-person coalition, and $v(1, 2, 3) = \$ 6.00$, if the coalition (1, 2, 3) is reported as a two-person coalition," though, of course, such a statement over looks the flavor of the instructions.

3　I say "include" rather than "are" because, while I have endeavored to list all the rules that seemed possibly relevant, there may have been customary features of the play which I overlook as trivial but which the players regarded as significant.

4　In this respect the Aumann—Maschler solution, (Aumann and Maschler, 1964), is superior because it accounts for the (0, 0, 0) outcomes, though not for the outcomes in the shaded spaces.

5　Even if one does not regard the experiments as independent and thus does not regard the one failure (in 21) of the null hypothesis as significant, it is still reasonable to ask why this *particular* case was the one that turned out to be in the five per cent that did not satisfy the null hypothesis. It could have been any one of the 21, but in fact it was this one, precisely where a deviation was expected.

6　Professor Maschler's notion of power also embodies this possibility, (Maschler, 1963).

REFERENCES

Aumann, R., and Maschler, M. The Bargaining Set for Cooperative Games. In M. Dresher, L. S. Shapley, and A. W. Tucker, (Eds.), *Advances in Game Theory*. Princeton: Princeton University Press, 1964. pp. 443–476.

Lieberman, B. Experimental Studies of Conflict in Some Two-Person and Three-Person Games. In J. Criswell, H. Solomon, and P. Suppes (Eds.), *Mathematical Methods in Small Group Processes*. Stanford: Stanford University Press, 1962. pp. 203–219.

Luce, R. Ψ Stability: A New Equilibrium Concept for n-Person Game Theory. *Mathematical Models of Human Behavior*. Stanford: Dunlap and Assoc., 1955. pp. 32–44.

Luce, R., and Raiffa, H. *Games and Decisions*. New York: Wiley, 1957.

Maschler, M. The Power of a Coalition. *Management Science*, 1963, **10**, 8–29.

Rappaport, A., and Chamma, A. *Prisoners' Dilemma*. Ann Arbor, University of Michigan Press, 1965.

Riker, W. H. Experimental Verification of Two Theories About Three-Person Games. In J. Bernd (Ed.), *Mathematical Applications in Political Science*. Vol. 3. University of Virgininia Press, 1967. pp. 52–66. (a)

Riker, W. H. Bargaining in a Three-Person Game. *American Political Science Rev.*, 1967, **LXI**, 91–102. (b)

Riker, W. H. and Zavonia, W. Rational Behavior in Politics: Evidence from a Tree-Person game. *Amer. Pol. Sci. Rev.*, 1970, **LXIV**, 48—60.

Schelling, T. *The Strategy of Conflict*. Cambridge: Harvard University Press, 1960.

Von Neumann, J., and Morgenstern, O. *The Theory of Games and Economic Behavior*. (3rd ed.) Princeton: Princeton University Press, 1953.

COALITION BEHAVIOR IN INESSENTIAL GAMES

RICHARD H. WILLIS[1]

University of Pittsburgh

The purpose of this paper is to illustrate the utility of the class of games called inessential for the development of descriptive coalition theory and for the experimental investigation of coalition behavior in small groups.

In this introductory section inessential games are discussed in relation to some recent descriptive theorizing about coalitions, and a distinction between deterministic and stochastic games is introduced. It is noted that inessential games and stochastic games both fall outside the scope of available descriptive theory. A number of hypotheses are formulated about coalition behavior in a class of inessential stochastic games. In the subsequent portion of the paper an experiment is reported which provides considerable support for these hypotheses.

Inessential games

About inessential games Luce and Raiffa (1957, p. 185) have this to say:
"It is conceivable that there are games in which no coalition of players is more effective than the several players of the coalition operating alone, in other words, that for every disjoint subset of players R and S,

$$v(R \cup S) = v(R) + v(S).$$

Such games are called *inessential*; any game which is not inessential is called *essential*. It is not difficult to show that a game is inessential if and only if the total payment to the set of all players is exactly the same as the sum of payments to all the individual players, i.e.

$$v(I_n) = \sum_{i=1}^{n} v(\{i\}).$$

Since nothing is gained by forming coalitions in inessential games, it is clear that we cannot expect any theory of coalition formation in that case, and so we shall be concerned only with essential games from now on."

When Luce and Raiffa say that we cannot expect any theory of coalition formation in the inessential case, they refer of course to normative theory. Actually, it would be more accurate to say that there *is* a normative theory of coalitions in inessential games—a very simple one—that recommends no expenditures on the part of participants in seeking either to form coalitions or to avoid them. This recommendation is based on the assumption that payoffs to coalitions are distributed equitably among coalition members, for then the expected payoff to any player is uneffected by his decision to enter into a coalition or play alone.

However, an adequate *descriptive* theory of coalitions in inessential games will be less simple and more interesting than the normative theory. In fact, such a descriptive theory is of special interest just because of the particular simplicity of the associated normative theory. Just because coalitions are neither advantagous or disadvantagous, extra-normative considerations will have their maximal impact on behavior. In the absence of a logical rationale, psychological factors should be revealed more clearly.

The game theorist has good reason to dismiss inessential games as trivial. The behavioral scientist, on the other hand, has good reason to consider them interesting and useful.

Descriptive coalition theory

Despite the fact that *n*-person game theory is concerned primarily with coalitions, it has been found to be of limited usefulness by behavioral scientists interested in coalition phenomena. One reason, of course, is the discrepancy between the normative and descriptive objectives. Another is that the "solutions" of *n*-person game theory do not generally allow the prediction of particular coalition structures.

As a result, recent attempts have been made to develop theoretical approaches to coalitions that would be more relevant for the description of actual behavior in small groups. All have taken inspiration from game theory while making little use of its technical superstructure. All have incorporated important extra-game-theoretic considerations. All have had considerable, albeit imperfect, success in predicting the behavior of experimental subjects (see, e.g. Gamson, 1964).

Among the earliest of the descriptive theoretical efforts was that of Theodore Caplow (1956, 1959), who restricted his attention to triads. Willis (1962) extended Caplovian theory to tetrads and provided an experimental test of the extension. Another descriptive theory of coalitions was developed by William Gamson (1961a, 1961b, 1964), while a related approach has been formulated in some detail by William Riker (1962). A key idea with both Gamson and Riker is that the most frequently formed coalition will be the least powerful one that is capable of winning. Caplow's analysis makes use, somewhat indirectly, of a related principle.

An important advantage of the Gamson and Riker formulations is their generality with regard to group size. They can be directly applied to groups larger than three, whereas Caplow's theory—as he developed it—is applicable only to three-person groups. Although the present author found it possible to extend a part of Caplow's analysis to four-person groups, a rather substantial increase in complexity was required which suggested that further extensions to larger groups would not be feasible. Another difference between the Caplow theory and the others is that Caplow assumes that participants are motivated to *control other participants* and to avoid being controlled by them, whereas Gamson and Riker assume that the concern is directly with *control over the decision* (e.g. the outcome of a vote).

Gamson's theory, which has been referred to as minimal resource theory (Gamson, 1964), can be taken as illustrative. We summarize it very briefly.

It applies to situations in which (a) there is a decision to be made and there are more than two social units attempting to maximize their share of the payoffs, (b) no single alternative will maximize the payoff to all participants, and (c) no participant has either dictatorial or veto power. These conditions, taken together, define a full-fledged coalition situation.[2] Predictions are based on information concerning (a) the initial distribution of resources, (b) the payoff for each winning coalition, (c) non-utilitarion strategy preferences, and (d) the effective decision point, i.e. the proportion of resources necessary to determine the decision (to win).

The *general hypothesis* of the theory is that "...any participant will expect others to demand from a coalition a share of the payoff proportional to the amount of resources that they contribute to a coalition." (Gamson, 1961b,

p. 566.) This expectation on the part of participants about one another is labelled by Gamson *the parity norm*. As used here, parity is very much in the spirit of *distributive justice* (Aristotle; Homans, 1958, 1961), or *equity* (Adams, 1963). Specifically, the parity norm is the expectation that coalition partners will demand equity or distributive justice in the division of any winnings.

The parity norm allows the prediction that the coalition formed will be the *cheapest winning coalition*, provided that the condition of reciprocal strategy choices is met. That is, that coalition will be formed—it is predicted—which has just barely the resources to determine the decision, provided that the coalition is otherwise acceptable to each potential member. Each participant prefers to join the less powerful of any two winning coalitions because his equitable share of the winnings will be larger.

An important limitation of Gamson's theory (as well as Caplow's and Riker's) is the requirement that there be a *critical quantity* of resources. Any participant or coalition possessing less than the critical quantity has no control over the decision and so *never* wins, while any participant or coalition possessing more than the critical quantity has complete control over the decision and so *always* wins.

Deterministic and stochastic games

In other words, the situations considered by the descriptive coalition theories under review are completely *deterministic*. Given a particular initial distribution of resources, chance or "luck" plays no role. The functional relationship between resources and probability of winning is a step-function, with a probability of zero up to the critical quantity and unity beyond. Voting situations provide the most obvious class of examples.

In many situations, however, the probability of winning is a joint function of resources and luck. Thus, even the team with the better players may be upset, and even the army that is substantially outnumbered may sometimes be victorious. These may be called, in the present context, *stochastic* coalition situations. Although the parity norm may still hold in a stochastic situation, the concept of a cheapest winning coalition becomes increasingly meaningless as the role of luck increases. When resources and luck jointly determine the likelihood of winning, as in the case of two baseball teams, a margin of safety in the form of a comfortable surplus of resources is a good thing to have.

In the limiting case, at the opposite extreme from the completely deterministic situation, the outcome is determined entirely by chance; all parties have an equal likelihood of winning despite apparent differences in resources. Here, obviously, the idea of a margin of safety is not applicable.

One intermediate case is particularly simple. This is the situation in which the probability of victory is exactly equal to the proportion of resources controlled. An example is a lottery in which different parties hold different numbers of tickets. The more tickets one holds, the greater the chance one has of winning. One holding twice as many tickets as another has twice the probability of being the winner. Such a situation will be recognized as an inessential game, for the expected value of the payoff to any coalition is exactly equal to the sum of the expected values for the coalition partners playing individually.[3]

In Figure 1 are plotted the three limiting cases just considered. Along the abscissa is plotted the proportion of resources controlled by an individual or a coalition, while the probability of winning the constant stake is plotted

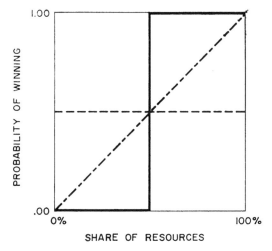

Figure 1 Functional relationships between share of resources and probability of winning, for three limiting cases

along the ordinate. The solid line shows a function for the kind of situation that Gamson, Riker, and Caplow treat; in this particular case the critical quantity is 50 per cent. The broken horizontal line shows the function for a case in which the probability of winning is constant (one half) and so unrelated to apparent differences in resources. The broken diagonal line shows the function for the situation in which the probability equals the proportion of resources controlled.

In Figure 2 are shown, for the sake of comparison, some curves related to the step-function of Figure 1. The center sigmoid curve is the 50 per cent

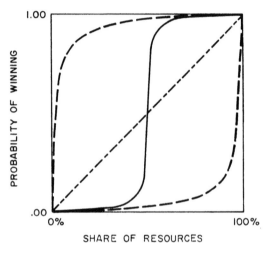

Figure 2 Functional relationships of some curves related to the step funktion of Figure 1

critical quantity step-function modified by the presence of a stochastic or "luck" component. Possession of at least the critical quantity of resources no longer guarantees victory, nor does possession of less than the critical quantity necessarily mean defeat, although the probability of winning changes quite rapidly in the vicinity of 50 per cent.

The upper, negatively accelerating curve in Figure 2 represents a stochastic version of the situation in which the critical quantity is so small as to approach zero. One interpretation runs as follows. There are an indefinitely large number of participants, each favoring a different outcome. Each wants to be elected leader, let us say. If time pressures demand that a decision be made immediately, any participant who can first gain a slight edge over the field—such as gaining even one or two supporters—greatly increases his chances of winning. Such a situation is unstable because the decision depends heavily upon the first minor perturbations of the initial balance.

The lower, positively accelerating curve characterizes a stochastic version of the situation in which the critical quantity is 100 per cent. As an interpretation, consider a voting group in which unanimity is required to reach a decision. The stochastic component aside, each member has veto power. To win, a party must control all or almost all of the votes. This situation can be described as ultrastable, for the status quo can be preserved almost indefinitely by a very small minority.

The linear function with unity slope, shown as a broken line in both figures, corresponds to the games played by subjects in the experiment reported below. Because coalescing is neither advantagous nor disadvantagous from a "rational" viewpoint, provided winnings are distributed equitably, the importance of psychological or social factors is maximized.

Rational man and social man

Let us construct two straw men—named Rational Man (RM) and Social Man (SM)—and make three assumptions about each in the context of coalition behavior in an inessential game. Each set of assumptions contains an *affective* (or motivational), a *cognitive*, and a *behavioral* assumption. For Rational Man, so-called, these assumptions are as follows:

1 Only manifest payoff has utility for RM.
2 RM believes that other group members will demand *at least equity*, in bargaining with potential coalition partners.
3 RM himself will demand *at least equity* in bargaining with potential coalition partners.

For Social Man, the corresponding assumptions are:

1 Only avoiding social isolation has utility for SM.
2 SM believes that other group members will demand *at most equality* in bargaining with potential coalition partners.
3 SM himself will demand *at most equality* in bargaining with potential coalition partners.

For a group composed entirely of Rational Men playing an inessential game, two propositions follow immediately from the assumptions:

1 Bargaining, if it occurs, will be exceedingly tight.
2 As a result of the tight bargaining, *no* coalitions will be formed.

For a group composed entirely of Social Men playing an inessential game, four propositions follow immediately from the assumptions:

1 Bargaining, which will most certainly occur, will be exceedingly loose.

10*

2 As a result of the loose bargaining, the maximum number of coalitions will be formed.

3 Coalitions will be randomly distributed among the various possibilities.

4 On the average, winnings will be divided between pairs of coalition partners equally, and will be unrelated to differences in contributions.

These contrasting pictures of group behavior are both too stark to show promise as descriptive models. Let us relax the assumptions and see what happens.

If we assume that all group members are intermediate between RM and SM, but closer to RM, the following propositions can be derived:

1 Bargaining will be relatively tight; winnings will be divided more nearly according to equity than equality.

2 As a result of the relatively tight bargaining, relatively few coalitions will be formed.

3 Equals will coalesce more often than non-equals, coalition strength held constant.

4 Coalitions will be formed more often between weaker members.

The first two propositions follow immediately from the relaxed version of the assumptions about RM. Proposition 3 derives from the fact that equity and equality amount to the same thing when partners contribute equally. This will facilitate agreement among potential partners. Proposition 4 follows from the fact that, the stronger the participant, the more it costs him to compromise on equity, and the more reluctant he will therefore be to enter into a coalition. Two additional reasons for expecting the weak to coalesce often, not deriving from the assumptions, are (a) the common fate of probably losing may arouse a reciprocal affiliation motive, and (b) in a triad, the coalescence of the two weaker members will maximize uncertainty in the information theory sense, and this may make the game more fun.

If we assume that all group members are intermediate between RM and SM, but closer to SM, the following propositions can be derived:

1 Bargaining will be relatively loose; winnings will be divided more nearly according to equality than equity.

2 As a result of the relatively loose bargaining, a relatively large number of coalitions will be formed.

3 Equals will coalesce more often than non-equals, coalition strength held constant.

4 Coalitions will be formed more often between weaker members.

The first two propositions follow immediately from the relaxed version of the assumptions about SM. The same reasoning used to arrive at the last two propositions before is applicable here. Relevant to the last proposition, it is more costly—in terms of manifest winnings—for a strong participant to compromise on equity in this group (because the compromise is closer to equality), but at the same time he cares less about such costs here. Accordingly, no prediction is made about the relative strength of the tendencies for weaker members to band together in the two cases. Nor is any prediction made about the relative strength of the Proposition 3 trends. The facilitative effect of an obvious solution to the problem of dividing winnings should be about equal in both instances.

Experimental hypotheses

The experiment brought subjects together in groups of three to play a series of games all fulfilling the condition that the probability of winning be equal to the proportion of resources controlled by the individual or coalition. In order to meld the two sets of theoretical propositions just presented into a set of four experimental hypotheses, it is only necessary to make the very reasonable assumption that all experimental subjects fall somewhere between the extremes of RM and SM. If we assume further that the typical male subject is closer to the RM end of the continuum than is the typical female subject, two additional experimental hypotheses can be formulated. These six hypotheses, ordered for convenience in discussing the experimental results, are:

Hypothesis 1 Fewer coalitions will be formed than in essential experimental games.

Hypothesis 2 Within a given experimental condition, coalition frequencies will be inversely related to coalition strength.

Hypothesis 3 Coalition strength held constant, equals will coalesce more frequently than will non-equals.

Hypothesis 4 Agreements between coalition partners about the division of winnings will be a compromise between equity and equality.

Hypothesis 5 Groups of males will form fewer coalitions than will groups of females.

Hypothesis 6 Agreements between coalition partners about the division of winnings will more closely approximate the condition of equity in groups of males than in groups of females.

METHOD

Subjects

Subjects were 168 undergraduates at the University of the Philippines—
84 males and 84 females—recruited from lower division Arts and Sciences
classes on a volunteer basis. From these were formed 56 three-person groups,
each containing members of one sex only. Experimenters were seven graduate students in sociology, one male and six females. Each experimenter ran
eight groups, four of males and four of females.

Task and design

Each group played 36 trials of a game of chance in which the object was to
earn as many points for oneself as possible. Over the 36 trials, eight different
experimental conditions were introduced, each condition characterized by
a different power structure. A power structure specifies a division of power
coefficients among group members, with coefficients summing to 10 in
every condition. The eight experimental conditions or power structures
were as follows:

$$A: 8 - 1 - 1$$
$$B: 6 - 2 - 2$$
$$C: 4 - 3 - 3$$
$$D: 4 - 4 - 2$$
$$E: 7 - 2 - 1$$
$$F: 6 - 3 - 1$$
$$G: 5 - 3 - 2$$
$$H: 5 - 4 - 1$$

The set of power structures exhausts the possible combinations of non-
zero integer coefficients that sum to 10. Each unit of power represents a
10 per cent chance of winning on a given trial. A coefficient of 5, for example,
means that the player has a 50 per cent chance of winning. On each trial the
winner received 100 points.

Players were allowed to form coalitions, if desired, during a one-minute
negotiation period which preceded each play of the game. If two players
coalesced, the coalition had a power coefficient equal to the sum of the two
individual power coefficients. Partners were required to agree beforehand on

the division of points in the event of winning. Coalitions were valid for one trial only.

Conditions A, B, C, and D were each represented by three consecutive trials among the total of 36, while six consecutive trials of Conditions E, F, G, and H were played. This allowed all possible assignments of power coefficients to specific group members to be made once each. The order of assignments within each condition was determined beforehand by chance.

Each of the seven experimenters ran eight groups, each group receiving the eight conditions in a different sequence. Sequences were chosen so that each experimenter's groups completed one replication of a balanced Latin square (Edwards, 1960, pp. 275–276). In a balanced Latin square, each condition is preceded and succeeded by each other condition an equal number of times. Such balancing will tend to minimize order effects.

Because there was an odd number of experimenters, it was possible to achieve only an approximate balancing of sex of subjects over sequences. Four experimenters ran odd-numbered sequences with male subjects and even-numbered sequences with females, while three experimenters used the reverse procedure.

The winning player or coalition on a particular trial was determined in the following way. On each trial ten playing cards were distributed among group members, each member receiving a number of cards equal to his assigned power coefficient for that trial. Cards were dealt face down. Then followed the one-minute negotiation period during which a coalition was perhaps formed. Coalition partners pooled cards. Then the experimenter determined the lucky number for that trial by chance. Subjects then turned up their cards and learned which individual or coalition won the 100 points. Talking among subjects was allowed only during the negotiation periods.

Subjects were informed that those "scoring better than average" would receive a package of good quality candy as a prize, and three such packages were in sight. Subjects were informed that the average score was 1200 points (i.e., one third of the total points), and those scoring better than 1200 were awarded candy. Subjects were not allowed to keep a running tally of their score.

RESULTS

Results will be discussed in terms of (a) the frequency with which coalitions were formed, (b) the distribution of coalitions within conditions, and (c) the division of payoff between partners.

Frequency of coalitions

In Table 1 are shown the frequencies with which coalitions were formed in
each condition and the corresponding percentages, for groups of each sex
separately and for both groups combined. For all groups and all conditions

Table 1   Frequencies with which coalitions were formed

		Frequency of Coalitions			% Trials Coalitions		
		M	F	M + F	M	F	M + F
A	8–1–1	54	56	110	64.3	66.7	65.5
B	6–2–2	53	62	115	63.1	73.8	68.4
C	4–3–3	43	42	85	51.2	50.0	50.6
D	4–4–2	46	44	90	54.8	52.4	53.6
E	7–2–1	101	99	200	60.1	58.9	59.5
F	6–3–1	93	100	193	55.4	59.5	57.4
G	5–3–2	89	95	184	53.0	56.5	54.8
H	5–4–1	77	97	174	45.8	57.7	51.8
	Σ or $\bar{X}$	556	595	1151	55.2	59.0	57.1

Note: For both sexes combined, there was a total of 168 trials for each of Conditions
A–D, and a total of 2 × 168 = 336 trials for each of Conditions E–H.

together, coalitions were formed on 57.1 per cent of the trials. How does
this figure compare with the rate of coalition formation in *essential* experimental games?

Vinacke and Arkoff (1957) had their male subjects play six games derived
from Caplow's typology of triads. Of these, four were essential (any two can
win) and two were inessential (one player all powerful). Coalitions were
formed on 93 per cent of all trials in the essential games, as compared to
32 per cent in the inessential games. In a later experiment using the same six
games (Vinacke, 1959), male and female groups formed coalitions on 89 and
78 per cent of the trials in the essential games, respectively, as compared to
32 and 46 per cent in the inessential games. In two three-person essential
games used by Lieberman (1962), the male subjects coalesced 87 and 93 per
cent of the time. Finally, in two four-person essential games played by equal
numbers of male and female groups (Willis, 1962), coalitions were formed
on 94 per cent of all trials. In summary, essential games typically induce
subjects to form coalitions about 85–90 per cent of the time.

The 57 per cent of coalition trials observed in this experiment easily qualifies as "fewer" than this baseline of 85–90 per cent, clearly confirming Hypothesis 1. Additional confirmation comes from the above-cited differential rates of coalescing in the essential and inessential games in the experiments by Vinacke and Arkoff, and Vinacke.

Support for Hypothesis 5 can be seen in Table 1 from the fact that, overall, males formed fewer coalitions than did females (55.2 vs. 59.0 per cent). The median test, applied to the numbers of coalitions formed by each of the 56 groups, revealed this trend to be statistically significant ($p < 0.05$). Again, the Vinacke study cited above is relevant. It lends additional support to Hypothesis 5 insomuch as males formed fewer coalitions than did females in inessential games—but more in essential games.

For both sexes combined, percentages of coalition trials in each condition range between 50.6 to 68.5. Let us dichotomize conditions into those with a highly uneven distribution of resources (A, B, E, and F) and those with a relatively even distribution (C, D, G, and H). All of the unevenly distributed conditions have a higher proportion of coalitions than any of the more evenly distributed. Furthermore, this pattern holds up perfectly for the proportions for the two sexes separately. The probability of a perfect four-four split occurring by chance alone is $4!4!/8! = 1/70$, and the probability of two such splits (as with each sex) is $(1/70)^2$. The observed relationship between the frequency of coalitions and the distribution of resources is highly significant. This between-conditions effect would appear to be an indirect manifestation of the within-conditions effect described by Hypothesis 2. When one group member is stronger than the other two together, the two weaker members coalesce especially often and thus increase the total number of coalitions for that condition. Direct evidence that this is happening is presented in Table 2.

Distribution of coalitions

Table 2 shows the frequency of each type of coalition within each condition, for each sex separately and for both combined. The ratio of each observed frequency to that expected by chance is also given.[4]

From a comparison of the O/E ratios within conditions, it can easily be seen that Hypothesis 2 receives strong direct support. There is a consistent "weakness effect," an inverse relationship between coalition strength and observed/expected frequency. For the two sexes separately, forty O/E ratios

Social Choice

Table 2 Frequency of type of coalition within each condition

Condition		M	F	M + F	M	F	M + F
		\multicolumn{3}{c}{Frequency}		\multicolumn{3}{c}{Observed/Expected}	

Condition		M	F	M + F	M	F	M + F
A	81	14	33	47	0.39	0.88	0.64
	11	40	23	63	2.22	1.23	1.72
B	62	18	29	47	0.51	0.70	0.61
	22	35	33	68	1.98	1.60	1.77
C	43	21	22	43	0.73	0.79	0.76
	33	22	20	42	1.53	1.43	1.48
D	44	21	20	41	1.37	1.36	1.37
	42	25	24	49	0.82	0.82	0.82
E	72	7	26	33	0.21	0.79	0.50
	71	31	28	59	0.92	0.85	0.88
	21	63	45	108	1.87	1.36	1.62
F	63	15	24	39	0.48	0.72	0.61
	61	26	35	61	0.84	1.05	0.95
	31	52	41	93	1.68	1.23	1.45
G	53	23	20	43	0.78	0.63	0.70
	52	16	31	47	0.54	0.98	0.77
	32	50	44	94	1.69	1.39	1.53
H	54	18	20	38	0.70	0.62	0.66
	51	24	36	60	0.94	1.11	1.03
	41	35	41	76	1.36	1.27	1.31

are tabulated and only three transpositions would be required to make the ordering perfect. Both differences in Condition D are in the wrong direction, and in Condition G the ratios for the 5–3 and 5–2 coalitions are in the wrong order for males. The likelihood of this level of consistency occurring by chance alone is so infinitesimal that Hypothesis 2 can be taken to be verified at a high level of statistical significance.

Although two of the three exceptions occur with males, still males in general showed the weakness effect to a more pronounced degree than did females. In a large majority of cases, 13 out of 16, the relevant differences in O/E ratios are larger for males. Furthermore, the three differences larger for females average 0.28 while the 13 differences larger for males average 0.53.

Do the stronger group members more often play alone by choice or necessity? Among all coalitions between non-equals, the stronger partner took the initiative only 41.1 per cent of the time, suggesting that stronger players play alone more often by choice than necessity. The bias is slightly more pronounced for males (38.9 per cent) than for females (43.0 per cent). When the Wilcoxon test was applied to data on each sex separately, this tendency was found to be significant at the 01 level for males and beyond the 05 level for females. When frequency of initiation was plotted against actual magnitudes of resource differentials, no clear relation emerged, except that in the two most extreme cases (7–1 and 8–1), the stronger partner initiated especially infrequently. The percentages were 11.1 and 32.2 for males and females, respectively.

Hypothesis 3—that equals coalesce more frequently—can also be tested by the data of Table 2, from certain between-conditions comparisons. Six kinds of comparisons are possible involving coalitions between equals and those of the same strength between non-equals, *viz.*, 2–2 vs. 3–1; 3–3 vs. 4–2 and 5–1; 4–4 vs. 5–3, 6–2, and 7–1. For each sex, the O/E ratio for the coalition between equals is the largest in each set, as predicted. This is highly significant ($p = 1/576$). Hypothesis 3 is strongly supported, and holds up for males and females equally well.

When comparisons involve only coalitions between non-equals, the magnitude of the difference between *male* partners in coalitions of a given strength turns out to be of little or no importance. Of the 13 relevant differences in O/E ratios, six are in one direction and seven in the other.

For females, however, all 13 differences are in the direction of *larger* O/E ratios for the *less* evenly distributed contributions! This is not only high significant, statistically, but also highly mystifying to a mere male investigator.

The weakness effect of Hypothesis 2 and the equality effect of Hypothesis 3 are not independent. Most of the time they operate in the same direction, making it impossible to obtain fully independent tests in this experiment. However, both effects are so clearly manifest that this partial confounding should cause little concern. Of special interest are those minority of instances in which the two effects are in opposition within a given condition. This happens six times for each sex. Only once is a coalition between exact equals larger than the other possible coalition(s)—Condition D, 4–4 vs. 4–2. For males and females both, the equality effect is much the stronger. No "strength in weakness" effect here! The weak player is excluded most often.

In the remaining cases of opposition between effects (7–2 vs. 7–1; 6–3 vs. 6–1; 5–3 vs. 5–2; 5–4 vs. 5–1 and 4–1), none of the stronger coalitions is between exact equals. This probably accounts for the fact that the weakness; effect is now the stronger nine times out of ten. Although exact equality outweighs weakness, weakness outweighs relative equality.

Division of payoff

Hypothesis 4 predicts that partners will divide points according to a compromise between equity and equality. Figure 3 plots division of payoff, for
each sex separately, as a function of the contribution made to the coalition
by the senior partner. If points were always divided equally, both curves
would lie along the abscissa; if points were always divided in proportion
to contributions, both curves would lie along the line marked *Equity*. The
equity-line also represents Gamson's parity norm.

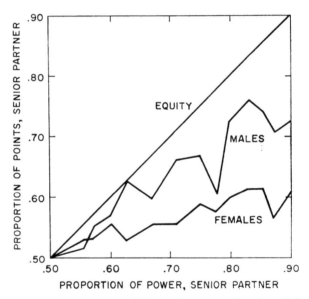

Figure 3   The division of payoff, for each sex, as a function of the contribution made to the coalition by the senior partner

Hypothesis 4, with one borderline exception, is uniformly confirmed by
the data points in Figure 3. Partners consistently divided points so as to give
more than equality to the senior partner but more than equity to the junior
partner. By and large, males divide slightly closer to equity than to equality,
while females are clearly nearer to the equality-line (i.e. the abscissa). The
separation between the two curves is large and consistent, a finding which
provides strong support for Hypothesis 6.

The bias in favor of junior partners helps account for the more frequent
initiation by weaker players; they typically increase the expected value of

their payoff by forming a coalition with a stronger player. Junior partners are typically more "rational" than senior partners.

Another aspect of the division of payoff is shown in Figure 4, where the proportion of 50–50 deals is plotted against the contribution of the senior partner. As expected, points are divided equally in almost all coalitions between equals, and the proportion of equal deals generally decreases as contributions become more and more unequal.

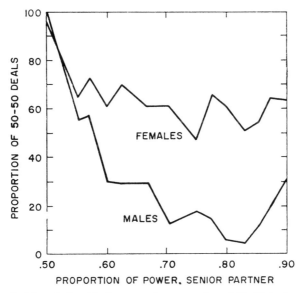

Figure 4 The relationship between the proportion of 50–50 deals and the contribution of the senior partner

Two facts stand out immediately in Figure 4. First, a rather large proportion of deals were of the 50–50 variety. In fact, over half (53.5 per cent) of all deals were of this kind. Even excluding coalitions between equals, the percentage is over two-fifths (43.6 per cent).

Second, equal division is much more frequent between females (66.0 per cent) than between males (40.1 per cent). When only coalitions between non-equals are considered, the difference becomes striking. Males split evenly 24.7 per cent of the time, while the percentage for females drops only six points to 60.3! These sex differences are clearly evident in Figure 4, where the two curves are separated by approximately 50 percentage points at several places. Although the configuration of Figure 4 is not independent of that of Figure 3, it represents some additional support for Hypothesis 6. Females are clearly the more socially oriented, while males are the more "rational" or task-oriented. A number of experimenters have observed sex differences of this general kind in a variety of contexts (e.g., Joseph and Willis, 1959; Vinacke, 1959; Bond and Vinacke, 1961).

One feature of Figure 4 is puzzling. Males, for some reason, begin making appreciably *more* 50–50 deals again as the contribution of the senior partner exceeds about 85 per cent.

DISCUSSION

All six hypotheses were confirmed. All in all, the assumptions made about the motivations and perceptions of subjects led to successful predictions about their coalition behavior in the inessential games used. The compromise model, which assumes that subjects are describable as hybrids of Rational Man and Social Man, remains tenable.

At first glance it may appear that the typical subject bears only a remote resemblance to Rational Man. The general picture which may seem to emerge is one of basically irrational behavior, where rationality is defined in terms of the experimenter-imposed task of earning as many points as possible. *Even males* form coalitions on a majority of trials and make 50–50 deals on one out of every four coalitions between non-equals.

Before concluding that subjects were behaving irrationally, however, it is necessary to note that rational and social motives are not actually in conflict in the games played. These games all meet the condition of *additivity* specified by Luce and Raiffa's definition of inessential games quoted at the beginning of this paper. Coalitions are not mutually advantagous, but neither are they necessarily disadvantagous since the coalition gets no less than the sum of its members' individual expectations. Thus, a participant's social motives can be gratified without decreasing his expected payoff. In fact, each and every subject can avoid social isolation most of the time without the diminution of anyone's anticipated payoff—provided that equity holds, either for each coalition or in the long run for each series of coalitions formed between particular subjects over the course of all trials.

In order to put rational and social motives truly into conflict, it would be necessary to use games in which the expected value of the payoff to any coalition is *less* than the sum of such values for members playing individually. Such games might be termed *subessential*. Because subessential games are capable of generating basic motivational conflict in subjects, they should prove highly useful for experimental research.

Whether or not a situation puts the two kinds of motives into inevitable conflict, Social Man has as much claim to *ends*-rationality as does Rational Man. The experimenter cannot justly dictate that winning points or money is more important for the subject than, say, avoiding social isolation. It becomes necessary, then, to assess the *means*-rationality of subjects, i.e., the extent to which their behavior is effective in accomplishing whatever it is that they want to accomplish.

In order to do this, it is necessary that a variety of possible "hidden" rewards, as well as such manifest ones as points or money, be taken into account. Techniques for assessing these hidden rewards must be refined and routinely incorporated into experimental studies of social interaction. The frequent failure by experimenters to do so in the past lends credibility to the claims of Scriven (1964), Ring (1967) and others who emphasize the artificiality and restricted meaningfulness of experiments in social psychology.

In the present instance, we cannot say that our subjects—even the females—were guilty of means-irrationality. Apparently, as anticipated, they had other motives besides that of winning points, and were, perhaps, employing strategies effective in gratifying these other motives. Forming coalitions may have been more fun than going it alone all the time, either because of an involvement in the negotiations or because of a preference for winning smaller amounts more often over winning the same total points in fewer, larger payoffs. Coalitions among the weaker players may have intensified the interest and suspense, for such coalitions in triads maximize uncertainly in the information-theory sense. The bias in favor of junior partners may have derived, not from the irrationality and poor bargaining skill of the senior partners, but rather from a desire to lend a helping hand to the underdog. Finally, offers to coalesce may often have been accepted because of the social cost of saying "No"; there is reason to believe such costs to be high in Filipino culture, but no reason to think they do not also exist in American culture.

We may say in conclusion that one of the most important and general implications of this study is that manifest rewards alone provide an inadequate basis for predicting the behavior of experimental subjects.

NOTES

1 The experiment reported in this paper was conducted while the author was a Rockefeller Foundation visiting professor at the University of the Philippines, while on leave from Washington University. It was made possible through the initiative and enthusiasm of seven sociology graduate students who wanted some experience in experimen-

tation. These students, who participated actively in the design of the experiment, as well as serving as experimenters, were Virginia Alvarez, Rodolfo A. Bulatao, Marlene Ligan, Amelita Liggayu, Elizabeth Quimpo, Ana Maria Rotor, and Maria Vida Ventura. Certain incidental expenses were met by the Rockefeller Foundation. A brief, preliminary refort of the experiment appeared previously (willis, 1969).

2   Inessential games obviously do not qualify as full-fledged coalition situations, because no possible coalition can benefit all its members, except possibly by chance.

3   It should be noted that inessential games can be deterministic (e.g. Caplow's 3-1-1 and 4-2-1 cases), and essential games can be stochastic (e.g. the winner is determined by chance, but the expected value of the payoff to at least one coalition is larger than the sum of the expected values to its members playing alone).

4   In converting the frequencies of Table 2 into O/E ratios, two kinds of adjustments were required. First, it was necessary to take into account the fact that only half as many trials were run of Conditions A–D as of Conditions E–H, just as in computing the percentages in Table 1. Second, it was necessary to adjust for the fact that, in any given Condition A–D, the coalition between equals could occur in only one way while the coalition between non-equals could occur in two ways. Thus, the expected frequency of the coalition between non-equals is twice that of the coalition between equals.

REFERENCES

Adams, J. S. Toward an understanding of equity. *Journal of Abnormal and Social Psychology*, 1963, **67**, 422–436.

Aristotle. *Nichomachean ethics.*

Bond, J. R., and Vinacke, W. E. Coalitions in mixed sex triads. *Sociometry*, 1961, **24**, 61–75.

Caplow, T. A theory of coalitions in the triad. *American Sociological Review*, 1956, **21**, 489–493.

Caplow, T. Further developments of a theory of coalitions in the triad. *American Journal of Sociology*, 1959, **64**, 488–493.

Edwards, A. L. *Experimental design in psychological research* (rev. ed.). New York: Holt, Rinehart & Winston, 1960.

Gamson, W. A. A theory of coalition formation. *American Sociological Review*, 1961, **26**, 373–382. (a)

Gamson, W. A. An experimental test of a theory of coalition formation. *American Sociological Review*, 1961, **26**, 565–573. (b)

Gamson, W. A. Experimental studies of coalition formation. pp. 81–110 in L. Berkowitz, (Ed.), *Advances in experimental social psychology*, Vol. 1. New York: Academic Press, 1964.

Homans, G. C. Social behavior as exchange. *American Journal of Sociology*, 1958, **63**, 597–606.

Homans, G. C. *Social behavior: its elementary forms.* New York: Harcourt, Brace & World, 1961.

Joseph, M. L., and Willis, R. H. An experimental analog to two-party bargaining. *Behavioral Science*, 1963, **8**, 117–127.

Lieberman, B. Experimental studies of conflict in some two-person and three-person games. In Joan H. Criswell, H. Solomon, and P. Suppes (Eds.), *Mathematical methods in small group processes*. Stanford, Stanford University Press, 1962, pp. 203–220.

Luce, R. D., and Raiffa, H. *Games and decisions*. New York: Wiley & Sons, 1957.

Riker, W. H. *The theory of political coalitions*. New Haven & London: Yale University ues. Press, 1962.

Ring, K. Experimental social psychology: Some sober questionabout some frivolous val- *Journal of Experimental Social Psychology*, 1967, **3**, 113–123.

Scriven, M. Views of human nature. In T. Wann (Ed.), *Behaviorism and phenomenology*. Chicago: University of Chicago Press, 1964, pp. 162–183.

Thibaut, J. W., and Kelley, H. H. *The Social psychology of groups*. New York: Wiley & Sons, 1959.

Vinacke, W. E. Sex roles in a three-person game. *Sociometry*, 1959, **22**, 343–360.

Vinacke, W. E., and Arkoff, A. An experimental study of coalitions in the triad. *American Sociological Review*, 1957, **22**, 406–414.

Willis, R. H. Coalitions in the triad: additive case, *Psychonomic Science*, 1969, **17**, 347-8.

BARGAINING BEHAVIOR IN AN ASYMMETRIC TRIAD

D. L. HARNETT and L. L. CUMMINGS

Indiana University and University of Wisconsin

The research reported in this paper represents one among a series of projects by the researchers investigating bargaining in conflict situations. Over the past two and a half years the researchers have engaged in a series of studies investigating bargaining in conflict settings involving aspects of both co-operation and competition; that is, where cooperation is necessary for agreement, but where the interests of individual bargainers conflict as to the nature of this agreement. The research presented here is a continuation of this research stream in a context designed to simulate one particular type of interaction among bargainers in a triadic relationship.

The type of bargaining paradigm we have chosen to study involves two bargainers of equivalent, but independent stature, each of whom must negotiate separate agreements with a third bargainer. This type of relationship can be represented by Figure 1. Both bargainers B and C must come to an agreement with A before a "solution" is reached. Gains to Bargainer A are obtained at the expense of Bargainers B and C. B and C are not competing directly with one another, but for a share of the total reward available. This type of setting has many real-world counterparts; e.g. interpretation can be in terms of relevance for market structures, such as two sellers facing a single buyer, or in terms of implications for under-standing superior-subordinate relations in a hierarchical setting. These are just a few of the more salient examples.

Our interest in conflict generation and resolution in the setting described above has focused on both structural and personal determinants of the processes as well as the results of bargaining. We have generated data relating to these variables in two types of bargaining relationships. In the first type, referred to as a *symmetric paradigm*, bargainers B and C assume indistinguishable bargaining roles (i.e. they are treated symmetrically). An *asymmetric bargaining paradigm* characterizes the second type of re-

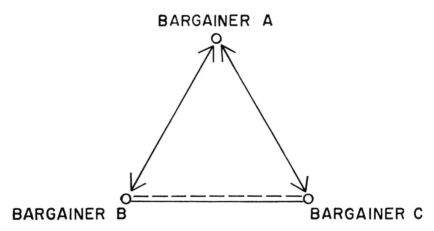

Figure 1 Asymmetric Bargaining Triad

lationship, where *Bargainers B and C are distinguished by variations in the structure of their bargaining position.* Only asymmetric results are reported in this paper; the symmetric condition is reported in another paper: Cummings and Harnett. (1969).

We have focused our attention on two structural determinants of bargaining. The first is *information*, which is concerned with the amount of knowledge a bargainer has about his opponents' rewards; i.e. about the desirability, value, or perhaps utility to his opponents of all possible agreements. Our interest is in investigating the effect on bargaining of variations in the amount of information available to Bargainer B relative to the amount possessed by Bargainer C.

The second structural determinant of interest is *communication*, specifically the tendency of the bargainers to transmit information, promises, or even threats during the negotiation process. We are interested in learning if the ability to communicate facilitates or hinders the bargaining process, how much information or misinformation is transmitted, and whether communication is generally beneficial or harmful to the individual bargainer.

Communications in our experiments were permitted between Bargainer A and either B or C, or between B and C.

In addition to investigating information and communication, we studied the influence of a number of personal characteristics on bargaining behavior. We administered a risk-taking propensity measure in an attempt to relate each bargainer's propensity to take risks to his bargaining behavior. Also, each bargainer was asked, prior to his participation, questions concerned with determining his expectations and aspirations regarding earnings in the experiment to follow. Answers to these questions were then related to performance in the ensuing bargaining. Finally, each bargainer was given, postexperimentally, a semantic differential instrument designed to measure several attitudinal factors which we felt provided additional insight into individual performance and satisfaction.

RELATED LITERATURE

The question of the allocation of rewards to the members of a group is a problem that has long intrigued economists, political scientists, sociologists, and recently, among others, mathematicians and psychologists. There are several streams of research which are especially relevant for the related bargaining question under consideration in this paper, the most important of which is the extensive theoretical and experimental research of Fouraker and Siegel (1960, 1963). The role of information has received special attention in their work, and they indicate that assumptions involving the amount of knowledge possessed by the participants are critical determinants of the bargaining outcomes.

The traditional assumption in the theoretical literature has been one of complete or perfect information, where each participant is assumed to be fully informed about his opponents desires. Under this assumption the even split of maximum joint profits among the bargainers in conflict is often specified as the apparent solution to the bargaining problem (Schelling, 1957). However, Fouraker (1957) states that "in many markets it may be inappropriate to assume complete knowledge of the cost and revenue functions for one or both firms. It may be more realistic to assume that the seller knows his cost functions, but does not have knowledge of the buyer's revenue functions, and the buyer, while aware of his revenue conditions, lacks knowledge of the seller's cost functions."

Both the Fouraker-Siegel research and the work of Schelling (1963) suggest that under some circumstances information may be harmful to a bargainer, since the bargainer with more information may be inclined to temper his demands because he knows what is reasonable or "fair." The bargainer with less information may be less likely to yield if a stalemate is imminent because he thinks his demands are reasonable when in fact they are not. Our own experimental research in this area (Harnett, Hughes, Cummings, 1968) indicated support for Schelling's hypothesis, as we found that generally the more completely informed bargainers agreed to less favorable terms.

If we note two additional characteristics of the experimental paradigm studied, our data takes on relevance for several issues in organizational behavior. First, in each of the five conditions Bargainer A possessed the *power* to terminate the bidding with the last offer if no agreement had been reached within the one hour time limit. Bargainers B and C could only either accept or reject this final bid. They could not make a counteroffer. Second, the reward structure of the game favored Bargainer A. While B and C's potential earnings ranged from $ 0 to $ 9.47, A's potential earnings from *each* of B and C ranged from $ 0 to $ 6.11. Thus, A possessed two sources of earnings with a potential total of $ 12.22. This again can be viewed as providing A with a source of *potential power* over B and C.

Given differential bidding power and differential rewards, let us, for the moment, think of Bargainer A in a position *superior* to B and C, the latter being *subordinate* to A on these two variables. Fiedler (1967) has suggested that such "position power" will be a crucial variable in explaining differences in group performance and subordinate affective reactions. Furthermore, the effects of these power differentials may be moderated by the communication network existing between A and B–C as well as between B and C (Leavitt, 1964, Chapter 15). In addition, our experimental variation of the magnitude and direction of information and communication allows us to examine an important question in the research on power. Namely, do differences in power between two parties (bargainers, super-subordinate dyads, etc.) have to be known by both parties in order to exhibit any effects on bargaining processes or results?

Adams (1965), and Porter and Lawler (1968) have raised questions about the relationship between the magnitude of a reward received and the satisfaction or affect experienced subsequent to its receipt. Equity and perceived contingency apparently play important roles in influencing this relationship. Our data allow us to examine directly the issue of the relation between expected earnings, actual earnings and post-bargaining satisfaction with earnings. We also will examine the manner and extent to which variations in information and communication moderate such relations.

HYPOTHESES AND DESIGN

We are interested in determining the influence of information and communication on bargaining, especially as these variables relate to the effect of a number of personal characteristics on the negotiation process. By designing a series of experiments in which the amount of information and/or communication permitted was systematically varied, we were able to investigate the singular effects of these variables as well as their interactional effects. Thus, we examined the role of information and communication as independent variables in determining variations in bargaining behavior *and* as moderators of the effects of risk-taking propensity on bargaining.

Our general hypothesis is that the ability of an individual to bargain successfully will be highly dependent on the amount of information and communication he has available. We expect that the more information a bargainer has about his opponents' rewards, the more realistically he will approach the negotiation problem. That is, he will be less likely to make unreasonable demands in his negotiations. On the other hand, he may earn less under these conditions. In effect, we are testing the Schelling hypothesis relative to the bargaining process.

We anticipate the effect of communication to be similar to that of information—it should encourage a more realistic attitude among bargainers and decrease the difficulty of successfully negotiating an agreement in a reasonable length of time. These effects, however, should vary depending on which bargainers are permitted to communicate, and on the amount of information available to each person. Without information, for example, communication may involve an exchange of knowledge concerning payoff structures, or suggestions for a method of compromising differences; i.e. act as a substitute for information. Completely informed bargainers, on the other hand, may concentrate their communications on more specific means for arriving at a given solution (e.g. threats, promises, or pleas to "be reasonable").

We investigated the effects of information, communication and risk-taking propensity in an experimental task involving price-quantity negotiations for the exchange of a fictitious good. For each three-man bargaining triad, Bargainer A was require to negotiate a *single* agreement with both Bargainers B and C.[1] As a result of these negotiations, and depending on the price and quantity agreed to, each player earned an amount of "profit." This profit served to provide incentive and to assure seriousness among the participants. A cash payoff, corresponding to the amount of profit earned in the bargaining, was made to each subject.

Subjects were tested in five different experimental variations of the basic three-man bargaining relationship. Throughout these conditions Bargainers B and C were differentiated by the amount of information and/or communication they possessed. By comparing the results of a sufficiently large number of subjects bargaining in the B and C roles, we thus were able to test for differences attributable to these variables. The five experimental conditions are labeled conditions 1–5.

Individual bargainers were either completely informed or had no information about the profit the other bargainers could earn. In all conditions, however, Bargainer A had complete information. Negotiations took place either with or without communication. By varying the amount of information and communication, we tested five combinations of these variables. Note that in each condition, Bargainers B and C are differentiated either in terms of information or communication availability.

Condition 1   In Condition 1, Bargainers A and B had complete information while Bargainer C had no information. No communication was permitted between any of the bargainers. We can represent this relationship as in Figure 2.

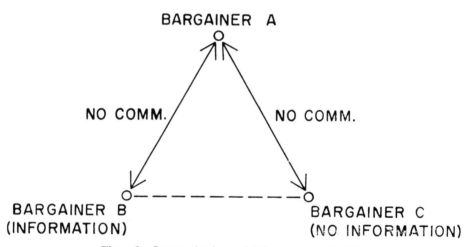

BARGAINER A

NO COMM.   NO COMM.

BARGAINER B   BARGAINER C
(INFORMATION)   (NO INFORMATION)

Figure 2   Communication and information in Condition 1.

Condition 2   This condition varied from condition 1 in the fact that communication was permitted between A and B and Bargainer B had no information, as shown in Figure 3.

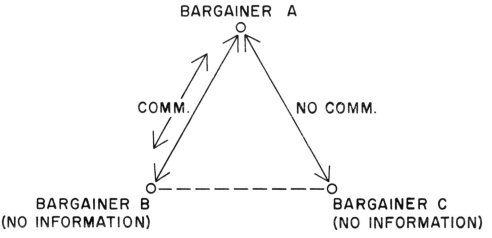

Figure 3 Information and Communication in Condition 2

Condition 3 Condition 3 was identical to condition 2 except that Bargainers A and B were both given complete information. Comparison of Bargainers B and C in Condition 3 allows the investigation of the effects of differential communication in the presence of information.

Condition 4 For Condition 4 we allowed Bargainer A to communicate with B and/or C; they could not communicate with him, but were permitted to communicate with each other. Information levels were identical to

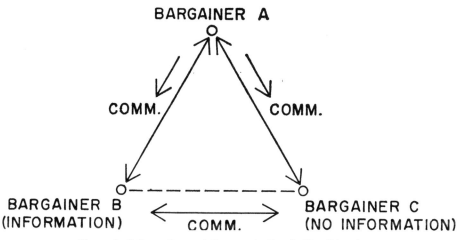

Figure 4 Information and Communication in Condition 4

condition 1. Comparison of Conditions 1 and 4 permits the investigation of the effects of adding one-way vertical and lateral communications, (see Figure 4.)

Condition 5   The only difference between Conditions 4 and 5 was that the communication stream between A and the other two bargainers was reversed. Comparison of Conditions 4 and 5 allows examination of the impact of the direction of communication in the triad.

EXPERIMENTAL METHODS

The data were collected in five experimental sessions, corresponding to the five conditions described above. All subjects, 156 male business school students at Indiana University, were told at the time of recruitment only that they would be paid for participating in a research project. They were assured the project would be without noxious stimuli, but were given no indication as to the nature of the experiment or the amount of money they could earn.

Each subject participating in a given session was randonly assigned to one of three rooms, corresponding to the three roles of Bargainers A, B, and C, and randomly assigned to a bargaining group. In their respective rooms the participants were given a set of mimeographed instructions, a table showing the various levels of profit they could achieve for each possible price-quantity agreement, and a sheet for recording the negotiations.[2] At the end of an instruction period of approximately twenty minutes, subjects were given an opportunity to ask questions. The experimental procedure, therefore, randomized subjects into groups of three, and into the role of Bargainer A, B, or C. Although recruiting and testing difficulties precluded randomizing subjects across conditions, the students appeared to be roughly comparable from condition to condition. Nevertheless, the fact that the data for all conditions were not collected simultaneously (i.e. each condition was on a different night) suggests that they may not, in fact, be comparable. For this reason our analysis of the differences between conditions will be informal and suggestive, rather than a more formal statistical approach.

The bargaining was arranged so that a subject could not see or talk to his bargaining opponents. Negotiations were conducted in silence with no communication permitted between participants except for written price-quantity offers and, when the experimental conditions permitted, written messages.

Bargainer A initiated the bargaining process by sending a written price-quantity offer to either B or C (or to both). His offer was taken by an experimental assistant to the appropriate opponent. This person then had the right to either accept the offer, in which case his part of the negotiations ended, or to reject the offer and send back a counteroffer. Bargainer A at that point then had the opportunity to accept this counteroffer, or reject it and start the process over again with a new offer. This process continued until Bargainer A reached an agreement with both B and C, or until the one hour time limit was ended. Each participant was informed prior to bargaining that if no agreement was reached within one hour between both A and B as well as A and C no one of the three would earn any profit.

Under complete information conditions, Bargainers B and C received not only their own payoff table, but that of Bargainer A as well. Bargainers under complete information were told exactly what information their opponents held; bargainers under incomplete information were given no knowledge of this nature. Communication was achieved by means of written notes. Each participant was given five slips of paper which he could use to write short messages; these messages were unrestricted, except they could not threaten physical violence, or reveal the identity of the bargainer, or suggest a division of profits postexperimentally. A bargainer experimentally permitted to communicate with both of his counterparts could allocate his five messages between the two as he pleased.

We studied the effects of information and communication by using a number of measures of the bargaining process. The dependent variables include:

1) Profit: The amount of money each bargainer earned.
2) Initial asking level: The amount of profit asked for in the first offer, or counteroffer.
3) Amount yielded: The amount a subject conceded from his second bid level to his final profit.[3]
4) The number of offers: The number of offers, or counteroffers, made before a solution was reached.

In addition to the above measures, three instruments were used to determine individual differences and postbargaining affective reactions.

a) Risk-taking propensity: This was measured through a variant on a 12 incident choice dilemma instrument developed by Kogan and Wallach (1964)[4] to assess the subject's willingness to recommend the undertaking of risky behaviors in hypothetical real-life dilemmas.

b) A semantic differential instrument (Scott, 1967)[4]: This measure was used to determine attitudinal differences on 1) the Bargaining Task, 2) me at the task, 3) my earnings, and 4) the other members of the bargaining group.

c) Aspiration measure: Before each experimental session began, all subjects were asked to indicate, on a form provided, 1) how much they thought they would earn in the two-hour session, 2) what would be a "fair" amount to earn, and 3) the lowest amount they considered acceptable payment for their time.

RESULTS

The results indicate substantial differences between the bargaining roles within a condition. In general, we received considerable support for our contention that adding information creates a more realistic bargaining attitude among participants, and that communication has an effect on negotiations similar to that of information. The sections to follow report our findings condition by condition. For each condition we present the results of single variable analysis regarding the effects of structural and personal variables on bargaining as well as the interactional effects of these variables on bargaining. Multiple stepwise R's are also reported indicating the amount of variance in profit accounted for by the pre-experimental measures.

Condition   1

Some of our most interesting results came in Condition 1, where Bargainer B had information, C had no information, and where there was no communication. The data of this condition strongly support the predictions described above relating to the Schelling hypothesis. Evidence of a more realistic attitude on the part of Bargainer B include the fact he generally asked for less profit on his initial bid, required fewer offers to complete an agreement, yielded less during the negotiations, and, in addition, earned significantly less profit for the session. Bargainer A was thus able to bargain more successfully with his opponent who had the greater amount of information. Both Bargainers B and C had approximately the same affect for their earnings, despite differences in these earnings. Bargainer B, however, had less affect for the task. A summary of these results is shown in Table 1.

A number of interactional relationships are especially interesting. We found that the relationship between duration of bargaining and amount earned by Bargainer B or C is significantly moderated by the presence or absence of information. Giving Bargainer B information of the sort described above changes the direction of the relationship between earnings

Table 1   Condition 1 Results

	Bargainer B (With Information) ($n = 11$)	Bargainer C (Without Information) ($n = 11$)	Significance
Profit Earned	$ 3.86	$ 4.46	$p < 0.05$
Initial Asking	$ 5.01	$ 6.81	$p < 0.001$
No. of Bids	8.00	11.55	$p < 0.01$
Amount Yielded*	$ 0.99	$ 2.00	$p < 0.03$
Affect-This Task	4.85	5.32	$p < 0.05$

Stepwise Multiple Regression on Profit Earned: Condition 1

Bargainer B ($n = 11$)		Bargainer C ($n = 11$)	
Variable	R	Variable	R
1. Lowest Acceptable	0.6323	1. R.T.P.	0.3837
2. R.T.P.	0.7442	2. Perceived Fair Earnings	0.4296
3. How Much Expected	0.7450	3. How Much Expected	0.5468
4. Perceived Fair Earnings	0.7496	4. Lowest Acceptable	0.5639

* Amount yielded = second bid minus profit earned. This holds for all conditions.

and number of bids. For bargainers operating without information, (C), there was a negative relationship $r = -0.469$ while for bargainers in the B role, there was a positive relationship $r = +0.538$. These correlations are significantly different at $p < 0.05$. Thus, it appears that naive (uninformed) bargainers start their bidding high in terms of profit to themselves. The longer they negotiate, the less favorable the outcome in terms of attained earnings. On the other hand, knowledgeable bargainers start lower in their bidding (at more realistic levels), and the more they negotiate the more they tend to raise their attained earnings.

The relationship between risk-taking propensity (RTP) and the number of bids actually shifts direction as the amount of information changes.[5] Bargainers in position C yielded a positive relationship between RTP scores and the number of bids during bargaining, $r = +0.366$, while those in the B role yielded a negative relationship, $r = -0.526$; the difference is significant at $p < 0.05$. So when information regarding Bargainer A's potential payoffs is available high risk-taking bargainers increase the number of bids during negotiations. When information is not available, high risk-taking bargainers tend to start higher, generate fewer bids and, as we noted earlier, have their first, naive bids accepted.

Information also significantly moderated the relationship between what a bargainer expected to earn (EE) and his actual earnings (AE). Bargainers without information (C position) exhibited a *negative* relationship between their RTP scores and the difference EE–AE, $r = -0.521$. When information is not available risk-taking bargainers thus tend to "give" in their bargaining from their expectation levels. The opposite was true of bargainers operating with information (B role), as they showed a *positive* relationship between RTP scores and EE–AE, $r = +0.418$. This difference is significant at $p < 0.05$.

We were interested in the question of how well the amount of profit an individual earned could be predicted from information gathered on him prior to his participation and from the number of bids he made. To explore this question we ran a stepwise multiple regression analysis on the B and C bargaining roles, using data gathered on each participant's RTP and his pre-experimental expectations about earnings (how much he expected, what he thought was fair, and the lowest he would accept). Because of the small sample sizes, the F-ratio in a number of cases was not significantly different from zero. We will report the multiple R for all variables entered in Conditions 1, 4 and 5, and leave interpretation of their predictive value to the reader.

As can be seen in Table 1, for Bargainer B (with information) the variables entered the stepwise regression in the following order; lowest amount of earnings perceived as acceptable, risk-taking propensity, how much the bargainer expected to earn and what he thought would be fair earnings. The R attained was approximately 0.75. It should be noted that for Bargainer C (without information), less variance in profit was accounted for ($R = 0.5639$) and the predictor variables entered the stepwise regression in a different order (risk-taking propensity, perceived fair earnings, expectations, and lowest acceptable earnings). The fact that RTP entered the stepwise regression first and accounted for greater variance in the dependent variable under the less structural condition (no information) is consistent with our earlier findings (Harnett, Cummings and Hughes, 1968).

Condition 2

For Condition 2 neither Bargainer B nor C had information, but Bargainers A and B did have the ability to communicate with each other. Thus we were testing the influence of communication, to see what effect distinguishing B from C in this manner would have. Our results are summarized in Table 2.

As we anticipated, the effect of adding communication to an uninformed bargainer was quite similar to giving him information. Since the communication process is at best an inefficient and/or inexact means for transmitting information, we did not expect its presence to alter bargaining results as significantly as differences in information itself did, in Condition 1. In general, this is what the data indicate. There was, for example, very little difference in initial asking levels, because most bargainers did not begin communicating until after their first offer. Nor did the average amount yielded in Condition 2 differ significantly between Bargainers B and C. The direction of the difference in yielding is interesting to note, however, as it was *opposite* to that of Condition 1; i.e. Bargainer B gave in the most in Condition 2, and the least in Condition 1. Such a result is not surprising in view of the fact that both bargainers had similar initial asking levels in Condition 2, but we expected B to be more realistic than C, and hence, to yield more.

The difference in profit earned was in the predicted direction (B earning less than C), but not statistically significant ($p < 0.15$). There was a significant difference in the number of bids, again in the predicted direction.

Table 2   Condition 2 Results

	Bargainer B ($n = 11$)	Bargainer C ($n = 11$)	Significance
Profit Earned	$ 4.36	$ 4.57	$p < 0.15$
Initial Asking	$ 7.19	$ 7.30	N.S.
No. of Bids	6.27	9.45	$p < 0.005$
Amount Yielded	$ 2.08	$ 1.87	N.S.

Differences between Bargainers B and C in the interactional effects exhibited by the predictor variables were generally in the *strength* of the relationships. Thus, as suggested earlier, communication variations do not generate as dramatic effects as informational variations. Most of the strong interactional relationships were in the B position. For example, the correlation between profit and affect for earnings was quite strong ($r = 0.842$), for players with communication, and fairly weak ($r = 0.306$), for bargainers without communication, the difference being significant at $p < 0.05$. The only two notable exceptions to this trend were for relationships not involving personal measures of the bargainers. Thus, it appears that permitting communication increased the consistency of the effect of these variables on the bargaining process.

The content of the messages between Bargainers A and B proved to be quite interesting. As expected, a great deal of information was transmitted. A's messages were generally concerned with informing B about A's payoff structure, explaining why B's demands were unreasonable (e.g. "your last offer gave me $ 0 profit, while you got $ 7.43"), or trying to justify his own demands. The interesting fact was that Bargainer B, for the most part, did not ask for this information, and often ignored it when he received it; he preferred to send messages explaining his own demands, inquiring about negotiations with Bargainer C, or telling A to "hurry up" with his offers. *Thus, Bargainers A and B both tended to handle information in their messages in accordance with Schelling's hypothesis; i.e., A tried to pass information (to weaken his opponent's bargaining power) and B tried to avoid it.*

Condition   3

Condition 3 was identical to Condition 2 except that Bargainers B and C were completely informed, rather than uninformed. As in Condition 2, communication was permitted between Bargainers A and B alone. If information does, as we expect, perform much the same function as communication in the Schelling hypothesis, then one would expect little differences attributable to the structural distinction between Bargainers B and C in Condition 3. That is, providing Bargainers B and C with equal information will tend to diminish the differences due to differential communication in Condition 2. This was the case for our data, as no significant differences were found between Bargainers B and C in profit earned, the number of bids, yielding, or in initial asking level. Again, communication seems to exert effects in the same direction as information but less dramatically.

The two bargainers differed on only two postexperimental attitudinal measures, both of which are predictable in light of our findings in Condition 2 on communication. The first concerned their attitude toward Bargainer A, B having a significantly higher opinion of A's interpersonal effectiveness than C. Similarly, B had significantly more affect for his earnings than did Bargainer C.

Both Bargainers A and B used their messages in Condition 3 not so much to transmit information about payoffs (as in Condition 2), but rather to present demands, make threats, or in general to indicate what they considered to be a "reasonable" or "fair" agreement. Bargainers in the A role usually tried to justify an amount equal to player B's earnings while B generally felt that A should earn less, perhaps even one-half as much as he (so that A's sum total would equal B's payment).

Condition 4

In Condition 4 we permitted communication from A to *both* B and C, and between B and C. Information levels were identical to those of Condition 1— Bargainer B being completely informed, Bargainer C uninformed. Thus, we opened the communication channels, and once again tested the effect of different information levels. *Our hypotheses were that the availability of communication would, as before, tend to eliminate profit differences between B and C, and that there would be significant variances in the negotiation process and in attitudes toward the bargaining itself.*

As exhibited in Table 3 profit differentials between B and C were quite small: eight out of ten were less than 40 ¢, and three of these were zero. The same tendency was true for the number of bids, as in four cases the number of offers was identical for B and C, and in only three cases did they differ by more than two. This similarity did not carry over to most of our other measures. Bargainers in the C position asked for more initially, yielded a larger amount, and were less satisfied with their performance in the task. It is particularly interesting to note that even though Bargainers B and C did not differ significantly in the amount of profit earned, B experienced greater positive affect regarding his earnings. This was presumably due to his ability to form reasonable expectations about and to compare his earnings with those of Bargainer A. Presumably through the effects of information, Bargainer B experienced greater positive affect for the bargaining task and toward himself at the task.

Measurement of interactional effects gave evidence of some strong relationships. These relationships tend to emphasize the importance, indicated earlier in Table 3, of how negotiations and attitudinal effects are influenced by information. Note in Table 3 the especially strong relationships involving

Table 3 Condition 4 Results

	Bargainer B (n = 10)	Bargainer C (n = 10)	Significance
Profit	$ 3.70	$ 3.64	N.S.
No. of Bids	6.00	5.60	N.S.
Amount Yielded	$ 1.28	$ 3.10	<0.005
Initial Asking	$ 5.73	$ 7.29	<0.025
Affect-Task	4.84	4.39	<0.10
Affect-Me at Task	5.96	5.01	<0.025
Affect-Earnings	5.67	4.67	<0.02

Pearson Product Correlations as Moderated by Information: Condition 4

	Bargainer B (n = 10) (Information and Communication)	Bargainer C (n = 10) (Communication only)	Significance
Profit-RTP*	−0.019	−0.884	$p < 0.05$
Profit-Affect, Me at Task	−0.339	0.637	$p < 0.05$
Profit-No. of Bids	0.726	−0.380	$p < 0.05$
Profit-Initial Asking	0.560	−0.561	$p < 0.05$
Yield-RTP*	−0.075	−0.788	$p < 0.10$
Lowest Acceptable-Task Affect	−0.892	−0.031	$p < 0.05$
Lowest Acceptable-Task Complexity	−0.906	0.049	$p < 0.02$

Stepwise Multiple Regression on Profit Earned: Condition 4

Bargainer B (n = 10) Variable	R	Bargainer C (n = 10) Variable	R
1. Lowest Acceptable	0.6122	1. RTP	0.8838
2. Perceived Fair Earnings	0.6566	2. How Much Expected	0.8887
3. RTP	0.7652	3. Perceived Fair Earnings	0.9549
4. How Much Expected	0.7875	4. Lowest Acceptable	0.9553

* Again a high RTP score indicates low risk-taking propensity and vice versa.

attitudinal variables. Profit and yielding were most highly related to these attitudinal factors for Bargainer C who was bargaining without information; for Bargainer B profit was most highly related to the number of offers.

Several trends in the correlational data reported in Table 3 are important. First, the association of RTP and profit earned seems to be significantly moderated by information availability, with RTP exhibiting a much stronger relationship with profit in the absence of information. We interpret this as generally supportive of the notion that the personal characteristics of the bargainers exhibit a much stronger impact upon bargaining behavior under relatively unstructured bargaining conditions. The same general trend appears in the relationship between yielding behavior and RTP. Second, the relationships between profit earned and 1) number of bids or duration of bargaining and 2) initial asking levels are strongly moderated by information availability. For Bargainers in the B position (with information and communication); the higher the initial asking levels and the longer the bidding, the greater the profit earned. The reverse holds for Bargainers in the C position (without information). Thus without information regarding the "meaning" of an offer to A in terms of his profits, Bargainers in the C position seem to hinder their bargaining outcomes by starting high and bargaining long. Third, pre-experimental feelings regarding the lowest amount of money the subject would consider acceptable for the experimental period seemed to exhibit an impact on postexperimental feelings toward the task only when the bargainer had information about his opponents' payoffs. The data indicate that the greater the lowest acceptable payment, the less the positive affect experienced and the less the perceived complexity of the bargaining task.

It can also be seen in Table 3 that considerably more of the variance in profit is accounted for when RTP enters the regression first and contributes substantially as a predictor variable (Bargainer C as compared to Bargainer B). When Bargainer A has communication with B and C, RTP apparently plays a more important role in determining profits on the less informed bargainer.

Messages in Condition 4 followed much the same pattern as those in Condition 3. Over two-thirds of the messages sent by A were directed to Bargainer C, as A attempted to "inform" C about what A thought was a "reasonable" offer, and why. A's messages to B also concentrated on reasonableness, but in this case A was much more likely to make demands or threats, rather than merely inform. The messages between B and C stressed coordinating their behavior in an attempt to persuade A to give them the best offer possible.

It is interesting to compare the profits earned by Bargainers B and C in Conditions 1 and 4. Note that both bargainers do worse in Condition 4, especially Bargainer C. This suggests that giving Bargainer A the ability to communicate but not allowing B and C to respond, *improves* A's bargaining

12*

position. A's position seems to be particularly improved by his ability to communicate with Bargainer C, who has no information. In this case, A can use his ability to communicate as a means to "inform" C, and hence weaken C's position not only relative to B, but relative to A as well.

Condition 5

Instead of allowing one-way communciation from A to either B or C (Conditon 4), in Condition 5 we reversed the flow of communication to allow messages between B and C, or from either B and C to A. Information remained as it was for Condition 4. Under these circumstances we would not hypothesize profit differences between B and C, but *we would hypothesize differences in the bargaining process and in attitudinal effects.*

Table 4 summarizes the results of Condition 5. Note that initial asking levels were higher for C bargainers, but these bargainers yielded more, and thus earned approximately the same profit as B bargainers. C bargainers perceived A as more effective, presumably because they had no "information" on which to judge his reasonableness; also, they were forced to yield more to A and required more effort (greater number of bids) to reach agreement.

Table 4   Condition 5 Results

	Bargainer B ($n = 9$)	Bargainer C ($n = 9$)	Significance
Profit	$ 4.32	$ 4.26	N.S.
No. of Bids	6.44	8.22	<0.12
Amount Yielded	$ 0.86	$ 2.09	<0.05
Initial Asking	$ 5.14	$ 6.93	<0.02
A's Effectiveness	4.02	5.13	<0.001

Stepwise Multiple Regression on Profit Earned: Condition 5

Bargainer B ($n = 9$)		Bargainer C ($n = 9$)	
Variable	R	Variable	R
1. RTP	0.6341	1. Perceived Fair Earnings	0.4277
2. Perceived Fair Earnings	0.7108	2. RTP	0.6860
3. How Much Expected	0.7288	3. Lowest Acceptable	0.8581
4. Lowest Acceptable	0.7362	4. How much Expected	0.8740

The regression results for Condition 5 are presented in Table 4. Once again, with RTP scores entering the regression, reasonably high levels of the variance of profits earned are explained. For both Bargainers B and C, RTP contributed the greatest increase in R^2. Note that as communication is changed from Condition 4 to 5, RTP changes as the most important influence on profits from the less informed to the more informed bargainer.

A comparison of the profit-earned figures in Table 3 and 4 illustrates once more the effect of one-way communication. Bargainers B and C both do substantially better in Condition 5, where they can communicate to A, but A cannot respond. Thus, even when A is fully informed, his bargaining power appears to be significantly influenced by whether he, or his opponents, have the sole power of communication.

SUMMARY AND CONCLUSIONS

We have attempted to specify some of the ways in which differentials in information and communication can influence the negotiation process as well as attitudes toward the bargaining results. Our data indicate strong support for the Schelling hypothesis about the value of information to bargainers. In addition, we found that communication has a unique effect on the attitude of the bargainers, but that its influence on bargaining results is quite similar to that of information although generally weaker.

A bargainer negotiating a single agreement with two opponents was found to be able to conclude a more profitable agreement with a completely informed adversary than with an uninformed one. The uninformed bargainers usually started negotiations at higher asking levels, took longer to reach agreement, and yielded more in their negotiations. Risk-taking propensity was found to be an important factor in explaining the amount of profit a bargainer earned.

The affect of permitting a bargainer to communicate with his opponent was found to be similar to that of providing information. Communication directed toward the uninformed bargainer thus tended to induce him to be more realistic, to take less time to reach an agreement, to perceive his bargaining opponent as more effective in the negotiation task, and have more aeffect for his earnings. Communication between informed bargainers tended to concentrate on threats, promises, or at least strong suggestions for a "reasonable" solution. An informed bargainer communicating with an uninformed opponent generally did not make such demands, but tended to pass information, hoping this information would encourage his adversary to make more reasonable offers. Uninformed bargainers did not usually seek information, almost as if they knew such information might weaken their bargaining position. Both informed and uninformed bargainers who lacked the power to communicate in a one-way communication channel appeared to have a distinct bargaining disadvantage relative to their position with this communication. Thus, not only did our bargaining results uphold Schelling's hypothesis, but the communication process and most attitudinal effects were in accordance with this theory.

NOTES

1 Experimental procedures are explained in greater detail in the section to follow, on experimental methods.

2 Due to space limitations the instructions and profit tables could not be included in the manuscript. Copies of each may be obtained from the authors.

3 Second bid (rather than first bid) was used in calculating yielding because of the extreme variances of the first bids. First bids seemed to reflect searching behavior rather than a stable aspiration level.

4 The authors gratefully acknowledge Professor Wallach's and Professor Scott's willingness to allow us to utilize these instruments.

5 A high RTP score indicates an aversion for risk while a low RTP score indicates a preference for risk.

REFERENCES

Adams, J. S. Inequity in Social Exchange, In L. Berkowitz (Ed.), *Advances in Experimental Social Psychology*, Vol. 2, New York: Academic Press, 1965, 267–299.

Cummings, L. L., and Harnett, D. L. Bargaining Behavior in a Symmetric Triad: The Role of Information, Communication, Power, and Risk-taking Propensity, *The Review of Economic Studies*, October 1969.

Fiedler, F. *A theory of Leadership Effectiveness*, New York: McGraw-Hill, 1967.

Fouraker, L. E. Professor Fellner's Bilateral Monopoly Theory, *The Southern Economic Journal*, 1957, **24**, 182–189.

Fouraker, L. E., and Siegel, S. *Bargaining Behavior*, New York: McGraw-Hill, 1963.

Harnett, D. L., Cummings, L. L., and Hughes, G. D. The Influence of Risk-taking Propensity on Bargaining Behavior, *Behavioral Science*, Vol. 13, No 2, March, 1968, pp. 91–101.

Harnett, D. L., Hughes, G. D., and Cummings, L. L. Bilateral Monopolistic Bargaining through an Intermediary, *The Journal of Business*, Vol. 41, No 2, 1968, pp. 251–259.

Kogan, N., and Wallach, M. A. *Risk-taking: A study in Cognition and Personality*, New York: Holt, Rinehart and Winston, 1964.

Leavitt, H. J. *Managerial Psychology* (Rev. ed.) Chicago: University of Chicago Press, 1964.

Porter, L. W., and Lawler, E. E. *Managerial Attitudes and Performance*. Homewood, Illinois: Irwin-Dorsey Press, 1968.

Schelling, T. C. Bargaining, Communication and Limited War. *Journal of Conflict Resolution*, 1957, **1**, 19–36.

Schelling, T. C. *The Strategy of Conflict*. Cambridge: Harvard University Press, 1963.

Scott, W. E. The Development of Semantic Differential Scales as Measures of 'Morale'. *Personnel Psychology*, 1967, **20**, 2, 179–198.

Siegel, S., and Fouraker, L. E. *Bargaining and Group Decision Making: Experiments in Bilateral Monopoly*. New York: McGraw-Hill Book Co., 1960.

A LEVEL OF ASPIRATION MODEL[1]
FOR GROUP DECISION MAKING

DONALD L. HARNETT

Indiana University

The research presented in this paper is primarily concerned with an experimental test of a descriptive model for studying group decision making, although the model is also conditionally normative. This model was designed to investigate the problem of finding a meaningful measure for aggregating individual preferences: one which avoids certain inconsistencies and the inadequacy of an ordinal scale (ranking) by considering strength of preference, yet one which does not encounter the interpersonal comparison problems common to an interval measure of utility.

The possibility of obtaining a meaningful measure of utility stronger than ordinality was suggested by von Neumann and Morgenstern (1947), whose numerical index of utility has the properties of both interval and ordinal scales. The implications of their research led Siegel (1956) to investigate the possibility of measuring utility on an ordered metric scale. Such a measure, which lies between an ordinal and an interval scale, not only ranks the alternatives, but ranks the relative distance between adjacent alternatives as well. This type of scale was shown to yield valuable data on individual values in Siegel's research on level of aspiration.

Siegel's hypotheses concerning level of aspiration were derived from assumptions similar to Simon's (1955) concerning the nature of individual utility functions.[2] That is, the utility of success and failure are assumed to be relatively large in relation to the difference between alternatives (goals), so that the utility function takes a large jump at the point separating success and failure. These assumptions, together with extensive theoretical and experimental research, led Siegel (1957, p. 257) to define level of aspiration as

"... the least upper bound of that chord (connecting two goals) which has maximum slope; i.e. the level of aspiration is associated with the higher of the two goals between which the rate of the utility function is a maximum."

Under this definition, utility measured on an ordered metric scale is sufficient to determine an individual's aspiration level. Becker and Siegel (1958) collected data supporting this hypothesis by obtaining an ordered metric utility function based on subject responses to hypothetical choices between various alternatives. For example, with three alternatives a subject ranks the alternatives and then decides whether he would prefer his second choice for sure, or a 50–50 chance between his first and third choices. Should he choose the former (i.e., the second choice), this would indicate that the largest distance in utility is between Choice 2 and 3, and that his second alternative is his aspiration level. Letting $U(X)$ represent the utility for alternative X, this result can be shown symbolically as follows:

$$\tfrac{1}{2}U(\text{1st choice}) + \tfrac{1}{2}U(\text{3rd choice}) < U(\text{2nd choice})$$

or

$$U(\text{2nd choice}) - U(\text{3rd choice}) > U(\text{1st choice}) - U(\text{2nd choice}).$$

For decision situations with more than three alternatives the subject is required to choose between probability combinations in a number of offers. If N is the number of alternatives to be scaled, then $\binom{N+1}{4}$ is the maximum number of probability combinations necessary; the exact number is usually considerably less and depends on the type of underlying ordered metric scale.

These developments concerning the interpretation and measurability of strength of preference on an ordered metric scale suggest a possible means of making interpersonal comparisons of utility and determining a criterion for "fair" group decisions—by comparing aspiration levels. A "fair" decision may be defined as one which satisfies more individuals than any other alternative, if one makes the assumption that group satisfaction depends only upon the number of individuals satisfied (i.e., reaching their level of aspiration).[3] Each group member is weighted equally, according to whether or not the decision alternative in question meets his aspiration level. Let $U_i(A_j)$ be the utility of the jth alternative to the

ith individual ($i = 1, 2, \ldots, N$) and define a satisfaction index $S_i(A_j)$ as follows:

$$S_i(A_j) = \begin{cases} 1 & \text{if } U_i(A_j) \geq L_i \\ 0 & \text{if } U_i(A_j) < L_i \end{cases}$$

for all i and j. If L_i is the aspiration level of the ith person, then it is assumed group satisfaction will be largest for the alternative which maximizes M_j where

$$M_j = \sum_{i=1}^{N} S_i(A_j).$$

By ordering all possible choices according to their value of M_j a complete ranking of alternatives can also be obtained. Although max M_j is not necessarily unique, the additional information may be sufficient to eliminate possible intransitivities under simple majority rule.[4]

Because the level of aspiration model considers strength of preference, this model is hypothesized to provide, under certain circumstances, a better characterization of group decisions than will majority rule.

The level of aspiration solution is predicted whenever conditions tend to favor an equitable or "fair" resolution of conflict. Usually such conditions are present whenever a majority might be expected to give serious consideration to the preferences of a minority because of the desirability or necessity of compromise. Consider, for example, a group of three where one individual strongly prefers Alternative Y to Alternative X, and two individuals rate them nearly equal, but would rank X slightly ahead of Y. Simple majority rule dictates X as the group solution, even though all three individuals might agree that Y is the better *group* solution. The level of aspiration model, in contrast, takes individual strength of preference into consideration and would name Y as the group solution. A test of the predictive properties of the level of aspiration model relative to the simple majority rule, for the case of three individuals and three decision alternatives, constitutes the empirical portion of the research presented in this paper.[5]

EXPERIMENTAL DESIGN

In order to test the predictive ability of the level of aspiration model in relation to simple majority rule, a series of experiments was designed to simulate certain conflict settings involving three bargainers and three alternatives. These settings, or designs, had to represent combinations of individual preference arrays and aspiration levels such that the level of aspiration model predicted one solution while simple majority rule predicted another. An experimental test of the level of aspiration model was arranged by grouping three subjects and having them choose between three alternatives in certain specifically designed decision situations.

With three bargainers and three decision alternatives, there are 56 different preference arrays possible, only 26 of which may result in possible discrepancies between the level of aspiration model and simple majority rule. If differences depending entirely on the labeling of alternatives are ignored, 6 different conflict situations remain from the 26. Two of these were eliminated from experimental consideration because they yield intransitive orderings under simple majority rule and thus do not provide a clearcut alternative solution to the aspiration level model. Of the 4 remaining combinations, the 2 below (with their associated aspiration levels) were considered most representative of the conflict situation desired and were used as the basic design for the experimental tests.

Experimental Setting A				Experimental Setting B			
Individual				Individual			
	I	II	III		I	II	III	
1	X	X	Y̲	1	X	Y̲	Z̲	
Rank 2	Y̲	Y̲	X	Rank 2	Y̲	X	X	— = level of aspiration
3	Z	Z	Z	3	Z	Z	Y	

Majority rule solution	X	X
Level of aspiration solution	Y	Y

The nature of the conflict situation, the type of decision rule imposed, and the amount of interpersonal contact were hypothesized to influence support for one of the two solutions. A tendency toward a majority solution should be quite strong in Experimental Setting A, since the majority solution is readily identifiable and accessible. Experimental Setting B, on the other hand, has no initial "obvious" solution, and therefore a greater tendency toward the level of aspiration alternative could be expected. The nature of the decision rule assumed to prevail (e.g., majority or unanimous rule) should also play an important role in determining group decisions—the larger the number required to agree, the greater will be the tendency toward a compromise solution. Finally, variations in interpersonal contact are expected to influence group outcomes due to an expected tendency toward "fairness" as increased interaction forces group members to defend their actions publicly. The other extreme, where the identity of bargaining opponents is kept anonymous (e.g., decisions are made by ballot), should minimize this tendency toward fairness.

Experimental tests were designed to introduce four of the eight possible combinations of these variables. The level of aspiration solution was expected to hold when at least one of the three variables favored such a solution. Arrangement of the experiments was thus in four designs, with the following variables and hypothesized solutions. (Variables with asterisks are assumed to favor the level of aspiration solution.)

Design	Variables			Hypothesized solution
	Experimental setting	Decision rule	Interpersonal contact	
I	A	Majority	Isolated bargaining (voting)	Majority rule
II	A	Majority	Face-to-face* bargaining	Level of aspiration
III	A	Unanimous*	Isolated bargaining (voting)	Level of aspiration
IV	B*	Majority	Isolated bargaining (voting)	Level of aspiration

Although a majority of cases are predicted to support the level of aspiration solution, some differences in the degree of agreement are expected—strength of support is hypothesized to increase from Design I to Design IV. Weakest support is predicted for Design I because this particular combination does not include any variables expected to favor the level of aspiration solution. The majority rule solution should hold in this case because two individuals are expected to impose their will on the third, the mere existence of a decision "fair" to all three persons being considered insufficient to induce either one to yield from his optimal choice. It would not be irrational to expect the level of aspiration model to hold, however, as the positive utility associated with the behavioral alternative of voting for a "fair" solution may bring the net utility for this alternative high enough to induce either Individual I or II (or both) to vote for it.[6]

Face-to-face bargaining in the identical situation should increase the tendency toward the level of aspiration solution, as the third party now has an opportunity to confront his opponents with his preferences and "appeal" for fairness. Hypothesized to aid this appeal and provide support for the aspiration solution is an expected natural reluctance for individual group members openly to reject what might be considered a fair solution. Needless to say, the assumption of such a natural reluctance is somewhat tenuous, especially in a competitive society such as ours, so that strong support for the aspiration model is doubtful.

The unanimity requirement in Design III should provide a stronger support for the level of aspiration model, because now Individuals I and II cannot impose their will on the third party. Realizing that Individual III is not likely to accept what he considers an unfair solution, Individuals I and II should concede after considering the probable consequences of a refusal to concede (a stalemate) and in view of the fact that a concession decision will still satisfy their aspiration levels. Nevertheless, the fact that two individuals must give in to a third still runs contrary to what one would expect in a decision situation, and thus weakens expected support for the level of aspiration solution and increases the possibility of a simple majority rule solution or a stelemate. The implicit possibility of a "stalemate alternative" (i.e., a status quo solution) will be eliminated in the present research by defining a lack of consensus under the stated decision rule to represent a decision for each individual's *worst* alternative.

Strongest support for the level of aspiration solution is predicted for Design IV. Here the setting is such that no initial majority rule solution exists, and at least one individual must vote for his second choice for the group to come to a decision. If one group member can yield to his second choice in this circumstance and still be satisfied with the outcome, clearly it will be to his advantage to do so rather than risk the possibility of a stalemate.

EXPERIMENTAL METHODS

For each of the experiments representing the four designs described above, the appropriate conflict characteristics were obtained by subject placements. These subjects were chosen because of their exhibited preferences for decision alternatives corresponding to those needed experimentally. The task for each group was to decide on the type of multiple-choice exam, out of three specified, they would prefer to take. Individual incentive was provided each participant by paying him in relation to his performance on the exam decided upon by the group. All three individuals had to take the same type of exam, and each person was paid ($ 0.50) for each question he answered correctly on this (eight-question) exam. Thus, competition was achieved by composing each group with individuals of different backgrounds and then offering them an appropriate array of exams from which to choose.

Arrangement of the volunteers into decision groups was determined in advance of the decision sessions by means of a questionnaire. This questionnaire asked each volunteer to rate his expected performance on an exam in each of 14 different areas by judging his performance in relation to a person with three or four college courses in that area. On the basis of these evaluations of expected performance, it was possible to arrange groups with a high likelihood of simulating the appropriate decision setting. Actual rankings and aspiration levels were obtained during the experimental session itself, so that this procedure produced only an approximation of the desired setting. It was therefore decided beforehand to consider as acceptable data only the decisions resulting from those groups where *actual* preferences and aspiration levels corresponded to the desired experimental setting.

The nature of the experiments for Design I, III, and IV dictated the testing of a large number of decision groups simultaneously, primarily to maintain the anonymity of individual group members. With a large number of subjects, group membership was kept secret by giving an individual information concerning his opponents' preferences while revealing only the fact that he was bargaining with other students in the same room. This was accomplished by using information sheets especially constructed for each experimental design and filled out for each participant in advance of his participation. These sheets described the nature of the experiments, listed the decision alternatives, and provided for each group member a brief summary of the preference strengths of his bargaining opponents.[7] Statements of the following type were used in describing preference strengths (Student 2 refers to a bargaining opponent):

Student 2 ranks the three exams in the following order:

1st choice (Best performance)	German
2nd choice (Next best performance)	mathematics
3rd choice (Worst performance)	chemistry

Student 2 would strongly prefer to take the examination in German, and of the three exams, he would expect satisfactory performance *only* on that one type. Although he does prefer mathematics to chemistry, he would expect an unsatisfactory score in both areas.

The information sheets asked each participant to list his own ranking of the alternatives, and to decide whether he would prefer having a 50–50 chance between taking his first- or third-ranked exams, or taking his second-ranked exam for sure. This part of the information sheet determined each person's actual ranking and aspiration level and was used to decide whether or not a particular group conformed to the desired setting.

Each group under isolated bargaining conditions (voting) was given five votes to reach a decision, with the outcome of each ballot being made known before the next vote was called for. If at the end of five votes a decision had not been reached, each participant had to take the one examination, of the three specified, which received his worst rating on the original questionnaire.

At the beginning of each group session a brief oral description of the nature of the experiment was given to all participants. It was impressed upon the subjects that they would make their decision by voting, and that their votes would be their only means for expressing their desires. Each participant was then given his instruction sheet; after sufficient time had been allowed for subjects to read this material and to fill out the required information, the balloting was started. When all groups had reached a decision (or after five votes), the proper exams were distributed. Students were free to leave as soon as they had finished their exam and had been paid.

Design II required separate experimental sessions for each group in order to facilitate observation of the face-to-face bargaining process. Procedures for these groups were similar to those described above. In the introductory remarks it was emphasized that participants could make their decision in any manner they wished, and that it need not be unanimous. Subjects were then given their information sheets, and when these had been filled out and collected the participants were instructed to begin discussions leading toward their decision.

DISCUSSION OF RESULTS

Although 144 students were selected to participate in the experiments, only 42 groups (126 subjects) were formed because a number of students failed to appear. An additional loss of 30 subjects (10 groups) resulted from unanticipated aspiration levels or rankings by 11 subjects. Eight of the 11 changed away from their expected ranking, and 3 away from their anticipated aspiration levels. All 3 of the latter changes resulted from an increase in aspiration levels, that is, from an expected aspiration level of Choice 2 to an actual aspiration level for Choice 1. The 8 changes from expected rankings were all by individuals with an aspiration level for their second choice and in each case involved an interchange of Choices 1 and 2.

Stalemate solutions resulted from two groups in Design III and one group in Design IV. These solutions were difficult to classify in terms of the research hypothesis; this behavior does not conform to the predicted simple majority rule solution, nor is clear support indicated for the level of aspiration solution. Since the model was designed to handle only those groups reaching a decision, stalemates will be counted as evidence neither for nor against the research hypothesis. After subtracting stalemates, there were 7 acceptable decision groups in Design I, 9 in Design II, 7 in Design III, and 6 in Design IV.

Design I

Setting A, majority rule, isolated bargaining.
Support for the predicted (simple majority rule) solution in Design I turned out to be stronger than originally assumed. Although strong support was anticipated, it had been expected that at least one or two individuals would choose the level of aspiration alternative because of its "fairness". As it was, every participant acted entirely in view of his own interests by voting for his first-ranked alternative, the result being a majority rule decision for all groups on the first ballot. A binomial test, with $P = Q = \frac{1}{2}$, was used to test the research hypothesis that experimental decisions would significantly favor the simple majority rule solution. The fact that all seven allowable groups made decisions consistent with simple majority rule permits rejection of the null hypothesis at $p = 0.008$ in favor of the research hypothesis.

In order to attain some idea of whether fairness was generally associated with the level of aspiration solution, each participant in Design I was asked (after the vote) to write on the back of his instruction sheet which examination he considered a "fair" solution for his group. A majority of subjects indicated they considered the level of aspiration solution as the fair decision. Especially significant, however, is the breakdown of evaluations between the two persons in the dominant position (Individuals I and II) and the person in the weak position (Individual III). Alternatives listed as fair by the 27 participants who had the proper ranking and aspiration level are shown in Table 1.

Thus, the position each person assumed in the conflict situation seemed to play an important role in determining what he considered a fair solution, but not in determining his vote. Note, in this regard, that 16 out of 27 participants (10 individuals in Positions I and II, and 6 in Position III) did not vote for the alternative they listed as fair. Most surprising is the fact that 6 of the 10 persons in the weak positions (Individual III) listed simple majority rule as the fair solution. These subjects usually stated, in effect, that it would be unfair for them to impose their will on two other persons, and that majority rule by itself is a fair decision method. This itself would not be quite as surprising if an approximately equal percentage of dominant individuals held a similar view. The fact that only 5 out of 15 agreed, however, seems to indicate a basic dissimilarity between the two groups.

Design II

Setting A, majority rule, face-to-face bargaining.
Four groups decided on the level of aspiration solution, and five decided on the examination supporting simple majority rule in Design II. A binomial test on this data does not permit rejection of the null hypothesis in favor of the research hypothesis that decisions will significantly support the level of aspiration solution ($p = 0.746$).

Table 1 Number of Persons listing the alternative solutions as "fair" in design I

| | Individual | | |
Fair solution	I, II	III	Total
Level of aspiration	10	4	14
Simple majority rule	5	6	11
Both of the above	2	0	2

Much of the support for the aspiration solution was hypothesized to result from Individual III's appeal for "fairness," but if Individual III considers simple majority rule fair, then this support is lost. In fact, group decisions at times did seem to depend largely on Individual III's evaluation of fairness, and Individual I or II (or both) often indicated some willingness to compromise. In view of the results of Design I, it therefore is surprising that the level of aspiration model received as much support in Design II as it did.

With only a few exceptions, the participants usually asked each other about their ranking, major in college, and sometimes the number of courses taken in the subject area in question. During the course of the discussions most persons offered an accurate representation of their preferences. (E.g., "I would prefer physics, but wouldn't mind economics.") A few, perhaps wisely, were reluctant to admit they had knowledge in more than one subject area even when their aspiration level was for Choice 2.[8]

Design III

Setting A, unanimous rule, isolated bargaining.
Six of the nine group decisions in Design III supported the level of aspiration model, one supported simple majority rule, and two ended in stalemates. The binomial test allows for rejection of the null hypothesis at $p = 0.062$. in favor of the research hypothesis that decisions will significantly favor the level of aspiration solution.

As expected, Design III provided support for the level of aspiration model and also resulted in the largest number of stalemates. Not anticipated, however, was the high degree of reluctance for Individuals I and II to yield to their second choice although in retrospect this does correspond to the results of Design I. In three of the six groups supporting the aspiration model all five votes were necessary before a decision could be reached. Only 2 of the 12 individuals who gave in to the aspiration solution did so on their first vote and only 2 on their second vote. The average individual in this set yielded in 3.16 votes, while it took, on the average, 4.00 votes for each of these groups to come to a decision. Results similar to these were obtained in a replication of Design III under slightly different conditions: out of six groups, there were four level of aspiration solutions and two stalemates. In this case, however, the two groups which were stalemated were allowed to meet and discuss their decision. Although no side payments were permitted (the payoff was for "extra" points toward their final grade), both groups were able to resolve their differences and unanimously agreed on the level of aspiration solution.

Design IV

Setting B, majority rule, isolated bargaining.
Strongest support for the level of aspiration model was obtained in Design IV. Six of the seven groups decided on the examination supporting the level of aspiration model, the seventh ending in a stalemate. The results of this design permit rejection of the null hypothesis in favor of the research hypo-

13*

thesis that decisions will significantly support the level of aspiration solution. The binomial test allows for rejection at $p = 0.016$ when stalemates are ignored.

The average number of votes necessary in this design for those groups coming to a decision was 3.14, and each decision took at least two votes. Participants appeared to recognize readily the essential nature of the conflict situation, although few seemed to note the existence of a simple majority rule solution. Most subjects interviewed believed the outcome depended primarily on who was willing to give in first, and that Individual I was the most likely candidate. One person in the role of Individual I waited until the fifth vote to change his vote. He remarked, quite logically, that he had nothing to lose by waiting until the last moment since he could have gained if either one of his opponents had decided to change his vote.

A number of interviews and a replication of this design indicated the importance of accurately assessing Individual III's aspiration level. For if Individual III foresees that he has little or no chance of gaining his first-ranked alternative, and if he has any incentive to actively pursue his second

Table 2   Decision results for designs I–IV

Design	Level of aspiration solutions	Majority rule solutions	Stalemates	Total	Level of significance for hypothesized solution
I	0	7	0	7	0.008
II	4	5	0	9	0.746
III	6	1	2	9	0.062
IV	6	0	1	7	0.016

alternative over his third, it would certainly be worth his while to do so, rather than hold out for Choice 1. Indeed, this is exactly what took place in the above-mentioned replication, the result being five out of six decisions for simple majority rule and only one for the level of aspiration solution. Of course, it was important in this latter study that Individual I recognized the weakness of III's position and was not in any hurry to change his own vote.

Summary

Table 2 shows the complete results for all four designs, together with the significance level for the hypothesized solution. The level of significance between designs, using a Fisher exact-probability test, is shown in Table 3.

As can be seen from the data in Tables 2 and 3, the hypothesized increase in strength of support for the level of aspiration solution from Design I to Design IV was for the most part upheld. Only the difference between Designs III and IV stands out in contrast to the predicted degree of difference, the deviation in this case due to the fact that both designs offered support for the model.

Conclusions

In view of the experimental results, it seems clear that the equity associated with the level of aspiration solution played an important part in determining most group decisions. The strength and nature of this "fairness," which appeared to depend largely on the nature of the conflict situation, influenced decisions, in general, in one of two ways.

Table 3 Level of significance of difference between designs

II	0.069		
III	0.002	0.121	
IV	0.004	0.042	0.539
Design	I	II	III

The first way, identified with Designs I and II, involved the "fairness" assumed to be inherent in a compromise solution. That is, a solution satisfying all participants was predicted to have special appeal even to group members who by virtue of their superior bargaining position could insist on a more favorable outcome. Although this aspect of fairness, as expected, did not find significant support under conditions of isolated bargaining and majority voting (Design I), the surprising fact was that not even one group decision supported the level of aspiration alternative.

Some support for the aspiration solution was found in Design II, indicating that face-to-face bargaining does tend to promote this type of fairness. In general, however, evidence supporting the importance of fairness of the sort where individuals voluntarily yield to a compromise solution was quite limited. Most participants based their decisions on their own personal rewards, thus favoring the majority rule solution. Simple majority rule was found to have a measure of fairness all its own, although this also depended on the role assumed.

The second and strongest influence of "fairness" resulted from Designs III and IV, where the combination of variables was such that no two individuals were able to insist on their first choice. The notion of fairness in these experiments seemed to give participants an opportunity to evaluate their chances of receiving the alternative they ranked first. Each person was able to assess his chances by noting the preferences of his opponents and considering whether it would be "reasonable" or "fair" to expect either one or both to give in. (E.g., "Would I yield in a comparable situation?") Most individuals would not yield to an unsatisfactory solution, nor would they expect their opponent(s) to do so either. Thus, the participant forced with choosing between a satisfactory second-ranked alternative or the possibility of a stalemate would be expected to yield. The importance of this aspect of fairness was substantiated by the support given the level of aspiration solution in Designs III and IV.

In general, the following conclusions were obtained from analysis of the data:

1   The mere existence of a solution fair to all was not sufficient to induce behavior toward the level of aspiration solution. Majority rule itself had some connotation of fairness and provided a stable outcome under isolated bargaining conditions.

2   A prominent majority rule solution appeared to offset some of the strength of the level of aspiration alternative because participants could more readily identify and attain this solution. When no initial majority rule solution was obvious, there was a strong tendency for subjects to search for a means to determine a "reasonable" solution, which in this case was the level of aspiration alternative.

3   The decision rule assumed to hold had a significant effect on the decision alternative selected. Majority rule lends support for the simple majority rule solution, while requiring unanimity favors the level of aspiration solution.

4   Increasing the amount of interpersonal contact increased the number of "fair" solutions, but did not result in significant support for the level of aspiration alternative.

NOTES

1   The research reported in this paper was supported by a Ford Foundation grant. The author is especially indebted to Lawrence E. Fouraker and Harold Bierman who, among others, made valuable contributions to this research.

2 Much of Siegel's (1956, 1957) research on level of aspiration, of course, stems from earlier work by Lewin, Dembo, Festinger, and Sears (1944). The relationship between the two is shown in Siegel's 1957 article.

3 The measurement assumptions in the present model do not allow for individual differences in *degree* of satisfaction, although this factor may well be relevant for most group decisions.

4 See Arrow (1951) for an analytical treatment of the problem of intransitivity under simple majority rule.

5 The relationship between level of aspiration and group decision making also was investigated experimentally by Fouraker in 1964; his model and decision setting, however, differ substantially from those presented in this paper.

6 Individuals I, II, III correspond to the individuals whose preference arrays comprise Experimental Settings A and B.

7 Since these sheets were all prepared in advance of each session, the preference strength attributed to each individual's opponents was an expected one. Only when these expectations were upheld were the data considered acceptable.

8 If any subject mentioned the possibility of side payments, an announcement was made that this would not be allowed. The possibility of implicit cooperation between friends was minimized by pairing volunteers who had little chance of knowing each other.

REFERENCES

Arrow, J. *Social Choice and Individual Values.* New York: Wiley, 1951.

Becker, S. W., and Siegel, S. Utility of Grades: Level of Aspiration in a Decision Theory Context. *Journal of Experimental Psychology*, 1958, **55**, 81–85.

Fouraker, L. Level of Aspiration and Group Decision Making. In S. Messick and A. H. Brayfield (Eds.), *Decision and Choice.* New York: McGraw-Hill, 1964. pp. 201–239.

Lewin, K., Dembo, T., Festinger, L., and Sears, P. Level of Aspiration. In J. McV. Hunt (Ed.), *Personality and Behavioral Disorders.* Vol. 1 New York: Ronald Press, 1944. pp. 333–378.

Von Neumann, J., and Morgenstern, O. *Theory of Games and Economic Behavior.* (2nd ed.) Princeton: Princeton University Press, 1947.

Siegel, S. A Method for Obtaining an ordered Metric Scale. *Psychometrica*, 1956, **21**, 207–216.

Siegel, S. Level of Aspiration and Decision Making. *Psychological Review*, 1957, **64**, 253–263.

Simon, H. A. A Behavioral Model of Rational Choice. *Quaterly Journal of Economics*, 1955, **99**, 99–108.

A UTILITY THEORY FOR THE BEHAVIOR OF THREE-PERSON INTERACTION SYSTEMS[1]

RICHARD OFSHE and LYNNE OFSHE

University of California, Berkeley

THE PROBLEM AND THE MODEL

In the following paper we will report on the development and empirical application of a model for the equilibrium behavior of three-person interaction systems. The context in which the members of the system interact is a laboratory situation known as the coalition game. The simplest description of a three-person coalition game is that it is an experimental game in which on each of a series of trials players attempt to form an alliance, and if successful, those participating in the alliance receive a payoff. The usual rule governing the formation of alliances is that only two of the players may enter into a coalition on any trial. The game may therefore be described as a mixed-motive game, since there are elements of competition in that no outcome satisfies everyone, and there are elements of cooperation in that two players must ally in order to win. What we mean by the equilibrium behavior of such an interaction system is the set of stable, probabilistically described strategies used by players in the game. We will propose and then demonstrate that such interaction systems stabilize over time and that the point at which they stabilize is that point which maximizes the expected utility of the participants in the interaction.

There are two quite different theoretical approaches that may be taken in attempting to analyze the situation outlined above. One line of attack would be to attempt to specify the set of strategies that players should adopt in order to maximize outcomes for all participants in the game. The problem is then to extract the maximum total payoff from nature (the experimenter, the society, etc.) and distribute this total among players in a manner that maximizes possible payoffs for all participants. Solutions of this type are truly solutions in the sense that they are directives for how the set of players should organize themselves in order to accomplish a certain end. In order to implement solutions of this sort, however, it is necessary for there to exist channels of communication between players, a mechanism for collective decision making and a procedure for enforcing decisions.

The alternative approach is to attempt to develop a formulation that will predict the manner in which each of the players *will* act, how the behaviors of one individual *will* affect the decisions of each of the other players and how their reactions *will* finally affect the first individual. Approaches of this type do not yield solutions of the sort described above. They result, when successful, in predictions of how the system of interacting players will behave under specified conditions. The line of analysis to be developed here is based on the assumption that individuals act so as to maximize expected utility in their decision making. We will show how a theory incorporating this assumption can be applied to a coalition game situation in a manner that takes account of actions and reactions among players and that identifies the strategies that maximize each player's utility. The three players in the game are viewed as separate decision makers who are continually affected by the behaviors of the other participants.

Although there exist numerous formal decision models which incorporate the concept of utility (for a discussion of various formulations, see Luce and Suppes' 1965 review of literature in this area), we will address the problem of constructing a model for the equilibrium behavior of three-person interaction systems by building on a line of research begun by Siegel and his associates (1964). Siegel developed a theory for decision making in the context of Humphreys' (1939) two-choice probability prediction experiment. A description of the general characteristics of experimental situations of this type is as follows: on each of a series of trials, a subject is required to predict the occurrence of one event from a set of possible events (there are at least two events in the set). Typically, the events occur with probabilities that are determined prior to the start of the experiment and are blocked over series of ten or twenty trials. Subjects are not aware of the probabilities with which the events will occur but are aware that the sequence of occurrences is determined prior to the start of the experiment. In the usual case, the probabilities with which the events occur sum to unity and one and only one event occurs on a given trial.

If, under these conditions subjects are instructed to predict which event will occur before each trial, it is well documented that after a learning period of variable length they will adopt a stable choice distribution in which events are predicted with approximately the same probabilities with which they occur (Luce and Suppes, 1965, pp. 392–393). However, for cases in which subjects are offered a payoff for making a correct prediction and are penalized for each incorrect decision, it is equally well documented that their stable-state distributions of choices between alternatives (i.e. choice strategies) are affected by the magnitudes of positive and negative payoffs associated with each alternative and depart from simple matching distributions (Luce and Suppes, 1965, pp. 394–395).

Considerable interest has been generated by the findings that individuals adopt matching strategies under conditions in which they are told to make as many correct predictions as possible, and that even under conditions in which a monetary payoff is offered for each correct prediction they still do not adopt strategies that maximize the number of correct predictions. Clearly, in order to maximize the number of correct predictions subjects should adopt a pure rather than a mixed strategy and should invariably predict the event with the higher probability of occurrence. The theory developed by Siegel and his associates postulates that individuals can be treated as if they are acting so as to maximize expected utility in their decision making. It can be shown to follow from this theory that the non-unity choice strategies adopted by subjects are those strategies which maximize the combination of utilities available for alternative actions.

In the particular experimental situation to which Siegel coordinated his theory, Humphreys' light-guessing experiment, the events that subjects attempted to predict were illuminations of one of a set of light bulbs and the payoffs for the correct or incorrect prediction of an event varied from ± 1 cent to ± 5 cents across different experiments. Siegel argued that in the experimental situation there were two sources of utility available to subjects. The more obvious utility factor was that of the utility of a correct choice. Presumably this utility varied directly with the magnitudes of the monetary rewards and penalties for correct and incorrect predictions. The second source of utility was that of choice variability resulting from the intrinsic boredom of a pure strategy (choosing the same light constantly), as well as from the greater satisfaction connected with being able to predict correctly the occurrence of the less frequent event.[2]

Building on the assumptions that individuals maximize expected utility and that in the light-guessing experiment this utility stems from two sources,

Siegel constructed a formal model of individual choice behavior. The model predicts the subject's stable-state behavior in a choice situation where the following factors are considered: the probabilities that the choices are reinforced; the marginal utility of a correct choice; and the marginal utility of choice variability. Although as derived by Siegel the model can apply to decisions involving any number of alternatives, only the derivation of the two-alternative case will be given here. It should be noted that this model will apply in cases in which the probabilities with which the events occur sum to more, or less, than one; that is, it can be applied when neither or both lights illuminate on some trials. (For a more detailed presentation of the model and a derivation of the k-alternative case, see Siegel et al., 1964). In deriving the model the following notation will be used:

π_i = the probability that the ith alternative occurs, $i = 1, 2$
a_i = the marginal utility of a correct choice of the ith alternative, $i = 1, 2$
b = the marginal utility of choice variability
α_i = the ratio of the marginal utility of a correct choice to the marginal utility of choice variability (a_i/b)
P_i = the stable-state probability that the subject chooses the ith alternative, $i = 1, 2$.

The purpose of this model is to enable predictions to be made for the subject's stable-state strategy, P_1 and P_2, from the values of the other variables. Employing the concept of mathematical expectation and the above definitions, it is obvious that the expectation that the subject's choice will be correct is the sum of the probabilities that he gets each light correct, or $P_1\pi_1 + P_2\pi_2$, and the expected utility of a correct choice is the sum of the expected utilities for all alternatives, or $a_1P_1\pi_1 + a_2P_2\pi_2$. Given the assumption that the utility of choice variability is proportional to the variance of the subject's choice, the interpretation of the utility of choice variability function is quite simple in the case of two alternatives. Assuming that with probability P_1 the subject chooses the first alternative and with probability $P_2 = 1 - P_1$ he chooses the second alternative, it is clear that the model of his choices is that of a sequence of Bernoulli trials with parameter P_1. Thus the variance of each choice is $P_1(1 - P_1)$, and it is assumed in the model that an individual's utility of choice variability is proportional to the variance of his (random) choice, that is $2bP_1(1 - P_1)$.

The expected utility, U, of P_1, the stable strategy of choosing alternative one with probability P_1, is assumed to be the sum of these two utility functions:

$$U = a_1 P_1 \pi_1 + a_2 P_2 \pi_2 + 2b P_1 (1 - P_1)$$
$$= -2b P_1^2 + (a_1 \pi_1 - a_2 \pi_2 + 2b) P_1 + a_2 \pi_2$$

It was assumed that the individual is maximizing his expected utility U, by his choice of a strategy, that is, by his choice of P_1. The problem is to find the value of P_1 which will maximize U in the above equation. Since U is concave downwards when graphed as a function of P_1, the maximum of U with respect to P_1 occurs when $\partial U/\partial P_1 = 0$:

$$0 = \frac{\partial U}{\partial P_1} = -4b P_1 + a_1 \pi_1 - a_2 \pi_2 + 2b$$

This equation can be solved for P_1; therefore, the maximum of U occurs when

$$P_1 = \left(\frac{a_1 \pi_1 - a_2 \pi_2 + 2b)}{4b} \right) = \left(\frac{1}{4} \right) \left(\frac{a_1}{b} \pi_1 - \frac{a_2}{b} \pi_2 \right) + \frac{1}{2}$$

and substituting α_i for a_i/b:

$$P_1 = (\tfrac{1}{4})(\alpha_1 \pi_1 - \alpha_2 \pi_2) + \tfrac{1}{2} \qquad\qquad P_2 = 1 - P_1 \quad (1)$$

This can be simplified in the case in which the utilities of the two alternatives are equal, that is, $a_1 = a_2 (\alpha_1 = \alpha_2 = \alpha)$:

$$P_1 = (\tfrac{1}{4}) \alpha (\pi_1 - \pi_2) + \tfrac{1}{2} \qquad\qquad P_2 = 1 - P_1 \quad (2)$$

These two sets of equations will predict the stable-state behavior of an individual given the probabilities of feedback and the values of the utilities.[3]

Siegel conducted an extensive research program designed to test the model. There were two distinct phases in the research. The first segment was composed of a series of experiments testing ordinal predictions from the theory, that is, experiments in which only a single variable (probability, payoff or intrinsic boredom) was altered between control and experimental conditions and the direction of the effect on behavior was predicted. In the second segment of the program, the model's ability to predict the values of stable-state choice strategies was tested. In order to predict probability values, it was necessary to measure the values of the α ratios. The method used by Siegel to accomplish this had two parts. The first step was to conduct an experiment (or set of experiments in cases in which $a_i \neq a_j$) with specified payoffs and feedback probabilities. Using the stable-state choice probabilities observed in this (measurement) experiment, the value of α could be found from equations (2) above. Theoretically, if the value of α is held constant and the feedback probabilities, π_i, are changed, the maximizing choice strategy will be different. The second step in the procedure for testing the model therefore called for conducting an additional (test) experiment in which the values of the feedback parameters were changed while the payoffs and boredom-inducing aspects of the experiment (that is, the α-determining variables) were held constant. The evaluation of the model's predictive power was based on the accuracy with which it could predict the choice strategies adopted by a new group of subjects under the changed experimental conditions. In the first tests of the model it was applied to data from three experiments in which $a_1 = a_2 =$ the marginal utility of ± 5 c, the values of π_1 were varied from 0.65 to 0.70 to 0.75 and the values of π_2 were varied from 0.35 to 0.30 to 0.25. The absolute mean error between the predicted and observed stable-state choice strategies for subjects in the three experiments was 0.011. In a second series of experiments, the model was tested under unequal α conditions in four experiments in which subjects were confronted with the problem of predicting the occurrence of one of three possible events. In these experiments $a_1 =$ the marginal utility of ± 5 c, $a_2 = a_3 =$ the marginal utility of ± 1 c and the π parameters were varied from $\pi_1 = 0.65$, $\pi_2 = 0.25$ and $\pi_3 = 0.10$ through $\pi_1 = 0.70$, $\pi_2 = 0.50$ and $\pi = 0.40$. The average absolute discrepancy between the observed and predicted choice strategies for subjects in the four different treatment conditions was 0.014.

The theory developed by Siegel has been recently applied to decision making in social situations. Ofshe and Ofshe (1970) have shown that it is possible to describe the situation confronting a player in a coalition game as a binary decision problem with a structure analogous to a probability prediction experiment. Consider a three-person coalition game in which a player's payoffs for forming alternative coalitions are specified in advance, potential coalition partners are not permitted to bargain over the division of payoffs and, in the absence of knowledge of the preferences of the other players, each player indicates his preference between alternative coalition partners on each of a series of trials. If on a given trial two players select one another, they have formed a coalition and are paid the predetermined amounts. Under these conditions, a player's problem is to predict which of the other players is going to select him in each trial. This constitutes the same general problem confronting subjects in probability prediction experiments.

Ofshe and Ofshe (1970) have demonstrated that much of the literature on choice behavior in the coalition game situation can be organized in terms of the effects of three causal variables: the probability of reciprocation of a choice; the rewards associated with formation of each alternative coalition; and equity considerations. These variables are believed to be interrelated in the same manner as the three variables affecting behavior in the light-guessing experiment: the probability of a correct choice; the payoffs associated with each alternative; and the basic monotony of the situation.

In a coalition game, an individual can win a reward only if his choice is reciprocated. This directly corresponds to a correct choice in the light-guessing experiment; an individual receives a payoff only if the light which he has chosen subsequently illuminates. Thus, it is obvious that a reciprocated choice in the coalition game is strictly analogous to a correct choice in the light-guessing experiment. Letting

a_i = the marginal utility of a reciprocated choice with participant i,
   $i = 1, 2$
P_i = the stable-state probability that the player chooses participant i,
   $i = 1, 2$

and

π_i = the probability that the player is chosen by participant i, $i = 1, 2$,
the expected utility of a reciprocated choice is $\pi_1 P_1 a_1 + \pi_2 P_2 a_2$. This function employs the same implicit assumptions that Siegel used in analyzing the light-guessing experiment.

The second utility considered in the light-guessing experiment, the utility of choice variability, may not seem to apply in this situation, for it could be argued that the game itself destroys boredom as well as any desire to choose the less frequently reinforced choice. However, there is a factor in this situation which is not operating the light-guessing experiment. Each time an individual forms a coalition, the other person is rewarded as well as himself. This means that if two players constantly form a coalition, the third player receives nothing. There is evidence that an equity norm causes a utility of choice variability. Lieberman (1962) points out that the results of one of his coalition game experiments "describe the behavior of three individuals in a situation where two have a clear incentive to unite forces to the detriment of the third. In a majority of choices [70 %] the two did just that. However, in a sizeable minority of choices [30 %] this prescribed behavior did not occur... Some subjects felt it was not fair to do this." Since this equity norm results in a subjective utility for varying choices, it is directly comparable to the utility of choice variability in the light-guessing experiment. Thus, letting

b = the marginal utility of choice variability,

the equations for the player's behavior can be derived in exactly the same manner as in Siegel's decision-making model for the light-guessing situation. Therefore, the following equations should describe an individual's choice behavior in the coalition game:

$$P_1 = \left(\frac{1}{4}\right)(\alpha_1\pi_1 - \alpha_2\pi_2) + \frac{1}{2} \qquad \text{(unequal payoffs)}$$

$$P_2 = 1 - P_1$$

$$P_1 = \frac{\alpha}{4}(\pi_1 - \pi_2) + \frac{1}{2} \qquad \text{(equal payoffs)}$$

$$P_2 = 1 - P_1$$

The assumptions employed in constructing this model are identical to those used by Siegel in his model for the light-guessing experiment; the only changes are in the substantive interpretation of certain variables.

Although it is possible to describe the coalition game and traditional probability prediction experiments in terms of the concepts of the same theory, this does not guarantee that the decision theory can be applied to the social decision problem. There are gross differences between the two situations that are ignored by the theory. The most radical difference between the two situations relates to the subject's perception of the environment. In the typical probability prediction experiment subjects are aware that the events that they must attempt to predict are determined in advance and are in no way dependent on their choices. A subject's choice on trial N cannot affect the event that occurs on trial $N + K$. This condition is substantially different in coalition game situations. Even in games in which the behaviors of all of the players except the subject are controlled by the experimenter, subjects operate with the belief that they can influence the choices of the other players and that these events are in no sense determined prior to the start of the experiment. In games in which three subjects interact without interference from the experimenter, it is of course possible for subjects to actually influence the coalition preferences of the other participants in the game.

RESULTS

In order to test the theory's power to predict social decision making, a research program paralleling Siegel's program was conducted in the context of the coalition game situation. Although subjects who participated in the experiments believed that they were participating in a three-person coalition game with two other human players, they were in fact playing with two robot players. The choices of the robot players were determined prior to the start of the experiment in the same manner as events are programmed in probability prediction experiments. The details of the experimental procedures can be found in Ofshe and Ofshe (1970). The research program had two segments. The first tested ordinal predictions from the theory, including one experiment in which the subjects' utility for equity was manipulated. The second segment was directed at testing the power of the model to predict subjects' stable-state choice strategies. The results of the second set of experiments are summarized in Table 1.

Table 1 Results of Experiments on Individual Decision Making in Coalition Games

Experiment	Formal Characteristics*				Predicted†		Observed†		|Discrepancy|
	π_1	π_2 :	a_1	a_2	P_1	P_2	P_1	P_2	
I	0.70	0.30 :	+5c −0	+5c −0	0.862	0.138	0.864	0.136	0.002
II	0.60	0.40 :	+5c −0	+5c −0	0.682	0.318	0.681	0.319	0.001
III	0.80	0.20 :	+5c −0	+10c −0	0.639	0.361	0.672	0.328	0.033
IV	0.70	0.30 :	+5c −0	+10c −0	0.556	0.444	0.539	0.461	0.017
V	0.60	0.40 :	+5c −0	+10c −0	0.407	0.593	0.440	0.560	0.033

* In all of the experiments designed to test the model the same manipulation of the equity variable was used. The manipulation consisted of a set of statements defining the norms appropriate to the conduct of the game. The experiments reported here were all conducted with male subjects. Experiments with female subjects were conducted and produced equivalent results. The results are not reported here since they are not necessary to discuss issues raised later in the paper.

† Predicted and observed *P* values refer to choice probabilities in stablestate. The procedures used to identify stable-state are discussed in Ofshe and Ofshe (1970).

The results of tests in the social, perceived interactive situation indicate that the greater complexity of the social situation in no way diminishes the predictive power of the model.[4] This result makes possible the further extension of the theory in order to predict the behavior of individuals engaged in truly interactive social situations, such as coalition games in which three players are free to choose one another without the experimenter introducing any control over the information subjects receive about the choices of the other players in the game. Note that in games of this sort it is possible for a player to influence another individual by demonstrating a desire to enter into a permanent alliance through simply choosing the other individual repeatedly and therefore for two players to develop a true alliance against the third individual. In games in which players interact with robots whose choice strategies are predetermined no such permanent alliance can be developed.

In the following section, the model will be generalized in order to predict the equilibrium behavior of systems of freely-interacting individuals; that is, generalized in order to predict the stable-state choice strategies of individuals participating in a coalition game in which there are three human players and in which the experimenter does not control the information that players receive about the choices of the other participants in the game.[5] The decision theory yields the prediction that each player will stabilize his choice behavior at a point that maximizes his expected utility with respect to the choice strategies of the other participants in the game and is able to specify the probability values of the choice strategies for all participants in the game. Since each player is predicted to attain a stable choice strategy, it is obvious that the system of interacting individuals will attain a state of equilibrium which is described by the choice strategies of the members of the system.

The basic form of the model considers the behavior of a single individual in a situation in which three factors are assumed to affect his behavior. The factors are (1) the probability with which he is chosen by the other players, (2) the marginal utility of the payoffs he receives for forming alternative coalitions, and (3) his marginal utility for an equitable distribution of the total payoffs in the game.

In order to apply this model, it is necessary to control the probabilities with which the relevant events occur. In the context of the coalition game, this means controlling the probabilities with which the individual is chosen by each of the other participants. Compare this situation to a three-person interaction system in which each individual is free to choose either of the other players. These two situations need differ only with regard to the probabilities with which an individual is chosen by each of the other players. That is, the experimenter no longer controls this component. The payoffs for forming alternative coalitions and the equity-inducing aspects of the game can be easily held constant across the two game situations. The behavior of the three separate individuals, 1, 2, and 3 can be described by the following equations of the basic model:

$$P_{1,2} = (1/4)(\alpha_{1,2}\pi_{2,1} - \alpha_{1,3}\pi_{3,1}) + 1/2 \quad P_{1,3} = 1 - P_{1,2}$$
$$P_{2,1} = (1/4)(\alpha_{2,1}\pi_{1,2} - \alpha_{2,3}\pi_{3,2}) + 1/2 \quad P_{2,3} = 1 - P_{2,1} \quad (1)$$
$$P_{3,1} = (1/4)(\alpha_{3,1}\pi_{1,3} - \alpha_{3,2}\pi_{2,3}) + 1/2 \quad P_{3,2} = 1 - P_{3,1}$$

where $P_{x,y}$ is the probability that player x chooses player y, $\alpha_{x,y}$ is player x's utility ratio for a coalition with player y, and $\pi_{y,x}$ is the probability that player x is chosen by player y.

Note that the derivation of predictions for free interactive behavior rests on the ability to determine the probabilities of reciprocation, $\pi_{y,x}$, in such situations. Assume that independent estimates are obtained for all α's in the above set of equations. (These estimates can be obtained from data generated in experiments in which subjects play against robots providing that payoff and equity variables are identical to the conditions of the free-interactive situation.) The only other term necessary to predict $P_{x,y}$ is $\pi_{y,x}$. The values of $\pi_{y,x}$ can be obtained as follows.

In free interactive situations, $P_{x,y}$ is equal to $\pi_{x,y}$. That is, for any player, say player one, the probability that he chooses player two is obviously identical to the probability that player two is chosen by player one. In any interaction system of the type being considered, the outputs of any one member ($P_{x,y}$) constitute half of the inputs of each of the other members ($\pi_{x,y}$). When all of the outputs of the three players are determined, it follows that all of the inputs for the three players are also determined. In terms of the above example, the notation would be as follows: $P_{1,2} = \pi_{1,2}$, where $P_{1,2}$ is a term in the equation which predicts player one's choice strategy and $\pi_{1,2}$ is a term in the equation for player two's choice strategy. The relations between the P and π values for the three players in a game are as defined below.

$$\pi_{1,2} = P_{1,2} \quad \pi_{1,3} = 1 - P_{1,2}$$
$$\pi_{2,1} = P_{2,1} \quad \pi_{2,3} = 1 - P_{2,1} \quad (2)$$
$$\pi_{3,1} = P_{3,1} \quad \pi_{3,2} = 1 - P_{3,1}$$

Substituting the set of equations above (set number 2) into the basic model's equations for the behavior of each of the three players in a game (set number 1), the following equations are obtained:

$$P_{1,2} = (1/4)(\alpha_{1,2}P_{2,1} - \alpha_{1,3}P_{3,1}) + 1/2$$
$$P_{2,1} = (1/4)\{\alpha_{2,1}P_{1,2} - \alpha_{2,3}(1 - P_{3,1})\} + 1/2 \quad (3)$$
$$P_{3,1} = (1/4)\{\alpha_{3,1}(1 - P_{1,\alpha}) - \alpha_{3,2}(1 - P_{2,1})\} + 1/2$$

14*

The equations in set number 3 can be arranged as a system of linear equations
as follows:

$$4P_{1,2} - \alpha_{1,2}P_{2,1} + \alpha_{1,3}P_{3,1} = 2$$
$$\alpha_{2,1}P_{1,2} - 4P_{2,1} + \alpha_{2,3}P_{3,1} = \alpha_{2,3} - 2 \qquad (4)$$
$$\alpha_{3,1}P_{1,2} - \alpha_{3,2}P_{2,1} + 4P_{3,1} = \alpha_{3,1} - \alpha_{3,2} + 2$$

Since the values of the utilities, $\alpha_{x,y}$, can be determined independently by
experimentation, these three equations can easily be solved for the values of
$P_{1,2}$, $P_{2,1}$ and $P_{3,1}$. Since α estimates can be obtained from experiments
in which one subject interacts with two robots, the method for estimating
the values of the α parameters does not call for using data obtained from
subjects whose behavior is then to be predicted. The solutions to the system
of equations are somewhat awkward; for example; the probability with
which player one chooses player two is given by the following equation:

$$P_{1,2} =$$

$$\frac{-32 + \alpha_{2,3}\alpha_{3,2}(2 - \alpha_{1,3}) + \alpha_{1,2}\alpha_{2,3}(3 - \alpha_{3,1}) + 8(\alpha_{1,3} - \alpha_{1,2}) +}{-64 + 4\alpha_{2,3}\alpha_{3,2} + 4\alpha_{1,2}\alpha_{2,1} + 4\alpha_{1,3}\alpha_{3,1} - \alpha_{1,2}\alpha_{2,3}\alpha_{3,1} -}$$
$$\frac{2\alpha_{1,3}(2\alpha_{3,1} - \alpha_{3,2}) + \alpha_{1,2}(\alpha_{2,3})^2}{\alpha_{1,3}\alpha_{3,2}\alpha_{2,1}} \qquad (5)$$

However, with values for the alphas, the evaluation of such equations is
trivial.

   Given that solutions for equations of type (5) are obtained for each of the
players in the game, it is obvious that the equilibrium behavior of the
interaction system is completely specified. The result of the above generalization of the model is the power to predict the behavior of a group of freely-
interacting individuals, in a complex social situation, by combining models
for the behavior of the group's member individuals. The behavior of each
group member is itself predicted from a utility-based theory of decision
making which postulates that actors can be treated as if they are acting to
maximize expected utility in their decision making.

   In much the same manner as the generalization of the theory was built on
basic work on individual decision making, the empirical test of the formulation was dependent on the experiments in which subjects operated in environments in which the behavior of their opponents was simulated by robots.
An overview of the procedure for testing the generalized version of the
theory is as follows. (Detailed descriptions of the research procedures are
available in Ofshe and Ofshe, 1970.) Subjects who participated in either

robot- or free-interaction games were instructed that they were going to participate in a coalition game in which they could win certain amounts of money for forming alternative coalitions. All participants were given identical instructions relating to the norms governing equity considerations. They were instructed that they were to be concerned solely with winning as much money as they could. Subjects were all briefed about the experiment under the same conditions. The briefings took place in a large room and there were always either six or nine subjects present during the briefing. It was explained to subjects that since they would be taken to individual cubicles from which the game would be played, and since there would be either two or three three-person games in progress simultaneously, it was impossible for them to know with which other two individuals they would be playing.

Subjects were taken individually to their respective cubicles. It was not until they had been separated from the other participants that they were informed about the payoffs that they would receive for forming alternative coalitions. There were two different sets of payoff arrangements. Some subjects were informed that they were to be paid five cents for forming either coalition and nothing if they failed to enter a coalition on a particular trial ($a_1 = a_2 =$ the marginal utility of $+5$ or 0). The remaining subjects were informed that their payoffs on each trial were five cents for one of the possible coalitions, ten cents for the other, and nothing if they were unable to center any coalition ($a_1 =$ the marginal utility of $+5$ or 0; $a_2 =$ the marginal utility of $+10$ or 0). It was pointed out to all subjects that they had no information on which to come to any conclusion concerning the payoffs that their potential partners were being offered for forming coalitions with them. Each subject was told that his potential partners might be receiving the same, more, or less money than he was receiving as a payoff for entering into a given coalition.

The play of the game was conducted over a computer controlled teletype system that connected players in different cubicles. The difference between robot-interactive and free-interactive games was solely whether the subject was made to interact with a pre-programmed robot or was actually permitted to interact with other subjects.

We shall report the results of the most complex of the experiments that were conducted to test the applicability of the model to free-interactive behavior. The structure of the coalition situation in which the research was carried out is reported in Figure 1.

The game situation described in Figure 1 is extremely interesting in terms of the monetary and equity influences that are likely to affect each player's choices. The game was one in which player one occupied a position in which he was offered five cents for forming one coalition and ten cents for the other, and both players two and three were in positions in which they received only five cents for any coalition. The three players were inter-connected such that a coalition with player two was a ten-cent alternative for player one and

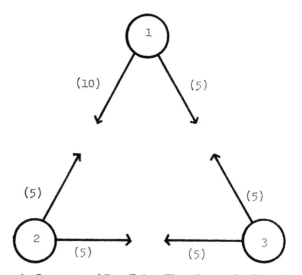

Figure 1   Structure and Payoffs in a Three Person Coalition Game*

* The notation for figures representing game structures should be read as follows: (X) defines a player; (X)—$\xrightarrow{(5)}$ defines the payoff that player X receives for a coalition with the player indicated by the directed line.

a coalition with player three was a five-cent coalition alternative for both players one and two. The game structure was one in which only player one had a clear monetary preference between his alternative coalitions. Players two and three were offered five cents for forming either of their possible coalitions and therefore were, on strict economic grounds, indifferent between alternative coalitions.

The factors that were expected to influence the behavior of the individuals with whom a player was in interaction introduced some interesting considerations. For example, although players two and three were in equivalent payoff positions (five cents for either alternative), they were in interaction with individuals who had quite different motivations to form coalitions with them. Player two was in interaction with players one and three. Player three was in interaction with players one and two.

For player two the motivations of his potential partners to ally with him were as follows. Since a coalition with player two yielded a ten-cent payoff for player one and his alternative coalition paid only five cents, he would be quite anxious to form an alliance with player two. Player three was paid five cents for forming either of his alternative coalitions, and therefore would be equally interested in either possible coalition.

For player three the situation was one in which no other player was greatly motivated to form coalitions with him. A coalition with player three yielded only five cents for player one. This was only one-half the amount that he was paid for a coalition with player two. Player two was paid five cents for forming any coalition and therefore was no more interested in a coalition with player three than he was in a coalition with player one. Indifference was the strongest economic motivation for either of his potential partners to form coalitions with player three.

Each player's equity considerations added to the complexity of the game structure. Consider player two for example. He is in the best position to form a permanent alliance with either of the others since he respresents player one's preferred alternative, and player three will be oriented to choose him since his other potential partner (player one) will not be greatly interested in forming coalitions with him. If player two has no concern about the welfare of the other individuals in the game, he will permit a permanent alliance to form with one of his possible coalition partners. This is, of course, highly detrimental to the excluded individual. If, as the theory predicts, player two is concerned about the welfare of the other players in the game, he will attempt to bring about conditions that equalize the number of coalitions that they are each able to enter. It is even conceivable that player two can arrange matters such that he will still be included in a coalition on every trial. Assume that player two has entered into a temporary alliance with one of the other players. Given the structure of the game, the excluded player will attempt to break the alliance by making consistent choices of player two. Player two is therefore put in a position in which, in order to include both of the other players in a more nearly equal number of coalitions, he must alternate in some manner between player one and player three. This strategy, however, involves some monetary risks for player two since it is possible that through imperfect coordination no coalition will form on some trials or that the other two players will enter into an alliance to his detriment.

Due to all of the above considerations, the game structure selected as the setting in which to conduct the research is considered to be a complex social situation in which each of the participants in the interaction system is faced with a decision problem that, for a number of reasons, is different from the decision problems faced by the other participants in the system. The test of the theory is its ability to predict the decision making of each player in the game and, therefore, the behavior of the system of interacting individuals.

Table 2 summarizes the formal characteristics of the experiment. There were a total of fourteen three-person groups participating in the experiment. Therefore, fourteen subjects occupied each of the structurally unique positions in the game. Although players in position numbers two and three were offered identical payoffs for forming alternative coalitions, the motivations of their potential partners to form coalitions with them were by no means identical. It is therefore necessary to consider players in these two positions to be confronted with quite different decision problems.

Table 2   Formal Characteristics of the Free-Interactive Game

Player	Payoffs for Coalitions with Players X and Y	Number of Trials	Number of Subjects	Sex of Subjects
1	2 = $ 0.10 3 = $ 0.05	60	14	Male
2	1 = $ 0.05 3 = $ 0.05	60	14	Male
3	1 = $ 0.05 2 = $ 0.05	60	14	Male

The most straightforward manner in which to report the behavior of the players in the game is to present graphs of the probabilities with which players in each position distributed their choices through time. Figures 2, 3, and 4 report these probabilities. In each case, the probability with which the player chose each of his potential partners is reported. Although the same information could be communicated by reporting probability values for only one alternative for each player, presentation of curves for choices of both alternatives makes it somewhat easier to understand the behavior of the subjects. The figures demonstrate that players in each of the three positions stabilize their choice behavior after a brief period of adjustment to the game.

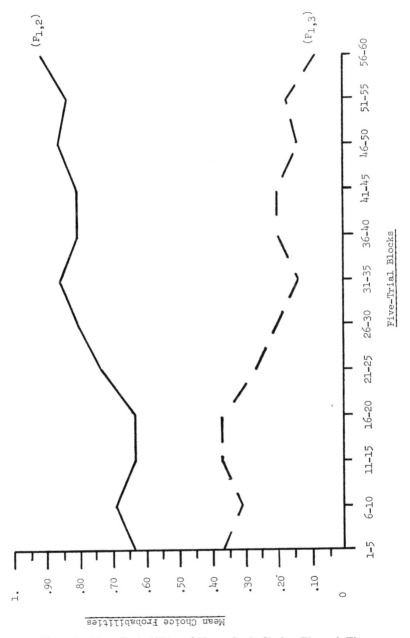

Figure 2 Mean Probabilities of Player One's Choices Through Time

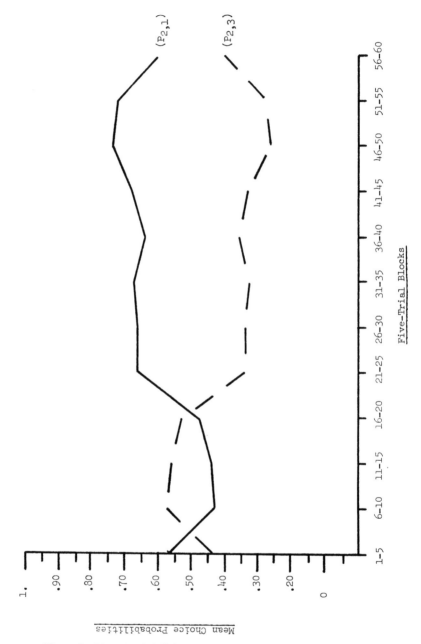

Figure 3   Mean Probabilities of Player Two's Choices Through Time

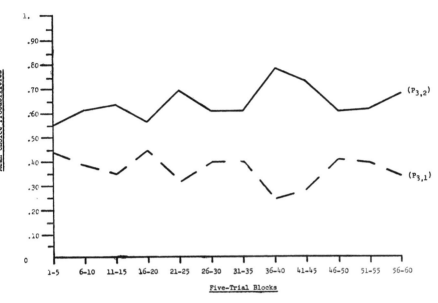

Figure 4 Mean Probabilities of Player Three's Choices Through Time

In order to test the model it is necessary to identify the portion of the experiment within which each player is considered to be displaying a stable choice strategy. Since there are no analytic procedures through which it is possible to unambiguously identify stable-state, the decision was made on the basis of inspection of the data. For player one, the stable-state period was identified as the last thirty-five trials of the experiment. For occupants of positions two and three the stable-state periods are taken to be the last forty iterations of the game for players in both positions.

Using these periods as the bases for calculations, the resulting stablestate choice strategies for occupants of the three positions are as follows:

$$P_{1,2} = 0.839 \quad \text{and} \quad P_{1,3} = 0.161$$
$$P_{2,1} = 0.671 \quad \text{and} \quad P_{2,3} = 0.329$$
$$P_{3,1} = 0.339 \quad \text{and} \quad P_{3,2} = 0.661$$

In the following section, the model's predictions for the stable-state choice strategies of players in the free-interactive game will be derived. *No* data from the free-interactive game are used in obtaining the predictions. Since the procedures for the robot- and free-interactive experiments differed only with regard to whether subjects interacted with robots or humans, it was possible to use the data from the robot-interactive experiments in order to estimate the α values necessary to predict behavior in the free-interactive experiments. The data from experiments I and II (see Table 1) were used in order to estimate α when $a_1 = a_2 =$ the marginal utility of $+5$ or 0. The data from experiments III, IV and V were used to estimate α_1 and α_2 when $a_1 =$ the marginal utility of $+5$ or 0 and $a_2 =$ the marginal utility of $+10$ or 0. Since there was more than the minimum data necessary to estimate α values for both the equal-α and unequal-α cases, a procedure developed by Siegel was used to obtain the best estimates from the available data. The method was based on the construction of a set of over-determined simultaneous equations and solving for the best estimate of α. The details of the procedure may be found in Siegel et al. (1964). Using this method, the estimate for α under conditions in which $a_1 = a_2 =$ the marginal utility of $+5$ or 0 is 3.49663. For unequal payoff conditions, when $a_1 =$ the marginal utility of $+10$ or 0 the estimate of α_1 was 3.02485 and when $a_2 =$ the marginal utility of $+5$ or 0 the estimate for α_2 was 1.58258.[6]

Although in order to estimate α it was necessary to hold the payoff and equity inducing aspects of the robot-interactive experiments and the free-interactive game situation constant across conditions, there was a gross difference between conditions. It was, of course, the truly interactive nature of the latter game. While it is quite impressive that the decision model can be used in order to predict behavior in non-social and social situations, in all previous work it was necessary to control the π parameters and therefore differences between research settings were primarily in the subjects' perceptions of the situation. In relinquishing control over the π parameters, the experimental situation is drastically altered. In free-interactive coalition games subjects are confronted not with fixed environments, but rather with the behaviors of individuals who can respond to the subject's past actions, presumably might be influenced to enter into permanent alliances and can attempts to influence the subject's behavior. The structure of the decision theory permits the formal inter-relation of players in a manner that reproduces the structure of game situation represented in Figure 1 and yields a number of unambiguous predictions about how this interaction system will behave if the theory is correct. The argument is quite clear; if individuals act so as to maximize expected utility and the values of the utilities have been adequately measured, then the interaction system should stabilize with subjects displaying predicted choice strategies, since these are the maximizing strategies given the maximizing behaviors of the other members of the system.

Predictions for each player's maximizing choice strategy are arrived at by introducing appropriate α values and by solving the system of linear equations that describe the interaction system. The system of linear equations is as follows:

$$4P_{1,2} - \alpha_{1,2}P_{2,1} + \alpha_{1,3}P_{3,1} = 2$$

$$\alpha_{2,1}P_{1,2} - 4P_{2,1} + \alpha_{2,3}P_{3,1} = \alpha_{2,3} - 2$$

$$\alpha_{3,1}P_{1,2} - \alpha_{3,2}P_{2,1} + 4P_{3,1} = \alpha_{3,1} - \alpha_{3,2} + 2$$

Inspection of Figure 1 reveals that player one is in an unequal-α situation in which he receives ten cents for a coalition with player two and five cents for a coalition with player three. Therefore, based an data from Table 1,

$$\alpha_{1,2} = 3.02485$$

$$\alpha_{1,3} = 1.58258$$

Players two and three are in equal-α situations since they receive five cents for either of their possible coalitions. Therefore,

$$\alpha_{2,1} = \alpha_{2,3} = \alpha_{3,1} = \alpha_{3,2} = 3.49663$$

Using these α values the model predicts that the choice strategy maximizing player one's expected utility is to choose players two and three with the following probabilities:

$$P_{1,2} = \frac{\begin{vmatrix} 2 & -\alpha_{1,2} & \alpha_{1,3} \\ \alpha_{2,3} - 2 & -4 & \alpha_{2,3} \\ \alpha_{3,1} - \alpha_{3,2} + 2 & -\alpha_{3,2} & 4 \end{vmatrix}}{\begin{vmatrix} 4 & -\alpha_{1,2} & \alpha_{1,3} \\ \alpha_{2,1} & -4 & \alpha_{2,3} \\ \alpha_{3,1} & -\alpha_{3,2} & 4 \end{vmatrix}}$$

$$= \frac{\begin{vmatrix} 2 & -3.02485 & 1.58258 \\ 3.49663 - 2 & -4 & 3.49663 \\ 3.49663 - 3.49663 + 2 & -3.49663 & 4 \end{vmatrix}}{\begin{vmatrix} 4 & -3.02485 & 1.58258 \\ 3.49663 & -4 & 3.49663 \\ 3.49663 & -3.49663 & 4 \end{vmatrix}}$$

$$= \frac{-6.21366}{-6.96479}$$

$$= 0.890$$

$$P_{1,3} = 1 - P_{1,2} = 0.110$$

Predictions for the maximizing choice strategies for players two and three can be derived in the same manner as outlined above.

Table 3 summarizes the model's predictions for the behavior of each participant in the interaction system and reports the observed stable-state choice strategies for subjects in each of the three player positions. The model predicts that for subjects in the player one position the optimizing choice strategy is to choose player two with a probability of 0.890 and player three

Table 3 Results of application of the generalized choice theory to data from a free-interactive coalition game

Player Position	Predicted Choice Strategy	Observed Choice Strategy	|Discrepancy|
1	$P_{1,2} = 0.890$ $P_{1,3} = 0.110$	0.839 0.161	0.051
2*	$P_{2,1} = 0.682$ $P_{2,3} = 0.318$	0.671 0.329	0.011
3*	$P_{3,1} = 0.318$ $P_{3,2} = 0.682$	0.339 0.661	0.021

* Note the similarity in predictions for the maximizing behaviors of players two and three. The model predicts that each will distribute his choices with probabilities of 0.682 and 0.318. Player two is predicted to choose player one with the greater probability, and player three is predicted to choose player one with the lesser of the two probabilities. The similarity in the values of these probabilities is accidental. The model does not always predict identical numeric strategies for players in identical payoff positions. For example, if player one's maximizing strategy was a selection of player two with a probability of 0.926 and player three with a probability of 0.074, the model's predictions for players two and three's maximizing strategies would be $P_{2,1} = 0.736$, $P_{2,3} = 0.264$, and $P_{3,1} = 0.338$, and $P_{3,2} = 0.662$.

with a probability of 0.110. Subjects in position number one choose player two with a probability of 0.839 and player three with a probability of 0.161. The absolute discrepancy between the predicted and observed choice strategies is 0.051. For subjects in the player two position the maximizing choice strategy is a 0.682 probability of a player one choice and a 0.318 probability of a player three choice. The observed strategy ($P_{2,1} = 0.671$ and $P_{2,3} = 0.329$) is discrepant from the predicted strategy by an absolute value of 0.011. For subjects in the player three position, the strategy that maximizes expected utility is to choose player one with a probability of

0.318 and player two with a probability of 0.682. The observed choice strategy of $P_{3,1} = 0.339$ and $P_{3,2} = 0.661$ is discrepant from the maximizing strategy by $|0.021|$. The mean absolute discrepancy between the predicted and observed choice strategies is 0.028.

The power of the model to predict the dynamics of the interaction system is obviously considerable. The decision theory on which it was based argues that all members of the system may be treated as if they are acting so as to maximize expected utility in their decision making, that each player will adopt a stable choice strategy, and consequently that the interaction system will arrive at an equilibrium point. In addition, the model predicts the precise optimizing strategy that each player will adopt, and consequently it specifies the equilibrium point to which the system will move.

NOTES

1 The authors share equal responsibility for the work reported in the following paper. The paper was prepared under grants from the National Science Foundation (G.S. 2152) and the Committee on Research of the University of California (Berkeley).

2 The existence of a utility for choice variation is argued for through the analysis of interviews with subjects in an experiment conducted by Siegel and Goldstein (1959) and by data reported by Goodnow (1955). One of the experiments reported in Siegel et al. (1964) was designed to demonstrate the effects of changing the subject's utility for choice variability. This was accomplished by varying the response format from one that was intrinsically boring to one that was intrinsically interesting. The predicted effect, adoption of a choice strategy closer to the strategy that maximized monetary gain, resulted from the experiment.

3 It should be noted that with certain combinations of feedback probabilities and utility values, the model can yield predictions for P_i greater than one or less than zero. Since P_i refers to a probability, it is meaningful only between the values of zero and one; consequently, it is necessary to impose a limiting condition on the model (i.e., $0 \leq P_i \leq 1$) and solve for the maximizing choice strategy within the range of possible values. Since the utility function is monotonically increasing, whenever the model yields a P_i greater than one it can be shown that the maximizing behavioral strategy is to choose the ith alternative with a probability of one. Analogously, when P_i is less than zero the maximizing strategy is to choose the ith alternative with a probability of zero.

4 The model has also been applied to decision making in conflict situations such as the prisoner's dilemma. For an analysis of the prisoner's dilemma literature in terms of the concepts of the theory and an application of the model to data from prisoner's dilemma experiments, see Ofshe and Ofshe (1970).

5 Although the generalization given here is for interaction in a three-person coalition game, it should be immediately obvious that the theory is applicable to n-person

systems in which each participant makes a binary decision on each trial. Also note that the restriction to binary decisions is not a limiting condition on the theory. It is applicable to k-alternative decisions. Therefore, given sufficient measurement data, it would be possible to predict the equilibrium choice distribution for interaction systems in which any number of individuals attempt to coordinate their choices to the choices of any number of other individuals.

6 It should be clearly understood that the data used to estimate α and the data against which the model's predictions are to be evaluated are completely independent. This extends to the subjects who participated in the robot-interactive and free-interactive experiments. Different sets of subjects were used in the different experiments. The only similarity between subjects was that they were all males and students at the same university.

REFERENCES

Goodnow, J. J. Determinants of choice-distribution in two-choice situations. *American Journal of Psychology*, 1955, **68**, 106–116.

Humphreys, L. G. Acquisition and extinction of verbal expectations in a situation analogous to conditioning. *Journal of Experimental Psychology*, 1939, **25**, 294–301.

Luce, R. D., and Suppes, P. Preference, utility, and subjective probability. In Luce, R. D., Bush, R. R., and Galanter, E. (Eds.), *Handbook of Mathematical Psychology*, Vol. III. New York: Wiley, 1965. pp. 249–410.

Ofshe, L., and Ofshe, R. *Utility and Choice in Social Interaction*. Englewood Cliffs, New Jersey: Prentice-Hall, 1970.

Siegel, S., Siegel, A. E., and Andrews, J. M. *Choice, Strategy and Utility*. New York: McGraw Hill, 1964.

Siegel, S., and Goldstein, D. A. Decision-making behavior in a two-choice uncertain outcome situation. *Journal of Experimental Psychology*, 1959, **57**, 37–42.

AN EXPERIMENTAL STUDY
OF THREE VOTING RULES

JACOB BIRNBERG and LOUIS PONDY

University of Pittsburgh and Duke University

As Lieberman (1965, p. 1) has pointed out, "How persons in interaction combine their individual preference patterns into a social choice is a fundamental question about which there has been much speculation, and an amount of mathematical work; *but there have been few, if any, empirical studies dealing directly with the question.*" (our italics) This paper reports the results of a laboratory experiment which was designed to contribute to one aspect of our empirical knowledge of the social choice question.

One of the common processes by which collectivities amalgamate individual preferences into a social choice is voting. Our specific interest is in the differential effects of various voting rules on the outcome of the group decision process. We shall not concern ourselves with other mechanisms for arriving at collective decisions, such as the exercise of personal power or persuasion, the imposition of a joint welfare function, interpersonal bargaining, or the reliance on precedents or commitments (Lieberman, 1965, p. 9).

Our reference to theories of collective choice will be limited to *positive* theories which attempt to explain and predict how groups actually make social choices through voting, not how they ought to do so. Thus, we exclude the work of Arrow (1963), Black (1958), Coleman (1966), Plott (1967), E. A. Thompson (1966), and others who have been concerned with the *normative* question.

However, it sould be pointed out that normative theories may become positive theories when the motivational basis of rationality is alleged in fact to be descriptive of the actors' motives, and thus become subject to empirical testing. A case in point is Buchanan and Tullock's (1962) comparative analysis of voting rules on the basis of their total costs (both "external costs" and "decision making costs") to the individual members of the collectivity.

RELATED EMPIRICAL RESEARCH

In a sense, the extensive research on the prisoners' dilemma has been concerned with the preformance of a specific voting rule—unanimity rule—under a variety of conditions. That is, the acceptable payoffs occur only if *both* players refuse to "confess." Similarly, the research on coalition formation has been concerned with which coalitions form under a specific voting rule, typically majority rule. Here we equate the required size of the minimal winning coalition with the voting rule in effect. Neither of these lines of investigation, however, has systematically studied the *comparative* effects of *different* voting rules.[1] Thus they bear only tangentially on the issue under consideration in this paper.

As a specific instance of Lieberman's more general statement, the literature is singularly devoid of *empirical* results which bear directly on the question of *comparative* preformance characteristics of different voting rules. The prime exception is Bower's (1965a and b) laboratory study of three man decision making groups. Each group was asked to select what its members collectively judged to be the best of 125 "investment alternatives." The 125 alternatives constituted a subset of 1000 alternatives defined by the combination of ten values of "sales," ten values of "profitability," and ten values of "risk." Quality of the alternatives was defined by a complex function of the three attributes. The function was unknown to the group members, but each member was given information on ten alternatives outside the subset of 125 available alternatives. In each group, each member had information which only partially overlapped that of the other two members. The group members communicated by written notes. After a thorough exchange of information and ideas, each group made its collective choice by voting. Half the groups operated under majority rule, and half under unanimity rule. Within each experimental subject, the group closest to the best alternative received thirty dollars. Under the "team" or cooperative condition, the prize money was to be divided evenly among the members of the winning group. Under the "foundation" or competitive condition, the prize money was to be divided $19/$10/$1 according to which group member's initial preference was closest to the group's final choice. Having an objective measure of group performance, Bower was able to assess the relative efficacy of the two voting rules under both conflict and cooperation. His findings relevant to our purposes were as follows:

1 Teams (cooperative condition) made better decisions when operating under unanimity rule than under majority rule.
2 Foundations (competitive condition) performed better under majority rule than under unanimity rule, *but only because of the high frequency of no-choice outcomes*. Using data only from those groups which reached decisions (truncated sample), foundations also performed better under unanimity rule than under majority rule.
3 For the truncated sample, the relative improvement due to a shift from majority to unanimity rule was greater for foundations than for teams.

A common expectation is that the performance characteristics of majority rule would be superior to those of unanimity rule, primarily because the conditions for agreement are more restrictive under unanimity and therefore optimum group choice is less likely. However, this overlooks the stimulating effects of unanimity on the search and evaluation processes. Bower ascribed the superiority of unanimity rule to the heightened pressures on each group member to exchange information and to search more intensively for better solutions. He supported this contention with supplementary data on the frequency of communication and the actual exchange of information.[2]

PERFORMANCE OF VOTING RULES IN LESS COMPLEX SITUATIONS

Bower's experiment leaves unanswered the question of relative performance characteristics of voting rules when the analysis of alternatives is less complex. Consider for example a set of alternatives for which the payoffs to each group member are certain. Suppose further that all members have complete and accurate information regarding the available alternatives, and that the payoffs are not perfectly correlated across group members.

In such a situation, communication and exchange of information can contribute nothing to the quality of search or analysis. The only function of communication in this case might be to facilitate coordination, bargaining, and coalition formation. Under these conditions, we would expect that voting rule to perform best which makes agreement among group members

15*

easiest, that is, which facilitates the "choice" phase of group decision. As Bower suggests, majority rule is likely to be superior to unanimity in this regard. If this is in fact true, it suggests that the relative advantage shifts from less restrictive to more restrictive voting rules as the group decision problem becomes more complex and uncertain.

The experiment described below was designed to investigate the performance characteristics of voting rules in such situations of relative simplicity and certainty. We have also chosen to test the effects of modified majority rule, wherein one specific person is given a blocking veto (or, equivalently, he has two votes to each of the other two members' one vote). This was done to reflect the hierarchical structure of many decision making groups.

DESCRIPTION OF EXPERIMENT

Subjects

The subjects were 36 students in the Master of Business Administration program at the Graduate School of Business of the University of Pittsburgh. They were formed into 12 "committees" of three members each.

Task

Each "committee" was asked to make 54 decisions regarding the allocation of resources among group members, plus three practice decisions at the beginning of the experiment. During each of the 54 trials, the group voted on three alternative plans: Plan R, which gave each member one "point;" Plan S, which gave two of the members two points and the third zero points; and Plan T, which gave one member five points and the other two members zero points. Thus there was an inverse relation between the total payoff of a given plan and the equality of payoff distribution.[3]

By rotating the two and five point payoffs so that all members had an equal opportunity to obtain them, there were nine distinct sets of allocation plans. The 54 trials were divided into three blocks of 18 trials each. Each of the distinct sets of allocation plans were presented twice during each block of 18 trials. The order of presentation was randomized within the first block of trials, and this same order was used for the second and third blocks of trials. Each group operated under three voting rules—majority rule, unanimity, and modified majority rule where person A had a veto. Six orders of three voting rules are possible, and each order was used twice during the 12 replications. No communication among group members was permitted during the experiment. The group members voted by passing marked ballots to the experimenter.

Under majority rule, if any two of the three members voted for the same allocation plan, that plan was used as a basis for distributing points. Under the unanimity rule, all three members had to vote for the same plan, and the payoffs followed the schedule described under the plan chosen, if any. Under the veto condition, person A and one other member had to vote for the same plan for it to be in effect. No payoffs of any kind were made if no plan received the required votes.

After each trial, if the group vote resulted in some decision, the experimenter reported which plan had been decided upon and allocated the payoffs accordingly. If no group decision resulted, then the subjects were informed of this, but were given no additional feedback regarding the individual choices made.

HYPOTHESES: FOUR MODELS OF VOTING BEHAVIOR

Our concern is not limited to which of the three voting rules is "best" in some collective sense. More specifically we are concerned with what type of group choice outcome is likely under each voting rule. For example, is a restrictive voting rule like unanimity likely to lead to agreement, if any, only on the allocation plan which promises a payoff to all members? Our hypotheses or predictions are embodied in four models described below. Each model posits a motivation for the *individual* voter, and aggregates the individual motivations into the most likely *group* choice.

Random choice model

Assume that each member votes for one of three plans at random. Then each plan is equally likely to be the group choice, but the probability of a "no-decision" outcome will vary with the voting rule in effect.

Under the unanimity rule the probability of agreement on any given allocation plan (i.e. R, S, or T) is 1/27 for all members must vote for the same allocation plan. The probability of "no decision" is 1–3 (1/27) or 8/9. For the majority rule similar analysis would show that the probability of any plan being selected is 7/27 and the probability of a "no decision" outcome is 2/9. Finally, for the veto rule the probability of any given plan being selected is 5/27 and the probability of "no decision" 4/9.

It is readily apparent that the probability of agreement on an allocation plan is strongly affected by the voting rule in operation. If people behave as if they are making random selections, then a simple majority rule procedure would yield agreement on the average 78 % of the time. The more stringent unanimity rule would result in agreement on the average only 11 % of the time.

Long run cooperative model

Total group payoff is maximized, in this experiment, if the group always successfully votes for Plan T. Under this plan, each member receives the maximum five point payoff one-third of the time, for an average payoff of 1 2/3 points per trial. (A given member, of course, could earn more than this, but only at the expense of the other members.)

In this model we assume that each person cooperates by always voting for Plan T. The predication of the long run cooperative model is that the group decides on Plan T 100 % of the time under all voting rules.

Short run competitive model

This model assumes that each person votes for the plan which gives him the maximum payoff on the trial in question. That is, each person tries to maximize *his own* payoff (not the group payoff, as in the previous model), without recognizing the need for cooperation with at least one of the other members. Under the unanimity rule, this model predicts that no agreement can ever be reached for all three members never receive their maximum payoffs on the same plan.

Under majority rule agreement is feasible for under Plan S (2–2–0 payoff schedule) two members may maximize their payoff. This will occur when the potential five point payoff goes to the member *without* a two point payoff. Such a payoff configuration will occur 1/3 of the time. The other 2/3 of the time no decision will be reached.

Under veto rule, Plan S is the only feasible outcome. This is possible only when the member with the veto has a two point payoff, and the five point payoff and the other two point payoff are divided between the other two members. This will occur 2/9 of the time. The remaining trials will yield no decision.

In summary, this model predicts no decision 100% of the time under unanimity rule, Plan S 1/3 of the time and no decision 2/3 of the time under majority rule and Plan S 2/9 of the time and no decision 7/9 under the veto rule.

Dominating Strategies Model

The preceding model is unnecessarily naive in that it assumes that each "player" forms no expectations whatsoever about each of the other players' likely choices. This model, based on quasi-game theoretic logic, assumes that each player votes for a plan which maximizes his payoff, contingent on the other players following a similar criterion.[4] As important element of this strategy is that each player attempts to eliminate certain plans which are dominated by other plans for all possible combinations of voting patterns by the other two players. Assuming that the other players are also rational in this sense, each player will be able to predict which plans the other players will not vote for, and will be able to adjust his strategy accordingly.

This choice procedure can be made clear by going through the analysis for a single case. Assume that each player is confronted by the payoff schedule or configuration which allots member C the zero payoff under Plan S and the five point payoff under plan T and that majority rule is in effect. The contingent payoff matrices are described in Table 1.

Since each player is assumed to be a rational, short term personal (competitive) maximizer, and since he knows his and all other payoffs, the reasoning might proceed as follows:

1 A reasons that he should *never* vote for plan T, since at best he can receive a 2 point payoff when B and C both vote for plan S, or a 1 point payoff when B and C both vote for plan R. But he will receive these payoffs when B and C both vote for R or S independent of his (A's) vote. That is, for each choice A makes (R, S, or T), there are nine possible payoffs to A depending on how B and C vote, so that each of A's choices can be described by a nine element vector. For the payoff configuration in footnote 5, and un dermajority rule, these vectors are:

$$A_R = (1, 1, 1, 1, 2, 0, 1, 0, 0)$$
$$A_S = (1, 2, 0, 2, 2, 2, 0, 2, 0)$$
$$A_T = (1, 0, 0, 0, 2, 0, 0, 0, 0)$$

Social Choice

Table 1 Contingent payoff matrices for majority rule vote (for payoff schedule described in figure 1)

A's Vote	B's Vote	C's Vote	Group Decision	Payoff to A	B	C
R	R	R	R	1	1	1
		S	R	1	1	1
		T	R	1	1	1
	S	R	R	1	1	1
		S	S	2	2	0
		T	none	0	0	0
	T	R	R	1	1	1
		S	none	0	0	0
		T	T	0	0	5
S	R	R	R	1	1	1
		S	S	2	2	0
		T	none	0	0	0
	S	R	S	2	2	0
		S	S	2	2	0
		T	S	2	2	0
	T	R	none	0	0	0
		S	S	2	2	0
		T	T	0	0	5
T	R	R	R	1	1	1
		S	none	0	0	0
		T	T	0	0	5
	S	R	none	0	0	0
		S	S	2	2	0
		T	T	0	0	5
	T	R	T	0	0	5
		S	T	0	0	5
		T	T	0	0	5

Since $(A_R)_i \geqq (A_T)_i$ and $(A_S)_i \geqq (A_T)_i$, for all i, both R and S are said to "dominate" the T choice, and T is eliminated since A can do at least as well by choosing R or S. But R and S do not dominate one another, and they are retained at this stage as possible choices. The other players, knowing that A will behave rationally, can depend on the fact that he will not choose Plan T.

2   By similar reasoning, B decides never to vote for plan T.

3   Player C, realizing that A and B will never vote T, decides to vote for plan R in hopes of receiving at least a 1 point payoff.

4   A, realizing that B will never vote for T and that C will always vote for R, decides to vote for S, since his payoff under an S vote is always at least as good as under an R vote, and is better (2 points) if B votes for S.

5   B goes through the same reasoning and votes for S.

6   Since both A and B vote for S, S is the group decision, and A and B each receive 2 points and C receives none. This particular three-person and non-zero-sum game has a unique, stable solution.

By a similar analysis, it can be easily shown that the group decision under majority rule for all other payoff configurations is always plan S.[5] Similarly, for votes under a rule of unanimity, it can be shown that there is a unique, stable solution at plan R for all payoff configurations. Finally, under veto rule, there is also always a stable voting solution for the three-person game. But the solution is plan R for some payoff configurations (1/3 of the time) and plan S for other payoff configurations.[6] Note that no "no decision" outcomes are predicted. These predictions of the Dominating Strategies Model can be summarized as follows:

1   Under unanimity rule the members will agree on **Plan R** 100% of the time.

2   Under majority rule the members will agree on **Plan S** 100% of the time.

3   Under veto the decision will be affected by the form of the payoff schedule being considered. As the results **Plan R** will be selected 1/3 of the time and **Plan S** 2/3 of the time.

RESULTS

Comparison of data and predictive models

Each of the twelve experimental "committees" voted 18 times under each voting rule, so that for each of the three voting rules, there were 216 votes taken on plans R, S. and T. There was a wide variation among the voting rules in the group decisions. As we might expect, the frequency of "no decision" outcomes was highest under unanimity and lowest under majority rule, since conditions for agreement were most stringent under the former voting rule and least stringent under the latter. The results are displayed in Table 2 along with predictions of the four models discussed above.

Table 2 Comparison of voting data with predictions of four models, for majority, unanimity and veto voting rules

Type of Voting Rule	Outcome	Predictions of Models				Data	
		Random Choice	L.R. Coop.	S.R. Comp.	Dominating Strategies	Percent	Number
Majority	Plan R	25.9%	0.0%	0.0%	0.0%	4.6%	10
	Plan S	25.9%	0.0%	33.3%	100.0%	63.3%	141
	Plan T	25.9%	100.0%	0.0%	0.0%	22.3%	48
	No Decision	22.3%	0.0%	66.7%	0.0%	7.8%	17
	Totals	100.0%	100.0%	100.0%	100.0%	100.0%	216
Unanimity	Plan R	3.7%	0.0%	0.0%	100.0%	37.5%	81
	Plan S	3.7%	0.0%	0.0%	0.0%	7.4%	16
	Plan T	3.7%	100.0%	0.0%	0.0%	0.0%	0
	No Decision	88.9%	0.0%	100.0%	0.0%	55.1%	119
	Totals	100.0%	100.0%	100.0%	100.0%	100.0%	216
Veto	Plan R	18.5%	0.0%	0.0%	33.3%	29.7%	64
	Plan S	18.5%	0.0%	22.2%	66.7%	51.8%	112
	Plan T	18.5%	100.0%	0.0%	0.0%	6.5%	14
	No Decision	44.5%	0.0%	77.8%	0.0%	12.0%	26
	Totals	100.0%	100.0%	100.0%	100.0%	100.0%	216

As can be seen from a casual comparison of data with the four sets of predictions, the long run cooperative model, which predicts group agreement on plan T 100% of the time, provides a singularly poor fit to the data. In fact, in the case of unanimity rule, not one single time out of 216 opportunities was plan T agreed upon! The groups do not appear to have followed a long run cooperative strategy. Only in the case of majority rule was there any incidence of agreement on plan T to speak of (22% of the time), and that was far below the prediction of the cooperative model.

Each of the other three models, *by itself*, is also a mediocre description of the actual voting behavior. For example, the dominating strategies model does not predict the incidence of "no decision" outcomes, but it does do a reasonable job of predicting the plans agreed upon, provided agreement was reached. However, since it is reasonable to assume that the groups may have followed more than a single strategy, we may be justified in fitting the data with some linear combination of the three sets of predictions. The coefficients in such a linear combination should be positive, fractional weights that sum to unity. This technique, of course, does not guarantee that all coefficients will be positive. In such a case, all pairs of two sets of predictions could be tried and the linear combination giving the best fit to the data chosen.

In fact, the best linear combination of all three sets of predictions does yield a negative coefficient. Trying pairs of predictions, it was found that the data were best explained by a linear combination of the random choice and dominating strategies models, with weights of 0.33 and 0.67, respectively.

Table 3 Comparison of observed voting frequencies with weighted predictions of random choice and dominating strategies models

	Voting Frequency Under Plan ...			
	R	S	T	No Decision
Majority Rule:				
Observed Data	0.046	0.653	0.223	0.078
Weighted Predictions	0.08	0.76	0.08	0.07
Unanimity Rule:				
Observed Data	0.375	0.074	0.00	0.551
Weighted Predictions	0.69	0.01	0.01	0.29
Veto Rule:				
Observed Data	0.297	0.518	0.065	0.120
Weighted Predictions	0.28	0.51	0.06	0.15

In other words, the "committees" behaved as if they were using quasi-game theoretic strategies 67 % of the time and random choice strategies 33 % of the time. A rationale for this weighted prediction is discussed later in the paper.

See Table 3 for the comparison of the data with this weighted prediction. The simple correlation coefficient between observed voting frequencies and weighted predictions is +0.84, significantly greater than zero at better than the 0.01 level.[7]

Effect of voting rules on committee decisions

Earlier in the paper we contended that committees operating under different voting rules would reach widely different decisions. The allocation alternatives ranged from a "small budget" evenly divided (Plan R) to a "large budget" unevenly divided (Plan T). The null hypotheses corresponding to this contention is, for example, that Plan R would be agreed upon with the same relative frequency under all three voting rules, and the same for Plans S and T and for the "no decision" outcome.

That is,

$$f_i(M) = f_i(U) = f_i(V), \quad i = \text{R, S, T, or } ND$$

where: M, U and V designate the voting rule in effect

f designates the outcome of the group decision (including the "no decision" outcome)

i designates the relative frequency of a given outcome under a specified voting rule

Votes were taken under each voting rule 216 times (18 votes by each of 12 committees). Out of 648 votes under all conditions, Plan R was the outcome 24 % of the time; Plan S, 41.5 %; Plan T, 9.5 %, and "no-decision", 25.0 % of the time. Thus, under the conditions of the null hypothesis, we would expect these same percentages to hold for all three voting rules. Examining Table 3, however, shows wide divergence of the three patterns from the marginal frequencies. If we assume all 648 votes to be statistically independent, a Chi-Square test of homogeneity may be performed. The analysis yields $x^2 = 325$, $df = 6$, significant at far beyond the $p = 0.001$ level. One might argue, however, that the 18 votes taken by a given committee operating under a given voting rule are *not* independent, thus invalidating the about analysis. If we take each such block of 18 votes to be an independent set, then there are 36 such independent sets (three voting conditions for each of the twelve committees). And each set is described by four relative frequencies corresponding to the four decision outcomes (i. e. 144 relative frequencies in all). The test of homogeneity can now be rephrased as follows: "For a given decision outcome, is the variation in relative frequency of the outcome *between* voting rules large relative to the variation in relative frequency *within* voting rules?" To answer this question, an analysis of variance was performed for each of the decision outcomes on the relative frequencies and the four analyses were pooled. The F-statistic was very large, i.e. F = 1470, for 12 and 132 degrees of freedom for the systematic and residual variances respectively.

Thus, it seems safe to conclude that voting rules do indeed have a highly significant effect on the outcome of group decisions under the conditions of our experiment. As we have already seen, these differences among the voting rules appear to be the result of some combination of random choice and quasi-game theoretic behavior by the individual members of the committees.

Given that significant differences exist among the voting rules, can we say anything about which voting rule is "best" in some sense? Since the function of the voting rule is to aggregate individual preferences into a group decision, one criterion of the rule's performance is the total number of points earned by the group members over each 18 trial block. A second criterion is the distribution of the total points earned among the three group members, i.e. the variability of individual shares. For this second criterion, we shall use a normalized range measure. That is, individual payoff variability is defined to be the difference between the largest and smallest individual point totals for a given voting rule, divided by the total points. Thus, individual payoff variability may range from zero, for a perfectly even distribution of points, to unity, for the case where one person receives all of the points. Other things being equal, we assume that one voting rule is better than another if it results in a larger total payoff and a smaller variability of individual pay-offs.

The majority rule resulted in the largest mean group payoff, 69.5 points, compared with 59.2 points for veto and only 25.6 points for unanimity. The differences among these means was significant at the 0.005 level. Similarly, while it did not have the smallest measure of variability, its score of 0.07 was very close to that of unanimity, 0.02, and significantly below that of veto, 0.22. The differences among these means was significant at the 0.001 level. (The normalized range measure of 0.22 correspond to about a 50%/ 25%/25% distribution of payoffs). Thus it would appear that, in balance, majority rule meets the tests of efficiency and equity better than the other two rules.

As a side note, the poor performance of the unanimity rule raises serious questions about group procedures which lay heavy stress on consensus formation. Because unanimity must be purchased with roughly *equal individual sharing* in any benefits over the short run, it may also result over the long run in inferior *aggregate* performance.

Order–of–presentation effects

As we have already indicated, each experimental committee operated under all three voting rules. There were two replications under each of the six possible orders in which the voting rules were tested. This was done primarily to control for the effects of practice on performance. However, the procedure also allows us to test whether there is an interaction between voting rule and the position in the sequence when a given rule was tested. In other words, we can ascertain whether practice improves performance more in the case of one voting rule than in that of another. This is relevant since our analysis to this point has assumed that the effects of practice are negligible both marginally and in interaction with voting rule.

To test order-of-presentation effects, we transformed the group decisions into the aggregate performance measure of total group points earned. Unanimity rule scored an average of 24.50 points per block of 18 trials when presented first, an average of 11.00 points per block of 18 trials when presented second and an average of 41.25 points per block of 18 trials when presented third. For majority rule these scores were 61.00, 68.75 and 78.75 respectively. Under veto they were 61.75, 59,75 and 56.00 respectively.

There appears to be a sizable increase in performance from the second to the third block of 18 trials. (The maximum number of points that could be earned over any 18 trial sequence was 90.) Performance under veto rule declines slightly with position in the test sequence, under majority rule increases by 18 points, and under unanimity decreases and then increases. However, an analysis of variance shows both the position-in-sequence effect and the interaction effect to fall just short of significance at the 0.05 level. The voting rule effect is, of course, highly significant, $p < 0.005$.

While the analysis of variance supports our earlier statistical procedures, the differences are sufficiently close to significance to warrant further study of the order-of-presentation effects on the performance of voting rules. To the extent that the data presented in this section are significant, they suggest that the superiority of majority rule over veto and unanimity rules increases with practice.

Further analysis indicates that improvement of majority rule with experience under other voting rules is due to the reduction by the group of the incidences of no-choice outcomes, rather than an upgrading of the quality of choices in cases in which agreement was reached. The incidence of "no decisions" fell from 17.7% when majority was first to 5.4% when it was second and 4.0% when it was used last. In contrast, the deterioration of performance under veto rule is due *entirely* to a substantial increase in "no-decision" outcomes when it appeared later in the sequence. No decisions rose from 5.5% to 11.2% and finally 19.5%. This may be due in part to a breakdown of trust under an uneven power distribution, after having voted under the more egalitarian majority and veto rules.

In general, trust appeared to be an important element in the absence of communication. When asked by the experimenter at the end of each session why he had not simply voted for Plan T throughout the trials in order to earn the greatest average payoff, the typical subject said that he could not trust his fellow committee members to vote for Plan T when *his* "turn" for a 5 point payoff came up. Had we asked each group member to cast a single vote which would be in force for the entire series of trials, the need for "trust-in-reciprocation" would be lessened and many groups might have agreed on Plan T. It seems reasonable that the equilibrium solution for such an extended game would be Plan T, although we have not attempted to prove it. For a further discussion of the importance of trust in coalition formation, see Lieberman (1964).

If a truncated sample is obtained by eliminating all decisions where no agreement was reached (similar to Bower's truncation procedure), the average number of points earned per trial under each voting rule is nearly constant as a function of position-in-test-sequence. These data were:

1 Majority rule $-4.11, 4.04, 4.56$
2 Unanimity rule $-2.06, 3.13, 3.18$
3 Veto $-3.68, 3.74, 3.87$

The average number of points earned per "successful" trial for each voting rule, when it was tested in the first block of 18 trials, is remarkably close to those predicted by the dominating strategies model. The fact that there was modest improvement on this measure in each voting rule with experience may merely indicate that the group members were extending their horizon beyond a single trial, thus transforming the situation into a multi-period game. Under such conditions, voting behavior more nearly consistent with the long-run, cooperative model would be rational. This of course is a highly tentative inference.

CONCLUSION

Our "committees" were similar to Bower's (1965a, 1965b) foundations in that partial conflict of interest existed among the group members, but we had no counterpart to his "teams". As in Bower's case, our committees performed better under majority rule (and under veto rule) than under unanimity. By truncating the sample (eliminating decisions with no-choice outcomes), this difference was reduced, but, contrary to Bower's finding, not reversed. This is consistent with our expectation, voiced earlier, that restrictive voting rules would improve the quality of group decisions only in those cases complex enough to involve substantial search and analysis. In simple, well-defined decision situations, such as that investigated by us, the pejorative effects of restrictive rules on the *choice* process tend to outweigh any positively stimulating effects on *search* and *analysis* processes. In addition to those effects related to Bower's study, we have demonstrated that the type of voting rule used may have a substantial effect not only on the aggregate quality of the decision outcome, but also on *nature* of the outcome according to whose interests are served by it.

NOTES

1   However, by varying the number of votes which each person has (i.e. the power distribution), studies of coalition formation have *implicitly* varied the voting rule, where the voting rule is defined as the number of *persons* required for group action. See, for example, the paper by William Riker in this volume.

2   One other finding of Bower's is of some interest. "Foundations" performed better than "teams", under majority rule and also (for the truncated sample) under unanimity rule.Thus, contrary to other research on the effects of intragroup competition (Deutsch, 1949), conflict among group members appears to have a positive effect on performance. Conflict, like restrictive voting rules, appears to intensify search and evaluation, even though it makes agreement more difficult. As one of us has argued elsewhere (Pondy, 1966, 1967), whether interpersonal conflict leads to more intensive joint search or to

withdrawal from the group depends upon the stability of the interpersonal relationships. Minor task conflicts, like those in Bower's experiment, generate pressures for joint search, and presumably lead to increased effectiveness. Major conflicts or conflicts which become "personalized" tend to disrupt group stability, induce rigidity and withdrawal, and lead to decreased effectness.

3   Unfortunately, because this project was not funded, no monetary rewards were able to be offered. We had to rely solely on the subjects' competitive instincts. This, of course, is potentially a major flaw in the experimental design. See the Appendix for the exact instructions given to the subjects.

4   We are indebted to Professor Robert Wilson of Stanford University for pointing out that the "dominating strategies" model is not game-theoretic in a pure sense. Under certain conditions, elimination of dominated strategies may not lead to unique equilibria. However, we believe that in this experiment, the dominating strategies model does lead to unique equilibria.

5   Since the above analysis is invariant under a permutation of the players, Plan S is the solution whenever the 2 and 5 point payoffs are available to *different* players. Plan S is also the solution when the 2 and 5 point payoffs are available to the *same* player, as in the payoff configuration below:

	A	B	C
Plan R	1	1	1
Plan S	2	2	0
Plan T	5	0	0

6   Plan R is the solution when the 2 and 5 point payoffs are available to *different* players (three payoff configurations), and Plan S when they are available to the *same* player (six payoff configurations).

7   There is some uncertainty as to the proper number of degrees of freedom. Since both the observed and predicted relative frequencies must sum to unity under each voting rule, it was felt that $n - 6 = 6$ degrees of freedom would be correct.

$$t = \frac{r\sqrt{df}}{\sqrt{1 - r^2}} = 3.8, \quad p < 0.01$$

APPENDIX

Instructions to subjects

This is an experiment on group decision making. You three are to select, by some voting procedure to be described later, a plan for dividing a payoff among yourselves. There will be 54 such trials or votes taken during the experiment. During each trial you will have to choose from among Plan R, Plan S, and Plan T. Under Plan R, each person will receive *one* point. Under Plan S, one person will receive *no* points, and the other two will receive *two* points each. Under Plan T, one person will receive *five* points and the others will receive *no* points. If you are unable to agree on a plan, then no one will receive any points. Each of you has the goal of trying to accumulate as many points as possible during the course of the experiment.

On the record sheet provided to you, you are to keep a record of your vote, the group decision, and your payoff for each trial of the experiment. These record sheets will be collected and compared at the end of the experiment.

Please do not communicate with one another during the experiment.

REFERENCES

Arrow, K. J. *Social Choice and Individual Values.* New York: Wiley, 1963.

Black, D. *The Theory of Committees and Elections.* Cambridge: Cambridge University Press, 1958.

Bower, J. L. The Role of Conflict in Economic Decision Making Groups. *Quarterly Journal of Economics,* 1965, **70**, 253–277. (a)

Bower, J. L. Group Decision Making: A Report of an Experimental Study. *Behavioral Science,* 1965, **10**, 277–289. (b)

Buchanan, J. M., and Tullock, G. *The Calculus of Consent.* Ann Arbour: University of Michigan Press, 1962.

Coleman, J. S. Foundations of a Theory of Collective Decisions. *American Journal of Sociology,* 1966, **71**, 615–627.

Deutsch, M. An Experimental Study of the Effects of Cooperation and Competition upon Group Processes. *Human Relations,* 1949, **2**, 199–231.

Lieberman, B. i-Trust: A Notion of Trust in Three-Person Games and International Affaris. *Journal of Conflict Resolution,* 1964, **8**, 271–280.

Lieberman, B. Combining Individual Preferences into a Social Choice. Research Memo SP-111.2, University of Pittsburgh, Department of Sociology, 1965.

Plott, C. R. A Notion of Equilibrium and Its Possibility Under Majority Rule. *American Economic Review,* 1967, **57**, 786–806.

Pondy, L. R. *Interpersonal Conflict in Organizations: Field Tests of a Formal Model.* Unpublished Ph. D. dissertation, Carnegie-Mellon University. 1966.

Pondy, L. R. Organizational Conflict: Concepts and Models. *Administrative Science Quarterly,* 1967, **12**, 296–320.

Riker, W. An Empirical Examination of Formal and Informal Rules of a Three-Person Game In B. Lieberman & D. Luce, (Eds.), *Proceedings of the Social Choice Conference,* forthcoming.

Thompson, E. A. A Pareto Optimal Group Decision Process. In G. Tullock (Ed.), *Papers on Non-Market Decision Making.* Charlottesville, Virginia: Thomas Jefferson Center for Political Economy. 1966, pp. 133–140.

CHAPTER 2.9

CHOOSING AMONG ALTERNATIVE DISTRIBUTIONS OF REWARDS[1]

LAWRENCE A. MESSÉ

Michigan State University

Suppose that you and another person are serving as subjects in an experiment and have completed a task which provides no basis for evaluative comparisons of performances. The experimenter then says that you alone must decide between two alternative distributions of rewards; that is, you must decide how much you and the other person are to be paid. One alternative (A) would, if chosen, give you $ 4 and him $ 1; the other alternative (B) would give both of you $ 2. Which alternative would you choose?

Some persons would probably choose alternative A, reasoning that, since good fortune provided one with the opportunity to make such a choice, he should make the most of it. Others would also choose alternative A, but for a different reason: the sum of rewards in alternative A ($ 5) is one dollar greater than the sum of rewards in alternative B ($ 4). Those persons who are interested in maximizing the amount of money available to a group, that is, in maximizing the social welfare, would choose alternative A, not because it gave them more per se, but because it gave the group more. On the other hand, some persons would choose alternative B since it gave both participants the same amount.

The example presented above is just one of eighteen such choices that a number of subjects in the present research had to make. Moreover, the decisions of each of these subjects actually determined the amount of money paid him and one other person with whom he was paired. This general procedure was used as a means of measuring the extent to which different senses

16*   243

of fairness affect the ways in which persons distribute rewards. Giving one person total control over the allocation of rewards—unilateral fate control in Thibaut and Kelley's (1959) terminology—allowed him to make choices without regard to the norm of reciprocity. Thus, a subject could choose in a self-interested manner without fear of reprisals, or he could choose a more equal distribution for reasons other than possible future rewards from the other. Therefore, a given subject's choices in the present research must have bene governed, to a great extent, by what he thought was fair.

THE SENSES OF FAIRNESS

For the purpose of the present research, the senses of fairness were defined as cognitive states which determine a person's satisfaction with the distribution of rewards in groups to which he belongs. Further, it was assumed that (a) every person has some sense of fairness which influences his actions, and (b) the sense of fairness can, and does differ from person to person.

A person, placed in the situation outlined above, would be satisfied with a given distribution of rewards to the extent that it did not offend his sense of fairness; moreover, he would be more likely to choose the alternative distribution which was more congruent with that sense. Thus, the senses of fairness are motivating mechanisms, or in other words, *behavioral dispositions* that affect the way a person acts.

The behavioral dispositions of fairness can take a number of different forms. As noted above, what one person feels is fair might be very different from the feelings of another; moreover, what a person feels is fair in one situation might be very different from what he feels is fair in another. This is so because each person's disposition is complex: it is the product of the interaction between a number of different cognitive elements, or subdispositions. Everyone probably has a mixture of all or most of these subdispositions present in his composite sense of fairness, but their relative strengths vary across persons, and situations within a person. Presented below are three subdispositions which are thought to be major contributors to most persons' composite senses of fairness.

a) *Self-interest* is the subdisposition to be concerned with one's own welfare. It can take two basic forms, *individualism* and *competition. Individualism* is the concern to obtain as much for oneself as possible, without regard for the welfare of the other; it is *self-interest* in an absolute sense.

Competition is the concern to obtain, as much as possible, an amount of reward greater than that of the other; it is *self-interest* in a relative sense.

It should be noted that the nature of the task used in the present study limited choices to those pairs of distributions in which an increase in reward to one person was always accompanied by some decrease in reward to the other. Because of this, it was impossible to separate choices motivated by *individualism* from those motivated by *competition*. For this reason, both were subsumed under the more general subdisposition of *self-interest*.

b) *Altruism* is the subdisposition to have the other obtain as much as possible. It operates when one acts to maximize the other's reward with no thought of either helping or hurting oneself. This subdisposition, as defined here, is highly congruent with the concepts of "altruistic love" advanced by Sorokin (1950a, 1950b, 1954) and altruism as viewed by Friedrichs (1957, 1960) and Macdonald (1966). However, it differs to a great extent from Sawyer's (1966) concept of altruism, which is discussed in greater detail below.

c) *Role symmetry.* In the two subdispositions presented above, the actor is primarily concerned with enhancing just one of the two rewards. Other subdispositions motivate the person to consider without distinction the rewards of both persons. Such subdispositions can be called role-symmetric in that interchanging the two persons' rewards would not affect the choice of the actor. Two such role-symmetric subdispositions follow:

1) *Equality* is the subdisposition to have both get the same reward. It operates when one acts to make the rewards of himself and the other more nearly equal.

Table 1 The motivating states of the subdispositions of the senses of fairness in terms of X, the reward to the actor, and Y, the reward to the other person

Subdisposition	Motivation
I. Self Interest	
A. Individualism	Maximize X
B. Competition	Maximize $(X - Y)$
II. Altruism	Maximize Y
III. Role Symmetry	
A. Equality	Minimize $(X - Y)$
B. Social Welfare	Maximize $(X + Y)$

2) *Social welfare* is the subdisposition to maximize the sum of rewards, irrespective of the exact distribution. Here the larger the total reward the better, without regard for who gets how much. It operates when a person acts to increase the amount of reward available without being concerned with how the money is divided.

Table 1 presents a summary of these subdispositions in terms of how they motivate a person to act in regard to his reward, X, and the reward of the other, Y.

Other theoretical treatments related to fairness

The subdispositions of fairness presented above are, in a sense, descriptions of different ways in which a given person can be concerned with his own welfare and that of others. A number of other theoretical treatments also address themselves to this problem. Two of these, Homans' (1961) concept of distributive justice and Sawyer's (1966) concept of interpersonal orientations, seemed most relevant so their relations to the senses of fairness are discussed below.

Distributive justice   The subdispositions *role symmetry* in general, and equality in particular seem to be special cases of distributive justice (Homans, 1961; and to some extent, Piaget, 1965). As defined by Homans, distributive justice, or equity, is that distribution of outcomes in a group where each member's profits (degree of psychological satisfaction minus the value forgone of other rewarding activities) are proportional to his investments (the time and effort it takes to master the skills needed to engage in the activities of the group).[2] Adams (1965) notes that a state of distributive justice for two persons, *P* and *O* can be represented by the equation,

$$\frac{P\text{'s Profits}}{P\text{'s Investments}} = \frac{O\text{'s Profits}}{O\text{'s Investments}}.$$

In the present study the investments of subjects were more–or–less equal, or at least indeterminant, since the task precluded evaluative comparisons. Under these conditions the above equation reduces the requirement for distributive justice to,

$$P\text{'s Profits} = O\text{'s Profits},$$

which is the *equality* form of *role symmetry*.

From this it follows that the above discussion of the senses of fairness applies, for the most part, to those situations where investments (or status) are equal. Where investments are unequal, *role symmetry* would still be concern for both rewards, but with distinctions between persons. However, the subdisposition would still imply symmetry in that both the high-investment and the low-investment person would choose a distribution which favored the former. Again, this differs from *self-interest* where the actor would favor himself, no matter what differences in level of investment, and from *altruism* where the actor would favor the other, no matter what differences.

Interpersonal orientations   Sawyer (1966) developed a conceptual measure (the Altruism Scale) that locates three "interpersonal orientations"—competition, individualism and cooperation—at points along a continuum he identifies as "altruism".[3] He defines:

P = one's own welfare
O = the welfare of the other, and
a = the magnitude of one's concern for the welfare of the other relative to one's concern for one's own welfare.

In Sawyer's scheme a person is considered to maximize the function $P + aO$, where the value of a identifies the direction and magnitude of relative concern for the other's welfare. Though a is a continuous variable, there are three particularly prominent values, each of which corresponds to one of the subdispositions of the present research:

$a = -1$: maximize $P - O$, the same as maximize X − Y,
$a = 0$:   maximize P, the same as maximize X,
$a = 1$:   maximize $P + O$, the same as maximize X + Y.

These three values are named competition, individualism, and cooperation. The subdispositions which correspond to the first-two values are also designated by these names, but the subdisposition which corresponds to cooperation is called, in the present research, *social welfare*.

The Altruism Scale assumes that a person always has some positive regard for his own welfare, and so there is not an exact, finite correspondence to the pure altruism subdisposition (maximize Y) of the present research. It could be approximated by maximizing $P + aO$, where a becomes very large, so that the weight placed upon the other's welfare becomes very great in relation to that placed upon one's own. However, such values of a (10, or 100, e.g.) would be far outside the normal range $(-1$ to $+1)$ defined by the three orientations noted above, and it appears unreasonable to attempt to measure pure altruism by this scale. Sawyer illustrates how values of *a* greater than 1.0 may lead to a mutually detrimental paradox, and from this he argues that −1 to +1 should be considered to constitute a normal range. In fact, the present research, as reported below, confirms the rarity of pure altruism.

As noted above, the Altruism Scale and the subdispositions are similar. However, the one major difference between them is very important, both conceptually and empirically. Unlike the Altruism Scale the subdispositions of fairness allow for the measurement of a preference for equality [by minimizing (X − Y)], which, as reported below, is a frequent response.

Thus, it would seem that the subdispositions of fairness have a great deal in common with both the concept of distributive justice and the system of interpersonal orientations. However they do seem to describe more completely that situation where investments are equal.

THE STRUCTURE OF REWARDS

As stated above, it is believed that a given peron's choice is determined by the interaction of his salient subdispositions with factors in the situation. One such relevant factor, and a focus of this research, is the structure of the alternative rewards from which a person must choose. For any group such a structure can be described by an *n*-dimensional coordinate system, where *n* = the number of group members and points = alternative distributions of rewards. In the present research, *n* = 2, so two axes were necessary and sufficient to describe the structure, and since all rewards were positive, points were limited to the first quadrant. Figure 1 is an example of such a coordinate system, where the abscissa describes the possible rewards to the person making the choices (the chooser), and the ordinate describes the possible rewards to the other (the receiver).

Note first that all points which denote equal rewards to both persons fall on the line that passes through the origin and has a slope of 1.0 (line *L* in Figure 1). All points which fall above this line denote distributions in which the receiver's reward is greater than those of the chooser (e.g. point *R* in Figure 1). Likewise, those points which fall below this line describe distributions in which the chooser's rewards are greater than those of the receiver (e.g., points *P* and *Q* in Figure 1).

Secondly, the sign of the slope of the line which connects any two points describes the nature of the differences in rewards of those two distributions: If the slope is positive (e.g. the slope of $\overline{PQ}$ in Figure 1) then the rewards to both persons differ in the same direction—that is, both are either higher or lower; if the slope is negative (e.g. the slope of $\overline{PR}$ in Figure 1), then the

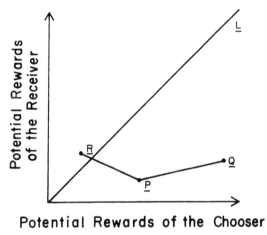

Potential Rewards of the Chooser

Figure 1   A coordinate system describing the reward structure of a two-person group.

difference between distributions in rewards to one person is the opposite of the difference in rewards to the other—that is, the distribution which provides the greater reward to one person provides the lesser reward to the other, and vice-versa. Since it seemed that the choice between a given pair of distributions is trivial if the line which connects them has a positive slope, the present research limited comparisions to those distributions whose connecting lines have negative slopes. This limitation also had the advantage of always providing subjects with a choice where the rewards in one distribution were more alike than were the rewards in the other distribution.

Given that in any comparison one distribution was more disparate than the other, it was thought best to hold constant this disparity. This had the advantage of presenting subjects with a standard to which a number of less disparate distributions could be compared. Moreover, two such standards were used: one in which the chooser received the greater reward, and the other which had the same values, but with the receiver now getting the greater amount. Thus, one standard was the mirror image of the other.

The more equal distributions with which these standards were paired (the alternative outcomes) also were varied in a systematic manner. First, the alternative outcomes differed in respect to relative welfare; that is, a given distribution of rewards could give the chooser more than the receiver, the same as the receiver, or less than the receiver. Secondly, the alternative outcomes differed in terms of social welfare; a given distribution could have a sum of rewards greater than that of the standard, equal to that of the standard, or less than that of the standard.

In sum, three dimensions of the reward structure were systematically varied in the present research: (a) the relative welfare of the standard distri-

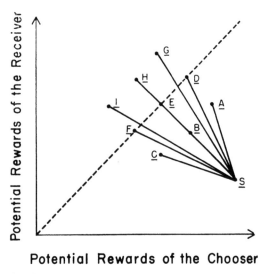

Potential Rewards of the Chooser

Figure 2   The nine Series X Comparisons—where the standard distribution gives the chooser more than the receiver.

bution; (b) the relative welfare of the alternative outcome; and (c) the social welfare of the alternative outcome. Since each dimension is independent of the other two, 18 unique comparisons between standard and alternative were generated (2 conditions of relative welfare of standard X 3 conditions of relative welfare of alternative X 3 conditions of differences in social welfare). The nine comparisons of alternative outcomes with the standard which gives the chooser more (the Series X comparisons) are described in Figure 2; the nine comparisons of alternative outcomes with the standard which gives the receiver more (the Series Y comparisons) are described in Figure 3.

Note that the two figures are mirror images of each other. Thus, in both series, comparisons $\overline{SA}$, $\overline{SB}$, and $\overline{SC}$ have alternative outcomes which give the greater reward to the person who also has the greater reward in the standard distribution; comparisons $\overline{SD}$, $\overline{SE}$, and $\overline{SF}$ have alternative outcomes which give the same reward to both no matter who receives more in the standard distribution; and comparisons $\overline{SG}$, $\overline{SH}$, and $\overline{SI}$ have alterna-

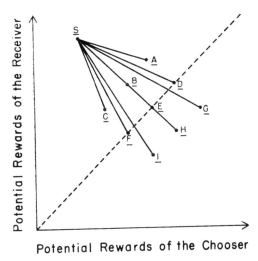

Potential Rewards of the Chooser

Figure 3 The nine Series Y comparisons—where the standard distribution gives the receiver more than the chooser.

tive outcomes which give the greater reward to the person who receives the lesser reward in the standard distribution. Also, in both series, comparisons $\overline{SA}$, $\overline{SD}$, and $\overline{SG}$ have alternative outcomes whose social welfare is greater than that of the standard distribution; comparisons $\overline{SB}$, $\overline{SE}$, and $\overline{SH}$ have alternative outcomes whose social welfare is equal to that of the standard distribution; and comparisons $\overline{SC}$, $\overline{SF}$, and $\overline{SI}$ have alternative outcomes whose social welfare is less than that of the standard distribution.

The exact amount of each reward used in the present research was selected to be congruent with this general structure. Since the experimental session was about one and one-half hours in length, an average reward of $2.50 seemed reasonable. For this reason, the values of the rewards in the two standard distributions were selected to be $4 and $1: in Series X the $4 was the reward of the chooser; in Series Y it was the reward of the receiver.

Table 2 The 18 choice situations classified by the relative welfares of the standard
distributions and the alternative outcomes

	Series X: X > Y in the Standard Distribution				
	Rewards in Standard Distribution		Increase or Decrease in Social Welfare of Alternative Outcome	Rewards in Alternative Outcome	
	X	Y		X	Y
			X > Y in Alternative Outcome		
A	$4	$1	+$1	$3.50	$2.50
B	$4	$1	0	$3.00	$2.00
C	$4	$1	−$1	$2.50	$1.50
			X = Y in Alternative Outcome		
D	$4	$1	+$1	$3.00	$3.00
E	$4	$1	0	$2.50	$2.50
F	$4	$1	−$1	$2.00	$2.00
			X < Y in Alternative Outcome		
G	$4	$1	+$1	$2.50	$3.50
H	$4	$1	0	$2.00	$3.00
I	$4	$1	−$1	$1.50	$2.50
	Series Y: X < Y in the Standard Distribution				
			X < Y in Alternative Outcome		
A	$1	$4	+$1	$2.50	$3.50
B	$1	$4	0	$2.00	$3.00
C	$1	$4	−$1	$1.50	$2.50
			X = Y in Alternative Outcome		
D	$1	$4	+$1	$3.00	$3.00
E	$1	$4	0	$2.50	$2.50
F	$1	$4	−$1	$2.00	$2.00
			X > Y in Alternative Outcome		
G	$1	$4	+$1	$3.50	$2.50
H	$1	$4	0	$3.00	$2.00
I	$1	$4	−$1	$2.50	$1.50

In respect to relative welfare in the alternative outcomes, when rewards differed, they always did so by exactly $ 1. Also, if the social welfare of an alternative outcome differed from that of the standard distribution, it always did so by $ 1. Table 2 presents the 18 comparisons, or choice situations, which were actually used to measure the senses of fairness.

Reading across a row of Table 2, the first column is the identification letter for a given comparison of distributions; note that these letters correspond to those used to identify the points representing alternative outcomes in Figures 2 and 3. The second and third columns contain the amounts of reward given the chooser and receiver in the standard distribution. The fourth column contains the amount the social welfare of the alternative outcome differs from that of the standard distribution. The fifth and sixth columns contain the rewards given the chooser and receiver in the alternative outcome. For example, Series X, comparison D, has standard distribution rewards of $ 4 for the chooser and $ 1 for the receiver, while the alternative outcome gives both persons $ 3. For this comparison the social welfare of the alternative outcome is $ 1 greater than it is in the standard distribution.

From a person's choices, it is possible to infer the strength of the various subdispositions—that is, it is possible to measure his composite sense of fairness—by comparing the two choice situations which are the mirror images of each other; in other words, the two situations where the values of X and Y in both distributions are interchanged from one to the other. In Table 2 (and Figures 2 and 3) each member of these pairs of situations is separated into the two different series, but identified by the same letter. For example, Series X, situation B, and Series Y, situation B, are the mirror image of each other. For each of these pairs, there are three ways to choose.

a) *Self-interest* Choose whichever gives you the most—i.e. standard distribution when it gives you more (Series X), alternative outcome when it gives you more (Series Y).

b) *Altruism* Choose whichever gives the other most—i.e. standard distribution when it gives him more (Series Y), alternative outcome when it gives him more (Series X).

c) *Role symmetry* Choose the same (standard distribution or alternative outcome) in both Series X and Series Y. Moreover, in three of the pairs, *equality* can be separated from *social welfare*. Choose the alternative outcome in both comparisons of pair (Series) X (situation) C–YC, pair XF–YF, and pair XI–YI, and you display a stronger motivation for *equality* than for *social welfare*; choose the standard distribution in both comparisons of these three pairs and you display a stronger motivation for *social welfare*.

HYPOTHESES

A number of predictions were made in regard to both the overall frequencies with which these senses of fairness would be displayed and the effects of differences in reward structure. In general, Homans' (1961) theory of distributive justice and the results of a number of empirical studies provided the bases for these hypotheses.

Frequency

As stated above, Homans (1961) theorizes that a person will be satisfied with a distribution of rewards to the degree that profits are proportional to investments. In terms of the present research equity was equal rewards since both investments and costs were assumed to be the same for all subjects. However, subjects were recruited by offers of monetary renumeration. Therefore, it was thought that they would be concerned with enhancing their own welfare, as well as with feelings of equity.

Thus, it seemed likely that most subjects would be motivated by two opposing subdispositions: on the one hand their *self-interest* would motivate them to maximize their own welfare; on the other hand, concerns with equity and social welfare would motivate them to choose *role-symmetrically*. However, a number of empirical studies (e.g. Arrowood, 1961; Adams and Jacobsen, 1964) have shown that subjects will work longer, harder, or better when they have been led to believe that they are being over-paid. These results imply that concerns with equity are somewhat stronger than *self-interest*. Therefore, it was predicted that *role-symmetric* responses would be more frequent than *self-interested* responses which, in turn, would be more frequent than *altruistic* responses.

The argument advanced above also is relevant to the prediction of differences in frequency between the two separate *role-symmetric* responses, *equality* and *social welfare*. Since investments were equal in the present research situation, equity is equality, and the number of *role-symmetric* responses attributable to *equality* should be greater than those attributable to *social welfare*. This hypothesis is supported further by the results of a bargaining study (Morgan and Sawyer, 1967) where pairs of subjects with potentially asymmetric payoffs tended to agree on equality even though this outcome yielded a relatively poor sum of rewards. Further support is provided by studies (Wright, 1942; Ugurel-Semin, 1952) which demonstrate that as children grow older they tend to divide rewards more equally.

Effects of reward structure

Taken as a whole the theory of distributive justice and the research findings presented above imply that there are normative constraints placed upon a person's *self-interest* such that he feels more or less compelled to be concerned with the welfare of the other. In fact, Homans (1961) proposes that a person will actually experience feelings of guilt when he perceives that a distribution of rewards is both inequitable and in his favor. It follows from this that a person might seek to rationalize his *self-interested* behavior so that violations of these norms would weigh less heavily on his conscience. In other words, he might look for factors in the situation which provide other reasons than naked *self-interest* for his behaving in a *self-interested* manner.

Two such factors might be the different conditions of relative and social welfare. Thus a person might choose the alternative outcome in a Series Y comparison because it divided rewards more equally, but choose the standard distribution in the mirror-image Series X comparison because the alternative outcome had a lower social welfare, or because it gave the other more than it gave him. Therefore, it was predicted that the frequency of *self-interested* and *role-symmetric* responses would be a function of the relative and social welfare of the alternative outcomes.

To be more specific, it was predicted that the frequency of *role-symmetric* responses would be greatest and the frequency of *self-interested* responses would be least when (a) the social welfare of the alternative outcomes of the Series X comparisons was greater than that of the standard distribution, and (b) the social welfare of the alternative outcomes of the Series Y comparisons was less than that of the standard distribution. Further, it was predicted that the frequency of *role-symmetric* responses would be least and the frequency of *self-interested* responses would be greatest when (a) the social welfare of the alternative outcomes of the Series X comparisons was less than that of the standard distribution, and (b) the social welfare of the alternative outcomes of the Series Y comparisons was greater than that of the standard distribution. When the social welfares were equal, it was predicted that the frequencies of *role-symmetric* and *self-interested* responses would be between the two extremes.

Likewise, it was predicted that *role symmetry* would be greatest and *self-interest* least when the reward of the chooser in the Series X alternative outcomes was greater than that of the receiver, and when the reward of the chooser was less than that of the receiver in the Series Y alternative outcomes. Further, it was predicted that *role symmetry* would be least and *self-interest* would be greatest when the reward of the chooser was less than that of the receiver in the Series X alternative outcomes, and when the reward to the chooser was greater than that of the receiver in the Series Y alternative outcomes. When rewards in the alternative outcomes were equal, it was predicted that *role symmetry* and *self-interest* would have frequencies which were between the two extremes.

METHOD

Subjects and recruitment

Since it was essential that subjects were placed in a meaningful situation where their choices actually mattered to them, an attempt was made to recruit persons who would be interested in a monetary reward. Therefore, it was crucial that they not just volunteered, but that they volunteered to "make some money." To this end, five undergraduate classes taught at the Chicago Circle Campus of the University of Illinois were approached for subjects. In each class students were asked to take part in an opinion survey and told that participants would be paid up to four dollars for their time. In this manner, 16 subjects were recruited for each of eight sessions. Therefore, 128 subjects were used, 64 males and 64 females.

Reward distribution booklet

The sets of distributions presented in Table 2 in terms of standard distributions and alternative outcomes, were given more neutral labels—Alternative A and Alternative B, respectively—and put in the form of an 18 page booklet, with one set per page, A sample from this Reward Distribution Booklet is presented as Table 3. The nine sets in Series X were randomized, and this order determined the page upon which a given choice appeared. This same order was used for the Series Y sets as well. Thus, a set and its mirror image appeared in the same position within each series.

Table 3   A sample choice situation

	Alternative A You get $ 4.00 and He gets $ 1.00	Alternative B You get $ 3.50 and He gets $ 2.50
1. Which alternative gives you the most? A or B? (Check one)	_____	_____
2. Which alternative, if either, gives the greater total to the two of you, together? Check A or B. If the two give the same total, check "Equal" <center>Equal</center>	_____	_____
3. Which alternative gives the two of you more nearly the same? A or B? (Check one)	_____	_____
Skip the question below: go on to the next page		

Choice XI:
Which alternative set of payments would
you rather see used? A or B? (Check one)   _____   _____

Remember: If this choice is the one drawn, you and he will be paid just the amounts you now choose.

Non-evaluative task

Subjects were presented with four separate questionnaires as the task used as the excuse to pay them. One instrument was a 134-item "Opinion Survey" which asked the subjects to respond to each statement on a seven-point scale ranging from strong agreement to strong disagreement. The first 30 items comprised the Rand Scale (Messe, 1968). The remainder of the Opinion Survey was composed of items from the "Personality/Altitude Schedule for use in Experimental Bargaining studies" (PAS) (Shure and Meeker, 1965), intermixed.

A second instrument, the "Temperament Inventory," was composed of 15 items from the PAS, and asked subjects to respond on a three-point scale. A third instrument was additional PAS items presented as 10 paired comparisons. The fourth instrument was the 30 item "Survey of Interpersonal Values" (Gordon, 1960).

Design and procedure

To insure both that choosers fully realized that they were paired with a real person, and that the identities of those paired together were kept from each other when the choices were being made, subjects were run in groups. In a given group, half the subjects were choosers and half were receivers; a given chooser, when responding, knew that he was paired with one of the receivers, but he could not tell exactly which one. For reasons of experimental control, every chooser within a given group had to be of the same sex. Likewise, the sex of every receiver in a group had to be the same.

The same procedure, outlined below, was used for all eight groups of subjects. For a group, subjects were randomly assigned to alternate seats in a classroom. Each subject was given a pencil, a folder that contained the personality inventories, and a sealed envelope that contained the Reward Distribution Booklet. First, the subjects were asked to open up their folders and complete the inventories. This task was completed in 35 to 40 minutes.

The experimenter then told the group that the remaining time would be spent determining how much each person in the group was to be paid. Subjects opened up their envelopes and the experimenter instructed them in the use of the Reward Distribution Booklet. He explained that the room had been divided in half, and each person in the front, a chooser, was to determine both his own payment and that of one person in the back, a receiver.

The experimenter then instructed the subjects in the use of the Booklet. He told the receivers that they too should make choices, but their responses would be hypothetical. He then demonstrated how payments would actually be made. Subjects were shown how one of each chooser's responses would be selected by chance, and this choice used to pay that chooser and his receiver.

Subjects went through the Booklet once, answering the first three questions on each page. Then, they went through the Booklet again, answering the fourth question, which indicated their choice of distributions. Finally, the experimenter collected the Booklets and paid the subjects. In all, a given session lasted about 1 hour and thirty minutes.

RESULTS

Following the procedure described above, the number of *role symmetric, self-interested, altruistic, equality,* and *social welfare* responses was tabulated for each subject. Since these were nine sets of mirror-image pairs, a subject's score for *role symmetry, self-interest,* and *altruism* could range from zero to nine, and his total across the three types of responses always equaled nine. Moreover, since there were three mirror-image pairs in which *equality* and *social welfare* were opposed, both these scores could range from zero to three and could total no more than three.

Since only their responses really determined rewards, just the data from the 32 males and 32 females who served as choosers are presented below. It should be noted that females had significantly higher *role symmetry* scores and significantly lower *self-interest* scores than did males. However, since the relative differences between frequencies and the effects of differences in reward structure were highly similar for both sexes, only the analysis based upon the combined sample are reported.

Frequencies

Table 4 presents the frequencies of the three general sense of fairness scores. As indicated, there were more *role symmetry* responses than *self-*

Table 4 Frequencies of responses based upon the three general senses of fairness

	Role Symmetry	Self-Interest	Altruism	Total Response
	Sense of Fairness			
Frequency	330	240	6	576

interested responses and more *self-interest* responses than *altruism* responses, and this overall difference in frequencies was significant ($X_r^2 = 98.2, df = 2, p < 0.001$; Friedman analysis of variance). Moreover, the difference between *altruism* and *self-interest* scores when compared alone was also significant ($z = 7.88, p < 0.00001$; sign test) as was the difference between *self-interest* and *role symmetry* scores ($z = 2.02, p < 0.03$; sign test).

In respect to the two general types of *role symmetry* responses, 312 were alternative outcome-alternative outcome choices and 18 were standard distribution-standard distribution choices, a significant difference ($z = 7.28,$

17*

$p < 0.00001$; sign test). The difference in frequencies of the *role symmetry* responses attributable solely to either *equality* (67) or *social welfare* (17) also was significant ($z = 2.99$, $p < 0.002$; sign test).

Effects of differences in reward structure

As noted above, a number of hypotheses were generated which predicted the effects of differences in reward structure on both *role symmetry* and *self-interest* scores. However, since the two scores correlated across subjects -0.988, the opposite of any statement made about *role symmetry* would be true of *self-interest*. Because of this, only the effects of differences in reward structure on *role symmetry* are reported below. Moreover, since the effects of differences in social welfare did not interact with the effects of differences in relative welfare, each variable is examined separately.

Effects of social welfare

A clear understanding of the effects of differences in social welfare is obtained only when *role symmetry* responses are separated into standard distribution-standard distribution choices and alternative outcome-alternative outcome choices. This is so because differences in social welfare between standard distributions and alternative outcomes should have the opposite effect on each type of *role symmetry* response.

As Table 5 indicates, this was indeed the case: as the difference in social welfare changed from favoring the alternative outcome though no difference to favoring the standard distribution, the number of alternative outcome-

Table 5 Frequencies of the two types of *role symmetric* responses classified by the social welfare of the alternative outcomes

Type of *Role Symmetric* Response	Social Welfare of Alternative Outcome			Total Responses
	Greater than Standard Distribution	Equal to Standard Distribution	Less than Standard Distribution	
Alternative outcome-Alternative Outcome	131	114	67	312
Standard Distribution-Standard Distribution	0	1	17	18

alternative outcome, *role symmetry* choices decreased; the overall difference in frequency was significant ($X_r^2 = 19.38, p < 0.001$; Friedman analysis of variance). The difference between the number of choices made when the social welfare favored the alternative outcome and when the social welfare was equal was significant ($p < 0.005$, sign test), as was the difference between the number of choices made when the social welfare was equal and when it favored the standard distribution ($z = 6.92, p < 0.00001$; sign test).

On the other hand, as the difference in social welfare changed from favoring the alternative outcome through no difference to favoring the standard distribution, the number of standard distribution-standard distribution, *role symmetry* choices increased; however, the overall difference in frequency was not significant ($X_r^2 = 2.10, p < 0.4$, Friedman analysis of variance). When examined separately, the difference in frequency between choices made when the social welfare favored the alternative outcome and when it was equal was not significant, but the difference in frequency between choices made when the social welfare was equal and when it favored the standard distribution was significant ($p < 0.001$; sign test).[5]

Effects of relative welfare

As with social welfare, it is important to differentiate between the two general types of *role symmetry* scores when the effects of differences in relative welfare are examined. Moreover, it is also important to note the series of the alternative outcomes whose relative welfares seem more relevant to a given type of *role symmetry* score. For alternative outcome-alternative outcome choices the relative welfares of the Series X alternative outcomes are crucial. This is so because a person who was interested in having a greater reward than the other would tend to choose the alternative outcome in Series Y, but only choose the alternative outcome in Series X when it gave him a greater reward. Likewise, the relative welfares of the Series Y alternative outcomes are crucial to standard distribution-standard distribution choices since a person who was interested in relative welfare would tend to choose the standard distribution in Series X, but only choose the standard distribution in Series Y when the alternative outcome also gave him the lesser reward.

Table 6 presents the two types of *role symmetry* scores classified by the relative welfare of the alternative outcomes of each series. As the relative welfares of the Series X alternative outcomes changed from favoring the reward of the chooser through equality to favoring the reward of the receiver, alternative outcome-alternative outcome choices tended to remain unchanged and then decline sharply. The overall difference was significant ($X_r^2 = 13.24$, $p < 0.01$; Friedman analysis of variance). However, the slight difference between the number of such choices made when relative welfares were equal and when they favored the chooser was not significant ($z = 0.18, p < 0.86$; sign test). The difference between the number of these choices made when relative welfares were equal and when they favored the receiver, on the other hand, was significant ($z = 5.62, p < 0.00001$; sign test).

Table 6 Frequencies of the two types of *Role Symmetric* Responses Classified by the Relative Welfare of the Subjects in the Series X and Series Y Alternative Outcomes

Type of *Role* *Symmetric* Response	Reward of Chooser			Total Responses
	Greater than Reward of Receiver	Equal to Reward of Receiver	Less than Reward of Receiver	
	Series X Alternative Outcome			
Alternative outcome- Alternative Outcome	122	128	62	312
	Series Y Alternative Outcome			
Standard Distribution Standard Distribution	2	3	13	18

As the relative welfare of the Series Y alternative outcomes changed from favoring the chooser through equality to favoring the receiver, the number of standard distribution-standard distribution choices increased. The overall difference was not significant ($X_r^2 = 2.54$, $p < 0.3$; Friedman analysis of variance). Here too, the number of choices when the relative welfare favored the chooser and when rewards were equal did not differ significanthy, but the difference between choices made when rewards were equal and when the relative welfare favored the receiver was significant ($p < 0.003$; sign test).

DISCUSSION

Frequencies

Each of the hypotheses concerning differences in frequencies was supported by the results: the modal sense of fairness was *role symmetry*, there were a substantial number of *self-interest* responses, and very few choices attributable to *altruism*. Within *role symmetry, equality* was favored over *social welfare* as a principle of allocation.

A somewhat unexpected finding was the almost total absence of altruism choices (6 out of 576). Since no chooser had more than one altruism score and no systematic pattern to these choices was apparent, it is likely that most, if not all, of these responses were merely errors. Three explanations of this finding seem plausible. First, it just might be that there are very few true altruists. This is congruent with the tendency for people to admire, to sanctify, and sometimes even to deify those who really seem to be altruists. Secondly, altruism implies a general desire to help others, but mainly to help others who are less fortunate. It is unlikely that any receiver was perceived as being in need, especially since subjects were recruited in the summer, a time when poorer students would be expected to work rather than attend school. Thirdly, *role symmetry*, in itself, is somewhat of an altruistic response in that a chooser gives up some of his reward to increase that of the receiver in one comparison of each mirror-image pair. Thus, a *role symmetry* response could satisfy a person's need to be altruistic at the same time it satisfied his desire for money.

As noted above, the tendency to respond with *role symmetry* in general and *equality* in particular might be a function of norms specific to a culture. For example, the present research found that *equality* was a more salient principle of allocation than was *social welfare*. White (1964), on the other hand, found that peasant children in the Yucatan Peninsula of Mexico, when presented with a bargaining game similar to that used by Morgan and Sawyer (1967), tended to agree on an outcome which maximized social welfare but distributed rewards with the greatest inequality. This was especially true when the experimenter was an American.

White's results imply that less affluent cultures might have different norms concerning the distribution of rewards than does middle-class America. In such cultures it seems reasonable that concerns with maximizing *social welfare* would take precedence over concerns with *equality*. However, there also is evidence that the norm of *equality* is common to more than just American culture. Ugurel-Semin (1952) found a tendency for older children to divide rewards equally in both Switzerland and Turkey. Since Turkish culture is probably about as dissimilar to American culture as is the peasant culture of Mexico, the results of these studies taken together imply that the findings of the present research have some generality, but one should be extremely cautious in extending them to other populations.

Relevance to theory

The results for frequency have relevance for two theories. As noted above, Homans' (1961) theory of distributive justice was the primary basis for the hypotheses of the present research. Therefore, the results indicate that the theory is a valid model of at least one type of social-choice behavior. Moreover, Homans derives three propositions about distributive justice which can be examined in terms of the present findings.[6]

Modified somewhat, these propositions are as follows: (a) if a man perceives an inequity against him, he will feel angry; (b) if a man perceives an inequity in his favor, he will feel guilty; (c) a man is more apt to act to lower his anger than to lower his guilt. Adams (1965) summarized research findings which bear on one or more of these propositions. He concludes that there is a reasonable amount of evidence in support of the first-two, but the third proposition lacks direct empirical confirmation.

The present research provides such a confirmation for the third, as well as for the first-two propositions. In respect to proposition (a), the number of times subjects were "angered" enough by the inequity against them in the standard distribution of Series Y to choose the alternative outcomes (552 out of 576) was significantly different from expected random behavior ($X^2 = 484.00$, $df = 1$, $p < 0.001$). In respect to proposition (b), the number of times subjects were made to feel "guilty" by the inequity in their favor in the standard distribution of Series X, and therefore chose the alternative outcomes (318 out of 576) also was significant ($X^2 = 6.25$, $df = 1$, $p < 0.02$). In respect to proposition (c), the number of times subjects acted to lower their "anger" (552) was significantly greater than the number of times they acted to lower their "guilt" (318) ($X^2 = 62.94$, $df = 1$, $p < 0.001$).

The results also have relevance for game theory when it is used as a descriptive model. To be specific, they call into question the assumption of game theory and most game experiments that utilities correspond to outcomes (e.g., Rapoport, 1966). For example, in a one trial Prisoner's Dilemma game, it is always better to compete since, no matter what the other does, a person always maximizes his reward by doing so. Thus, if outcomes correspond to utilities, game theory would predict that a person would compete in this situation irrespective of what the other does. Further, for the same reason, it should be irrelevant whether or not the person knows the choice of the other: he should always maximize his utility by maximizing his reward.

In some respects the Series X comparisons are equivalent to a Prisoner's Dilemma game where the person knows in advance that the other has chosen cooperatively. If a person in the present research chose the standard distribution, it would be as if he were competing in that Prisoner's Dilemma situation; if he chose the alternative outcome, it would be as if he were cooperating. The subjects in the present research chose the alternative outcome 318 times out of 576. Thus, it is as if they had cooperated 55 per cent of the time in a situation where game theory predicts competition. From this, it seems obvious that utilities do not always correspond to outcomes, unless those outcomes take into account the utility for some people of conforming to the norm of fairness.

Effects of differences in reward structure

It was predicted that differences in reward structure would have an effect on responses to the extent that they did or did not give persons a reason in addition to *self-interest* for choosing in a self-interested manner. Although the results did not conform exactly to the specific hypotheses, they still were congruent with this basic premise. It is apparent from the data that, contrary to predictions, for standard distribution-standard distribution responses, situations where the social welfare of the alternative outcome exceeded that of the standard distribution were equivalent to situations where the social welfares were equal; and likewise, for both types of responses, situations where the relative welfare of the alternative outcome favored the chooser were equivalent to situations where rewards were equal.

However, there was one condition of social welfare (where it favored the standard distribution) which did affect standard distribution-standard distribution responses in a manner different from the other two conditions. Likewise, both types of *role symmetry* responses were affected by one condition of relative welfare (where the alternative outcome favored the receiver) in a manner different from the other two. Thus it seems that these two conditions provided the best rationale for choosing the more disparite standard distribution. In some cases these two conditions gave subjects an excuse to choose *self-interestedly*, while the other conditions did so to a much lesser extent. This implies that the norm of *role symmetry* is more powerful than at first thought since not all potential reasons for its violation were equally attractive to the subjects.

CONCLUSION

It is a fundamental fact of social science that men can live together because they develop norms, or rules of conduct, which guide their interpersonal relations. Such rules can only serve their purpose to the extent that members of the group are willing to conform to them. The present research indicates that the norm of fairness, manifested in *role symmetry*, has, to some extent, the power to affect behavior.

It might be argued that the situation used to study the senses of fairness presented subjects with trivial decisions; that is, their behavior might have been very different if they had to choose among distributions of rewards which involved thousands of dollars, or even just hundreds of dollars. This is certainly a possibility, but it is somewhat beside the point. Persons in real life make relatively few decisions that would be equivalent to choosing among distributions which involve hundreds of dollars. Instead they tend to make many, rather pedestrian decisions which certainly affect welfares, but when taken alone do so to a small extent. It is precisely these sorts of everyday decisions, hopefully modeled by the choice situations, which are mediated to some degree by the senses of fairness. If so, then the present research indicates that, among other reasons, men can live together and function as a group because they conform to a norm which says that they should consider the welfare of others.

NOTES

1 This paper is an adaptation of the author's doctoral dissertation presented to the faculty of the Department of Psychology, Division of Social Scienes, of the University of Chicago. The research was supported by United States Public Health Service Grant MH 05350, "Experiments in the Resolution of Interpersonal Conflict", Jack Sawyer, principal investigator. The author wishes to thank Dr. Sawyer, both for making the necessary funds available, and for his assistance during all phases of this

research. Additional support was provided by USAF Office of Scientific Research Grant F 44620–69–C–0114. The assistance of Susan Messé and Maryann Taranowski is also gratefully acknowledged.

Thanks also go to Roger L. Dominowski and I. E. Farber, Department of Psychology, and Robert L. Hall, John W. Martin, William S. Place, James Wilkins, and Joseph Zelan, Department of Sociology, The University of Illinois, Chicago Circle Campus, for their help in recruiting subjects.

2 The more general concept of status (social worth) might be a useful substitute for investments in this definition. Investment can be viewed as one determinant of achieved status; there are others, such as quality of output, which might also be relevant to distributive justice. Moreover, by limiting oneself only to considerations of investments, the possibility of distributive justice based upon an ascribed-status system is also overlooked.

3 The author acknowledges Sawyer's system as the theoretical basis for the above discussion of the senses of fairness, and the Altruism Scale (the instrument developed to measure interpersonal orientations) as the methodological starting point for the choice situation booklet used in the present research.

4 It could be argued that $P + a0$, $a > 0$, implies a concern for equality, especially when $a = +1$, since the formula then indicates a dual concern for self and other. If this is indeed the case, then the altruistic orientation corresponds to the *equality* subdisposition, but there is no orientation which corresponds to the *social welfare* subdisposition.

5 Notice that the 17 standard distribution-standard distribution choices made when the social welfare favored the standard distribution are the *social welfare* scores reported above.

6 For some reason Homans elevated only one of these to the status of a formal proposition. However, since the other two seem of equal importance, no distinction is made between them here.

REFERENCES

Adams, J. S. Inequity in social exchange. In L. Berkowitz (Ed.), *Advances in Experimental Social Psychology*. Vol. 2. New York: Academic Press, 1965.

Adams, J. S., and Jacobsen, P. R. Effects on wage inequities on work quality. *Journal of Abnormal and Social Psychology*, 1964, **69**, 19–25.

Arrowood, A. J. *Some effects of productivity of justified and unjustified levels of reward under public and private conditions*. Unpublished doctoral dissertation, University of Minnesota, 1961.

Friedrichs, R. W. *An exploratory study of altruism*. Unpublished doctoral dissertation, University of Wisconsin, 1957.

Friedrichs, R. W. Alter versus ego: an exploratory study of altruism, *American Sociological Review*, 1960, **XXV**, 496–508.

Gordon, L. W. *Manual for the Survey of Interpersonal Values*. Chicago: Science Research Associates, 1960.

Homans, G. C. *Social Behavior: Its Elementary Forms.* New York: Harcourt, Brace & World, 1961.

Macdonald, S. L. *Altruism: a study of means and ends.* Unpublished honors thesis, Radcliffe College, 1966.

Messé, L. A. *Parameters of fair play: an investigation of differences in the just distribution of rewards,* Unpublished doctoral dissertation, University of Chicago, 1968.

Morgan, W. R., and Sawyer, J. Bargaining, expectations, and the preference for equality over equity. *Journal of Personality and Social Psychology,* 1967, **6**, 139–149.

Piaget, J. *The Moral Judgment of the Child.* Trans. M. Gabain. New York: The Free Press, 1965.

Rapoport, A. *Two-Person Game Theory: The Essential Ideas.* Ann Arbor: University of Michigan Press, 1966.

Sawyer, J. The Altruism Scale: a measure of cooperative, individualistic, and competitive interpersonal orientation. *American Journal of Sociology,* 1966, **LXXI**, 409–420.

Shure, G. H., and Meeker, R. J. A personality/attitude schedule for use in experimental bargaining studies. Technical Memorandum (TM-2543), Systems Development Corporation, Santa Monica, California, 1965.

Sorokin, P. A. Affiliative and hostile tendencies of college students. In P. A. Sorokin (Ed.), *Explorations in Altruistic Love and Behavior: A symposium.* Boston: Beacon Press, 1950.

Sorokin, P. A. *Altruistic Love, a Study of American Good Neighbors* and *Christian Saints.* Boston: Beacon Press, 1950.

Sorokin, P. A. Dynamics of interpersonal friendship and enmity. In P. A. Sorokin (Ed.), *Forms and Techniques of Altruistic and spiritual Growth: a Symposium.* Boston: Beacon Press, 1954.

Thibaut, J. W., and Kelley, H. H. *The Social Psychology of Groups* New York: Wiley, 1959.

Ugurel-Semin, R. Moral Behavior and moral judgments in children. *Journal of Abnormal and Social Psychology,* 1952, **47**, 463–474.

White, W. L. Cross-cultural bargaining and game behavior. *Proceedings of the IX Congress of the Inter-American Society of Psychology,* 1964, 555–561.

Wright, B. Altruism in children and the perceived conduct of others. *Journal of Abnormal and Social Psychology,* 1942, **37**, 218–233.

CONTROL OF COLLECTIVITIES AND THE POWER OF A COLLECTIVITY TO ACT

JAMES S. COLEMAN[1]

Johns Hopkins University

The distribution among the members of formal control over a collectivity's actions is an important element of constitutions. The exercise of such control is mediated by decision rules, which may be very complex, involving preliminary decisions by sub-collectivities within the larger collectivity. Framers of constitutions pay very special attention to the distribution of control and to the form of the decision rules, for these determine in large part the power of various members of the collectivity as well as the power of the collectivity vis-a-vis the members. Illustrations that give some intuitive feel for this are easily found. The bicameral form of the U.S. Congress, with equal representation of states in one, and equal representation of individuals in the other, and with a requirement that legislation be affirmed by both bodies, is one example—because there were, and are, two types of members of the United States, individual citizens as members and states as members. This paradoxical state of affairs, in which a federal body has a members both the constituent states and the members of these constituent states, was arrived at as one aspect of the resolution of the problem of sovereignty of states vs. sovereignty of the nation, and obviously reflects the outcome of a struggle between states with many persons and states with few, a struggle documented by numerous political historians.

Another example of a decision rule reflecting the different status of individual members and giving a heuristic sense of the power of the collectivity to act is the United Nations Security Council. The Security Council originally had eleven members, including five permanent, taking action upon a positive vote of seven of the eleven members, not a bare majority of six, but only under the condition that the positive votes include those of each permanent member. This innocuous-sounding procedure masks two points that become obvious upon some further examination of the rule: first, that the permanent members have allocated no power to the Security Council whatsoever, because each retains a veto; and second, that the relative control of the body's action by the permanent and temporary members is very skewed indeed, since no action can be taken without the vote of a permanent member, while an action can be taken without the votes of as many as four of the six temporary members.

Despite the importance of these formal structures for controlling the action of collective bodies, little theoretical work has been devoted to their analysis. In this paper, I will develop modes of analysis that offer some answers to the questions posed by constitutions, providing some mathematical analysis of situations which, though they can be stated quite precisely (as they are in constitutions) have hardly been subject to such analysis.

THE SHAPLEY–SHUBIK MEASURE OF POWER

There has been one major approach to the problem of describing the power of members of a collectivity by analysis of the decision rule, a measure proposed by Shapley and Shubik (1956). Subsequent to that work, there have been several applications made of the Shapley-Shubik measure, and numerous discussions of the measure, but little serious analysis of the problem of collectivity control and collectivity power other than by applications of this measure.

I propose here to examine in some detail both the problem of the distribution of control of the actions of a collectivity by its members and the problem of the power of the collectivity to act. One useful way to begin this is by examination of the Shapley-Shubik measure, which has some remarkable properties, and which is unique in these properties. In presenting a measure for the power of a member in a game, or any collectivity with a well-defined decision rule, Shapley and Shubik propose a measure that has the following three properties:

a)   The measure of a member's power inheres in his structural position in the collectivity defined by the rules, and in any relabelling, the procedure will reassign to members power measures according to the structural position, and not the new labels assigned to them.

b) The measures of power are additive: if total control over the actions of the collectivity is counted as unity, then the sum of the measures of power of members will sum to one. If $\phi_i(N)$ is the measure of power of individual i in collectivity N, and the members of the collectivity are labelled $i = 1, \ldots, n$, then

$$\phi_1(N) + \cdots + \phi_n(N) = 1$$

c) If an individual has a given amount of power in one collectivity x, and a given amount of power in another collectivity y defined over the same members but with a different constitution (as an example, the power in the House of Representatives and in the Senate of an individual citizen from a given sized congressional constituency in a state of a given size), then his power in the combined collectivity (e.g. the Congress) is the sum of this power in the two separate collectivities.

The remarkable point about the measure developed by Shapley as a measure of the value of a game to a player and used by Shapley and Shubik as a measure of power in a collectivity is that it is the *only* measure fulfilling these conditions. Yet this remarkable fact should be noted and set aside; the crucial question about measures of power in a collectivity (or control of the collectivity's actions) should derive from considerations of the internal structure of the measure, and whether this structure corresponds to what one believes ought to be entailed by a measure of power. Consequently, I will examine the internal structure of this measure—as, of course, many have done before now—preliminary to discussing more generally the questions of control of a collectivity's action by its members and the power of the collectivity itself to act.

As a way of introducing consideration of the Shapley-Shubik measure, its background is important. Shapley developed the measure as a measure of the value of a game to its players—reasoning that the expected value of the game for a player is the value that he can expect to get out of it, and that this in turn is directly dependent on *his* value to the winning of the game—that is, his contribution to the coalitions that constitute winning coalitions. The measure is more general than this, because it allows for the fact that in a game, the outcome may be something other than a situation in which the winning coalition wins all—but that is not important for the application to power in collectivities. What is important is that the measure was first obtained as a measure of the value a player can associate with a given game, and that it is based on the important identity between value and power: the value a player associates with a game, the value that he can expect to get from it, is precisely what he can expect to realize from the game, which in turn is his power to affect the outcome of the game.[2]

The origin of the Shapley-Shubik measure of power is important because it gives some sense of the motivation behind the measure, and its intended original purpose. The measure was then adapted as a measure of power in a collectivity by setting the overall value of the game as 1, and determining that a coalition received the value of the game (normalized to unity as indicated) if the coalition was sufficient, according to the rules of the collectivity, to obtain passage of an action by the collectivity. This general orientation is somewhat different, as indicated above, from the usual problem of power in a collectivity, for the usual problem is not one in which there is a division of the spoils among the winners, but rather the problem of controlling the action of the collectivity. The action is ordinarily one that carries its own consequences or distributions of utilities, and these cannot be varied at will, i.e. cannot be split up among those who constitute the winning coalition.[3] Instead, the typical question is the determination of whether or not a given course of action will be taken or not, that is, the passage of a bill, a resolution, or a measure committing the collectivity to an action.

The Shapley measure of value, converted by Shapley and Shubik to a measure of power, is in mathematical form, given by the following expression:

$$\phi_i(N) = \sum \frac{(s-1)!\,(n-s)!}{n!}\,\delta_i(S) \tag{1}$$

where the summation is taken over all subsets of the collectivity of which i is a member,

s is the size of the subset of coalition S of which i is a member,

n is the size of the collectivity as a whole, and

$\delta_i(S)$ is 1 if the subset S including i is a winning coalition but is not a winning coalition without i, and zero otherwise.

Let us consider the total collectivity. In this collectivity, there are $n!$ different orders in which members can cast votes. Consider for each of these orders that each vote is cast in favor until exactly the necessary number of votes for passage is obtained, and then all the remainder are cast against. If we were to list all these sequences, in each one the member whose vote is the last positive vote can be designated as the determining member. In a simple majority voting system in a collectivity with an odd number of members, this would be the member casting the $(N+1)/2$ vote. Since each member is in this position the same number of times, the power of each is $1/n$.

If we count the number of times member i is in this position, and divide by the total number of sequences, this will give the proportion of times he was in a winning position. This is the measure of power, $\phi_i(N)$. It is possible now to reverse the sequence of voting. Then if his positive vote made him the determining member for the positive coalition in the forward sequence, his negative vote would put him in the determining position for a winning negative coalition in the reverse sequence. Thus whether considering positive or negative coalitions, the proportion of times his vote is the determining one is the same, and is $\phi_i(N)$. Obviously the sum of $\phi_i(N)$ over all n members will be one, since in every sequence there is one and only one member whose vote is deciding. Almost as obviously, the member's power in two subcollectivities sum to give his power in the larger collectivity: Consider a collectivity's decision to be the result of decisions by two (or more) subcollectivities. Then if we write these $n!$ sequences, it is again possible to designate the member's vote that determines the outcome in the larger collectivity, even though it does so by determining the outcome of the subcollectivity. Thus for the collectivity as a whole, there are n measures, $\phi_i(N)$, which sum to one and are measures of individual power. But the proportion of times that subcollectivity N_j (with n_j members) is determining is simply the sum of the n_j values of $\phi_i(N)$ for its members. Thus the measure of power of the subcollectivity as a whole is $\phi(N_j)\ [=\sum_{i\varepsilon N_j}\phi_i(N)]$, and the measure of the member's power in the subcollectivity is $\phi_i(N)$, the same as his measure of power in the larger collectivity.[4]

These considerations show that the Shapley-Shubik measure has the properties indicated earlier in condition (ii) and (iii), though of course they do not show that it is the only measure with these properties. But it is useful to examine some implicit assumptions of the measure. It counts each order equally, and since all persons are equally likely to be in a given position, and the vote in a given position is positive in exactly half of the $n!$ orders, it assumes each member is equally likely to vote positive or negative. Secondly, if we look at the list of the $n!$ orders that have been written down, and pick out one in which member i is the determining voter, and regard as the set S (with s members including himself) this particular coalition, then there are other orders in the list in which he is still in the determining position for this same coalition S, but the other members of S and the members of the losing coalition are ordered differently. Altogether, there are $(s-1)!\,(n-s)!$ such orders, for this same coalition S, with him in the determining position. Each of these orders is counted once in forming the measure.

This last property of the measure produces some curious results that can best be seen by example. Thus I will apply this to an example treated by Shapley and Shubik, the original U.N. Security Council, to show the results of this property. There are two types of members, five permanent, with a veto, and six temporary, without, and the voting rule is taken with a majority of seven or more and no vetoes. Since there are only two types of members, I will not show all 11! orders, but only those for which #5 (the last-numbered permanent member) and # 11 (the last-numbered temporary member) are determining. There happen to be 7,939,680 different orders in which #5 is determining, so that I will not list all these, but will merely indicate which orders they include. Those orders for which #5 is determing are:

composition of coalitions positive (determining) negative	number of different orders in these positive and negative coalitions
123467(5)891011	$6!4! = 720 \cdot 24 =$ 17,280
123468(5)791011	17,280
123469(5)781011	17,280
1234610(5)78911	17,280
1234611(5)78910	17,280
123478(5)891011	17,280
123479(5)681011	17,280
1234710(5)68911	17,280
1234711(5)68910	17,280
123489(5)671011	17,280
1234810(5)67911	17,280
1234811(5)67910	17,280
1234910(5)67811	17,280
1234911(5)67810	17,280
12341011(5)6789	17,280
1234678(5)91011	$7!3! = 5040 \cdot 6 \ =$ 30,240
1234679(5)81011	30,240

and 18 more combinations each
involving 3 different members
from the set of 6 temporary members

12346789(5)1011	$8!2! = 40320 \cdot 2 =$ 80,640
123467810(5)911	80,640
	80,640 each (× 13)

and 13 more combinations each
involving 4 different members
from the set of 6 temporary members

1234678910(5)11 $9!1! = 362,880 \cdot 1 = 362,880$

1234678911(5)10   362,880

                                                362,880 each ($\times$ 4)

and 4 more combinations each
involving 5 different members
from the set of 6 temporary members

123123467891011(5) $10!0! = 3,628,800 \cdot 1 = 3,628,800$

Altogether, this gives the following tabulation for member #5:

6–4 coalitions 15 different coalitions	17,280 orders for ea. =	259,200
7–3 coalitions 20 different coalitions	30,240 orders for ea. =	604,800
8–2 coalitions 15 different coalitions	80,640 orders for ea. =	1,209,600
9–1 coalitions 6 different coalitions	362,880 orders for ea. =	2,237,280
10–0 coalitions 1 different coalitions	3,628,800 orders for ea. =	3,628,800
57 different coalitions		7,939,680
		different orders

For member #11, the only coalitions in which he is a determining member are those which include all five permanent members and one temporary member, as follows:

123456(11)78910 $6!4! = 720 \cdot 24 =$ 17,280

123457(11)68910   17,280

123458(11)67910   17,280

123459(11)67810   17,280

1234510(11)6789   17,280

5 different coalitions   86,400 different

                                               orders

According to the Shapley–Shubik measure, the relative power of member #5 and member #11 is 7,939,680 : 86,400, or over 90 : 1, since this is the ratio of the number of differently-ordered coalitions in which these two are the determining members. Adding all the orders in which the five permanent members are determining and all those in which the six temporary members are determining, we can arrive at the proportion of power

18*

held by the permanent five and the temporary six. This is 0.987 for the five, and 0.013 for the six, a result arrived at by Shapley and Shubik in their paper.

This disparity arises from two sources: the greater number of coalitions in which #5 (or the other permanent members) is a determining member, and the greater number of different orders for a given coalition, for most of the coalitions in which #5 is a determining member. For example, in the coalition of the whole, in which #5 is a determining member, there are 210 times as many different orders as in the one type of coalition in which #11 is the determining member. Thus, if for example, #5 was a determining member only in this coalition, and #11 was a determining member only in a single coalition of the 6–4 type, then #5 would have a power index 210 times that of #11, even though both were determining in only one distinct coalition. Such a disparity seems inappropriate, for it is implicitly based on the assumption that the probability that a coalition will form is proportional to the number of different orders that can exist in that coalition. It seems more reasonable to assume that each distinct coalition has the *same* probability of forming. The difficulty, of course, in doing this is that if each distinct coalition is counted only once, with no attention to the order of its members, then there may be several members who could cast the determining vote. The question then arises, to whose credit should it be counted?

Such questions as this arise with any measure of power other than the one which Shapley and Shubnik propose. Its virtue lies in the mathematical properties it exhibits, which prevents this and other questions from arising. Nevertheless, some other questions must be asked about the measure, in view of its properties as just illustrated in the example. First, one might ask whether too high a price has been paid for the mathematical properties, since the resulting measure seems to have at least one unreasonable property, its dependence on the different orders of members of a coalition. Beyond that, however, it is useful to reexamine just what a concept of power should be, just whether it should have the properties taken implicitly as desirable, and whether the Shapley-Shubik measure does indeed have the properties which such a measure should have.

The Shapley measure was initially developed in a context of zero-sum and non-zero sum games, in which there is some "value" of the game, or good which constitutes the expected outcome if the game is rationally played. The Shapley measure of value is a measure of how that value could be expected to be divided among the players, given that each exercised rationally the power given him in the rules or constitution of the game. This realization of value would be arrived at through division of the winnings by the winning coalition.

But the situation posed by decisions in collective bodies is ordinarily quite different. The decision governs an *action* to be taken—or not taken, depending on the outcome—by the collectivity, an action that has a fixed profile of consequences for the members. Thus, since it is not a question of a battle over the division of spoils, as assumed by the Shapley value, one is not concerned directly with the power of members *vis à vis* one another. Instead, several other concepts are important. One is the power of the group to act. Such power may be very small, if there are very few vote outcomes that lead to action, or very large if most outcomes lead to action. Second, there is the power of the member *vis à vis* the acting collectivity; his power to *prevent* action of the collectivity, and his power to *initiate* action of the collectivity—or, in short, his degree of control over the collectivity's actions, in both positive and negative directions. Now it may be useful to compare members of the collectivity with regard to their power to initiate action or their power to prevent action—but since each is exerting that power on the collectivity, the functional comparisons, which pertain directly to the collectivity's action, are between the collectivity's power to act and each member's power to initiate or prevent action.

THE POWER OF COLLECTIVITIES TO ACT

The power of collectivities to act, as provided by a set of constitutional rules, lies in the ease with which individual members' interests in collective action can be translated into actual collective action. If each member has a veto power over the collectivity's action, then this power to act is very small; if any member can initiate action, as in giving a fire alarm, the collectivity's power to act is very great. One might ask why members would devise a constitution that gave a collectivity only very little power to act; but the answer is obvious to anyone who has ever been a member of a collective body: The power of a collectivity to act is the power to act in accord with the aims or interests of some members, but often against the aims or interests of others. Thus for a collectivity of a given size, the greater the power of the collectivity to act, the more power it has to act against the interests of some members.

We may develop a measure of the power of a collectivity to act by using some, but not all, of the ideas behind the Shapley-Shubik measure. That is, we retain the idea of examining all possible subsets, but we count a distinct subset only once, not according to its number of possible different orders. The subset S has the value $v(S) = 1$ if the subset, under the rules of the constitution, is sufficient to make the collectivity act, that is, sufficient to pass a positive action. Otherwise, the value of the subset, $v(S)$, is zero.

In a collectivity of n members, there are 2^n distinct partitions of the collectivity into two subsets, that is, 2^n different subsets favoring the action (including the subset with no members, and the coalition with all members), and for each of these, a complementary subset consisting of the remaining members. For collectivities of five and six members, lists of the distinct partitions are included as Appendix A, for reference use in later examples. Thus a natural measure of the power of the group to act under the constitutional rules is merely the sum of $v(S)$ over all distinct subsets or coalitions S, divided by 2^n:

$$A(N) = \frac{\Sigma v(S)}{2^n} \tag{2}$$

If a collectivity operated under a decision rule in which each member has a veto, that is a unanimity decision rule, the power is at a minimum for this size collectivity, since only the coalition of the whole will give action: $A(N) = 1/2^n$. If the collectivity has an odd number of members, and the decision rule is a majority rule, then exactly half the coalitions will be equal to or greater than the member required for action, $(n + 1)/2$, and $A(N) = 1/2$. In the case of the U.N. Security Council, with a veto for five members and a rule of 2 out of 6 for the other six, there are 57 coalitions out of 2048 in which the collectivity will act, and $A(N) = 57/2048 = 0.0278$.

In a collectivity with an even number of members, where $n/2 + 1$ positive votes are necessary for action, then the power of the collectivity to act is slightly less than $1/2$, since all the coalitions with exactly $n/2$ members fail, whereas it would be necessary for half of them to pass if $A(N)$ were to equal $1/2$. Since there are $n!\left(\dfrac{n}{2}!\dfrac{n}{2}!\right)$ distinct coalitions with exactly half the members, then for an even-membered group with a majority rule,

$$A(N, n/2 + 1) = \frac{1}{2} - \frac{1}{2^{n+1}}\left(\frac{n!}{\dfrac{n}{2}!\dfrac{n}{2}!}\right) \tag{3}$$

More generally, if the decision rule requires a positive vote by m out of n members for passage of an action, then the power of the collectivity is the sum of all those combinations of n members, taken m or more at a time, divided by 2^n;

$$A(N, m) = \frac{\sum_{k=m}^{n} \frac{n!}{k!(n-k)!}}{2^n} \qquad (4)$$

It is interesting to write the expression for the power of the United States to act through legislation. If legislation must pass a committee in the House of Representatives of n_1 members, a committee in the Senate of n_2 members, then pass both bodies by a majority and obtain the President's signature, or pass both by a two-thirds vote without the President's signature, then the total number of subsets or coalitions is $2^{n_1+n_2+100+435+1}$. If the power of the two committees to act, as calculated by Equation (4), is $A(N_1)$ and $A(N_2)$ respectively, then the power of the nation to act through legislation is:

$$A(N) = \frac{A(N_1)A(N_2)}{2^{n_3+n_4}} \left[\frac{1}{2} \sum_k \frac{n_3!}{k!(n_3-k)!} \sum_j \frac{n_4!}{j!(n_4-j)!} \right. $$
$$\left. + \frac{1}{2} \sum_h \frac{n_3!}{h!(n_3-h)!} \sum_r \frac{n_4!}{r!(n_4-r)!} \right] \qquad (5)$$

where the limits of summation are, for k and j,

$$\frac{n_3+1}{2} \leqq k \leqq n_3, \qquad \frac{n_4+1}{2} \leqq j \leqq n_4,$$

and for h and r,

$$\frac{2n_3}{3} \leqq h \leqq n_3, \qquad \frac{2n_4}{3} \leqq r \leqq n_4,$$

and where n_3 and n_4 are the sizes of the House and Senate.

Equation (5) includes, in the first term within brackets, all those partitions of Senate and House from a majority vote up to the total, multiplied by 1/2, which is the power to act of a collectivity consisting of one person, in this case the President, plus all those partitions of Senate and House from a 2/3 majority to unanimity, which are sufficient for passage without the President's assent.

The concept of the power of a collectivity to act can be applied also to those situations in which a public good, or a public bad, can be supplied by only one or a few members of a collectivity. For example, if one person in a community can pollute a stream, then the power of the community to act in polluting the stream is obtained by summing all those partitions except those in which no members are positive:

$$A(N, 1) = 1 - \frac{1}{2^n}. \tag{6}$$

Thus, unless n is very small, $A(N, 1)$ will be close to 1.0. This reflects the difficulties that arise in preventing the creation of public nuisances: the "action of the collectivity" can be initiated by one person, or a few, and does not require assent from the other members of the community. In contrast, the decision rule for those collective actions that can restrain the public nuisance is ordinarily at least a majority vote, a rule that gives the collectivity much less power to act.

However, only a portion of the total problem is treated by examining the power of the collectivity to act. The power of individual members to prevent action or to initiate action must be examined as well. It is to the first of these that I now turn.

THE POWER OF MEMBERS TO PREVENT ACTION

The Shapley-Shubik measure derives a member's power from the number of ordered subsets in which he is the determining member. In the modified context under consideration here, his power as an individual member vis-à-vis the collectivity should derive from the number of subsets (distinct in membership, not in ordering) in which he is a determining member in initiating or preventing the group's action. Since we have just examined the collectivity's power to act, it is natural to examine his power to prevent its action. Following the conception described above, and labelling individual i's power to prevent action $P_i(N)$, it is:

$$P_i(N) = \frac{\sum_S [v(S) - v(S - [i])]}{\sum_S v(S)}, \tag{7}$$

that is, his power to prevent action is the number of subsets in which he is a determining member, divided by the number of subsets in which the collectivity acts. For the special case in which all members have identical roles, and there is a decision rule with m out of n votes necessary for collective action, $P_i(N)$ is a function only of n and m. In this case, $P_i(N)$ can be expressed as $P_i(n, m)$. In this simple case, a reasonably direct way of calculating $P_i(n, m)$ can be given, from the fact that the numerator of Equation (7) is the number of partitions in which his defection would convert passage to failure, and in a simple collectivity with n members and m required for passage, this is the number of combinations of the other $n - 1$ members partitioned so that exactly $m - 1$ of them are positive, or in other words, the combination of $n - 1$ things taken $m - 1$ at a time, or $\dfrac{(n - 1)!}{(m - 1)! \, (n - m)!}$.

The denominator is the sum of the number of combinations of n things taken k at a time, for k from m to n. Thus

$$P_i(n, m) = \frac{\dfrac{(n - 1)!}{(m - 1)! \, (n - m)!}}{\displaystyle\sum_{k=m}^{n} \dfrac{n!}{k! \, (n - k)!}}, \tag{8}$$

or simplifying,

$$P_i(n, m) = \frac{1}{n \displaystyle\sum_{k=m}^{n} \dfrac{(m - 1)! \, (n - m)!}{k! \, (n - k)!}}$$

In the case of the U.N. Security Council, the number of partitionings in which the Council acts is 57, and the number in which any of the first five members is determining is also 57, so that

$$P_1(N) = \frac{57}{57} = 1.0.$$

The power of any of the six temporary members to prevent action is calculated similarly: There are five coalitions out of the 57 in which any one of the temporary members can be deciding, so that

$$P_6(N) = \frac{5}{57} = 0.088.$$

In each case, $P_i(N)$ can be conceived as a fraction of $A(N)$: It is that proportion of all partitions in which the collectivity acts that member i can prevent action. If the proportion is 1.0, as it is when member i has veto power, the collectivity's power to act is exactly counterbalanced by the individual member's power to prevent action. If it is less than one, the member's power to prevent action is only that fraction of the collectivity's power to act.

THE POWER OF MEMBERS TO INITIATE ACTION

By similar considerations, the power of individuals to initiate action may be conceived. The number of partitions in which the individual is determining is the number in which he can, by changing his direction of action, change a negative collective action to a positive one, and thus initiate action. As a measure of the member's power to initiate action, it should be compared to the total number of partitions in which no action occurs.

$$I_i(N) = \frac{\sum_S (v(S + [i]) - v(S))}{\sum_S (1 - v(S))}. \tag{9}$$

For the special case in which all members have identical roles, and the collectivity has a decision rule with m of n required for action, $I_i(N)$ can be written as a function of n and m, $I_i(n, m)$. The method for calculation of $I_i(n, m)$ may be found by considerations similar to those used for finding $P_i(n, m)$. The numerator of Equation (9) is the number of partitions in which individual i's addition would convert failure to passage, and in the simple collectivity, this is merely the number of combinations of the other $n - 1$ members partitional with exactly $m - 1$ positive, or $\dfrac{(n - 1)!}{(m - 1)!\,(n - m)!}$.
The denominator in this case is the total number of partitions of the whole collectivity in which fewer than m members are positive, or $\displaystyle\sum_{k=0}^{m-1} \frac{n!}{k!(n - k)!}$.
Thus after simplifying,

$$I_i(n, m) = \frac{1}{n \displaystyle\sum_{k=0}^{m-1} \frac{(m - 1)!\,(n - m)!}{k!(n - k)!}} \tag{10}$$

In the case of a permanent member of the U.N. Security Council, the numerator is as for $P_i(N)$, and the denominator is $2048 - 57$, to give

$$I_1(N) = \frac{57}{2048 - 57} = 0.0286,$$

and for the temporary members,

$$I_6(N) = \frac{5}{2048 - 57} = 0.0025.$$

Thus the power to initiate action is small for the permanent as well as the temporary members. The permanent members of the security council, in devising this constitution, in effect sacrificed the power of the collectivity to act ($A(N)$), as well as their own power to initiate action, and in return kept complete power to prevent action by the collectivity.

Example Change in U.N. Security Council Rule.

The United Nations Security Council changed its size and its voting rule, increasing the total size to 15 (10 instead of 6 temporary members), and changing the voting rule from 7/11 with no vetoes to 9/15 with no vetoes. It is useful to examine changes in the power of the Council and of the permanent and temporary members by this action. Calculations are below:

$$A(N^*) = \frac{\sum\limits_{k=4}^{10} \dfrac{10!}{k!(10-k)!}}{2^{15}} = \frac{848}{32,768} = 0.0259$$

$$P_1(N^*) = 1.0$$

$$P_6(N^*) = \frac{84}{848} = 0.099$$

$$I_1(N^*) = \frac{848}{32,768 - 848} = 0.0266$$

$$I_6(N^*) = \frac{84}{32,768 - 848} = 0.0026$$

Table 1 compares the structure of power before and after the change. It is evident that the change has been relatively minor. The power of the Council to act has reduced very slightly, as has the power of permanent members to initiate action. The power of the temporary members to prevent action has increased slightly, and their power to initiate action has increased even more slightly.

Since there is a larger number of temporary members, 10 rather than 6, one might be tempted to add their power to prevent or initiate action in the two cases, and compare the sums, which would show a greater difference. This temptation must be resisted, however, because the sum of members' power has no operational meaning. Each member's power is power *vis à vis* the collectivity's action, and it must be maintained as such. Only later, after having examined the power of subcoalitions within the collectivity, will we be in a position to discuss the power of more than one temporary member.

Table 1   Power structure of U.N. Security Council

Before and After Expansion		Before Change $5 + 6 = 11 : 7/11$	After Change $5 + 10 = 15 : 9/15$
Power of Council to act	$A(N)$	0.0278	0.0259
Power of permanent member to prevent action	$P_i(N)$	1.0	1.0
Power of temporary member to prevent action	$P_6(N)$	0.088	0.099
Power of permanent member to initiate action	$I_i(N)$	0.0286	0.0266
Power of temporary member to initiate action	$I_6(N)$	0.0025	0.0026

Example   A simple five-man collectivity with differing decision rules. Some sense of the way in which these measures of collectivity power and member power vary can be obtained by examining their variation as the decision rule changes from one in which a single member can initiate action (as in the case of creation of a public nuisance, or turning in a fire alarm) to one in which a single member can veto action.

Case I: One man necessary to initiate action:

$$A(N, 1) = \frac{2^5 - \dfrac{5!}{0! \, 5!}}{2^5} = \frac{31}{32}$$

$$P_i(N) = \frac{1}{31}$$

$$I_i(N) = \frac{1}{32 - 31} = 1$$

Case II: Two men necessary to initiate action:

$$A(N, 2) = \frac{\displaystyle\sum_{k=2}^{s} \frac{5!}{k!(5 - k)!}}{2^5} = \frac{26}{32} = \frac{13}{16}$$

$$P_i(N) = \frac{\dfrac{5!}{2!\,3!}\cdot\dfrac{2}{5}}{26} = \frac{4}{26} = \frac{2}{13}$$

$$I_i(N) = \frac{4}{32-26} = \frac{2}{3}$$

Case III: Three men necessary to initiate action:

$$A(N, 3) = \frac{\displaystyle\sum_{k=3}^{s}\dfrac{5!}{k!(5-k)!}}{2^5} = \frac{16}{32} = \frac{1}{2}$$

$$P_i(N) = \frac{\dfrac{5!}{3!\,2!}\cdot\dfrac{3}{5}}{16} = \frac{6}{16} = \frac{3}{8}$$

$$I_i(N) = \frac{6}{32-16} = \frac{3}{8}$$

Case IV: Four men necessary to initiate action:

$$A(N, 4) = \frac{\displaystyle\sum_{k=4}^{s}\dfrac{5!}{k!(5-k)!}}{2^5} = \frac{6}{32} = \frac{3}{16}$$

$$P_i(N) = \frac{\dfrac{5!}{4!\,1!}\cdot\dfrac{4}{5}}{6} = \frac{4}{6} = \frac{2}{3}$$

$$I_i(N) = \frac{4}{32-6} = \frac{4}{26} = \frac{2}{13}$$

Case V: Five men necessary to initiate action:

$$A(N, 5) = \frac{\dfrac{5!}{5!\,0!}}{2^5} = \frac{1}{32}$$

$$P_i(N) = \frac{1}{1} = 1$$

$$I_i(N) = \frac{1}{32-1} = \frac{1}{31}$$

The tabulation of group and member power with these five decision rules shows the symmetry between rules which require m and $n - m + 1$ votes for passage.

Table 2 Power structure with different decision rules in collectivity of five members

		Number of members necessary for passage				
		1	2	3	4	5
Power of collectivity to act	$A(N, k)$	$\dfrac{31}{32}$	$\dfrac{13}{16}$	$\dfrac{1}{2}$	$\dfrac{3}{16}$	$\dfrac{1}{32}$
Power of member to prevent action	$P_i(N)$	$\dfrac{1}{31}$	$\dfrac{2}{13}$	$\dfrac{3}{8}$	$\dfrac{2}{3}$	1
Power of member to initiate action	$I_i(N)$	1	$\dfrac{2}{3}$	$\dfrac{3}{8}$	$\dfrac{2}{13}$	$\dfrac{1}{31}$

Example Acting power of the United States

The acting power of the United States can be calculated through use of equation (5). If the House and Senate Committees involved (N_1 and N_2 in equation (5)) use a majority decision rule of an odd number of numbers for passing a bill out from committee, then $A(N_1) = A(N_2) = 0.5$. The quantity $\dfrac{1}{2^n} \sum \dfrac{n!}{k!\,(n-k)!}$, where the sum is taken over $m > n/2$, is 0.5, and the same sum for $m \geq 2n/3$ is 0.000437 for the Senate, and 1.6×10^{-12} for the House. Thus the full description of the power to act is

$$A(N) = 0.5 \cdot 0.5\,[0.5 \cdot 0.5 + 0.5 \cdot 0.5 \cdot 0.000437 \cdot 1.6 \times 10^{-12}] = 0.03125.$$

This power to act is in effect equivalent to the power of a simple collectivity of five members in which each member had a veto, leading to one affirmative partition out of 32. The effect on the measure of acting power of the House and Senate override of the presidential veto is negligible. The reason for this is that the proportion of partitions in which more than 2/3 of members are positive is very small, only about 0.0004 in the Senate, and 1.6×10^{-12} in the House. Thus the acting power of the U.S. in legislation is not at all affected by the existence of the veto override.

The actual power of the country to act is, of course, affected by this rule, because the probability of the Senate and House having more than 2/3 of their members in favor of an action is not accurately given by the proportion of partitions in which more than 2/3 are positive. This derives from the fact that the members' votes are not cast independently with probability 0.5, as this model implicitly assumes. There is a high degree of interdependence.

An estimate of the interdependence, and the effective number of independent numbers in the House and Senate could be obtained by estimating the variance of p (where p is the proportion of members voting positive) over all bills, and then equating this to the binominal variance, pq/n, for unknown n. An approximation to this may be obtained by use of an empirical regularity that has been observed in many political elections in countries with two-party systems and single-member constituencies: the variance of p over different constituencies is about 0.0187. Setting this equal to pq/n, and letting $p \approx 0.5$, gives $n \approx 13$. Thus the constituencies act as if they are composed of 13 independent members, each with the same probability (probabilities alike, within and between constituencies) of voting for a given party.

If 13 is taken as the "effective" size of the House and Senate, assuming that they behave with the same degree of interdependence as do those voting bodies that have been studied (and the widespread uniformity of this variance, 0.0187, suggests that they do), then the acting power added by the veto override is no longer negligible. The proportion of partitions in a simple collectivity of size 13 that are greater than 2/3 positive (9 or more positive) is 0.1334. Thus the estimate of $A(N)$ with this modification (but still assuming the House and Senate act independently) is:

$$A(N) = 0.5 \cdot 0.5 \, [0.5 \cdot 0.5 \cdot 0.5 + 0.5 \cdot 0.1334 \cdot 0.1334] = 0.0335$$

Thus according to this calculation, the veto override adds acting power of 0.0022, or contributes $0.0022/0.0335 = 0.066$ of the total acting power of the nation in legislation.

THE POWER OF COMBINED FORCES

In initiating action of a collectivity, or in preventing a collectivity from acting, the individual's power is not limited to his unilateral action. Nor is it the case that his power can merely be added to that of other members to obtain their combined power. For example, in the U.N. Security Council with 11 members, any five of the temporary members can combine to block action, the set of five having exactly the same power to prevent collective action as any one permanent member. Yet the sum of the individual power of five temporary members prevent action is not 1.0, but 0.44. Even less could one add, for this purpose, the earlier measure of Shapley and Shubik, despite its apparent property of "additivity." For example, the sum of the power of five temporary members, by that measure, is only 0.011, compared to a power of 0.197 for a permament member, although the power of such a bloc to prevent action is in fact identical to that of the permanent member.

In order to determine the power of a given subset C, it is necessary to treat them as if they were a single entity and analyze the power $P_c(N)$ and $I_c(N)$ just as was done by use of equations (7) and (9) for $P_i(N)$ and $I_i(N)$. The relevant equations are:

$$P_c(N) = \frac{\sum_S (v(S) - v(S - C))}{\sum_S v(S)}, \tag{11}$$

$$I_c(N) = \frac{\sum_S (v(S + C) - v(S))}{\sum_S (1 - v(S))}. \tag{12}$$

where C is a given subset of members of N.

The power of a subset C of which i is a member always includes his individual power, so that the preventive power he gains by joining such a bloc is given by $P_c(N) - P_i(N)$. He gains this power, of course, at the cost of giving up some autonomy over his own vote, as I have discussed elsewhere [1968]. His power *within* the subset C, to induce it to prevent or initiate action of the larger collectivity, may be calculated from considerations similar to those with which we began: the power of the subset C to prevent action of the larger collectivity with him as a member minus the power of the subset C without him as a member to prevent such action is the basis of his power to induce the subset to take a negative position, and similarly for his power to induce the coalition to initiate action. This power is likely to be reflected in the decision rule within this subset for determining its bloc vote, although the actual decision rule used may reflect this relative power only imperfectly.

It is useful to examine one property of $P_c(N)$ as C increases in size, approaching N. It is clear that when C includes all n members of the collectivity N, then it is a determining member for every partition of N. It is able to initiate action in all those partitions for which $v(S) = 0$, and able to prevent action for all those partitions in which $v(S) = 1$. Thus $P_N(N) = 1$, and $I_N(N) = 1$. As a consequence, then for any member i with $P_i(N) < 1$

or $I_i(N) < 1$, or both, there is an increase in $P_c(N)$ from $P_i(N)$ to 1 as C (including i) increases in size, and an increase in $I_c(N)$ from $I_i(N)$ to 1 as C increases in size. If all members other than i are alike, as in a simple committee or other voting body with undifferentiated members, then this increase can be described simply as a function of the size of C. If the members are differentiated, as in the U.N. Security Council, or in federal legislation in the U.S., $P_c(N)$ and $I_c(N)$ change as a function of the number of members of each type. It is useful to examine $P_c(N)$ and $I_c(N)$ in examples of both these kinds.

Example The power of blocs in a simple five-man collectivity.

In the simple five-man collectivity examined in an earlier illustration, we may examine $P_c(N)$ and $I_c(N)$ for subsets C varying in size from 1 to 5, and for each decision rule. A tabulation may be made, as shown in Table 3, by examining the list of partitions of five-members collectivities given as Appendix A.

Table 3

Numerator and Denominator for $P_c(n, m)$ for $n = 5$, $m = 1, 2, 3, 4, 5$, and Size of Subset $C = 1, 2, 3, 4, 5$

Number Necessary for Passage (m)	Number of Partitions Winning	Number of Winning Partitions by Removal of Specific Subsets C				
		i	i,j	$i,j,k,$	i,j,k,l	i,j,k,l,m
1	31	1	3	7	15	31
2	26	4	10	18	26	26
3	16	6	12	16	16	16
4	6	4	6	6	6	6
5	1	1	1	1	1	1

Numerator and Denominator for $I_c(n, m)$ for $n = 5$, $m = 1, 2, 3, 4, 5$, and Size of Subset $C = 1, 2, 3, 4, 5$

Number Necessary for Passage (m)	Number of Losing Partitions	Number of Losing Partitions That Win by Addition of Specific Subsets C				
		i	i,j	i,j,k	i,j,k,l	i,j,k,l,m
1	1	1	1	1	1	1
2	6	4	6	6	6	6
3	16	6	12	16	16	16
4	26	4	10	18	26	26
5	31	1	3	7	15	31

As Table 3 illustrates, there is a symmetry between the power to prevent action and the power to initiate action under decision rules which require m and $n - m + 1$ votes respectively, for action to occur. That is, this example suggests that in a simple collectivity with decision rule requiring m votes for collective action.

$$I_c(n, n - m + 1, j) = P_c(n, m, j).$$

Comparison of equations (13) and (14) given below will show that this equality holds for simple collectivities of any size. Figure 1 shows the increase in power to prevent or initiate action under different decision rules, as the size of the subset C increases from 1 to 5.

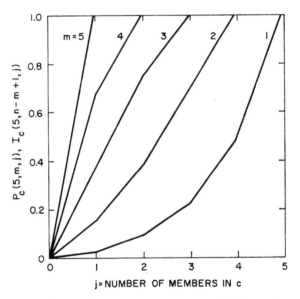

Figure 1 The increase in power to prevent or initiate action under different decision rules, as the size of the subset C increases from 1 to 5

Example   Three kinds of coalitions within the U.N. Security Council.
In the U.N. Security Council, there are three different kinds of coalition possible: within the set of permanent members, within the set of temporary members, and between one or more permanent members and one or more temporary members. For convenience using the list of partitions of five and six member collectives given as Appendix A, the number of partitions in which coalitions of various kinds can block or initiate action can be found by inspection. The tabulation is given in Table 4.

Table 4

Numbers of Partitions of U.N. Security Council (11 Members)
in Which Coalitions of Different Composition Can
Prevent Action or Initiate Action

Number of Passing Partitions	Number of Failing Partitions
57	1991

a. Coalitions Within the Set of Six Temporary Members

Size of C	No. of Partitions Blocked	No. of Partitions Initiated
1	5	5
2	13	7
3	22	7
4	41	7
5	57	7
6	57	7

b. Coalitions Within the Set of Five Permanent Members

Size of C	No. of Partitions Blocked	No. of Partitions Initiated
1	57	$1 \cdot 57 = 57$
2	57	$3 \cdot 57 = 171$
3	57	$7 \cdot 57 = 399$
4	57	$15 \cdot 57 = 855$
5	57	$31 \cdot 57 = 1767$

c. Coalitions between permanent and temporary members (Only initiation is shown because one permanent member can block all 57 passing partitions)

Number of Temporary Members	Number of Permanent Members				
	1	2	3	4	5
1	$62+5=67$	$3\cdot62+5=191$	$7\cdot62+5=439$	$15\cdot62+5=935$	$31\cdot62+5=1927$
2	$64+7=71$	$3\cdot64+7=199$	$7\cdot64+7=455$	$15\cdot64+7=967$	$31\cdot64+7=1991$
3	71	199	455	967	1991
4	71	199	455	967	1991
5	71	199	455	967	1991
6	71	199	455	967	1991

Social Choice

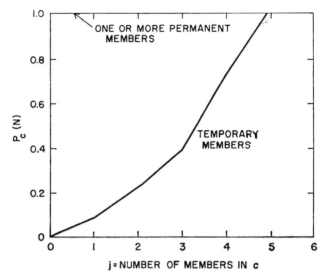

Figure 2 Power of U.N. Security Council members as given by the decision rule, in all possible coalitions, temporary members

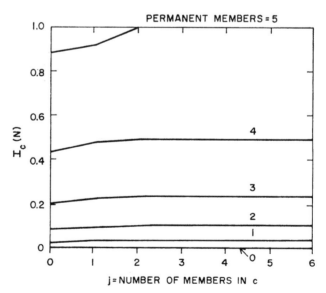

Figure 3 Power of U.N. Security Council members as given by the decision rule, in all possible coalitions, permanent members

Table 4, and accompanying Figures 2 and 3, show the power of U.N. Security Council members (11-member council) as given by the decision rule, in all possible coalitions. The possibility of coalition, either with other permanent members or with temporary members, does not affect the power of permanent members to prevent action, for that power is already absolute, through the veto. It greatly affects, however, the power of temporary members to do so, for that power rises rapidly as the number of temporary members in a coalition increases from one to five (and of course it increases to 1 if a coalition includes a permanent member).

The possibility of coalition among the permanent members increases sharply their power to initiate action, which rises to 0.886 with five permanent members, in the absence of any temporary members. The addition of one or two temporary members increases slightly the power of the coalition, as the slight rises in the lines of Figure 3 shows. Overall, it is clear that the temporary members gain little power through coalition with one another except for purposes of preventing action, where their power in combination is strong. They gain much power through coalition with permanent members, but because they add little to the permanent members' power, their power within that coalition, to determine its position, will be very small. For example, in a coalition between one temporary and one permanent member, the temporary member gains power to initiate action in 62 partitions (67–5), while the permanent member gains power to initiate action in only 10 (67–57). The temporary member gains the power to block action in 52 partitions (57–5), while the permanent member gains no preventive power. As a consequence of this difference in value of the two members to the coalition, the decision rule within the coalition should give differential power to the two.

THE VALUE ADDED BY COALITION

Since membership in a coalition reduces a member's autonomy of action in casting his vote, unless he has complete control of the coalition, it is useful to ask the circumstance under which it will be to the benefit of all members of a potential coalition to join. This circumstance will prevail when the power of the coalition is greater than the sum of the power of the members individually—for if that is the case, some decision rule can be found such that the fraction of control over the collectivity's action held by each member, multiplied by the coalition's power, is greater than his individual power in the absence of coalition, for every coalition member.[5] The condition for a coalition to be mutually beneficial in preventing collectivity action is:

$$P_c(N) > \sum_{i \in C} P_i(N),$$

and the condition for a coalition to be mutually beneficial in initiating collectivity action is

$$I_c(N) > \sum_{i \in C} I_i(N).$$

This condition, for P or I, holds in Figures 1 or 2 wherever the curve of $P_c(N)$ or $I_c(N)$ is concave upward. There is value added (i.e. power added) by a coalition of temporary members of the Security Council for coalition size up through five members, by the accelerating increase of $P_c(N)$ with increase in size of C. There is power added for initiating action by coalitions among permanent members of the Council. And there is a slight amount of power added for initiating action by coalitions between permanent members and one or two temporary members, as Table 4 shows. Figure 1 and Table 3 show that in the simple collectivity of 5 members, power to prevent action is gained by coalitions when $m = 1$ or 2, and power to initiate action is gained by coalition when $m = 4$ or 5.

From considering these examples, it appears that a more direct way of calculating $P_c(N)$ and $I_c(N)$ may be devised when the collectivity is a simple one with all members undifferentiated. In this case, with a decision rule requiring m positive votes for action, the power of a coalition of j members to prevent and initiate action may be labelled $P_c(n, m, j)$ and $I_c(n, m, j)$ respectively, since P and I are functions solely of n, m, and j. The power of the coalition to prevent action may be calculated by considering the number of partitions in which the collective action fails if the votes of the coalition members are missing from the positive side and entered on the negative side, minus the number of partitions in which the collective action fails before this change is made. This difference divided by the total number of partitions in which collective action succeeds $[\sum_S n(S)]$, is the power of the coalition to prevent action. The numerator is simply the number of failures contributed by defection of the coalition, and the denominator is the number of affirmative partitions, which is $\displaystyle\sum_{k=m}^{n} \frac{n!}{k!\,(n-k)!}$.

The number of partitions in which the action fails, out of all the 2^n partitions is merely $\displaystyle\sum_{k=0}^{m-1} \frac{n!}{k!\,(n-k)!}$. The number of partitions of $n - j$ numbers in which the action fails is $\sum_{k=0}^{m-1} \dfrac{(n-j)!}{k!\,(n-j-k)!}$, but each of these represents 2^j in partitions in the original set of partitions, so that

$$P_c(n, m, j) = \left[2^j \sum_{k=0}^{m-1} \frac{(n-j)!}{k!(n-j-k)!} - \sum_{k=0}^{m-1} \frac{n!}{k!(n-k)!} \right] \frac{1}{\sum\limits_{k=m}^{n} \dfrac{n!}{k!(n-k)!}}$$

or simplifying by combining terms under the summation sign,

$$P_c(n, m, j) = \left[\sum_{k=0}^{m-1} \frac{2^j(n-j)!\,(n-k)\cdots(n-j-k+1) - n!}{k!\,(n-k)!} \right]$$

$$\times \frac{1}{\sum\limits_{k=m}^{n} \dfrac{n!}{k!(n-k)!}} \tag{13}$$

From similar considerations, $I_c(n, m, j)$ may be calculated, recognizing that the partitions in which the collective action passes are those in which $m \le k \le n$, and the j numbers are now arbitrarily entered on the positive side (so that only $m - j$ others are necessary for passage). The equation for $I_c(n, m, j)$ is:

$$I_c(n, m, j) = \left[2^j \sum_{k=m}^{n} \frac{(n-k)!}{(k-j)!\,(n-k)!} - \sum_{k=m}^{n} \frac{n!}{k!(n-k)!} \right]$$

$$\times \frac{1}{\sum\limits_{k=0}^{m-1} \dfrac{n!}{k!(n-k)!}}$$

Or simplifying by combining terms under the summation sign,

$$I_c(n, m, j) = \left[\sum_{k=m}^{n} \frac{2^j(n-k)!k \ldots (k-j+1) - n!}{k!(n-k)!} \right] \frac{1}{\sum\limits_{k=0}^{m-1} \dfrac{n!}{k!(n-k)!}}$$

$$\tag{14}$$

Both these formulas, $P_c(n, m, j)$ as given by equation (13), and $I_c(n, m, j)$ as given by equation (14), are valid only over certain ranges of coalition size. If $j > n - m$, then the coalition can block all actions, and $P_c(n, m, j) = 1$. If $j \ge m$, then the coalition can initiate action against any opposition, and $I_c(n, m, j) = 1$. Equations (13) and (14) are valid for all coalitions smaller than these, that is, $j \le n - m$ for $P_c(n, m, j)$, and $j < m$ for $I_c(n, m, j)$.

CHANGES IN POWER OF THE COLLECTIVITY TO ACT AS A RESULT OF COALITION

The power of the collectivity to act, $A(N)$, is determined by the decision rule of the collectivity, as shown in an earlier section. But when two or more members act as a single member through coalition, this may change the power of the collectivity to act, depending on the decision rule used by the coalition itself. For example, in the U.N. Security Council, if a coalition forms between three permanent members, so that they agree to vote alike, and they agree to decide internally without a veto, by a majority of two out of three, then this reduces the effective number of permanent members to three, and reduces the total number of partitions of the Security Council vote to 2^9, or 512.[6] The number of affirmative partitions remains at 57, so that the acting power of the collectivity becomes 57/512, or four times its value when no coalitions existed. If, on the other hand, five of the temporary members (the optimum number for increase in preventive power) formed a coalition using a majority rule for voting within the coalition, then the Security Council in effect is reduced to seven members, one with no power and the other six with equal power. There are 2^7, or 128, partitions, and two of them (the first six members positive, and the seventh either positive or negative) are affirmative partitions, so that $A(N) = 2/128 = 32/2048$, which is less than the acting power of 57/2048 without that coalition. This reduction in acting power of the collectivity is directly due to the power added by the coalition of five members as discussed in the preceding section. It follows from the fact that the coalition members, in determining a decision rule within their coalition, can create a decision rule more restrictive than the 2 out of 6 decision rule that obtains in the absence of coalition. The majority rule, 3 out of 5, is more restrictive, and in effect reduced the number of affirmative partitions from 57 to 32.

It appears, then, that the power of coalition lies in the power of the coalition members to determine for themselves an internal decision rule that differs from the decision rule that implicitly obtains for the coalition when its members are acting individually. When the coalition's decision rule is more restrictive on affirmative action than the implicit decision rule when they act individually, the power of the total collectivity to act will decrease as a result of the coalition. When it is less restrictive (as in the example of a majority rule governing a coalition of three permanent members who have individual vetoes in the absence of coalition), then the power of the total collectivity to act will be increased.

BEHAVIORAL POWER

This analysis is concerned wholly with the study of formal power as given by the constitutional rules of a collectivity. Yet even in the analysis of formal power, assumptions about members' behavior is implicitly made. By the device of counting each partition of the collectivity once, and adding the number of partitions in obtaining measures of power, it is implicitly assumed that each member has equal probability of voting for or against a collective action (except in the case of formal coalition, in which case their vote is completely dependent, voting as a bloc). This is appropriate for the analysis of formal power as given by a constitution, that is, for an analysis of organizational rules. It does not, however, provide a basis for behavioral prediction of the collectivity's action, when further information exists about the members. In particular, the two assumptions made in the analysis of formal power, equal probabilities of positive and negative votes by each member, and independence of votes among members, may be empirically investagated, and the collectivity's action predicted by the use of such information.[7]

The way in which this may be done in the case of differing probabilities of positive and negative votes is evident by recognizing that each of the partitions counted once in the present analysis is a partition in a binomial distribution which has a weight of $p^k(1 - p)^{n-k}$, where k is the number of positive votes in that partition, and p is the probability of a positive vote from a member. If all members have $p = 1/2$, then each partition has equal weight, and the above analysis holds. If all have the same p, but $p \neq 1/2$, then each partition should be weighted by $p^k(1 - p)^{n-k}$, where k is the number of positive votes in the partition—or, what is the same thing, the probability of outcomes with m or more positive members may be obtyined by using the binomial distribution, i.e., by replacing in the relevant equations those terms of the form $\sum_{k=m}^{n} \dfrac{n!}{k!\,(n-k)!}$ with $\sum_{k=m}^{n} \dfrac{n!}{k!\,(n-k)!} p^k(1 - p)^{k-n}$.

If different members have different probabilities of voting positively, but all remain independent, a more detailed calculation must be made, weighting each partition separately. If p_i is the probability of a positive vote by member i, then each partition must be weighted by $\prod_{i \in S} p_i \prod_{j \notin S} (1 - p_j)$.

If there is interdependence among the votes of members of the collectivity—that is, something between total independence and a formal coalition—then the analysis becomes more difficult. If this interdependence is uniform, and in a simple undifferentiated collectivity, then it does not affect the relative power of individuals, but can affect the power of the collectivity to act, depending on the decision rule. In such a situation, stochastic models for interdependence of action, as discussed in Coleman (1964, Chapter 11), may be useful. For situations that are more complex, either in the formal structure of the collectivity or in the form of the interdependence among members, more complex models must be developed.

APPENDIX A
DISTINCT PARTITIONS OF FIVE—AND SIX-MEMBERED COLLECTIVITIES

S N-S

0/12345	1234/5	45/6123	1245/36
1/2345	1235/4	46/1235	1246/35
2/3451	1254/3	56/1234	1256/34
3/4512	1543/2	123/456	1345/26
4/5123	5432/1	124/563	1346/25
5/1234	12345/	125/634	1356/24
12/345		126/345	1456/23
13/452	0/123456	134/562	2345/16
14/523	1/23456	135/624	2346/15
15/234	2/34561	136/245	2356/14
23/451	3/45612	146/623	2456/13
24/513	4/56123	146/235	3456/12
25/134	5/61234	156/234	12345/6
34/512	6/12345	234/561	12346/5
35/124	12/3456	235/614	12356/4
45/123	13/4562	236/145	12456/3
123/45	14/5623	245/613	13456/2
124/53	15/6234	246/135	23456/1
125/34	16/2345	256/134	
134/52	23/4561	345/612	
135/24	24/5613	346/125	
145/23	25/6134	356/124	
234/51	26/1345	456/123	
235/14	34/5612	1234/56	
245/13	35/6124	1235/46	
345/12	36/1245	1236/45	

NOTES

1   Any views expressed in this paper are those of the author. They should not be interpreted as reflecting the views of The RAND Corporation or the official opinion or policy of any of its governmental or private research sponsors. Papers are reproduced by The RAND Corporation as a courtesy to members of its staff.

This paper was prepared for presentation at a conference on social choice to be held at the University of Pittsburgh, Pennsylvania, September 9–12, 1968.

2 This measure of value assumes a game in which there is full possibility of dividing the winnings among the members of the winning coalition, a division that will take place according to the contribution of each member to winning (in a sense to be defined shortly). This assumption is not valid for collectivities in which a proposed action is to be accepted or rejected, as in political bodies, for each action carries a fixed distribution of consequences. Thus as a measure of the "value of the game" to members of a collectivity, the Shapley measure would not be valid. However, this difference between political actions to be decided by a collective decision, and games in which there is a division the winnings among the members of a winning coalition does not affect the validity of the measure as a measure of power.

3 Certainly it is the case that in some collective actions, such a division of the spoils does in fact occur. A convention has some of these attributes, for there are spols to be distributed among those delegations that support the winner, and particularly those delegations that cast the deciding ballots in favor of the winner. But this is an unusual case, in which there is a winning nominee, who does have spoils to distribute.

4 If the subcollectivity's power is normalized to one, then his measure of power in the subcollectivity is $\phi_i (N)/\phi(N_j)$, which is the same measure as would be obtained by applying Eq. (1) to the subcollectivity N_j rather than to the collectivity N.

5 This addition of power to the power of the members assumes, however, that the appropriate decision rule is used by the coalition. For a coalition may have, as a coalition, a high amount of preventive or initiating power, but that power not be transmitted to the members through an inappropriate decision rule in the coalition.

6 The majority rule here is used in illustration, because by counting each partition equally, one implicitly assumes equal probabilities of a member voting positively or negatively. If a "member" consists of a coalition C, and its probability of voting positively, as given by $A(C)$, is not $1/2$, then the different partitions must be weighted by $A(C)$ or $1 - A(C)$ depending on whether the coalition C is positive or negative in that partition.

7 Another implicit assumption of this analysis of formal power is the isolation of collective decisions from one another. Once this isolation is no longer assumed, then the possibility exists of trading control over one collective decision for control over another. But in the analysis of such systems of exchange, it is necessary first to carry out an analysis of formal power, as done here, in order to know exactly what constitutional power each member has as his initial resources in such an exchange market. The examination of such systems in the presence of variations in formal power of the kind examined above will be carried out in subsequent work.

REFERENCES

Coleman, J. S. *Introduction to Mathematical Sociology*, New York: The Free Press, 1964.

Coleman, J. S. *The Benefits of Coalition*. John Hopkins University, Baltimore, Maryland, mimeographed, 1968.

Luce, R. D., and Rogow, A. A. A Game Theoretic Analysis of Congressional Power Distributing for a Stable Two-Party System. *Behavioral Science*, 1956, **1**, 83–95.

Luce, R. D., and Raiffa, H. *Games and Decisions*, New York: Wiley, 1957.

Shapley, L. S. A Value for n-Person Games. In H. W. Kuhn and A. W. Tucker (Eds.), *Contributions to the Theory of Games II, Annals of Mathematical Studies*. Vol. 28. Princeton: Princeton University Press, 1953.

Shapley, L. S. and Shubik, M. A Method for Evaluating the Distribution of Power in a Committee System. *American Political Science Review*, 1954, **48**, 787–792.

INDIVIDUAL PREFERENCES, COLLECTIVE DECISIONS, AND SOCIAL WELFARE[1]

BLISS CARTWRIGHT,[2] STEPHEN LITTLECHILD,[3] and JACK SAWYER

Northwestern University

When individual preferences are combined to reach collective decisions, how well are the individual preferences satisfied? What average level of satisfaction is achieved, and how equally or unequally is it distributed among individuals? The answer depends upon two factors—the structure of the original individual preferences, and the collective decision procedure used to combine them.

The present research employs computer simulation to determine empirically just how the level and distribution of satisfaction is influenced by three decision criteria and by a variety of individual preference structures. In exploring these questions, this research intends also to illustrate how simulation techniques can be applied to collective decision problems.

Individual preference structure Assume that each of a number of persons has a certain preference for each of a number of issues or actions the group is jointly to decide upon. Let the preferences range, through several gradations, from negative to indifferent to positive. The resulting set of preferences has three particularly prominent characteristics that the present research varies, to determine their effect upon the level and distribution of satisfaction:

1) *Size:* the number of persons and of issues.
2) *Distribution:* how preferences on an issue are distributed over individuals.
3) *Correlation:* the correlation, over issues, between the preferences of one person and the preferences of another.

Collective decision criteria Each of the three collective decision criteria specifies a rule for combining individual preferences to form a group outcome. The first criterion regards simply the direction of a person's preference (for, against, indifference). The second criterion considers preference on a scale from -9 to $+9$. The third criterion uses the same scale, but minimizes a squared function that gives more weight to extreme preferences.

The first rule represents a collective decision where every individual (unless he chooses to abstain) has an equal weight. Each person simply votes his preference regardless of its strength and regardless of any possible gain to himself or others. But in fact, preferences do vary in intensity. On any issue, some persons care more than others, and any person cares more about some issues than others. This is often reflected by differential participation in particular decisions.

The second and third rules represent situations that consider different intensities, and admit the possibility of vote-trading or other forms of cooperation. These criteria do not specify the processes by which departures from unweighted, independent voting might occur, but they do determine the potential changes in utility that could occur. They determine limits to the possible benefits of cooperation.

Thus this research explores how aggregate welfare is influenced by decision rules that consider simply whether an individual opposes or favors an issue, as well as by rules that also consider the intensity of his preference. For each decision criterion, and for different individual preference structures, computer simulation is used to determine the average level of satisfaction the rule produces, and how evenly the rule distributes satisfaction across persons.

SIMULATION MODEL AND METHOD

The computer simulation first generated individual preference matrices with specified variations in size, distribution form, and correlation among persons over issues. Then it applied to each set of generated preferences the three decision criteria. The following model specifies the representation of preferences, outcomes, and utilities.

THE MODEL

The model assumes an underlying continuum of strength of preference‘ ranging, on each issue, from strongly opposed through indifferent to strongly favorable. Each individual has a specified preference for each issue. The matrix of preferences of all individuals on all issues constitutes the individual preference structure.

Let w_{ij} = the weight person i places on issue j, where $i = 1, \ldots, m$ and $j = 1, \ldots, n$.

Arbitrarily $-9 \leq w_{ij} \leq 9$, and

$$w_{ij} \begin{cases} > 0 \\ = 0 \\ < 0 \end{cases} \text{indicates that person } i \text{ wants issue } j \text{ to} \begin{cases} \text{pass} \\ \text{tie} \\ \text{fail} \end{cases}$$

The purpose of the simulation is to specify, from the matrix of individual preferences, a particular outcome for each issue:

Let z_j = the outcome of issue j, where

$$z_j = \begin{cases} 1 \\ 0 \\ -1 \end{cases} \text{indicates sisue } j \begin{cases} \text{passes} \\ \text{ties} \\ \text{fails} \end{cases}$$

The way the simulation specifies outcomes is to consider the utility of possible outcomes:

Let $u_i(z_1, \ldots, z_n)$ be the utility to person i of a set of outcomes

$$(z_1, \ldots, z_j, \ldots, z_n)$$

The particular utility function is specified through use of the weights w_{ij} that represent the individual preferences. The utility of an outcome for an individual is given by multiplying the outcome $z_j(-1, 0, +1)$ by the weight w_{ij} (-9 to $+9$). I.e.

Define $u_i(z_1, \ldots, z_n) = \sum_j w_{ij} z_j$

Thus, if the outcome is in the direction the person prefers (pass or fail), then the signs of the outcome z_j and the preference w_{ij} agree, and the utility is positive. If the sign of the outcome and the person's preference disagree, then the utility is negative. The absolute value of failure and passage of an issue is the same to an individual; the positive utility when outcome and preference agree is the same in magnitude as the negative utility when outcome and preference disagree. The utility of a tied outcome is zero, half way between that of passing and failing.[5] The magnitude of either the positive or negative utility is directly given by the preference weight w_{ij}; in particular, if $w_{ij} = 0$, then a person is indifferent to the outcome, and has zero utility for any outcome.

The simulation proceeds by determining that outcome for which the discrepancy between the utility for it, and the utility for the most desired outcome, is a minimum.[6] Therefore,

Let u_i^* be the utility to person i of the most preferred set of outcomes

$$(z_1, \ldots, z_j, \ldots, z_n)$$

Thus $u^* = \max u_i(z_1, \ldots, z_n)$

$$z_1, \ldots, z_n$$

Then let $d_i(z_1, \ldots, z_n)$ be the discrepancy in utility between what the person i most desires and a given set of outcomes.

Thus $d_i = d_i(z_1, \ldots, z_n) = u^* - v_i(z_1, \ldots, z_n)$

Collective decision criteria

The structure of individual preferences is assumed always to involve an underlying continuum, but the first rule, like most voting procedures, does not consider it in arriving at decisions. The second and third rules provide two prominent alternative ways to consider intensity of preference. The linear rule considers mean utility only, minimizing the mean discrepancy between preferred and obtained outcomes. The squared discrepancy rule considers the variance in the discrepancies for different individuals, and tends to make the discrepancies of all persons more nearly equal.

1 Signed preferences Only the sign of the individual's preference is considered; these are counted as -1 (against), 0 (indifferent), and $+1$ (for). The possible outcomes, in all three rules, are counted as -1 (fail), 0 (tie), and $+1$ (pass). When only direction of preference is considered, choosing the outcome that minimizes the discrepancy in utility (on a -1, 0, $+1$ scale) between actual and most preferred outcomes simply amounts to a majority rule. An issue passes if there are more persons for it than against it, ties if the two frequencies are equal, and fails if there are more against it.

Thus, $z_j = \text{sign} \sum_i \text{sign } w_{ij}$

$$\text{where sign } x = \begin{cases} x/|x|, & x \neq 0 \\ 0, & x = 0 \end{cases}$$

This criterion disregards strength of preference; an issue weakly favored by a bare majority can pass even though it is strongly opposed by a large minority. Thus this criterion can produce a decision where total dissatisfaction (measured on an underlying continuum of intensity) exceeds total satisfaction.

2 Linearly-weighted preferences Each individual's preference is considered on a scale from -9 to $+9$. Then outcomes $(z_1, \ldots, z_n)$ are chosen to minimize discrepancy between the utility of desired and obtained outcome. The z_j's are those that solve

$$\underset{z_1, \ldots, z_n}{\text{Min}} \sum_i d_i(z_1, \ldots, z_n) = \sum_i [u_i^* - u_i(z_1, \ldots, z_n)],$$

$$\text{subject to } z_j = -1, 0, +1$$

Since u_i^* is a constant, this amounts to maximizing $\sum_i u_i(z_1, \ldots, z_n)$. The z_j's that maximize this function are simply

$$z_j = \text{sign} \sum_i w_{ij}$$

Thus, an issue passes if the algebraic sum of the preferences is positive, ties if the sum is zero, and fails if the sum is negative. This is a weighted voting rule.

3 Squared discrepancies The same -9 to $+9$ scale is used as for the linear criterion; the only difference is that the outcome is chosen to minimize the square of the average discrepancy between the utility of the actual and preferred outcomes. This criterion chooses z_j to

$$\underset{z_1, \ldots, z_n}{\text{Min}} \sum_i d_i^2 = \sum_i [u_i^* - u_i(z_1, \ldots, z_n)]^2$$

$$\text{subject to } \quad z_j = -1, 0, +1$$

The relation between the squared and linear criterion can be seen by analyzing the variance of the discrepancies:

$$\text{Variance } (d_i) = \sum (d_i^2) - \sum (d_i)^2$$

$$= \sum_i \frac{d_i^2}{m} - \left(\frac{\sum d}{m^i} \right)^2$$

Thus, $\sum_i \dfrac{d_i^2}{m} = \text{Var} \, (d_i) + [\text{Mean} \, (d_i)]^2$

Thus the squared discrepancy criterion gives equal weight to the square of the mean discrepancy and to the variance of the discrepancies over individuals. The first of these equally-weighted parts corresponds to the linear criterion.

Table 1 Illustrative application of three criteria to a 5 × 5 matrix of individual preferences

Persons	Issues A B C D E	Utility of Most Preferred Outcome (u_i^*)	Utility of Actual Outcome (u_i) Signed Criterion	Linear Criterion	Squared Criterion	Discrepancy in Utility (d_i) Signed Criterion	Linear Criterion	Squared Criterion
1	0 −6 −2 −4 8	20	20	10	0	0	10	20
2	3 5 8 −2 2	20	−9	9	0	29	11	20
3	7 −7 −5 −6 −3	28	15	−9	4	13	37	24
4	−4 9 5 1 3	22	−12	11	−4	34	11	26
5	−9 −1 −4 6 −9	29	−10	−10	9	39	39	20

Criterion	Outcomes (z_j)				
Signed	0	−1	−1	−1	+1
Linear	−1	0	+1	−1	+1
Squared	−1	−1	+1	−1	−1

	Signed	Linear	Squared
Mean Discrepancy	23.0	21.6	22.0
S.D. of Discrepancy	14.4	13.3	2.5

Thus the squared criterion will produce mean discrepancies that are larger than those of the linear criterion—but more nearly equal across individuals.

Table 1 illustrates the calculation and implications of these three criteria. It shows how the outcome for an issue may differ under the three criteria. The first issue, for example, has equal frequencies of positive and negative preferences, but a greater negative total. The second issue has a majority of negative preferences, but equal positive and negative totals. Outcomes from the squared criterion may differ from either of the others, as it minimizes a function that includes the variance as well as the mean.

The utility of the most preferred set of outcomes is the same under all three criteria, and is simply equal to the absolute sum of the weights on separate issues. If every issue is decided in the direction the individual prefers (as for person 1 under the signed criterion), then his actual utility equals the maximum possible, and the discrepancy is zero. Since the linear criterion produces different outcomes from the signed criterion, individual discrepancies differ under the two criteria.

Over all individuals, the linear criterion must always produce a mean discrepancy smaller, or at least as small as that of any other criterion. The squared criterion, however, tends to produce discrepancies whose variance over individuals is smaller than that of the linear criterion.

Individual preference structure

Size Two sizes of preference matrices were employed: those with 5 issues and 5 persons, and those with 20 issues and 20 persons.

Distributions Three distribution shapes were used: normal, uniform, and dichotomous. All three were symmetric distributions, but they vary in how spread out or concentrated the probability is. The normal concentrates probability around the mean; uniform distributes it evenly; and the dichotomous distribution concentrates it all at two separate points. The normal distribution has a mean of zero and a standard deviation of 3, except that probability lying outside ± 3 standard deviations was concentrated at those points, to produce a range of -9 to $+9$. The (nearly) uniform distribution was generated by selecting a random digit from 0 through 9, then randomly affixing a $+$ or $-$ sign. This provides a range from -9 to $+9$, with equal probability on all points except 0, which has twice the probability of other points. In the dichotomous distribution, random digits 0 through 4 were -1, and random digits 5 through 9 were called $+1$. All random digits were computer-generated.

20*

Correlation The procedure described above for distributions yields a preference matrix with an expected value of zero for the correlation between each pair of persons. For the normal distribution, the following alterations were made. First, a matrix of preferences was constructed just as above, producing an expected correlation of zero. Then to the vector comprising each person's preferences was added a single fixed vector, also from the normal distribution. The addition was weighted, and the sum is given by p (fixed vector) $+(1 - p)$ (random vector). The weight was the same for an entire preference matrix, but six levels of p were employed: 0 (independence), 0.1, 0.3, 0.5, 0.7, and 0.9.

Computation

A CDC 6400 was used first to construct preference matrices with the characteristics previously specified, then to solve for the optimal outcomes z_j under each decision criteria, and finally to evaluate, for each combination of criteria and preference matrix, the value of the mean and variance of the discrepancy between actual and preferred outcomes.

Optimal z_j for decision criterion 1 (signed preferences) and 2 (linearly weighted preferences) can be straightforwardly calculated. Criterion 3 (squared discrepancies) was approximated by the convex programming problem

$$\text{Min} \sum_i d_i(z_1, ..., z_n)^2$$

subject to $-1 \leq z'_j \leq 1$.

In all cases reported here, most of the resulting z'_j lay at plus or minus 1. Those few lying between ± 1 were rounded to values of -1, 0, or $+1$, in order to obtain the vector minimizing squared discrepancies.

The convex programming routine used was the Sequential Unconstrained Minimization Technique (SUMT) of Fiacco and McCormick (1964). A subroutine to generate appropriate random matrices was added. Total computer time (central processor) was about 10 minutes.

RESULTS OF COMPUTER SIMULATION

Table 1 shows the results of runs on 18 preference matrices. Six of the distributions were normal, six were uniform, and six were dichotomous. Of each six, three contained 5 issues and 5 persons, and the other three contained 20 issues and 20 persons. Thus for each combination of size and distribution shape, there were three random replications. Table 2 averages over the three replications which are shown in full in Appendix Table A. Table 2 shows the mean discrepancy and the variance across persons in discrepancy for each of the three criteria: signed preferences, linearly weighted preferences, and squared discrepancies. Since Table 2 shows discrepancies between preferred and actual outcomes, smaller means and variances are both desirable. To make the values comparable among distributions, the utilities expressed in the original metric (-9 to $+9$, or -1 to $+1$) have been divided by the average deviation for that distribution.

Table 2 Mean and variance in discrepancy for three collective decision criteria

Distribution and Size	Criterion					
	Signed Preferences		Linearly-weighted Preferences		Squared Discrepancies	
	Mean	S.D.	Mean	S.D.	Mean	S.D.
Normal						
5 × 5	0.45	0.51	0.41	0.54	0.53	0.37
20 × 20	0.88	0.31	0.83	0.33	0.84	0.28
Uniform						
5 × 5	0.61	0.42	0.58	0.45	0.62	0.23
20 × 20	0.84	0.25	0.82	0.24	0.82	0.23
Dichotomous						
5 × 5	0.64	0.42	0.64	0.42	0.67	0.31
20 × 20	0.83	0.18	0.83	0.18	0.83	0.16

Note: Each cell contains the means, over three replications from different randomly chosen preference matrices, of the discrepancy mean and standard deviation divided by the average deviation of the original preference.

Decision Criteria

Mean discrepancy is similar for the three criteria. Necessarily, however, the linearly-weighted criterion always yields the lowest (sometimes tied) value, because the linear function expressly minimizes mean discrepancy. When there are 20 issues and 20 persons, the variances are also similar among decision criteria. For 5 issues and 5 persons, however, the variance for the squared discrepancy is substantially less than the variance for the linearly-weighted criterion. The standard deviation is smaller for squared discrepancy in eight of the 5 × 5 matrices (Appendix A) and tied in the ninth; on the average, the standard deviation for the squared discrepancy criterion is about a third smaller. This reduction in variance is accomplished with a rather small increase in mean discrepancy. Thus, where the number of persons and issues is small, it may be possible to achieve substantially greater equality of distribution with very little reduction in total satisfaction.

Preference Structures

Size   The effect of size is highly consistent. For each of the three distributions, and for each of the three criteria, the discrepancy is lower in smaller sizes, but more evenly distributed in larger sizes. Smaller samples tend to reduce mean discrepancy because they increase the likelihood that most of the preferences on a given issue will be in the same direction. The expected mean preference on each issue is zero in either size matrix, but greater departures are expected in smaller samples, because the standard error of a proportion (or mean) varies inversely with sample size. When most of the preferences are in the same direction, then it is possible to satisfy more persons, and so the mean discrepancy is smaller. At the same time, however, the variance among persons is greater, partly because each person's discrepancy results from only five issues rather than twenty.

Distribution   For the dichotomous distribution, the signed preference and linearly weighted preference criteria necessarily give identical results, because in a two-point distribution there are no differential weights for the linear criterion to consider. The square criterion is also highly similar, though not necessarily idential.

The three differently-shaped distributions—normal, rectangular, and dichotomous—were included mainly to extend the range of conditions under which the criteria were evaluated. On the whole, the previously-described general results held in each distribution separately. In all three distributions, mean discrepancies for the three criteria were similar. In all distributions, variances were substantially smaller for the squared than linear criterion, for the 5 × 5 matrices.

Correlation   Table 3 presents the results for the correlated normal distribution. These analyses all employed 20 × 20 matrices, and the uncorrelated case is repeated from Table 2 for comparison. Each level of correlation had three replications, which are averaged in Table 3, but shown in full in Appendix Table B. Necessarily, the mean and variance in discrepancy both decrease as the systematic component becomes larger in relation to the random component. Ultimately, if the random component were zero, then all preferences would be perfectly correlated, and could all be satisfied simultaneously, so that both mean and variance in discrepancy would be zero. The decrease both in mean discrepancy and in the variance is greater for the first addition of systematic variance than for later additions. On the average, the mean discrepancy drops by two-thirds when the fixed component is raised only to 0.3. Apparently the advantages of increasing satisfaction and of distributing it more evenly can both be promoted without requiring uniform preferences.

Table 3 Mean and variance in discrepancy at various levels of correlation among preferences

Component		Criterion					
		Signed Preferences		Linearly-weighted Preferences		Squared Discrepancies	
Random	Fixed	Mean	S.D.	Mean	S.D.	Mean	S.D.
1.0	0.0	0.88	0.311	0.83	0.336	0.84	0.279
0.9	0.1	0.72	0.316	0.68	0.279	0.68	0.245
0.7	0.3	0.29	0.164	0.27	0.149	0.27	0.147
0.5	0.5	0.10	0.081	0.095	0.081	0.095	0.081
0.3	0.7	0.044	0.050	0.039	0.036	0.039	0.036
0.1	0.9	0.020	0.016	0.019	0.016	0.012	0.016
0.0	1.0	0.00	0.000	0.00	0.000	0.00	0.000

Note: Each cell contains the mean, over three replications from different randomly chosen preference matrices, of the discrepancy mean and standard deviation divided by the average deviation of the original preference distribution. All preference matrices were 20 × 20.

DISCUSSION

In summary, the salient findings include the following:

1) Only a small potential increase in mean utility can be expected from any vote-trading, bargaining, or other scheme that departs from the simple rule that each person votes his own preference on every issue.

2) Smaller numbers of persons and issues permit higher mean utility, but distribute it less evenly.

3) When the number of issues and persons is small, a substantial gain in the equality of distribution can be obtained with a very small sacrifice in total utility.

4)   The largest increment to mean utility and to equality of distribution occurs in the difference between moderate concensus and random agreement rather than in the difference between moderate concensus and complete uniformity of preferences.

5)   The above results hold across three symmetrical distributions that represent extremes in degree of centrality or distribution of preferences.

The following discussion examines these findings, speculates upon their implications, and suggests further analyses.

Total Utility is Relatively Constant

The relatively small differences among the three schemes set limits for the advantage to be gained by any possible modification from the practice of each person voting his preference on all issues. The room for cooperation, over the present distributions, is not large. The aggregate welfare is nearly a constant sum, regardless of distribution. Thus there are relatively few modifications that would improve total welfare.

The present analysis arrives at the minimum discrepancy without the necessity of specifying which individuals would modify their votes in order to make an issue pass that would otherwise fail. But in actual vote-trading (or, comparably, cooperative trading in any interpersonal relation) exchanges are only consumated where both persons gain over the status quo. A multi-person exchange would be consumated only if all stood to gain. This restriction to mutually beneficial exchanges further limits, perhaps substantially, the gains in utility that could be achieved in practice.

Equality May Be Inexpensive

If various distributions do not alter mean utility greatly, then it is not too important to made fine discriminations on this variable. Further distribution could then be made nearly equal without the total utility being greatly affected. The present results indicate that with a small number of persons and issues considerably more even distribution could be achieved with very little loss in total utility.

The linear criterion considers solely the mean discrepancy, whereas the squared criterion weights equally the variance of the discrepancies and the square of their mean. Yet the mean discrepancy for the squared criterion is not much larger than for the linear. Other things equal, both a larger mean utility and a smaller variance is desirable. The precise weighting is a value question, and some of the implications are explored by Rescher (1966). Knowledge of the trading relation between the two quantities can determine the relative cost. In the present research, it appears that, at least for smaller sizes, equality does not cost much in total utility.

A Little Consensus Goes a Long Way

Two features are notable in the findings for correlated preferences. One is that consensus is more helpful than preference-combining schemes, both for increasing mean utility and for reducing variance. As Table 3 showed, neither the linear or squared criterion reduced mean discrepancy much from that of the simple voting of preferences. But correlated preferences, which reflect consensus among persons about which issues are favored and opposed, greatly reduced both discrepancy mean and variance.

The second feature of these findings is that the change in mean and variance occurs largely with the introduction of the first systematic components. Most of the gain in increased mean utility and decreased variance occurs by the time the systematic component has been raised to 30%. This indicates the greatly increased opportunity for joint satisfaction when some positive consensus exists.

Further Explorations

Several added steps could profitably be undertaken. All the present distributions are symmetrical around an indifference point, so that positive and negative preferences are balanced. Asymmetrical distributions, and perhaps particularly combinations of distributions of varying asymmetry, may be expected to give different results. They may well make equality harder to achieve and more costly of total utility than it is here.

Future trials should also evaluate how much mean discrepancy is increased when variance alone is considered and made as close to zero as possible. Just how much (in mean utility) would complete equality cost?

The other major half of the model should be tested. The present scheme merely decides which issues should pass, tie, and fail, to minimize the criteria. These linear and squared criteria do not specify *which* persons should vote for and against each issue. (Some will have to change from their natural preference, if it has been possible to achieve better results by the latter two mechanisms.) The second part of this procedure provides for assigning votes of individuals on issues, within the restriction of which issues pass, tie, or fail, according to minimizing infidelity—the extent to which a person's votes depart from his preference. This model is sketched out in Appendix C.

Finally, both parts of the model should be evaluated not only against further computer simulation, but against actual collective decision processes.

APPENDIX A

Values for separate replicates averaged in Table 2: Mean and variance in discrepancy for three collective decision criteria

Distribution and Size	Criterion					
	Signed Preferences		Linearly-weighted Preferences		Squared Preferences	
	Mean	S.D.	Mean	S.D.	Mean	S.D.
Normal						
5 × 5	0.32	0.65	0.32	0.65	0.44	0.42
5 × 5	0.70	0.23	0.60	0.32	0.60	0.31
5 × 5	0.32	0.64	0.32	0.64	0.56	0.39
20 × 20	0.87	0.35	0.84	0.40	0.86	0.31
20 × 20	0.82	0.30	0.77	0.29	0.78	0.27
20 × 20	0.95	0.29	0.88	0.31	0.89	0.26
Uniform						
5 × 5	0.52	0.35	0.50	0.37	0.53	0.25
5 × 5	0.52	0.34	0.52	0.34	0.53	0.27
5 × 5	0.80	0.56	0.73	0.63	0.79	0.16
20 × 20	0.82	0.23	0.80	0.22	0.80	0.22
20 × 20	0.84	0.28	0.81	0.27	0.81	0.23
20 × 20	0.87	0.24	0.85	0.22	0.85	0.22
Dichotomous						
5 × 5	0.64	0.45	0.64	0.45	0.68	0.30
5 × 5	0.72	0.39	0.72	0.39	0.72	0.39
5 × 5	0.56	0.41	0.56	0.41	0.60	0.25
20 × 20	0.85	0.19	0.85	0.19	0.85	0.15
20 × 20	0.80	0.19	0.80	0.19	0.80	0.19
20 × 20	0.85	0.16	0.85	0.16	0.85	0.14

Note: Each cell contains the mean, over three replications from different randomly chosen preference matrices, of the discrepancy mean and standard deviation divided by the average deviation of the original preference distribution.

APPENDIX B

Values for separate replicates averaged in Table 3: mean and variance in discrepancy at various levels of correlation among preferences

Component		Criterion					
		Signed Preferences		Linearly-weighted Preferences		Squared Discrepancies	
Random	Fixed	Mean	S.D.	Mean	S.D.	Mean	S.D.
0.9	0.1	0.79	0.33	0.76	0.31	0.77	0.29
0.9	0.1	0.62	0.30	0.59	0.24	0.60	0.17
0.9	0.1	0.74	0.33	0.67	0.30	0.68	0.26
0.7	0.3	0.24	0.15	0.24	0.13	0.22	0.13
0.7	0.3	0.32	0.18	0.20	0.13	0.30	0.13
0.7	0.3	0.29	0.17	0.28	0.18	0.28	0.18
0.5	0.5	0.11	0.08	0.10	0.08	0.10	0.08
0.5	0.5	0.11	0.07	0.11	0.06	0.11	0.06
0.5	0.5	0.08	0.10	0.08	0.10	0.08	0.10
0.3	0.7	0.04	0.05	0.04	0.03	0.04	0.03
0.3	0.7	0.05	0.06	0.04	0.04	0.04	0.04
0.3	0.7	0.05	0.05	0.04	0.04	0.04	0.04
0.1	0.9	0.013	0.02	0.012	0.02	0.012	0.02
0.1	0.9	0.021	0.02	0.021	0.02	0.010	0.02
0.1	0.9	0.027	0.02	0.025	0.02	0.012	0.02

Note: Each cell contains the mean, over three replications from different randomly chosen preference matrices, of the discrepancy mean and standard deviation divided by the average deviation of the original preference distribution. All preference matrices were 20×20.

APPENDIX C

Individual voting patterns

Consider the following problem: subject to ensuring predetermined outcomes on each issue, how should each person vote?

One possibility is to define for each person a utility function $v_i()$ on his own voting pattern $(x_{i1}, \ldots, x_{ij}, \ldots, x_{in})$. This might indeed take the same form as his outcome utility function, i.e.,

$$v_i(x_{i1}, \ldots, x_{in}) = \sum_j w_{ij} x_i$$

Analogous to the previous criteria would be the following welfare criteria for individual voting.

1 *Linear criterion* maximize the sum of individual voting utilities, i.e.

$$\text{Max}_{x_{ij}} \sum_i v_i(x_{i1}, \ldots, x_{in})$$

$$\text{subject to} \quad \sum_i x_{ij} \begin{cases} > 0, z_j = 1 \\ = 0, z_j = 0 \\ < 0, z_j = -1 \end{cases}$$

$$x_{ij} = -1, 0, +1$$

2 *Squared Criterion* minimize the sum of squares of individual voting discrepancies. Defining

$$v_i^* \equiv \text{Max}_{x_{ij}} v_i(x_{i1}, \ldots, x_{in})$$

and $e_i(x_{i1}, \ldots, x_{in}) = v_i^* - v_i(x_{i1}, \ldots, x_{in})$

we have

$$\text{Min}_{x_{ij}} x_j \sum_i e_i^2 = \sum_i [v_i^* - v_i(x_{i1}, \ldots, x_{in})]^2$$

$$\text{subject to} \quad x_{ij} \begin{matrix} > 0, z_j = 1 \\ = 0, z_j = 0 \\ < 0, z_j = -1 \end{matrix}$$

$$x_{ij} = -1, 0, +1$$

Like (3), equation (6) can also be approximated by a convex programming problem, and solved as before.

The overall decision criterion is of the general form

$$\text{Max} \ W(\ldots z_j \ldots; \ldots x_{ij} \ldots)$$

In this model it takes the special form

$$\text{Max} \ M_1 W_1(\ldots z_j \ldots) + M_2 W_2(\ldots x_{ij} \ldots)$$

where M_1, M_2 are elements from a non-Archimedean field, with $M_1 \gg M_2$. The effect is to choose the outcomes to maximize W_1 and then, subject to these, to choose individual voting patterns to maximize W_2. Three possible forms for W_1 are suggested in the paper, i.e.,

(1) $W_1(z_1, \ldots, z_n) = \sum_j \text{sign} \sum_i \text{sign} \ w_{ij}(z_1, \ldots, z_n)$

(2) $W_1(z_1, \ldots, z_n) = \sum_j \sum_i w_{ij} z_j$

(3) $W_1(z_1, \ldots, z_n) = \sum_i (u_i^* - \sum_j w_{ij} z_j)^2$

Similarly, two forms for $W_2(...x_{ij}...)$ are suggested. A variety of other such weighting functions are possible, including those with preference given to certain individuals or groups or individuals.

NOTES

1 Presented at the Conference on Social Choice, Department of Sociology, University of Pittsburgh. September 1968.

2 Now at Yale University.

3 Now at Graduate Centre for Management Studies, University of Birmingham.

4 The authors are grateful to A. Charnes for his valuable suggestions on formulating the programming model, and to Fred M. Phillips for writing several subroutines. This research was partially supported by United States Public Health Service Grant MH 14305, "Experiments in the Resolution of Interpersonal Conflict."

5 In practice, a tie may perhaps be considered closer to failure than to success, but the present formulation is more convenient, and should not seriously distort the results, since in the present analysis very few issues tied.

6 In summing over individuals the discrepancy between preference and outcome, the present analysis implicitly makes interpersonal comparison of utility. Thus to apply the present criteria would involve conceptual and measurement problems not treated here. The comparison of decision criteria nonetheless appears useful.

REFERENCES

Rescher, N. *Distributive Justice*. Indianapolis: Bobbs-Merrill, 1966.
Fiacco, A. V., and McCormick, G. P. The sequential unconstrained minimization technique for non-linear programming, a primal-dual method. *Management Science*, January 1964, vol. 10, number 2.

SECTION 3

NORMATIVE STUDIES

INTRODUCTORY DISCUSSION

The problem of amalgamating preferences into a social or group choice is a very general one and subsumes many different phenomena: some that have conventionally been considered political, some economic, and some that are considered sociological or social psychological. The papers of the previous sections dealt with topics such as power, coalition formation, and level of aspiration. The five papers of this section deal with normative questions— how one should appropriately or effectively merge preferences. Interestingly, all the papers of the section deal with some aspect of behavior that we conventionally call political. And it is not surprising, for the practice and study of politics, if it can be characterized singularly at all, may be said to be the practice and study of the amalgamation of preferences into a social choice.

The paper by Davis and Hinich presents quite a rigorous treatment of two candidate electoral competition where two persons are competing for votes from a total population whose preferences are described by a bimodal mixture of two multivariate distributions. The authors discuss the relationship of these distributions to political parties and discuss the strategies that should be adopted to increase the likelihood of obtaining a majority of votes in an election.

David Chapman's paper analyzes the role of political parties in election processes and contrasts the situation in which all persons contribute directly to decision making to the situation in which participation is mediated by party activity.

Douglas Rae's paper describes an estimate of decisiveness and indecisiveness of n-party systems. He describes a way of determining the degree to which actual elections produce outcomes that will enable those elected to govern decisively.

Robert Wilson's paper examines some details of the relationship between the theory of games and collective decision processes. It has been argued that solution theory may be considered to offer prescriptions for the production of reasonable social choices, and an n-person game, described in characteristic function form, can also be expressed in the language of the social choice literature. Wilson argues that no system of vote trading will produce satisfactory solutions and the relationship of Arrow's thoreme to solution notions is discussed. John Chamberlin also analyzes political choice processes using game theoretic notions. He conceives of the platform selection process an an n-person game and attempts to find equilibrium conditions for the process of platform selection in a two party system that uses a majority decision rule.

CHAPTER 3.1

SOME EXTENSIONS TO A MATHEMATICAL MODEL OF DEMOCRATIC CHOICE[1]

OTTO A. DAVIS and MELVIN J. HINICH

Carnegie-Mellon University

1 INTRODUCTION

Recent years have witnessed on increasing recognition of the importance of the entire problem of social choice. One aspect of this recognition is the appearance and growth of a still small body of literature which is devoted to the construction of analytic models of democratic choice. Prominent examples include the work of Black (1958), Black and Newing (1951), Buchanan and Tullock (1962), Downs (1957) and Tullock (1965, 1967). There are several common threads in this literature. First, the analysis is based upon the assumption of "rational" voters who have well defined preferences. Second, the general methodological approach involves choice between paired comparisons which are sometimes interpreted as competing candidates or parties. Third, much of the work can be characterized as being a one dimensional "spatial" model.[2]

This paper is an extension of previous work (Davis and Hinich (1966, 1967, 1968)) which is similar to the literature referenced above in the sense that it too utilizes the first two of the above three points but differs in that it is a multi-dimensional spatial model. In order for the analysis presented in this paper to make sense, it is necessary to review briefly certain of the salient aspects and assumptions of the model which is to be extended here.

2 THE MODEL

There are only two basic parts in the model. First, there is a simple rule which is taken to represent the decision mechanism of a voter confronted with choosing between competing candidates who, in turn, are viewed as being nothing more than collections of policies. Second, there is a probabilistic representation of the distribution of preferences across the population. For the results presented in this paper, a bimodal mixture of two distributions is assumed to be required to represent adequately the preferred positions of the total population. It is also desirable to point out that issues, though not necessarily utility, are measured on a cardinal scale which is the usual practice in economic models. However, utility (or disutility) need not have a cardinal measure although for certain purposes it is convenient and insightful to assume such a measure.

It is appropriate to begin the review of the formal model by considering individual preferences. Assume that each individual in the voting population perceives n issues which are relevant to an election. Each voter is assumed to have a most desired or most preferred position on each of these issues. Thus the column vector $x' = (x_1, \ldots, x_n)$ denotes the most preferred position of a given voter for each of the relevant issues. In other words, if the ith issue is monetary support of the government for higher education, then x_i represents the number of dollars which the given individual desires to see the government spend on higher education. Since any issue, such as governmental support for higher education, can be divided into sub-issues and since different individuals can perceive the sub–issues in various ways, the assumption that n dimensional vectors can be taken to represent the most preferred position of individual voters is heroic.

Obviously, except in the most trivial case, all voters cannot be allowed to enjoy their most preferred position. Provision must be made for the "loss" which a voter must feel when governmental policy differs from that which he most prefers. Let the column vector $\theta' = (\theta_1, \ldots, \theta_n)$ represent governmental policy. The loss function is defined as follows:

$$(x - \theta)' \, A(x - \theta) = \|x - \theta\|^2 \tag{2.1}$$

where A is a positive definite $n \times n$ matrix and the term on the right hand side of the equality defines the notation which will be used here.[3] Note that this loss function is quadratic in θ. Arguments as to why the assumption of a quadratic loss is acceptable can be found in Davis and Hinich (1966).

The definition of the loss function (2.1) makes easy the specification of voting rules. Suppose that there are two candidates competing in an election where the first has a platform represented by the column vector $\theta' = (\theta_1, \ldots, \theta_n)$ and the second has a platform represented by the column vector $\phi' = (\phi_1, \ldots, \phi_n)$. Consider the voter whose most preferred position is represented by x. This voter casts his ballot for the first candidate if

$$\|x - \theta\|^2 < \|x - \phi\|^2 \tag{2.2}$$

and for the second if

$$\|x - \theta\|^2 > \|x - \phi\|^2 \tag{2.3}$$

so that a voter is presumed to select that candidate for which his loss is least.[4] The intuitive meaning of these voting rules is that a person selects that candidate whose platform is closest to his own position.

It is now necessary to characterize the total population. For the purpose of this paper suppose that the total population of voters can be exhaustively and exclusively divided into two groups or parties. It will be assumed that there are certain similarities between the members of these two groups. In particular, presume that the taste of the members of the first party are sufficiently similar that they share the matrix A used in definition (2.1) of the loss function. To avoid ambiguity, this matrix will be subscripted and denoted A_1. This assumption can be interpreted as meaning that the members of the first party have identical intensities of preference about the various issues. Of course, despite the assumed identical intensities of preference, it is desirable to allow for divergence of opinion. Accordingly, it is assumed that the preferred positions (the x) of the members of the first party can be described by a multivariate normal distribution $N(\mu_1, \Sigma_1)$ with mean column vector $\mu_1' = (\mu_{11}, \ldots, u_{1n})$ and covariance matrix Σ_1. Taken together, these assumptions mean, for example, that the first party can have members who desire large expenditures on education and others who desire small (even negative) expenditures, but all members must feel equally intense about the issue.

For simplicity the same assumptions are made with respect to the members of the first party. They too share a matrix A used in (2.1) and this matrix will be subscripted and denoted A_2. Similarly, the preferred positions (the x) of the members of the second party are described by a multivariate normal distribution $N(\mu_2, \Sigma_2)$ with mean column vector $\mu_2' = (\mu_{21}, \ldots, \mu_{2n})$ and covariance matrix Σ_2.

Now suppose that the proportion of the total population of voters which are members of the first party is α, $0 \leq \alpha \leq 1$, so that the proportion which are members of the second party is $\beta = 1 - \alpha$. The density function for the preferred positions of the total population of voters is the bimodal function

$$f(x) = \alpha N(x|\mu_1, \Sigma_1) + \beta N(x|\mu_2, \Sigma_2) \tag{2.4}$$

where $N(x|\mu, \Sigma)$ is the multinormal density with the indicated vector of means and covariance matrix. This definition (2.4) implies that the mean preferred position for the total population is

$$\mu = \alpha\mu_1 + \beta\mu_2 \tag{2.5}$$

which is the weighed average of the mean vectors of the two parties. The covariance of $f(x)$ is

$$\Sigma = \alpha\Sigma_1 + \beta\Sigma_2 + \alpha\beta(\mu_1 - \mu_2)(\mu_1 - \mu_2)' \tag{2.6}$$

where Σ is obviously *nxn*. Observe that, as a general rule, definition (2.4) can be taken to mean that $f(x)$ is a bimodal density. This bimodal characterization (2.4) of the total population and the provision for the loss matrices A_1 and A_2 constitute the "theme" of this paper. These assumptions distinguish this paper from the other Davis and Hinich papers.

Recalling from above that the members of the first and second parties are assumed to share the loss matrices A_1 and A_2 respectively, and that both of these matrices are assumed to be positive definite, consider the following definitions:

$$(x - \theta)' A_1(x - \theta) = \|x - \theta\|_1^2 \tag{2.7}$$

$$(x - \theta)' A_2(x - \theta) = \|x - \theta\|_2^2 \tag{2.8}$$

so that the notational subscript on the right hand side of (2.7) identifies the loss functions of members of the first party and that of (2.8) identifies the loss functions of members of the second party.[5] Note that the voting rules (2.2) and (2.3) must be given subscripts whenever $A_1 \neq A_2$.

Given the above definitions of the relevant loss functions, the voting rules (2.2) and (2.3) which are now applicable in terms of these loss functions, and the definition (2.4) of the density of the preferred positions of the total population of voters, it is now possible to state expressions which indicate the proportion of the vote going to each of the two competing candidates in an electoral contest. Suppose that the two candidates have platforms θ and ϕ respectively. Imagine choosing a voter at random and determining which of the candidates he would select. The argument is that the probability that a randomly selected voter would choose the candidate with platform θ, given the opposition platform ϕ, can be interpreted as the proportion of the total vote going to the candidate with platform θ under the assumption that there are no abstentions. Hence, the expression

$$r(\theta|\phi) = \alpha P(\|x - \theta\|_1 < \|x - \phi\|_1) + \beta P(\|x - \theta\|_2 < \|x - \phi\|_2) \qquad (2.9)$$

indicates the proportion of the total vote going to the candidate with platform θ, given the opposition platform ϕ. Obviously, since there are no abstentions and $f(x)$ is continuous

$$(r\phi|\theta) = 1 - r(\theta|\phi) \qquad (2.10)$$

is the proportion of the vote going to the candidate with platform ϕ.

It is sometimes convenient to view $r(\theta|\phi)$ in a somewhat different form than that given by (2.9). The argument in Davis and Hinich [4] demonstrates that

$$\begin{aligned} P(\|x - \theta\|_1 < \|x - \phi\|_1) &= P(y_1 > t_1) \\ P(\|x - \theta\|_2 < \|x - \phi\|_2) &= P(y_2 > t_2) \end{aligned} \qquad (2.11)$$

where y_1 and y_2 are defined as follows

$$\begin{aligned} y_1 &= \frac{(x - \mu_1)' A_1(\theta - \phi)}{\|\theta - \phi\|_1^*} \\ y_2 &= \frac{(x - \mu_2)' A_2(\theta - \phi)}{\|\theta - \phi\|_2^*} \end{aligned} \qquad (2.12)$$

and t_1 and t_2 are given by

$$\begin{aligned} t_1 &= \frac{\|\theta - \mu_1\|_1^2 - \|\phi - \mu_1\|_1^2}{2\|\theta - \phi\|_1^*} \\ t_2 &= \frac{\|\theta - \mu_2\|_2^2 - \|\phi - \mu_2\|_2^2}{2\|\theta - \phi\|_2^*} \end{aligned} \qquad (2.13)$$

where the starred norms are given by

$$\begin{aligned} \|\theta - \phi\|_1^* &= (\theta - \phi)' A_1 \Sigma_1 A_1(\theta - \phi) \\ \|\theta - \phi\|_2^* &= (\theta - \phi)' A_2 \Sigma_2 A_2(\theta - \phi) \end{aligned} \qquad (2.14)$$

so that

$$r(\theta\phi) = \alpha P(y_1 > t_1) + \beta P(y_2 > t_2) \qquad (2.15)$$

is an alternative form of (2.9). One can also see from (2.12) or from the argument in Davis and Hinich (1966) that under the assumptions here both y_1 and y_2 are normally distributed with mean zero and unit variance.[6]

3 TO POLARIZE OR TO COALESCE

Having described the basic elements of the model which is to be extended here, it is appropriate to put the results which are developed in this section into perspective by reviewing one of the theorems developed in Davis and Hinich [4]. This theorem assumes

$$A_1 = A_2 = A \tag{3.1}$$

so that all voters in the total population have the same intensity of preference on all of the issues although preferred positions differ and can be described by a continuous distribution $f(x)$. Also assume that A remains positive definite and that the covariance matrix Σ has its eigenvalues bounded away from zero and infinity as n (the number of indices or issues) goes to infinity. If the two candidates have platforms

$$\theta = \mu$$
$$\phi = \mu + \varepsilon 1, \quad \varepsilon \neq 0, \quad 1' = (1, ..., 1) \tag{3.2}$$

so that one candidate's platform is the mean and the other's platform is not the mean, then the theorem states that

$$P(\|x - \mu\| < \|x - \phi\|) \to 1 \text{ as } n \to \infty \tag{3.3}$$

where the 1 in (3.3) is the number one. In other words, as the number of issues grows large the proportion of the vote which goes to a candidate whose platform is the mean preferred position approaches one. To put it another way, as the number of independent issues increases while the dispersion of preferred points remains bounded, the total population coalesces around the mean preferred position when faced with a forced choice between the mean and some other position.

This section develops two limit theorems which are somewhat similar to the one outlined above. Under one set of conditions the population polarizes. Under another set it coalesces. Both theorems are based upon assumptions which differ from those above. In particular,

$$A_1 \neq A_2 \tag{3.4}$$

is allowed. For the first theorem the platforms

$$\theta = \mu_1; \quad \phi = \mu_2 \tag{3.5}$$

are assumed. This assumption can be interpreted as meaning that the candidates have been selected by a primary within their own party, where the means μ_1 and μ_2 are dominant under the assumptions. Thus the candidates "represent" their respective parties.

The first theorem concerns polarization. The interpretation of this theorem requires the utilization of an interpretation of the theorem discussed above. In the selection of the candidates in the primaries the members of each party tend more and more as the number of issues increases to vote for a candidate whose platform is the mean preferred position of the members of that party until in the limit the platform of the mean position simply swamps any other platform in any two candidate contest. In the limit the platform of the mean position attracts all of the votes for the nomination In this sense, the members of both of the assumptions and this interpretation it is quite reasonable to use $\|\mu_1 - \mu_2\|_1^2$ and $\|\mu_1 - \mu_2\|_2^2$ to represent the approximate utility loss which any member of one party might feel if the candidate of the other party won the election and enacted his platform.

Let ε represent a scalar. Let μ_{1i} and μ_{2i} represent the ith component of the vector of the mean preferred position of the members of the first and second parties respectively.

Theorem 1 For a given $\varepsilon > 0$ and integer $i^* \geq 1$, suppose that $|\mu_{1i} - \mu_{2i}| > \varepsilon$ for all $i \geq i^*$. Given the previous assumptions, $\|\mu_1 - \mu_2\|_1^2 \to \infty$ as $n \to \infty$ and $\|\mu_1 - \mu_2\|_2^2 \to \infty$ as $n \to \infty$.

Proof With no loss of generality let $i^* = 1$. Define

$$\delta = \mu_1 - \mu_2 \qquad (3.6)$$

for notational simplicity and let δ_i represent the ith component of δ. For any $n \times 1$ vector $a \neq 0$, it follows from (2.6) that

$$a'\sum a > \alpha\beta(a'\delta)^2 \qquad (3.7)$$

since $a'\Sigma_1 a$ and $a'\Sigma_2 a$ are necessarily positive. By assumption $\delta_i^2 > \varepsilon^2$ for all i. Let a_i represent the ith component of a. Choose $a_i = \pm 1/\sqrt{n}$ with the sign selected so that $a_i\delta_i > 0$ for each i. Thus

$$(a'\delta)^2 = \left(\sum_i a_i\delta_i\right)^2 > \left(\sum_i \varepsilon/\sqrt{n}\right)^2 = n\varepsilon^2 \qquad (3.8)$$

and also

$$a'a = \sum_i a_i^2 = 1 \qquad (3.9)$$

by construction. Therefore, for the vector a of unit length it follows from (3.7) and (3.8) that

$$a'\sum a > \alpha\beta n\varepsilon^2 \qquad (3.10)$$

and since the maximum eigenvalue of Σ is the maximum of $v'\Sigma v$ for all $v'v = 1$, inequality (3.10) implies that the maximum eigenvalue must be greater than $\alpha\beta n\varepsilon^2$. This maximum eigenvalue thus goes to infinity as $n \to \infty$. Let λ_1 and λ_2 represent the minimum eigenvalues of A_1 and A_2 respectively. Then from the properties of eigenvalues

$$\|\mu_1 - \mu_2\|_1^2 = \|\delta\|_1^2 > \lambda_1\delta'\delta$$
$$\|\mu_1 - \mu_2\|_2^2 = \|\delta\|_2^2 > \lambda_2\delta'\delta$$

(3.11)

where the equalities are merely definitional. Moreover, since by assumption $\delta_i^2 > \varepsilon^2$ for all i

$$\lambda_1\delta'\delta > \lambda_1 n\varepsilon^2; \quad \lambda_2\delta'\delta > \lambda_2 n\varepsilon^2$$

(3.12)

obviously obtains. Combining (3.12) and (3.11),

$$\|\mu_1 - \mu_2\|_1^2 \to \infty \text{ as } n \to \infty$$
$$\|\mu_1 - \mu_2\|_2^2 \to \infty \text{ as } n \to \infty$$

(3.13)

is the result.   QED

It is clear that Theorem 1 requires some interpretation. From the above discussion of the theorem proved previously in Davis and Hinich (1966) it is clear that with a large number of issues (or n) the voters within each party will always select the mean preferred position of their own party. It is in this sense that the voters within each party "prefer" their party's mean. Therefore, with a large number of issues (Σ_1 and Σ_2 as well as A_1 and A_2 must remain nonsingular), voters within each party will always cast their ballot for the mean preferred position of their own party in an election in which the choice is one of the two means. Under the assumed conditions with a large number of issues, voters never select the candidate of the opposition party. Hence, the majority party always wins the election and its mean preferred position is adopted by the government. When the two means differ and there is a large number of issues, the overall population polarizes around the two means.

How is the situation perceived by the voters within the two parties? From the previous argument it is reasonable to use $\|\mu_1 - \mu_2\|_1^2$ and $\|\mu_1 - \mu_2\|_2^2$ as approximations to the utility losses which will be experienced by the members of the first and second parties respectively if the opposite party is the majority and thus wins the election. Recall the basic assumption that these means μ_1 and μ_2 differ for $i \geq i^*$. Theorem 1 establishes that these losses approach infinity as n approaches infinity. Therefore, with a large number of issues or with a very sophisticated population so that many indices are needed to measure the issues, the members of the losing party are most unhappy about the outcome of the election. One can speculate that this situation is not likely to be stable. Not only does the minority party have no chance of winning the election, but the costs of losing are infinitely high. Thus there may be a movement, perhaps violent, to alter the system. Polarization is not likely to be conducive to a democratic form of government.

On the other hand, consider a situation in which new issues become relevant to the electorate and these issues have the property that the distribution of preferred positions for the total population is unimodal and symmetric for these additional issues. What is to be argued here is that the total population coalesces around the mean preferred position for the total population.

Imagine an electoral contest between two candidates in which one adopts a platform θ defined as follows

$$\theta = \mu = \alpha\mu_1 + \beta\mu_2 \tag{3.14}$$

and the other adopts a platform ϕ which satisfies the following condition for all $i \geq i^*$

$$|\mu_i - \phi_i| \geq \varepsilon, \quad \varepsilon > 0 \tag{3.15}$$

where μ_i and ϕ_i represent the ith component of the vectors μ and ϕ respectively and ε is a positive scalar. Let μ_{1i} and μ_{2i} represent the ith component of the vectors u_1 and μ_2 respectively.

Theorem 2   Assume that for all $i \geq i^*$, $\mu_{1i} = \mu_{2i}$. Suppose that one platform θ is given by (3.14) and the other platform ϕ satisfies (3.15) for all $i \geq i^*$. Then, given ϕ and the assumptions defining the model, the proportion $r(\mu|\phi)$ of the vote going to the candidate with platform $\theta = \mu$ goes to one as $n \to \infty$.

Proof   With no loss of generality, let $i^* = 1$. Let a be an n component column vector which satisfies $a'a = 1$. Assuming that the eigenvalues of Σ_1 and Σ_2 are bounded away from infinity because of the presumed lack of colinearity between issues, it is clear from (2.6) that $a'\Sigma a < \infty$ as $n \to \infty$ since $\mu_{1i} - \mu_{2i} = 0$ for all $i \geq i^*$. Consider the definition (2.15) of $r(\theta|\phi)$. The plan here is to demonstrate that $P(y_1 > t_1) \to 1$ as $n \to \infty$. It will be obvious that the same argument applies for $P(y_2 > t_2)$. Consider the definition (2.13) of t_1. Due to the definition (3.14) and the assumption $i^* = 1$, $\|\mu - \mu_1\|_1^2 = 0$ since $\mu_1 = \mu$ so that

$$t_1 = -\frac{\|\phi - \mu\|_1^2}{2\|\mu - \phi\|_1^*} \tag{3.16}$$

obtains. Since utility is defined only up to a monotonic transformation, there is no loss of generality in assuming $\Sigma_1 \leq A_1^{-1}$ so that $A_1\Sigma_1A_1 \leq A_1$. Referring to the definition (2.14) of $\|\theta - \phi\|_1^*$, this assumption means that

$$\frac{\|\phi - \mu\|_1^2}{2\|\mu - \phi\|_1^*} \gtreqqless \frac{\|\phi - \mu\|_1}{2} \tag{3.17}$$

obviously holds. Now let λ_1 represent the minimum eigenvalue of A_1 and observe that $\lambda_1 > 0$ due to the assumption that A_1 is positive definite. Thus λ_1 is bounded away from zero as $n \to \infty$. Using the well known property of eigenvalues one can write

$$\frac{\|\phi - \mu\|_1}{2} \gtreqqless \frac{1}{2}\sqrt{\lambda_1\sum_i(\phi_i - \mu_i)^2} \tag{3.18}$$

where the Σ in (3.18) represents the operation of summation. Given the assumption (3.15) and using Σ just as above,

$$\frac{1}{2}\sqrt{\lambda_1\sum_i(\phi_i - \mu_i)^2} \gtreqqless \frac{1}{2}\sqrt{\lambda_1\sum_i\varepsilon_i^2} = \frac{1}{2}\sqrt{\lambda_1 n\varepsilon^2} \tag{3.19}$$

and the last term on the right obviously goes to infinity as $n \to \infty$. Combining the above steps, $t_1 \to \infty$ as $n \to \infty$ so that

$$P(y_1 > t_1) \to 1 \text{ as } n \to \infty \tag{3.20}$$

obviously obtains. The same argument applies for the other distribution so

$$P(y_2 > t_2) \to 1 \text{ as } n \to \infty \tag{3.21}$$

is obviously true. Therefore,

$$r(\mu|\phi) = \alpha P(y_1 > t_1) + \beta P(y_2 > t_2) \to 1 \text{ as } n \to \infty \tag{3.22}$$

clearly follows.   QED

The above theorem obviously needs some interpretation. Its intuitive meaning is that if many new issues become relevant to the campaign and if there is enough "agreement" between the members of the two parties for the means of the preferred positions to be the same on these new issues, then the overall mean becomes dominant in an extreme way in that it will attract almost all of the votes and all in the limit. In this sense the two parties coalesce. The middle takes over. The parties tend to resemble one another. One can speculate that this type of situation is very conducive to democracy. One can also suggest that Theorem 2 provides a strategy for obtaining agreement when there is disagreement between two parties. What one can do is to find new relevant issues upon which agreement can be obtained and this process will help to bring overall agreement and a compromise at the overall mean. Of course, the strategy is not without danger since Theorem 1 demonstrates that if there is no agreement on the new issues there will be polarization.

Finally, it should be observed that while both Theorems 1 and 2 were concerned with situations in which there were only two parties, it is obvious that the methods of the proofs allow easy extensions to situations in which there are many parties. In this sense the Theorems are rather general.

4   A DEFINITION OF COHESIVE POPULATIONS

Observe that the factors t_1 and t_2 defined by (2.13) involve two metrics. Explicitly,

$$\|x\|_1 = \sqrt{x'A_1x}$$
$$\|x\|_2 = \sqrt{x'A_2x}$$

and

(4.1)

$$\|x\|_1^* = \sqrt{x'A_1\Sigma_1A_1x}$$
$$\|x\|_2^* = \sqrt{x'A_2\Sigma_2A_2x}$$

(4.2)

so that one metric is defined by the matrices A_1 and A_2 respectively and the other is given by the matrices $A_1\Sigma_1A_1$ and $A_2\Sigma_2A_2$ respectively. It was observed earlier that the ordinality of utility means that the matrices A_1 and A_2 are defined only up to a scalar multiplication so that there is no loss of generality is assuming

$$\|x\|_1^* = \sqrt{x'A_1\Sigma_1A_1x} \leqq \sqrt{x'A_1x} = \|x\|_1$$
$$\|x\|_2^* = \sqrt{x'A_2\Sigma_2A_2x} \leqq \sqrt{x'A_2x_2} = \|x\|_2$$

(4.3)

since suitable scalar multiplications could always make the inequalities hold without altering the assumed preference orderings.

Interest here is centered on the special class of situations in which

$$\|x\|_1^* = \sqrt{x'A_1\Sigma_1A_1x} = \sqrt{x'A_1x} = \|x\|_1$$
$$\|x\|_2^* = \sqrt{x'A_2\Sigma_2A_2x} = \sqrt{x'A_2x} = \|x\|_2$$

(4.4)

can be arranged after suitable scalar multiplications of A_1 and A_2 at least for all those vectors x in the space of interest about μ. Of course, if the equalities are true for all x then

$$A_1\Sigma_1A_1 = A_1; \quad A_2\Sigma_2A_2 = A_2$$

(4.5)

or to put it in another equivalent way

$$A_1 = \Sigma_1^{-1}; \quad A_2 = \Sigma_2^{-1} \tag{4.6}$$

also obtains.

Clearly (4.5) or (4.6) imply a very special class of situations. Accordingly, there is some necessity in obtaining an intuitive understanding of what is implied. Probably the best approach is to make the simplifying assumption that the matrices are diagonal. In other words, assume that non-diagonal elements are zero. Let a_{ii} represent the ith diagonal element of either A_1 or A_2 and let σ_{ii} represent the ith diagonal element of the corresponding matrix Σ_1 or Σ_2. Then (4.6) clearly means that $a_{ii} = 1/\sigma_{ii}$ for $i = 1, ..., n$. Since the relative size of the a_{ii} indicate the intensity of feeling on the corresponding issue, the inverse relationship $a_{ii} = 1/\sigma_{ii}$ means that for those issues upon which the members of the population feel strongly there is a small variance about the mean preference so that there is considerable agreement within the particular party as to what is preferred. Conversely, when the a_{ii} is relatively small the σ_{ii} is relatively large. Thus there is considerable disagreement about what is desired within the particular party whenever the issue is not considered to be very important and the members do not feel so strongly about it. Intensity of preference and the dispersion of the preferred positions are inversely related.

Populations or parties whose members share a common loss matrix which can be transformed by a scalar to be made equal to the inverse of its covariance matrix will be called cohesive. In other words, (4.6) defines two cohesive parties.

It must be admitted that the assumption that parties are cohesive is very strong. Not only does it require the presumption that all members of each party share the same A matrix in their loss functions, which is rather stringent and non-intuitive, but it also requires (4.6) to be satisfied. Nevertheless, there are some (admittedly weak) justifications for the assumption of cohesion. One can argue that on those issues which are most important to our society, such as the nature of our governmental institutions, social processes arrange for something very near a consensus by the time citizens reach voting age. Thus there is little variance in opinion about these most important issues. One can argue further that more transient issues, where there is greater diversity of opinion and fewer social processes to arrange for greater agreement, are likely to be judged not nearly so important so that the intensity of preference is not likely to be nearly so strong. Of course, one cannot push this argument too far and it remains that the presumption that parties are cohesive is a strong assumption.

In the developments which follow the assumption of cohesion is made whenever it will add to the analysis and simplify the proofs. Insofar as one is concerned with applying the theory, it is not necessary for the population to be cohesive. All that is required is for "approximate cohesion" to obtain for vectors in a region about the mean preferred position.

5 THE CASE OF TWO PARTIES OF EQUAL SIZE

One of the most interesting and important cases of two party competition is the instance where each of the parties has roughly the same strength so that the competition is fierce and it is costly for either of the candidates to make a mistake. It is especially important in this case to try to determine whether dominant strategies exist, to explore the nature of such strategies if they do exist, and to determine the conditions for their existence. Accordingly, in the developments which follow the possibility of primaries and other intraparty competition placing constraints upon a candidate's selection of a platform is ignored and attention is centered solely upon this issue of dominance. In addition, in a theoretical sense this notion of "equal strength" is probably best translated and represented by the assumption that the parties are of equal size. Therefore, the following developments assume that $\alpha = \beta = 1/2$.

In an election where one candidate has platform θ and the other platform ϕ, the proportion of the vote going to the candidate with platform θ is given by (2.15). It was observed earlier that under the assumptions here where the preferred positions of the members of each of the two parties are described by multivariate normal distributions, the variables y_1 and y_2, defined by (2.12), are distributed normally with mean zero and unit variance. Using the property of symmetry of the $N(0, 1)$ distribution, recalling the definition (2.13) of t_1 and t_2, and definining $k_1 = -t_1$ and $k_2 = -t_2$, it follows that

$$P(y_1 > t_1) = P(y_1 < k_1)$$
$$P(y_2 > t_2) = P(y_2 < k_2)$$

(5.1)

where k_1 and k_2 are given by

$$k_1 = \frac{\|\phi - \mu_1\|_1^2 - \|\theta - \mu_1\|_1^2}{2\|\theta - \phi\|_1^*}$$
$$k_2 = \frac{\|\phi - \mu_2\|_2^2 - \|\theta - \mu_2\|_2^2}{2\|\theta - \phi\|_2^*}$$

(5.2)

due to the definition (2.13) of t_1 and t_2. Due to (5.1) it is now possible to write (2.15) in an altered form

$$r(\theta|\phi) = \alpha\Phi(k_1) + \beta\Phi(k_2) \qquad (5.3)$$

where $\Phi(k)$ is the cumulative distribution function of the $N(0, 1)$, the unit normal.

While $r(\theta|\phi)$ is the probability that a voter who is selected at random will cast his ballot for the candidate with platform θ, given that the other candidate has platform ϕ, this probability can be interpreted as the proportion of the total vote which goes to the candidate with platform θ. Thus $r(\theta|\phi) > 1/2$ is a necessary and sufficient condition for the candidate with platform θ to win the election over his opponent with platform ϕ. It is this condition which provides much of the analytical power in the following developments.

Consider the set of platforms defined by

$$\theta = \lambda\mu_1 + (1 - \lambda)\mu_2, \quad 0 \leq \lambda \leq 1 \qquad (5.4)$$

where λ is a scalar so that this set of platforms constitute the line connecting the mean preferred positions of the members of the two parties. Theorem 5.2 of Davis and Hinich (1966) indicates that if $A_1 = A_2 = A$ and if the platforms of the two candidates are restricted to the line defined by (5.4), then there exists a point (platform) defined by

$$\theta^* = \lambda^*\mu_1 + (1 - \lambda^*)\mu_2 \qquad (5.5)$$

which dominates all other points on the line (5.4) in the sense that

$$r(\theta^*|\theta) > 1/2, \quad \theta \neq \theta^* \qquad (5.6)$$

always obtains. This platform θ^* was only shown to exist and was not identified except in an example, but it was observed that θ^* need not always be the mean preferred position $(\alpha\mu_1 + \beta\mu_2)$ of the overall population. In addition, Theorem 5.1 of Davis and Hinich (1966) demonstrated that if $A_1 = A_2 = A$ and the platform ϕ is not on the line defined by (5.4), then there exists a platform θ on the line defined by (5.4) such that $r(\theta|\phi) > 1/2$. Taken together, these two theorems suggest that θ^* must be a dominant platform. Indeed, Davis and Hinich (1966) made this conjecture. As it turns out there are conditions under which θ^* is dominant, but dominance is not always a characteristic of a total population which is made up of a mixture of two multivariate normal distributions. The developments in this section are largely devoted to examining conditions under which θ^* is or is not a dominant platform. In addition, when θ^* is not dominant bounds are obtained for the region in which other points can win when competing against θ^*.

The following analysis can be considerably simplified without a loss of generality by some changes in the notation. Consider the operation of subtracting the mean preferred position μ_1 from the preferred positions of all voters in the total population. Then the mean preferred position of the members of the first party becomes

$$0 = \mu_1 - \mu_1 \tag{5.7}$$

and that of the second party becomes

$$u = \mu_2 - \mu_1 \tag{5.8}$$

while the restriction $\alpha = \beta = 1/2$ means that

$$\mu = \tfrac{1}{2}u \tag{5.9}$$

is now the mean preferred position of the voters in the total population. Under this notation

$$
\begin{aligned}
k_1 &= \frac{\|\phi\|_1^2 - \|\theta\|_1^2}{2\|\phi - \theta\|_1^*} \\[2mm]
k_2 &= \frac{\|\phi - u\|_2^2 - \|\theta - u\|_2^2}{2\|\phi - \theta\|_2^*}
\end{aligned}
\tag{5.10}
$$

become the definition of k_1 and k_2.

Consider the case where strategies are constrained to competition between platforms which are a linear combination of the means of the preferred positions of the members of the two parties. In particular, let

$$\phi = \lambda u, \qquad 0 \le \lambda \le 1 \tag{5.11}$$

be the platform of one candidate and

$$\theta^* = \lambda^* u \tag{5.12}$$

be the platform of the other candidate where

$$\lambda^* = \frac{1}{1 + \dfrac{\|u\|_1^2 \, \|u\|_2^*}{\|u\|_2^2 \, \|u\|_1^*}} \tag{5.13}$$

defines λ^*.

Theorem 3 Let θ^* be defineb by (5.12) and ϕ be given by (5.11). Then $r(\theta^*|\phi) > 1/2$ for all $\phi \neq \theta^*$.

Proof The objective is to show that

$$r(\theta^*|\,\phi) = \alpha\Phi(k_1) + \beta\Phi(k_2) > 1/2 \tag{5.14}$$

for all $\phi \neq \theta^*$ where ϕ and θ^* are defined by (5.11) and (5.12) respectively. Since under the assumptions $\alpha = \beta = 1/2$, (5.14) is true if and only if

$$\Phi(k_1) + \Phi(k_2) > 1 \qquad (5.15)$$

and since $\Phi(k)$ is the cumulative density function of the unit normal

$$\Phi(-k) = 1 - \Phi(k) \qquad (5.16)$$

for all k. Therefore, if and only if

$$k_1 + k_2 > 0 \qquad (5.17)$$

will (5.15) obtain. This condition (5.17) is used again and again in the proofs which follow. Using definition (5.10) and substituting (5.11) and (5.12)

$$\frac{\lambda^2 \|u\|_1^2 - \lambda^{*2}\|u\|_1^2}{2|\lambda - \lambda^*|\ \|u\|_1^*} + \frac{(1-\lambda)^2\ \|u\|_2^2 - (1-\lambda^*)^2\ \|u\|_2^2}{2|\lambda - \lambda^*|\ \|u\|_2^*} > 0 \quad (5.18)$$

is merely a restatement of (5.17). By noting that multiplication by $2|\lambda - \lambda^*|$ simplifies the expression and preserves the inequality, and by collecting terms in (5.18)

$$(\lambda - \lambda^*)(\lambda + \lambda^*)\frac{\|u\|_1^2}{\|u\|_1^*} - (\lambda - \lambda^*)(2 - \lambda - \lambda^*)\frac{\|u\|_2^2}{\|u\|_2^*} > 0 \quad (5.19)$$

is obtained as an equivalent expression. There are two cases to be considered. Suppose $\lambda > \lambda^*$. Then division of (5.19) by $(\lambda - \lambda^*)$ preserves the direction of the inequality and collecting terms gives

$$(\lambda + \lambda^*)\left(\frac{\|u\|_1^2}{\|u\|_1^*} + \frac{\|u\|_2^2}{\|u\|_2^*}\right) > 2\frac{\|u\|_2^2}{\|u\|_2^*} \qquad (5.20)$$

as an expression which is equivalent to (5.19). If one divides both sides by the terms within the second parentheses from the left and rearranges the right hand side according to (5.13), then

$$\lambda + \lambda^* > 2\lambda^* \qquad (5.21)$$

is obtained. Hence, (5.20) is true if and only if (5.21) holds. However, (5.21) is true because of the assumption $\lambda > \lambda^*$ and therefore (5.14) also holds. By repeating the same argument the result can be seen to be true for the case $\lambda < \lambda^*$.   QED

Theorem 3 needs some interpretation. It demonstrates that even in the case in which the loss matrices are different so that $A_1 \neq A_2$, there exists a dominant platform which is identified by (5.12) and (5.13) if the two candidates are constrained to choose a platform which is a linear combination of the two mean vectors of the preferred positions of the members of the two parties. In other words, if the candidates must choose a platform which can be represented as a point on the line which connects the means of the two parties, then there exists a single point which is dominant in the sense that the candidate selecting it will be certain to obtain a majority of the votes as long as the other candidate does not select the same platform. Candidates always tie if they select the same platform. Therefore, when strategies are constrained a limited kind of dominance is insured.

There is some interest in examining this platform even though it is dominant in only a limited sense. Under the assumptions and notation used here, (5.9) identifies the mean preferred position of the members of the total population. Intuitively, one might think that this mean should be the dominant platform. Definition (5.13) reveals, however, that this "dominant" platform need not be and in general is not identical to the overall mean. If and only if

$$\frac{\|u\|_1^2}{\|u\|_2^2} = \frac{\|u\|_1^*}{\|u\|_2^*} \tag{5.22}$$

does the platform which is dominant along the line coincide with the mean preferred position of the total population. Otherwise, a candidate gains by being a little closer to one or the other of the mean preferred position of the two parties. If the two parties are cohesive, which is defined by $A_1 = \Sigma_1^{-1}$ and $A_2 = \Sigma_2^{-1}$ then the line-dominant strategy and the overall mean are identical if and only if $\|u\|_1 = \|u\|_2$ or, to put it another way, if suitable scalar transformations can arrange $A_1 = A_2$.

Unfortunately, the notion that strategies are constrained to the line segment joining the means of the two populations is critical to the proof of the existence of a dominant platform. Later examples will show that overall dominance need not exist. For the moment, however, it is interesting to examine a case where there is true dominance in the sense that no constraints need be placed upon the allowable platforms.

Theorem 4 Assume $A_1 = A_2 = A$ and $\Sigma_1 = \Sigma_2 = \Sigma$ so that $\lambda^* = 1/2$ and $\theta^* = (1/2) u$. Under these assumptions $r(\theta^*|\phi) > 1/2$ for all $\phi \neq \theta^*$ so that θ^* is a dominant platform against all alternatives.

Proof The objective is to show that (5.14) obtains for $\theta^* = (1/2) u$. Since the normality assumption is made throughout the paper, (5.14) will obtain if and only if (5.17) is true. Substituting from (5.10) it follows that $r(\theta^*|\phi) > 1/2$ if and only if

$$\frac{\|\phi\|^2 - \tfrac{1}{4}\|u\|^2}{2\|\phi - \tfrac{1}{2}u\|^*} + \frac{\|\phi - u\|^2 - \tfrac{1}{4}\|u\|^2}{2\|\phi - \tfrac{1}{2}u\|^*} > 0 \tag{5.23}$$

22*

where the subscripts on the metrics have been dropped since $A_1 = A_2 = A$ and $\Sigma_1 = \Sigma_2 = \Sigma$. Since $\|\phi - \frac{1}{2}u\|^* > 0$ for all $\phi \neq \frac{1}{2}u$, multiplication by twice this quantity preserves the inequality and yields

$$v(\phi) = \|\phi\|^2 + \|\phi - u\|^2 - \frac{1}{2}\|u\|^2 > 0 \qquad (5.24)$$

which is true if and only if (5.23) obtains. Differentiating v with respect to ϕ gives

$$\frac{\partial v}{\partial \phi} = 2A\phi + 2A(\phi - u) \qquad (5.25)$$

and since A is positive definite A^{-1} exists and therefore it is obvious that the unique minimum to $\partial v/\partial \phi = 0$ is $\phi = \frac{1}{2}u$. Therefore,

$$v(\phi) > v(\tfrac{1}{2}u) = 0, \quad \phi \neq \tfrac{1}{2}u \qquad (5.26)$$

obtains so that (5.24) and the preceeding inequalities are true and

$$r(\theta^*| \phi) > \tfrac{1}{2}, \quad \phi \neq \theta^*, \quad \theta^* = \tfrac{1}{2}u \qquad (5.27)$$

obtains.   QED

Some words of explanation are obviously in order. Theorem 4 establishes sufficient conditions for the overall mean to be a dominant platform when the preferred positions of the population of voters is described by an equally weighed combination of multinormal distributions. As a rule this combination of distributions results in the mixture being a bimodal density and the overall mean is between rather than at either of the modes. Nevertheless, the overall mean dominates under the postulated conditions and the candidate which selects it to be his platform is certain of at least a tie in the election. One might also observe that the overall mean can be at a point where the mixed density is relatively thin and in such a situation relatively few voters have preferred positions which are in a neighborhood of the overall mean.

Attention should be given to the fact that the conditions for overall dominance of the mean against any other strategy or platform are only sufficient. At this time one can only speculate that the conditions are rather stringent since necessary and sufficient conditions have not been obtained. While it is true (see Davis and Hinich (1966, 1968)) that the mean is always dominant in situations in which a single multinormal distribution is adequate to describe the preferred positions of the voters in the population, this dominance is no longer guaranteed when a mixture of two multinormal distributions is required to describe adequately these preferred positions. The following example illustrates this fact and casts some light upon the situation.

Let $n = 2$ and $A_1 = A_2 = I$ where I is the 2×2 identity matrix. Let the mean preferred position of the first party be given by $0' = (0, 0)$ and that of the second party be given by $u' = (1, 1)$. Under these assumptions

$$\|u\|_1 = \|u\|_2 = \sqrt{2} \qquad (5.28)$$

is easily computed. Let the variance-covariance matrices be given by

$$\Sigma_1 = \begin{bmatrix} 2 & 0 \\ 0 & 1 \end{bmatrix}, \quad \Sigma_2 = \begin{bmatrix} 1 & 0 \\ 0 & 2 \end{bmatrix} \qquad (5.29)$$

so that

$$\|u\|_1^* = \|u\|_2^* = \sqrt{3} \qquad (5.30)$$

is also easily computed. From (5.13) it follows that $\lambda^* = 1/2$ so that (5.12) yields $\theta^* = \frac{1}{2}u = (1/2, 1/2)'$. Since by assumption $\alpha = \beta = 1/2$, it is obvious that the overall mean $\mu = \frac{1}{2}u = (1/2, 1/2)'$ so that the point which would be dominant if platforms were constrained to the line segment connecting the means of the two parties is the mean of the overall distribution. Suppose that one candidate adopts θ^* as his platform. Let the other candidate select $\phi' = (1/2, 1/4)$ as his platform. The following calculations can easily be checked.

$$\|\phi\|_1^2 - \|\theta^*\|_1^2 = -\frac{3}{16}$$

$$\|\phi - u\|_2^2 - \|\theta^* - u\|_2^2 = \frac{5}{16}$$

$$\|\phi - \theta^*\|_1^* = \frac{1}{16} \qquad (5.31)$$

$$\|\phi - \theta^*\|_2^* = \frac{1}{8}$$

It follows from (5.10) that $k_1 = -3$ and $k_2 = 5/2$. Thus

$$k_1 + k_2 = -\tfrac{1}{2} < 0 \qquad (5.32)$$

and the steps preceeding (5.17) establish that in this situation

$$r(\theta^*|\phi) < \tfrac{1}{2} \qquad (5.33)$$

so that the candidate with platform θ^* obtains less than a majority and the candidate with platform ϕ wins the election. Thus the platform $\phi = (1/2, 1/4)'$ dominates the platform $\theta^* = (1/2, 1/2)'$ and ϕ is not on the line segment joining the means of the two parties. Theorem 5.1 in Davis and Hinich

(1966) establishes that in this situation there exists a point on the line segment which joins the two means which dominates any point not on the line segment. Theorem 3 above establishes that $\theta*$ dominates all points on the line segment. It follows that there is no overall dominant strategy in this situation. There is, instead, a set of intransitivity. Dominance is not guaranteed when the overall distribution consists of a mixture of two multinormals.

There is some interest in finding a bound such that a platform defined by the best point on the line segment connecting the two means is certain to win over a platform which is beyond that bound. In other words, one would like to find bounds to an area in which unconstrained candidates should choose to compete. While such a bound has not been determined for the general situation, it can be found for the special case of cohesive parties.

Define

$$c = \cfrac{1}{\cfrac{1}{\|u\|_1} + \cfrac{1}{\|u\|_2}} \tag{5.34}$$

and let $\theta* = \lambda*u$ where $\lambda*$ is defined by (5.13). Consider the inequality

$$\|\phi - \lambda*u\|_1 + \|\phi - \lambda*u\|_2 > 4c \tag{5.35}$$

and the following theorem can be stated.

Theorem 5   Let $A_1 = \Sigma_1^{-1}$ and $A_2 = \Sigma_2^{-1}$ and consider any platform ϕ which satisfies (5.35). Then $r(\lambda*u|\phi) > 1/2$.

Proof   Note that cohesive parties are assumed so that $\|u\|_1^* = \|u\|_1$ and $\|u\|_2^* = \|u\|_2$ so that from (5.13)

$$\lambda* = \cfrac{1}{1 + \cfrac{\|u\|_1}{\|u\|_2}} \tag{5.36}$$

so that

$$c = \lambda*\|u\|_1 = (1 - \lambda*)\,\|u\|_2 \tag{5.37}$$

obviously obtains. By definition $\|\theta*\|_1^2 = \lambda*^2\|u\|_1^2$ and $\|\theta* - u\|_2^2 = (1 - \lambda*)^2\,\|u\|_2^2$. Some manipulation will show that

$$\|\phi\|_1^2 - \lambda*^2\,\|u\|_1^2 = \|\phi - \lambda*u\|_1^2 + 2\lambda*\,(\phi - \lambda*u)'\,A_1u \tag{5.38}$$

$$\|\phi - u\|_2^2 - (1 - \lambda*)^2\,\|u\|_2^2 = \|\phi - \lambda*u\|_2^2 + 2(1 - \lambda*)\,(\phi - \lambda*u)'\,A_2u$$

is true. From the Schwarz inequality it follows that

$$
\begin{aligned}
(\phi - \lambda*u)'\,A_1u &> -\,\|u\|_1\,\|\phi - \lambda*u\|_1 \\
(\phi - \lambda*u)'\,A_2u &> -\|u\|_2\,\|\phi - \lambda*u\|_2
\end{aligned}
\tag{5.39}
$$

is true. Therefore,

$$\|\phi - \lambda^* u\|_1^2 + 2\lambda^*(\phi - \lambda^* u)' A_1 u > \|\phi - \lambda^* u\|_1^2 - 2\lambda^* \|u\|_1 \|\phi - \lambda^* u\|_1$$

$$\|\phi - \lambda^* u\|_2^2 + 2(1 - \lambda^*)(\phi - \lambda^* u)' A_2 u \tag{5.40}$$

$$> \|\phi - \lambda^* u\|_2^2 - 2(1 - \lambda^*) \|u\|_2 \|\phi - \lambda^* u\|_2$$

follows from (5.38) and (5.39). By definition for the case here

$$k_1 = \frac{\|\phi\|_1^2 - \lambda^{*2}\|u\|_1^2}{2\|\phi - \lambda^* u\|_1}$$

$$k_2 = \frac{\|\phi - u\|_2^2 - (1 - \lambda^*)^2 \|u\|_2^2}{2\|\phi - \lambda^* u\|_2} \tag{5.41}$$

since the parties are cohesive. Now note that if inequalities (5.38) are divided by $\|\phi - \lambda^* u\|_1$ and $\|\phi - \lambda^* u\|_2$ respectively, and if inequalities (5.40) are divided by these two terms respectively, and if definitions (5.41) are applied to the left hand sides of (5.38), then (5.38) and (5.40) jointly yield

$$2k_1 > \|\phi - \lambda^* u\|_1 - 2\lambda^* \|u\|_1$$

$$2k_2 > \|\phi - \lambda^* u\|_2 - 2(1 - \lambda^*) \|u\|_2 \tag{5.42}$$

so that if inequalities (5.42) are added and appropriate substitutions are made from (5.37)

$$2k_1 + 2k_2 > \|\phi - \lambda^* u\|_1 + \|\phi - \lambda^* u\|_2 - 4c \tag{5.43}$$

and by hypothesis (5.35) the right hand side of (5.43) is positive. Therefore

$$k_1 + k_2 > 0 \tag{5.44}$$

and by the argument preceeding (5.17) it follows that

$$r(\lambda^* u| \phi) > 1/2 \tag{5.45}$$

is true.   QED

Theorem 5 establishes a bounded area within which one might expect the candidates to compete. At least for the case of cohesive parties, one expects candidates to select platforms within this bounded area if at all possible since platforms outside the area expose the candidate to the possibility of certain defeat if the opposition is clever enough to select $\theta^* = \lambda^* u$ for its platform. It is unfortunately true, however, that even in the case of cohesive parties the line dominant platform θ^* need not be dominant overall so that platforms ϕ which do not satisfy (5.35) can win the election. The following simple example illustrates this fact.

Imagine two parties whose members have loss matrices which can be written as follows

$$A_1 = \begin{bmatrix} 4 & 0 \\ 0 & 1 \end{bmatrix}, \quad A_2 = \begin{bmatrix} 1 & 0 \\ 0 & 4 \end{bmatrix} \tag{5.46}$$

so that there are only two issues which are relevant to the campaign. Assume that the parties are cohesive so that $\Sigma_1 = A_1^{-1}$ and $\Sigma_2 = A_2^{-1}$. Let the mean of the preferred positions of the members of the first party be $0' = (0, 0)$ and that of the second party be $u' = (1, 1)$. Assume, as usual, that the parties have equal strength to that $\alpha = \beta = 1/2$ and the mean of the overall population of voters is $\mu = \frac{1}{2}u = (1/2, 1/2)'$ so that from (5.36), recognizing that $\|u\|_1 = \|u\|_2 = \sqrt{5}$, it follows that $\lambda^* = 1/2$. Thus $\theta^* = \lambda^* u = (1/2, 1/2)'$ and the best platform on the line segment joining the two means is the mean of the overall population. Suppose that one candidate selects $\theta^* = \mu = (1/2, 1/2)'$ as his platform. Let the other candidate select $\phi' = (0, 1)$ as his platform. The following calculations can be checked easily.

$$\|\phi\|_1^2 - \tfrac{1}{4}\|u\|_1^2 = -\tfrac{1}{4}$$
$$\|\phi - u\|_2^2 - \tfrac{1}{4}\|u\|_2^2 = -\tfrac{1}{4} \tag{5.47}$$

From (5.41) it is obvious that in this instance $k_1 + k_2 < 0$ so that by the usual argument $r(\theta^*|\phi) < 1/2$ and the candidate with platform ϕ wins over the one with platform θ^*. Therefore, the overall mean is not always dominant even with cohesive parties. The platform $\phi = (0, 1)'$ selects the mean of the first party for the issue for which the members of that party care relatively more and the mean of the second party for the issue for which its members feel intensely. In the postulated example the strategy of "giving each what he wants most" is superior to the strategy of seeking a compromise on each of the issues by selecting the overall mean $\mu = \theta^* = (1/2, 1/2)'$.

There are conditions, aside from those established by Theorem 4, in which the selection of the overall mean is a very good strategy. Probably the most trivial of these conditions is the equivalence of the mean preferred positions for the members of both parties. Under this condition (with the normality assumption) the mean of each of the parties is dominant within the party and since they are identical they are the overall mean which therefore must be dominant for the total population. As has been shown above, however, there is no certainty that the overall mean is dominant when the population has preferred positions which are such that a bimodal mixture of two distributions is required for an adequate representation. In fact, when the parties are cohesive and bimodal there can arise a strange situation in which the mean preferred position of one of the individual parties becomes the dominant platform.

Theorem 6 Let $A_1 = \Sigma_1^{-1}$ and $A_2 = \Sigma_2^{-1}$. In situation one assume $\|u\|_2 \neq 0$. Then $\theta^* = \lambda^* u \rightarrow u$ as $\|u\|_1 \rightarrow 0$. In situation two assume $\|u\|_1 \neq 0$. Then $\theta^* = \lambda^* u \rightarrow 0$ as $\|u\|_2 \rightarrow 0$. In both situations θ^* becomes dominant in the limit.

Proof Consider situation one where $\|u\|_2 \neq 0$. Let $\|u\|_1 \rightarrow 0$. From (5.36), $\lambda^* \rightarrow 1$ so that $\theta^* = \lambda^* u \rightarrow u$. From (5.34), $c \rightarrow 0$. For all $\phi \neq \lambda^* u$,

$$\|\phi - \lambda^* u\|_1 + \|\phi - \lambda^* u\|_2 > 0 \qquad (5.48)$$

so that Theorem 5 yields the limiting result $r(\lambda^* u|\phi) > 1/2$. A similar analysis applies for situation two. QED

Theorem 6 clearly needs some interpretation. It must be admitted that the notation which has been used here does not help to suggest the proper interpretation. Consider the quantity $\|u\|_1^2$. It is helpful to recall the notational convention introduced in (5.7) and (5.8). Thus

$$\|u\|_1^2 = \|u - 0\|_1^2 = \|\mu_2 - \mu_1\|_1^2 \qquad (5.49)$$

so that $\|u\|_1^2$ is interpreted as the utility loss felt by an individual in the first party whose preferred position is the mean preferred position of the members of his party (0 or μ_1 according to the convention) when he is faced with the alternative of the mean preferred position (u or μ_2 according to the convention) of the second party. Theorem 6 states that as this loss $\|u\|_1^2$ goes to zero the mean preferred position of the second party becomes the dominant platform for the election. Now how can this loss go to zero? Imagine that for some issues (denoted by i) the means are identical so that $\mu_{1i} = \mu_{2i}$ while for other issues (denoted by j, $i \neq j$) they are different so that $\mu_{1j} \neq \mu_{2j}$. Then $\|u\|_1^2$ can approach zero if the loss matrix A_1 is altered in such a manner that less and less weight or intensity of preference is given to those issues j In which the two means are different. In the limit these issues j are given no weight so that the members of the first party do not care about them. Thus the mean preferred position of the second party becomes the dominant platform. Of course, proper interpretation does not require that one go all the way to the limit. The result should hold when one is "near" the limit.

The interpretation is clearly symmetric. Thus as the utility loss felt by a member of the second party whose preferred position is the mean of his party goes to zero when faced with the alternative of the mean preferred position of the first party, the latter mean becomes the dominant platform. One should observe, of course, that the assumption of cohesive parties is made here so that the preferred positions become more "spread out" on those issues which are given less and less weight.

6 CONCLUDING REMARKS

The unifying theme of this paper has been the examination of two candidate electoral competition when the preferred positions of the total population are such that a bimodal mixture of two multivariate distributions is required as an adequate characterization. The two distributions have been termed parties. While the mean is always the dominant platform or strategy in a population whose preferred positions can be characterized by a single multivariate normal distribution, this characteristic cannot be always guaranteed for a bimodal mixture of two normals. Sometimes platforms quite different from the overall mean dominate it. This fact does not imply that the overall mean is no longer of interest, but it does indicate that greater attention needs to be given to the conceptual and empirical question of determining what constitutes an adequate representation of the distribution of preferred positions.

NOTES

1 This research was supported by grants from Resources for the Future and the National Science Foundation. Appreciation is also due to the Ford Foundation for providing a Faculty Research Fellowship for one of the authors.

2 Tullock (1967) is a notable exception in that a two dimensional model is presented. The term "spatial" gives clear and deserved recognition to Hotelling (1929) whose famous work on the location of firms along a road had important but largely unrecognized implications for analyses of party competition.

3 As a matter of notational convention, the fact that the norm $\|.\|$ does not have a subscript means that it is taken with respect to the matrix A so that $\|x\|^2 = x'Ax$. Obviously, $\|x\| = \sqrt{x'Ax}$ is a convention.

4 The situation of equal loss of indifference where $\|x - \theta\| = \|x - \phi\|$ for $\theta \neq \phi$ has zero probability if x has a continuous distribution, as is assumed here, so that it can be ignored.

5   It is important to understand the notational convention. Whenever the A's are looked upon as being the same so that $A_1 = A_2 = A$ no subscript will be used on the squared norm so that $\|x\|^2 = x'Ax$. However, if $A_1 \neq A_2$ is allowed, then subscripts identify the norm so that $\|x\|_1^2 = x'A_1x$ and $\|x\|_2^2 = x'A_2x$.

6   The star (*) on the norms (2.14) is a part of the notational convention. Thus if $A_1 = A_2 = A$ and $\Sigma_1 = \Sigma_2 = \Sigma$ so that no subscripts are necessary $\|x\|^* = \sqrt{x'A\Sigma Ax}$. If $A_1 \neq A_2$ or $\Sigma_1 \neq \Sigma_2$ is allowed, subscripts are necessary so that $\|x\|_1^* = \sqrt{x'A_1\Sigma_1 A_1 x}$ and $\|x\|_2^* = \sqrt{x'A_2\Sigma_2 A_2 x}$.

REFERENCES

Black, D. *The Theory of Committees and Elections.* Cambridge: Cambridge University Press, 1958.

Black, D., and Newing, R. A. *Committee Decisions With Complementary Valuation.* London: William Hodge, 1951.

Buchanan, J. M., and Tullock, G. *The Calculus of Consent.* Ann Arbor, University of Michigan Press, 1962.

Davis, O. A., and Hinich, M. J. A Mathematical Model of Policy Formation in a Democratic Society. J. Bernd (Ed.), *Mathematical Applications in Political Science II.* Dallas: Southern Methodist University Press, 1966.

Davis, O. A., and Hinich, M. J. Some Results Related to a Mathematical Model of Policy Formation in a Democratic Society. J. Bernd (Ed.), *Mathematical Applications in Political Science III.* Charlottesville: University Press of Virginia, 1967.

Davis, O. A., and Hinich, M. J. On the Power and Importance of the Mean Preference in a Mathematical Model of Democratic Choice. *Public Choice,* 5, 59–72, 1968.

Downs, *An Economic Theory of Democracy.* New York: Harper, 1957.

Hotelling, H. Stability in Competition. *Economic Journal,* 1929, 39, 41–57. Reprinted in G. J. Stigler and K. E. Boulding (Eds.), *Readings in Price Theory.* Chicago: Irwin, 1952.

Tullock, G. *The Politics of Bureaucracy.* Washington: The Public Affairs Press, 1965.

Tullock, G. *Towards a Mathematics of Politics.* Ann Arbor: University of Michigan Press, 1967.

SOME TYPES OF PARTY COMPETITION AND THEIR FUNCTION IN SOCIAL CHOICE

DAVID CHAPMAN

University of Lancaster

SUMMARY

In order to elucidate some of the functions of party competition in social choice, the operation of a party system is compared with that of a direct democracy. These functions are: to reduce the requirement for citizens' participation; to obtain a more integrated policy as the social choice; to promote responsiveness of the social choice to the needs of each section of citizens; to stabilise the social choice over time; to promote consent among the citizens for the social choice. Models are then constructed to assess and compare two-party and multi-party competition in their effectiveness in performing the latter three functions. Departing from the tradition of models with a policy set placed on a left-to-right scale along which electors have single-peaked preferences, these models generate the policy set by *allocation*, i.e. the set of alternatives out of which each competing party chooses its policy, consists of variations in the allocation of the nation's limited resources between the needs of the various sections of electors. A further feature of the models is that electors are influenced in their voting decisions not only by party policy, but also by their "party identification", which, as in the real world, may vary in strength from elector to elector. It is shown that, with two-party competition, there is an equilibrium policy on which both parties converge. This is that policy which, for either party, maximises its votes by allocating the resources between the sections of electors so that the marginal return in votes for resources is the same for each section. With multi-party competition, however, different parties tend to diverge in policy; the policy of the government coalition is indeterminate, since it is uncertain which parties will form the coalition, and what will be the result of the bargaining between these parties concerning the policy they will jointly adopt. It is concluded that, as represented by the models, multi-party is less effective than two-party competition in performing the last of the three functions in social choice stated above. A third type of party competition, that for majority preference in a multi-party situation, is then described. This is provided by an electoral system in which preliminary ballots are used to reduce the number of competing parties to two, the government party then being elected in a final ballot between these two parties. Under this system, despite the multi-party context, the government party faces competition similar to that in a two-party situation.

SECTION 1: SOCIAL CHOICE THROUGH A PARTY SYSTEM COMPARED WITH THAT THROUGH DIRECT DEMOCRACY

It is paradoxical that while, in real-world democracies, preference aggregation is carried out by party systems, much of the theoretical writing about voting and social choice is concerned with direct democracy.[2] Direct democracy seems to be regarded as a prototype of social choice, illuminating its problems by showing clearly the relationship between individual preferences and the social decision. It would be justifiable to consider such direct democracy models to be applicable to reality, if one could regard elected representatives or parties merely as means of transmitting information on the citizens' preferences, simply communication channels with no effect on the social decision. If viewed in this way, parties obscure the fundamentals of social choice, which therefore can better be investigated by constructing models of direct democracy. But while such an initial simplification may give useful insights, it is important to extend the models by the specific inclusion of parties in the social choice procedure, if, as seems to be the case, they play an active role, and affect the nature of the social decision.

Comparison of a party system with a direct democracy is useful in elucidating the effect and function of parties in social choice. To make this comparison, we will first briefly discuss the working of a direct democracy. In fact no modern state is run as a direct democracy, though there is some limited use of referenda. But by use of electronic communication, some form of direct democracy could perhaps be devised, which was practicable, if not desirable, in a collectivity of the size of a nation. Thus the whole nation could serve as a legislature, making decisions by simple majority of those voting, any group of citizens above a certain number having the right of proposing legislation.

In the absence of empirical evidence, we can only theorise about the results of this. If we make the assumption that each citizen is concerned only with his own self-interest, the following problems might be expected to arise.

1) In such a direct democracy, it is likely that many proposals would be put forward to modify or add to existing legislation, so that, to exert influence on the social decision, citizens would need to vote frequently, and to have information on the likely effects of the many measures proposed. But due to the small chance that any individual citizen would affect the social decision, he would have very little motive to take the trouble of voting, or to acquire information on the measures put forward.

2) A further problem concerns the degree of integration of the series of measures passed by a direct democracy. For the different issues dealt with may be interdependent, the success of one measure depending on the decision taken on other issues perhaps at a later date. Hence to be most effective, legislation may need to be planned as an integrated whole. But this is unlikely to be achieved where successive measures can be sponsored by different groups, and passed by differently-composed majorities.

3) A third problem concerns the interests of the minority. For where each piece of legislation is passed by a majority, proposals which a minority intensely desires but a majority weakly opposes will fail, while proposals severely harmful to a minority but slightly beneficial to a majority will be enacted. It is possible that each citizen may in the long run be harmed by this, the relatively slight benefit he gains, on average, on those issues in which he is in the majority, being outweighed by severe losses on issues in which he is in the minority. Such all-round long-term losses would be mitigated or avoided if vote-trading ("log-rolling") occurred over different issues, i.e. there were agreements where one set of citizens voted in favour of a proposal slightly against its interests but greatly to the benefit of certain other citizens, who in return supported a later proposal of great benefit to the first set but slightly against their own interests. But in fact, where the number of voters is large, as it is in a nation, vote-trading across issues would be extremely difficult to organise; and the difficulty would be even greater if voting were secret, since then it could not be known whether any individual voter had fulfilled his part of the agreement. A perhaps more practicable

way of avoiding this self-defeating outcome could be to construct a complex "package" of legislation on many different issues, such that for a majority of citizens, each citizen in this majority benefited from the package *as a whole*, though many individual items in it might be to his disadvantage. The package would then be put forward as one proposal and passed at a single vote. But even if, under direct democracy, it were worth while for any group to undertake the labour of designing and promoting such a package, the problem of the minority would still remain, though in a different form. For the package would reflect the interests of the majority voting for it, and might be severely detrimental to the minority. Instead of harm being done diffusely to many different minorities each on different issues, harm might be done to one compact minority. Thus the package might bring the social decision closer to Pareto-optimality, but at the cost of greater inequity.

4) A further problem concerns the instability of the social choice over time. For the social choice at any given time can be considered as a decision for one of the many social alternatives, each social alternative being one possible set of measures, one on each issue. The instability problem would occur if the different citizens' preference rankings of the social alternatives were such that there existed no "majority alternative" (i.e. no alternative which, as compared with *any* other alternative, would be preferred by a majority), in other words, if majorities were cyclical.[3] If no majority alternative exists, it is likely that the set of measures imposed by, and favourable to, one majority, will at some later date be revoked by another majority and replaced by a set more favourable to them, which might later be changed by another majority, and so on. Thus the social choice would be unstable over time, benefiting now one majority, now another, so that any individual citizen might experience sharp changes in his level of welfare, downwards as well as upwards, over time. Now it seems likely that the citizens' preference rankings of the social alternatives would in fact be such that majorities are cyclical, and no majority alternative exists, since this set of social alternatives between which citizens are choosing is a set of *allocations*[4], essentially the different ways of dividing the nation's limited resources between the satisfaction of the needs of different citizens. Therefore this problem of the instability over time of the social choice, seems likely to occur.[5]

5) Due to the various unsatisfactory features mentioned above, the problem is likely to arise of insufficient consent among the citizens for the implementation of many of the measures passed, and even of lack of consent for direct democracy itself, as a procedure.

Let us now consider the situation where the social choice is made *indirectly* by election of parties i.e. through a party system. The functions of parties in social choice can thus be seen as ways of dealing with the above five problems, as follows.

1) The introduction of parties drastically reduces the amount of activity, in acquiring information on social alternatives and in voting, which is required of citizens if they are to exert a given level of influence over the social choice. This reduction in costs is achieved, as it is in the economic sphere, by a form of division of labour. For under direct democracy, to exert influence on the social choice, individuals would need to inform themselves about a large number of social alternatives, and to vote on them. But under a party system, the task of sifting through the vast number of social alternatives and of judging their impact on the citizens is carried out by specialised bodies—the parties, so that in the election, the citizens are presented with a relatively simple choice to make, between at most a few alternatives instead of between many. This function of parties, though important, is mentioned only in passing, and will not be further analysed in this paper.

2) A party system produces a more integrated set of measures as the social decision, i.e. as government policy. Especially if single-party government comes about, the set of measures will be planned as an integrated whole, at least over the period of one legislative term. Again, this function of a party system, though important, is merely mentioned here, and will not be further analysed.

3) Another function which a party system performs, at least under certain conditions, is to produce a social choice which is responsive to the needs of each section of electors, and not simply to the needs of a majority.

4) If the models of this paper are valid, a party system can function to stabilise the social choice over time. With a party system, at least under certain conditions, government policy is determinate, *given* the electors' policy preferences. If electors' preferences do not change over time, neither does government policy, despite any change of party in power.

5) A party system can help to maintain consent for the social decision under conditions where the interests of different citizens conflict.

This paper is concerned to develop a model to examine how, and to what extent, party systems perform the last three functions. The same basic model will be used to examine both a two-party and a multi-party system, to compare the extent to which they might be expected to perform these functions.

This basic model of party competition for votes has two main features. First, the set of possible policies (i.e. social alternatives) out of which a party chooses its policy, is assumed to consist of alternative *allocations*, i.e. of ways of dividing the nation's limited resources between the satisfaction of the competing needs of different sections of electors.[6] A model using such a policy set has a clearer empirical meaning then one which requires a party to choose a point solely on one left-to-right continuum, as in much theorising about party competition. Further, this assumption seems realistic. The second feature of the model is that electors are influenced in their voting decision not only by the respective party policies, but also by *non-policy* factors, such as party loyalty or "identification". This is a political analogue of brand loyalty in economics, and again, this appears realistic.[7]

SECTION 2: TWO-PARTY COMPETITION

We first consider a two-party system, to examine by means of a model of its working the effect of two-party competition on the social choice, i.e. on government policy. The electoral system under which the two parties are competing for votes is assumed to be that of proportional representation by party lists in one nationwide electoral district (as in Israel). Voting is compulsory, so that it is not very unrealistic to assume 100 per cent turnout in the model, and to neglect any effects of differences in turnout between sections of electors. This electoral system is chosen because it results in a relatively simple model, but the conclusions of the model could be extended without much modification to two-party competition under *other* electoral systems.[8]

2.1   Outline of the model

The main assumptions of the model can be explained, and the argument roughly outlined, as follows. As mentioned above, an elector's voting choice is assumed to be influenced not only by his preferences for the party on grounds of policy, but also by his *non-policy preference* (NPP) for the party, i.e. his preference for the party for any reasons *other than* its policy. These non-policy reasons might be: a tradition in the elector's social group of voting for that party; the presence in the party of politicians of his own race or religion; the personal appearance of its leader, and so on. A further assumption is that a party is unable in its policy to discriminate effectively between individual electors, but can deal with them only in broad categories or *sections* (e.g. farmworkers), giving or withdrawing certain benefits for a section as a whole, so that each elector in the section is affected equally. It is assumed that, in any one section, some electors have a stronger NPP in favour of one party, and some in favour of the other, and all to varying degrees. The result of this is that for every marginal increase in the benefit of its policy for a section, a party is rewarded with a marginal increase in votes from that section, from those electors whose strength of NPP is such that they previously were "just on the verge" of switching their vote to the party. The argument of the model is that, in order to increase its votes, a party seeks a policy which allocates the limited national resources between the different sections of electors so as to equalise for each section the marginal return in votes for resources. It is shown that, in a two-party system, this margin-equalising, vote-maximising policy is the same for both parties. There is one determinate policy which both parties will adopt, so that whichever party wins, government policy is the same.

The assumptions of the model are set out in detail below, followed by the proof of the above conclusions.

2.2 Assumptions of the model

Assumption 1: party behaviour Competition takes place between two parties, party A and party B. Each party prefers government office (which goes to the party with a majority of seats) to opposition. Whether in office or opposition, it prefers more seats to fewer. Thus it seeks to maximise votes.

Assumption 2: elector behaviour An elector's voting choice is influenced by his non-policy preference (NPP) for a party, i.e. his preference for the party for reasons other than its policy, as well as by the benefit to him of the party's policy. He votes for that party for which the sum of the benefit to him of its policy, *plus* his NPP for it, is greater. (The benefit he ascribes to the government party is simply his level of benefit during the legislative term preceeding the election. The benefit he ascribes to the opposition is the benefit he would have derived, if it had been enacted, from whatever policy the opposition was advocating during the same term.)

Assumption 3: the electorate consists of large sections The electorate can be divided into *sections*. (A section is defined as a set of electors each of

23*

whom is alike in all his needs which government activity can help to satisfy, and each of whom the government must, for reasons of administrative practicability, treat in the same way in respect of these needs. Thus each elector in the same section will have the same preferences between alternative policies). Each section is assumed to comprise a sufficiently large number of electors for it to be justifiable to treat the size of any majority a party might obtain within the section, as a continuous variable.

Assumption 4: the distribution by NPP difference of the electors in a section
By subtracting an elector's NPP for party B from his NPP for party A, we obtain his *NPP difference*. The shape of the curve of the distribution of the electors in any one section by NPP difference need not be the same as that of another section, but it is assumed that in each case it is a smooth, unimodal, but not necessarily symmetrical curve, with greater-than-zero frequency at the point of zero NPP difference (such as Figure 1). There is an upper limit on the degree of steepness of any part of this curve, further explained on page 359. (Concerning the units along the horizontal scale of Figure 1, an elector's NPP difference is measured in units of benefit, as follows. If x units is the maximum amount of benefit by which he will tolerate A's policy to be worse for him than B's policy, and still vote for A, then his NPP difference is said to be x units. Within any one section, the policy preferences of the electors being the same, the units of benefit of different electors are placed on the same scale by regarding as equal, for each elector in the section, the gain in benefit from increasing the resources going to each elector in the section from y to $y + 1$ units.)

Assumption 5: the set of alternative policies open to each party   The set of alternative policies out of which a party must choose a policy, consists of the alternative ways of allocating the nation's fixed amount of resources between the satisfaction of the needs of the different sections of electors.

Assumption 6: lower limit on the amount of resources allocated to a section
Due to the administrative difficulties of drastic change from current policy, there is for each section a lower limit below which a party cannot reduce the resources it allocates to the section.

Assumption 7: decreasing marginal returns in benefit for resources   A section of electors receives a decreasing amount of benefit for each successive extra unit of resources which the policy of a party devotes to its welfare. The benefit received by a section of electors depends only on the amount of resources allocated to it, and is independent of which party has allocated it.

2.3   Proof that both parties adopt the same policy

As a preliminary to this proof, it is necessary to explain certain marginal
rates of return which characterise the effect of a party's policy upon a single
section of electors, such as that section the NPP–difference distribution of
which is shown in Figure 1. Suppose that one party (let us say party B)
varies its policy so as to increase its benefit to the section, while party A
keeps its policy constant. B will therefore receive an increasing number of

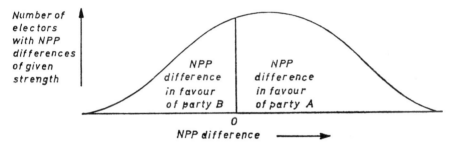

Figure 1   Distribution of electors in section i by NPP difference.

votes from the section. At the point where B's policy has x more units of
benefit than A's policy for each elector in the section, B receives the votes
not only of those electors in it who have an NPP difference in favour of B,
but also of those with an NPP difference in favour of A of up to x units.
(See Assumption 2). At this point, B's marginal return in votes for increased
benefit (MVB for short) is proportional to the height of the distribution at x.
(i.e. the frequency of electors of NPP difference such that they are just on the
verge of switching their votes). In order to increase the benefit to the section,
B increases the amount of resources allocated to it, there being at any point
a certain marginal return in benefit for resources (MBR), which by Assumption 7, decreases as more resources are allocated. As will be shown below,
in order to maximise votes, B takes into account a further rate—the marginal
return in votes for resources (MVR) in respect of the section. At any point,
this is clearly the product of the MBR and MVB, since extra resources give
extra benefit and extra benefit gives extra votes.

   We will now prove that each party will adopt that policy by which it
allocates the resources between the sections so that, *when this policy is
followed by both parties*, the MVR for the party is the same for each section.
Let us refer to this policy as *m*. That such a policy exists, can be shown as
follows.

Suppose both parties adopt the same policy, but one for which the MVR is *not* equal for all sections. Suppose then that both parties increase, by the same amount as each other, the resources for sections with high MVR, and reduce resources for those with low MVR. Thus by Assumption 7, MBR will decrease for the former and increase for the latter. But provided both parties still adopt the same policy as each other, then for any section the MVB of each party stays the same as before, and the same as that of the

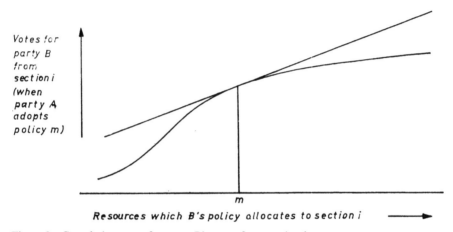

Votes for party B from section i (when party A adopts policy m)

m

Resources which B's policy allocates to section i ⟶

Figure 2   Cumulative curve for party B's votes from section i.

other party, reflecting always the frequency of occurrence in the section of the same electors—those with zero NPP difference. Thus, since MVR is the product of MBR and MVB, if both parties simultaneously increase resources to those sections with high MVR and reduce resources to those with low MVR, a policy *m* will be reached such that, for both parties, MVR is the same for all sections. (It is assumed that the lower limit on resources for a section stated in Assumption 6, allows resources for the latter sections to be reduced low enough.)

Let us now consider the votes which one party, let us say party B, would receive from a single section, as B varies its policy, while party A maintains policy *m* throughout. We can derive from the section's NPP difference distribution curve (such as Figure 1), a cumulative curve such as Figure 2, showing the votes received by B, as it increases the resources it allocates to the section, starting at the lower-limit allocation stated in Assumption 6.

The slope of this cumulative vote curve depends partly on the shape of the NPP–difference distribution curve, relating votes to benefit, and partly on Assumption 7, relating benefit to resources. Those parts of the distribution curve which are upward-sloping (giving increasing MVB) tend to produce a cumulative vote curve *concave* to points above it. On the other hand, Assumption 7 (decreasing MBR) tends to produce a cumulative vote curve *convex* to points above it. Thus the flatter the distribution curve, the more of the vote curve will be convex. Now it was stated in Assumption 4 that there is an upper limit on the steepness of any part of the distribution curve. This limit is assumed to be such as to produce a cumulative vote curve which is convex at the point where the level of resources is that specified in policy *m*, and which is such that its other parts, whether convex or not, lie below a tangent drawn at this point.

Let us now consider all sections in the electorate, and suppose that party B varies its policy, moving from *m* to some other policy *g*, while A remains at *m*. Now when at *m*, B will by definition of *m* receive the same marginal return in votes for resources from each section. In moving to *g*, B will give a certain amount more resources to some sections, and will receive from each of them an *average* return in votes for resources which (due to the fact that the cumulative vote curves lie below the tangents at *m*) is *less* than this marginal return at *m*. But since by Assumption 5 the total of resources is fixed, B must also reduce by the *same* amount the resources to some other sections, and again due to the shape of the cumulative vote curves, will lose votes from each of them at an average rate in votes for resources removed, which is *greater* than the marginal return at *m*. Hence a party will obtain more votes with policy *m* than with any other policy, provided the other party also adopts *m*.

Now in each seeking to maximise its proportion of votes from the same electorate (see Assumption 1), the parties are playing a zero-sum game. That the game has a "saddle-point" where both parties adopt *m*, can be shown as follows. Party B's minimum payoff when it adopts *m* is greater than its minimum payoff when it adopts any other policy. But B's minimum payoff when it adopts *m* occurs when A also adopts *m*, which for A also gives a greater minimum payoff than any other policy. Thus, following the maximin principle, both parties will adopt the same policy *m*, which equates for each section of electors the marginal return in votes for resources.[9]

We can further deduce from this model not merely that parties converge in policy, but also what sort of policy they converge on. This "equilibrium policy" is one which allocates more to a section of electors the higher is its

NPP difference distribution at the point of zero NPP difference, i.e. the higher the proportion of electors in the section who have no preference between the parties on non-policy grounds. This conforms with the commonsense expectation that either party will favour a section more if it has a high proportion of electors of marginal allegiance, potential floating voters whose votes are easily lost or gained, than it would if the section's votes could be gained only with difficulty.[10]

2.4 The two-party model and the functions of parties in social choice

Coleman (1966) commented on the need, in a "reasonable" method of aggregating individual preferences, for the reflection of intensity of preference. This model indicates how intensity of preference is taken into account under a two-party system. For in the model, if the government has to decide between any given pair of social alternatives, its choice reflects not only the number of electors by which each alternative is preferred, but also (1) their respective intensities of preference, and (2) the proportion of electors in either group who have no party bias, i.e. no preference between parties on non-policy grounds. Thus the government will choose the alternative preferred by the minority if it is sufficiently intense in its preference and/or high in its proportion of electors without party bias. Because of this feature of its working, the two-party system of the model can perform certain functions in social choice, as stated in Section 1 above. These functions are as follows.

1) It functions to produce a social choice which is responsive to the needs of each section of electors, and to obviate the problems of the neglect of minority interests which seemed likely to afflict the theoretical direct democracy discussed in Section 1. One might expect that since the government party depends for its election and re-election on retaining the votes of a majority, it would follow a policy designed to benefit some compact majority of sections without regard to the minority. But instead, due to the fact that the electors' vote depends in part on non-policy factors, it seeks a majority of votes drawn from all sections in the electorate. Thus the government responds positively to the needs of each section, and there are no "neglected" sections in the sense that, if the total of resources available were to increase, each section would receive at least some increase in its allocation, in order to equate the marginal return in votes at a higher level of benefit for each section.[11]

2) Since both parties adopt the same policy, then whichever party wins, government policy is the same. Thus the two-party system functions to

stabilise government policy from term to term, even if the party in office changes. The social choice is stabilised over time despite the fact that, as in the theoretical direct democracy discussed in Section 1, the set of social alternatives is generated by variations in *allocation*, and hence (as explained in note 4) citizens' preferences between the social alternatives *alone* (i.e. leaving out the non-policy factors which influence their preference for a party-plus-policy) must create cyclical majorities. A model on these lines, where voting is affected by non-policy preferences as well as by party policy, appears to provide some explanation of the fact that the much-discussed paradox of voting does not seem in practice to produce the pro-blems for democracy which one might expect.

3) This model seems relevant to a further problem in the theory of social choice—that of *consent*: how is it that a collectivity can continue to function, avoiding rebellion and obtaining the consent of its members to the social decision, despite the fact of their conflicting interests as to what this decision should be?[12] It seems likely that a citizen's witholding of consent tends to follow from a sense of deprivation, either deprivation relative to the amount received by others in society, or (which is perhaps more im-portant) relative to what he himself received in the past. If so, the two-party system of this model will function to promote consent in two ways: (1) by producing a social decision which responds to the needs of each section of electors; (2) by promoting stability over time of the social decision, and thus maintaining each section of electors at their accustomed level of welfare.

SECTION 3: MULTI-PARTY COMPETITION

A multi-party (i.e. more-than-two-party) system will now be examined. A model will be constructed of its working to investigate its effect on the policy of individual parties and on the policy of the government. The electoral system under which these more-than-two parties are assumed to be competing is the same as that for the two-party system previously modelled, i.e. proportional representation with party lists, in one nation-wide electoral district, with compulsory voting.

3.1 Assumptions of the model

The assumptions of this model are the same as those of the previous one (see 2.2 above), except for the following elaborations.

In this model, where coalition governments are possible, the concept of a party's *policy* to which electors react, has to be more complex, if the electors are to distinguish the policy of a party from that of the coalition of which it forms a part. Thus the model takes into account a party's policy promises, as well as its actual performance. A party is assumed to make two policy decisions per legislative term. At the *beginning* of the term, if it is in office, alone or in coalition, it decides alone or jointly with its coalition partners, on the government policy for the term. If it is in opposition, it decides what policy to advocate during the term as a counter-proposal to that of the government. At the *end* of the term, each party, whether government or opposition, makes a pre-election promise about its policy for the *succeeding* term. (As in the previous model, a policy still consists of one alternative allocation of the nation's resources between the different sections of electors).

Elector behaviour also, has to be more complicated than in the previous model. At the election at the end of term t, an elector is assumed to vote for that party for which the sum of the following, is greatest:

1) his non-policy preference (NPP) for the party

2) in the case of a government party, the benefit he derived from government policy during term t; or, in the case of an opposition party, the benefit he would have derived, if it had been enacted, from the policy the party *proposed* for term t

3) the benefit for him of the policy the party promises for term $t + 1$

4) in the case of a government party, but *only* when the government policy in term t has been worse for him than the policy the party had promised for term t, a negative quantity $-(da)^k$, where d is the benefit for him of the promised policy, less that of government policy, a is positive and depends reciprocally on the size of the benefit unit used, and k is greater than unity.

The effect of 4) is to give a marginally increasing penalty for a "broken promise", whereby a party, by joining a coalition with a policy different from the one it had promised, would tend to lose votes from those sections for which the coalition policy is worse than the party's promised policy.

As in the previous model, electors in any one section differ in their degree of non-policy preference for the different parties. If there are n parties, and the degree of NPP of each elector for each party is represented by a point in n-dimensional space, each dimension representing strength of NPP for one party, then it is assumed that these points are distributed as a single cluster, i.e. are distributed throughout the space with smoothly changing density, there being one position where points are at maximum density,

with density falling off continuously as one travels out from this position
in any direction. The assumption is also made (corresponding to the limit
in steepness of distribution curve of Assumption 4 of the two-party model)
that there is a limit on this rate of decrease in density, which will be further
explained in 3.2 below.

3.2 The policies of the parties

In order to investigate what policies the parties will adopt in a multi-party
situation, we will first consider the effect of party policy on the vote of a
single section of electors. Suppose there are three parties, A, B and C. An
elector's NPP for each party can be represented by a point in three-dimen-
sional space, such as the cube of Figure 3. If all three parties adopt the same

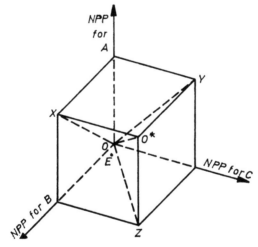

Figure 3 NPP of electors in one section for each party, represented in three dimensions

policy, then NPP must be the only factor affecting voting, and so each
elector will vote for that party for which he has the strongest NPP. Electors
located above the planes O*XO and O*YO have their strongest NPP for A
and will vote for A, electors to the left of planes O*XO and O*ZO will vote
for B, and so on. The same thing is illustrated more simply by Figure 4,
which is a view of the same cube from the direction O* to O, and represents
in two dimensions the same division of the section's vote. These planes, or
lines, dividing at any time the electors who vote for one party from those

who vote for another, will be referred to as the *margins* between the parties
at that time. If one party, let us say party A, changes to a policy x units
more beneficial to the section, it will shift the AB and AC margins x units
downwards, gaining from B and C the votes of those electors located just
below, to x units below, the planes O*XO and O*YO in Figure 3, or below
the line XOY in Figure 4. How many votes A gains from each party depends
on how densely these areas are populated with electors. For instance, if
electors are distributed with the centre of the cluster at E to the left of the
line O*O, then A gains relatively few votes from C but more from B.

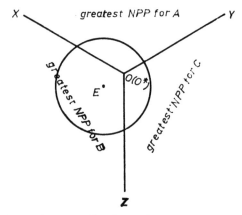

Figure 4   NPP of electors in one section for each party, represented in two dimensions

As with the previous model, the effect of a party's change in policy can
be characterised by certain marginal rates of return. As a party allocates
more resources to a section, the benefit of its policy increases with a *decreas-*
ing marginal return in benefit for resources (MBR). (See Assumption 7 of
2.2) Increased benefit brings increase in votes, the marginal return in votes
for benefit (MVB) depending on the density with which electors are located
on the party's margins. Thus MVB might either increase or decrease with
increasing benefit, depending on whether or not the margins are approaching
the centre of the cluster. But as mentioned in 3.1, a limit is assumed on the
rate of change in this density. This limit is such that, where MVB is increasing, this rate of increase is sufficiently small for it to be swamped by
the decrease in MBR, so that the marginal return in votes for resources
(MVR) *de*creases as the party allocates more resources to the section.

It will be shown that in such a model (provided certain highly plausible
asymmetries exist) the parties are under pressure to diverge in policy in

order to gain votes. This tendency to diverge may be to some degree reduced, but not eliminated, by an opposite pressure to converge due to the expectation of forming a government coalition. For simplicity in exposition, we will at first suppose that only the factors in favour of divergence are in operation. The argument will later be modified (in 3.3 below) to take into account the weaker pressure to adopt more similar policies.

The argument concerning divergence in policy can be simply outlined by comparing multi-party competition for votes with two-party competition. The important difference lies in the fact that, in the two-party situation, both parties must be competing in a given section for the *same* set of electors on the single margin between them, while in the multi-party situation, the set of electors who are on the margin of one party will be a *different* set, even if partly overlapping, from those on the margin of another party. For instance, for A they will be on the AC and AB margins, while for B they will be on the BC and AB margins. Since each party has a different set of such electors in the section, the sets need not form the same proportion of the section. The consequence of this will be demonstrated below, that different parties, in order to gain votes by each equating its MVR for each section, may be obliged to diverge in policy.

This problem will be considered by means of a simple example of a multi-party situation, where there are three parties, A, B and C, and an electorate consisting of only three sections, sections 1, 2 and 3. The situation is illustrated in Figure 5, which shows the way in which the electors in each of the three sections are distributed in respect of NPP for each of the three parties. In the real world, different sections of society tend to differ somewhat in their party allegiance and this example reflects this. In section 1, the distribution clusters in such a way that a high proportion of electors have their greatest NPP for A. Similarly, section 2 has a high proportion with greatest NPP for B and section 3 for C.

In order to consider whether it is in the interests of the parties to diverge in policy, let us suppose the following situation, existing shortly before an election *e*. During the previous term *t*, the government has enacted, and the opposition advocated, the same policy *f*, which is such that, for party A, the MVR is the same for each section. We suppose that each party, in considering what policy to promise for the succeeding term $t + 1$, is concerned only to maximise votes in election *e*.[13]

Since the MVR from any section decreases with more resources, and since A is equating its MVRs, A will lose votes by any policy shift, and will have no incentive to change its policy, provided the other parties do not

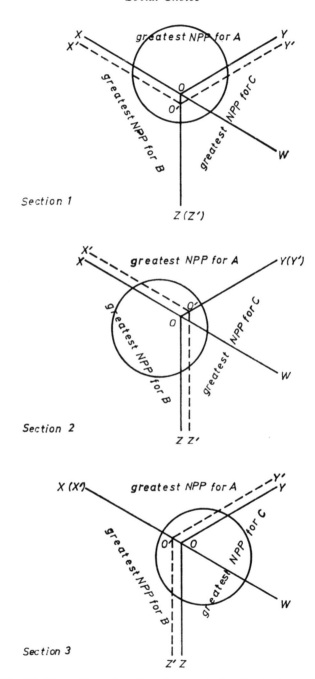

Section 1

Section 2

Section 3

Figure 5 Final division of the votes after adjustments of policy by the parties

change theirs. However it can be shown as follows that for the other parties it would be advantageous to diverge from the common party policy f, since for them it does not equate the MVRs.

Suppose that party B is considering whether to promise f. It is clear from Figure 5 that in section 1, B would have a lower MVB than A, since there are fewer electors along line XOZ then along line XOY. In section 2, B would have a higher MVB than A, while only in the case of section 3 does MVB appear to be about the same for both parties. Now the MBR for any section is the same for both A and B, their promised policies being the same. Thus B's MVR, being the product of MVB and MBR, must be less than that for A for section 1, and greater for section 2. But for A the MVR of each section is equal. Thus for B the MVR of different sections must be unequal, being low for section 1 and high for section 2. Thus B would obtain more votes by promising a policy which allocated less resources than policy f to section 1 and more to section 2, and would continue to gain votes by changing the promised allocation until it equated the MVR for each section.

For similar reasons, C would gain votes by promising a policy which allocates more than policy f to section 3, and less to section 1. The final division of the votes of each section after the parties have made their adjustments, is shown in Figure 5 by the lines joining X', Y' and Z' to O'.

The above example is a simple one, but the same general argument applies where there are more parties, or more sections, or both. The conclusion can be stated as follows. Let us refer to the party for which an elector has the strongest NPP as the party towards which he is *biased*. Let us refer to an elector who has an NPP for party i which is equal to his NPP for some other party j, and greater than or equal to his NPP for any other party, as an elector *marginally biased* to i. (For example, electors along the line XOY are marginally biased to A.) Under multi-party competition, if the sections differ in the proportions of their electors marginally biased to the various parties, then the parties will diverge in policy. The sections will clearly tend to differ in this way if they differ in the proportions of their electors biased to the various parties. This, it seems, is frequently the case in the real world, where different economic groups tend to differ in their party allegiances. Downs (1957) came to similar conclusions about the tendency to policy divergence where there is multi-party competition in left-to-right ideological space. It is interesting to observe that the same conclusion holds for multi-party competition when the policy set consists of alternative allocations.

3.3   The policy of the government

We now consider the implications of this tendency to divergence in party policy, for government policy under a multi-party system. The same three-party example will be used, and it will be supposed that no party obtains a majority of votes, so that the government must be a coalition of two parties. These must agree on a single coalition policy for the term following their election, despite the fact that before the election they had differed in the policies they promised for that term. Thus two questions arise: which two parties will form the coalition, and what policy will they jointly adopt?

Now any given party i will, if its votes are subsequently not too much reduced thereby, prefer joining a government coalition to not joining (see Assumption 1 of 2.2), and will seek as a coalition partner a party j which will agree to a coalition policy as near as possible to the one which i has promised, since, as explained in 3.1 above, i will tend to lose votes at the next election from those sections for which the coalition policy is worse than the policy i has promised. A further reason to seek such a partner might be that the policy which i promised at the last election, having been designed to win votes for i then, would still be a good vote-winner for i at the next election. How near a coalition policy party j will agree to, will depend on the strength of j's desire for government office, on what offer j has from the third party k, and on the cost of compromise in terms of votes, which in turn depends on how close j is to i in policy. Thus a bargaining process will go on to arrive at a coalition. Though, other things being equal, a given coalition is more likely to be formed the nearer are the two parties in policy, this bargaining process is indeterminate in outcome. Further, the policy agreed on by the coalition which eventually forms, will be some compromise between the promised policies of its two members, and again, this compromise, being the result of bargaining between parties with somewhat conflicting interests, will be indeterminate.

As mentioned in 3.2 above, the anticipation of forming such a government coalition may lead parties to diverge less in the policies they promise. Thus if before election e, party A expects subsequently to form a coalition government with B, then instead of designing its policy promise solely to maximise votes at election e, it would promise a policy somewhat more like B's, and thus, by reducing the discrepancy between its promised policy and that of the anticipated coalition, reduce the number of votes which it would lose at election $e + 1$ from those sections for which the coalition policy would be worse than A's promised policy. But since, as such discrepancy increases, it brings a marginal increase in "disfavour", and hence a marginal vote loss, which increases from a value of zero at the outset, the effect of this anticipation will be only to *reduce* the tendency to diverge from B, and not to eliminate it. Further, it will not eliminate the tendency to diverge from C.

Thus, in general, with multi-party competition, government policy is indeterminate for two reasons:

1) parties have different policies, and it is not certain which parties will form the government coalition,

2) given the parties which form the coalition, the compromise policy they agree to adopt is even then not determinate.[14]

This can be illustrated from our three-party example. If A and B form the coalition, the government policy will be favourable to sections 1 and 2. If B and C form the coalition, government policy will favour sections 2 and 3. But in neither case would the policy be determinate. Thus with a coalition of A and B, A would bargain for a coalition policy more in favour of section 1, and B for one more in favour of section 2.

SECTION 4: TWO-PARTY VERSUS MULTI-PARTY COMPETITION AS A MEANS OF SOCIAL CHOICE

We now compare two-party and multi-party competition as represented by these models, in their performance of three functions in social choice, those of response to the needs of each section, stability of social choice over time, and promotion of the citizens' consent.

1) In the models, both two-party and multi-party competition function to produce a social choice (i.e. government policy) which responds positively to the needs of each section of electors. But with multi-party competition it seems likely that the responsiveness, though still positive, is more variable from section to section, there being a greater tendency for the government to allocate a very low level of resources to some sections and a high level to others, for reasons unconnected with their respective intensities of need, however such relative intensities may be judged. This is explained as follows. The amount of resources which a party allocates to a given section depends on its proportion of electors who are marginal for the party, i.e. whose votes could be gained or lost by a marginal increase or decrease in the benefit of the party's policy. The higher this proportion, the more resources the party allocates to the section in order to reduce the differences between the sections in their marginal returns in votes for resources. This can be

illustrated from Figure 5, for both two-party and multiparty competition. In the case of two-party competition (let us say between A and B), the electors marginal for both A and B in any section lie along the line XW. If we assume that the distribution is symmetrical, the proportion of marginal electors will be greatest when the section is equally divided into electors biased to A and to B. The more unequally divided is the section, the less dense will be the part of the distribution which the line XW traverses, and the smaller the proportion of marginal electors, and so the smaller will be the amount of resources allocated to the section, both by A and B. Under three-party competition, the situation is more complicated. The electors marginal for party A will be those lying along the line X'O'Y', and those marginal for B will lie along X'O'Z', and so on. Here the effect, for a given section, of inequality between the parties in their share of electors biased towards them, is both erratic and exaggerated. Up to some point, if a party has more than an equal share of supporters in a section, it will allocate more resources than if the section were divided equally between the parties; if it has a very large share it will allocate less. In cases where a party has a less-than-equal share of supporters, it allocates less to the section than if it had been equally divided, and the party tends to respond to a *given* degree of inequality in a very exaggerated fashion as compared with the response which would be made by a party under two-party competition. Thus, if this model is valid, though we can rely neither on two-party nor on multi-party competition to produce a government policy which gives an allocation which some benevolent outside observer would consider "just" or "equitable" (see note 11, to 2.4 above), multi-party competition seems likely to give a *less* equitable allocation than the other type, since it tends to give a very low level of resources to some sections, and a high level to others, for reasons unconnected with their relative intensities of need.

2) With two-party competition, the social choice is stabilised over time, since there is an equilibrium policy which both parties adopt, so that whichever party wins in successive elections, government policy is the same. But under a multi-party system, as was pointed out above, government policy is indeterminate, partly in that it is uncertain which parties, each tending to differ in policy, will form the government coalition, and partly because, given the members of the coalition, the compromise policy on which they agree, is not determinate. Hence the social choice is likely to be unstable over time, not only when there is a change in the parties forming the coalition, but also (though to a less extent) when the same parties remain in the government from one term to another.

3)   The view was put forward above that a citizen's witholding of consent tends to follow from a sense of deprivation, either relative to the amount received by others, or relative to what he himself received in the past. If so, multi-party competition as represented in this model is likely to perform less effectively than two-party competition in promoting consent among the citizens for the social choice, for two reasons: (1) it produces a less equitable allocation between sections; (2) it gives less stability over time in the social choice, and thus is less effective in maintaining each section at their accustomed level of welfare.

**SECTION 5: COMPETITION FOR MAJORITY PREFERENCE
IN A MULTIPARTY SITUATION**

If two-party competition is indeed desirable, either on account of the properties which this model attributes to it, or for other reasons, it seems important to ask whether there is any way in which it can be guaranteed that competition of this type occurs. It is well known that the "Anglo-Saxon" simple-majority single-member-district electoral system, though it might have some tendency to produce two-party competition, does not ensure it, but it may be possible to design electoral systems which are effective in guaranteeing this.

If the previous models are valid, the presumed advantages of two-party competition lie in the fact that the government is formed by a single party which is competing for the votes of the *whole* electorate with a single opponent, and which therefore is led to design its policy with the object of obtaining a majority drawn from all sections of electors, rather than aiming to maintain a minority of support by seeking votes primarily from a restricted set of sections. The problem can thus be stated as follows. If in a given country more than two parties are already in existence, or if it is likely that third parties may arise and disrupt the two-party pattern if it already exists, how can it be provided, in such a multi-party context, (1) that there is government by a single party, and (2) that this party, in order to obtain or retain office, must compete for votes against a single opponent in a contest which is decided by majority vote of the whole electorate?

As a solution to this problem, an electoral system is suggested below, which uses one or two preliminary ballots to reduce the number of competing parties to two, and elects the government party in a final ballot between these two parties. The rules of the system, which will be referred to as the

24*

majority-preference system, are set out in some detail. Such detailed specification of the system needs to be justified, since it is clear that this is not the only scheme which would conform to the requirements stated above. The scheme is presented in detail since then the practicability of its general principle can more easily be judged. If only the general principle were stated, it might not receive whatever consideration it deserves, either because the reader could not see any method of implementing it, or because of drawbacks, in fact avoidable, in the methods which happened to occur to him. Of course, this detailed presentation runs the opposite risk, that the general principle might be dismissed because of some inessential but objectionable feature of the present scheme. However, this proposal should be regarded merely as a tentative basis for discussion. It might be possible to modify it to eliminate snags, without abandoning the main features of the scheme.

This majority-preference electoral system is designed to produce, as the basis for a parliamentary system of government, a single-chamber legislature. It contains a single government party, and opposition parties. Each party has seats in proportion to its votes in the first ballot of the election (let us say six seats for each one per cent of votes), except that the government party has a certain minimum of seats (let us say 150). In order to enable their party to govern, each member of the government party is given a weighted vote in the legislature, so as to provide the party with an absolute majority of votes of some fixed size (let us say, of 55 per cent). Thus if, for example, the government had 220 seats in a legislature of 600 seats, then each member of the government party would need to be given a vote with a weight of 2.111. The party would then command 55 per cent of the total votes in the legislature, provided it retained the support of all its members.

The method of election is as follows.[15] The whole country is treated as one electoral district. Each party competing in the election presents a single list of candidates. The ballot paper bears the names of the parties, not of the individual candidates.

A first ballot is held, and if needed, one or two further ballots to elect the government party. In any ballot, a party must get at least one-half the votes cast to be elected as government. If no party has half the votes in the first ballot, a second ballot is held. Any party may apply to enter the second ballot. The second ballot may be either between two parties (in which case it is final), or between three parties. A two-party ballot, between the applying party with most first-ballot votes and the applicant with next most votes, is held if the latter party obtained more votes than the total obtained by all parties other than these two, *or* if only two parties have applied. Otherwise, the second ballot is held between three parties. If more than three have applied, only the three applicants with most first-ballot votes may stand. If no party has half the votes in the second ballot, a third ballot is held. Any party may apply to enter the third ballot. If more than two apply, only the two applicants with most second-ballot votes may stand.

Seats are allocated to each party according to its votes in the first ballot, by the "largest average" method, as follows. Suppose there are 600 seats to be allocated. Each party gets one seat for each one-sixth per cent of votes. Any remaining seats are allocated one by one, a seat being given to that party which, if all were to get one more seat each, would then have the highest average of votes per seat. If the government party gets less than the prescribed minimum (150 seats as suggested above) it is given extra seats to bring it up to this minimum.

Such are the formal rules of the majority-preference system.[16] What then might we expect to be the results of its working in practice?

The scheme can be described, somewhat paradoxically, as a method of providing two-party competition in a multiparty context. Even though many parties might be competing, and might obtain seats in the legislature, single-party government is produced, and the government party will expect competition of the "two-party" type, i.e. to have to contest in the final ballot against one other party for majority approval from the whole electorate.

In this paper, the advantages of two-party competition have been argued on the basis of a model in which the set of alternative policies consisted entirely of variations in allocation. Though allocation seems to be the most import antfactor generating the policy set in the real world, it appears that issues also exist on which the alternatives can be expressed as points on a left-to-right linear scale, concerning which the electors' preference rankings are jointly single peaked. Now as demonstrated by Downs (1957) two-party competition on such issues tends to produce a government policy which is a stable equilibrium at that point most preferred by the median elector on the scale. Thus, on the basis of a model combining both allocation issues and "left-to-right" issues to generate its policy set, it can be argued that the majority-preference system, in providing two-party competition, produces a government policy which is stable over time, not only in its allocation but also in its position on left-to-right issues. Concerning these latter issues, this equilibrium policy is positively responsive to the preferences of electors on any point of the scale, in this sense: even if, for a given group of electors, the policy is not at the point they most prefer, nevertheless they influence the outcome, since the fact that they have votes leads the parties to adopt a policy which is nearer to this pont than it would be if they had none. Just as a case can be made for the relative equity of this equilibrium policy in its allocation (see Section 4 above), so also it can be argued, on the basis of perhaps not unreasonable assumptions about the relative intensity of preference of different electors concerning movement along this scale, that the median position on a left-to-right issue is the least displeasing to the electorate as a whole, and is the most equitable. It seems likely also that this median position would be the most effective in maintaining general consent.

If these models are valid, one can expect that the majority-preference system will produce two main parties, each nationally based, with a policy designed to seek votes in all sections of the electorate, and that insofar as the other parties are seeking government office, it will exert pressure on them to adopt a similar policy. As long as there is some well-established party prepared to adopt such a policy, then no party which is extremist in some ideological dimension, or which is sectionalist, appealing to a particular interest, will achieve office as government, though it might obtains a proportion of seats.

Some comment is called for on the purpose of the provision for representation of parties in proportion to votes in the first ballot. By maintaining "third" parties in existence, and by reducing the entry barrier against new parties, this provision functions to increase party competition. At the same time, the provision for repeated ballots has the result that if any third party succeeds in offering an effective challenge against the government, then this competition (assuming the government party avoids elimination before the final ballot) will be of the two-party type analysed above. Perhaps more important is the possible function of provision for third parties, in promoting consent for the system. For it could be expected that those third parties which received seats would frequently be ideologically extremist parties. Now under two-party competition obtained by penalising third parties out of existence (e.g. by the simple-majority single-member-district system) the fact that their favourite party could not gain representation might alienate such extremist electors from the system. Even under the usual type of multi-party system obtaining under proportional representation, such electors might feel antagonistic because their party, though it gained representation, was excluded from power, never being allowed to join the government coalition. But under the majority-preference system, extremist electors could, by their votes in the first ballot, obtain representation for their most-favoured party, without having to sacrifice, as they would in the other systems, all influence over which of the other parties achieves government office. The fact that their favourite party, though represented and thus able to put its case, could not gain the preference of the majority, might lead them to accept the legitimacy of not allowing it government office, especially since, through their votes in subsequent ballots, they still have influence, as effective as that of any other electors, over which of the other parties is elected as government.

NOTES

1　Presented at the Conference on the Descriptive and Normative Aspects of Social Choice, Department of Sociology, University of Pittsburgh, September 1968.

2　For example, Musgrave (1959), Leibenstein (1962), and Shubik, (1966).

3　See Black (1958) and Arrow (1963).

4　No allocation can be a majority alternative, since for any allocation, there must be some other allocation which gives less to some minority of citizens and motre to the rest, and which is thus preferred by a majority. See Ward (1961).

5　It should be pointed out that this problem, and also problems (1) and (3) might be mitigated to some extent, in so far as citizens were altruistic, taking into account the interests of other citizens in deciding how to vote, and being willing to invest more effort in acquiring information and in voting, than would be rational on a purely self-interested basis. Altruism however seems unlikely to be strong enough completely to overcome these problems.

6　Concerning the interpretation of this assumption into a statement about the real world, the way a particular allocation is to be achieved is not necessarily through direct allocation by the government of goods and services to the various electors, but might be by means of taxes or subsidies, or by government regulation of the market or of the degree of inflation or deflation.

7　See Campbell et al. (1960), which emphasises that real-world electors are influenced by their "party identification" as well as by their perceptions of party policy.

8　This paper is intended only to analyse and compare the effect of two-party and multi-party systems on government policy, taking such systems as given. It does not seek to explain how it comes about that there are two parties, or more than two. The writer is currently working on models similar to these in this paper in respect of assumptions about elector behaviour, etc., in order to investigate the influence of the electoral system on the number and size of parties.

9　In the above model the proof of party convergence in policy is based on the assumption that the electorate is composed of *non-overlapping* sections (for example, occupational ones). But the model can be elaborated as follows to accommodate sections which overlap (for example, the section of motorists would overlap with many occupational sections). Thus the definition of a section (see Assumption 3 in 2.2) is altered to: a set of electors each of whom is alike in *one or some* of those needs which government activity can help to satisfy, etc. A set of electors who are alike in *all* their government-satisfiable needs (who in this model would typically be in the "overlap" of two or more sections) is here re-defined as a *subsection*.

The significance of this is that a party cannot allocate more resources to a particular need of a subsection (let us say to the motorist-needs of the motorist-firemen) without also allocating more to the nonfireman motorists. It is assumed that, if an elector belongs to more than one section, the benefit he receives from resources allocated to the needs he has as a member of one section, is independent of whatever amount is allocated to the needs he has as a member of any other section. The proof of party convergence in policy is as follows. An MVR-equating policy m is defined by a hypothetical procedure similar to that described above for non-overlapping sections. Let us consider a cumulative vote curve for the votes received from any subsection i by one party when it varies its policy as follows (while the other party remains at m.) Starting at the policy m, the party simultaneously varies the resources allocated to some or all of the sections of which subsection i is a member, perhaps giving less to some while it gives more to others, subject to the proviso that the resources to the different sections are varied in *constant proportions*, i.e. so that for any two different points g and h through which the party travels as it varies the allocation of resources, the ratio of the difference in resources between m and g to the difference between g and h, is the same for each section. It is assumed that, for any subsection, the distribution of its electors by NPP difference is sufficiently flat or dispersed to ensure that any such cumulative vote curve drawn for the subsection is such that all parts of it other than m lie below a tangent drawn through m. It follows from this that if a cumulative curve is drawn for the votes received from *the whole electorate* (i.e. from the total of all subsections) by one party when it varies its policy, starting at m, re-allocating *in constant proportions* the fixed total amount of resources between the sections (while the other party remains at m), then all parts of this curve other than m will lie below a tangent drawn through m. It follows from the definition of m that the slope of the curve at m, and thus of the tangent, will be zero. Thus each party maximises votes at m, provided the other party also adopts m. Thus on the maximin principle, both parties adopt m.

10 This two-party model can be elaborated by further assumptions which permit additional conclusions to be deduced about the nature of the equilibrium policy. (See Chapman, 1967 and 1968.) These assumptions concern (1) the effect of the amount allocated to a section on its members' productivity, (2) the electors' memory for benefits received over past terms, which is assumed to influence their voting, (3) altruism of electors, where their vote is influenced by the benefits received by members of other sections. The following conclusions are derived: the equilibrium policy allocates more to a section to the extent that (1) its members give a greater marginal increase in productivity for resources allocated to them (2) they have a longer memory for benefits received from a party, and (3) the section has a greater number of altruistic sympathisers in other sections.

11 This is not to say that government policy must be one that would be considered fully equitable (e.g. in the judgement of some benevolent outside observer). For as pointed out above, the policy reflects not only the intensity of preference of different sections, but also their relative proportions of electors without party bias, and thus if some sections are low in the latter they will receive an "inequitably" low allocation.

12 See Coleman (1966) for a fuller statement of this problem.

13 In fact a party may also be concerned with the impact of its promised policy on its votes in election $E + 1$. The modification which this introduces into the argument is discussed in 3.3.

14 In 3.2 and 3.3, it is assumed that each party, in trying to maximise votes, does so on an individualistic, go-it-alone basis, without co-operating with a second party to increase its winnings from a third (even if it finally forms a government coalition with the second party). But two parties might be able, by such co-operation, each to obtain more votes than they would by an individualistic strategy. For example, A and B could co-operate in designing their policies, no longer trying to win votes from each other, but concentrating on increasing their joint winnings from C by the following agreement. A should promise a policy which gained votes from C by reducing the differences between the sections in MVR along line $Y'O'$ and so was more beneficial to sections 1 and 3. B should promise a policy also designed to win votes from C, but by reducing the differences in MVR along line $Z'O'$, thus favouring sections 2 and 3. The coalition government formed after the election by A and B should adopt a policy equating MVR along line $Y'O'Z'$, and so favour section 3. But the agreement which A and B finally arrive at is the result of bargaining between them and is not determinate, since for any one possible agreement, there may be others more advantageous to one party and less to the other, while still being better for each than its best individualistic strategy. Though such co-operative strategy by any two parties would result in a government policy different from that under individualistic strategy, the *general* conclusion of the model still holds, i.e. that the government policy is indeterminate, varying according to which set of parties it is which follow the co-operative strategy, and according to the result of the bargaining within this set of parties.

15 Some comment is required about two features of this method of election—the single national electoral district, and the provision for successive ballots. The single district is suggested because it is the simplest way to achieve the required type of party competition. But a modified form of the majority-preference system can be designed which represents electors by small electoral districts, if this is desired. In this, part of the legislature is elected from candidates put up by the parties in small electoral districts, and part from national lists run by the same parties in a national district. One party is elected as government by one or more ballots in the national district, and its members (those elected in either type of district) are given a weighted vote in the legislature to enable the party to govern. Concerning the provision for successive ballots, this method is suggested because it is perhaps a more familiar procedure—for example it is used to elect the President in France. But if repeated ballots are regarded as a drawback, a single-ballot method can clearly be designed, in which the elector numbers the parties in order of his preference. Each party would receive seats in proportion to its first-preference votes, and to elect one party as governmentthe lower preferences would be used, if necessary, instead of holding any further ballots.

16 In the theoretical models of this paper, the existence of strongly competing parties has simply been assumed. But in the real world, competition might not always be adequate. This suggests that it might be desirable to have some provision to promote competition, and especially to promote the growth of an opposition party with enough support to have some likelihood of defeating the government party in the final ballot at the next election. Thus it might be provided that both government and opposition parties should be given state aid, each in proportion to the number of its members in the legistature. This state aid might take the form of a subsidy, and of access at state expense to mass communication facilities, such as qroadcasting time, advertising space in privately-owned newspapers, etc.

REFERENCES

Arrow, K. J. *Social Choice and Individual Values*. (2ⁿᵈ Ed.) New York: Wiley, 1963.

Black, D. *The Theory of Committes and Elections*, Cambridge: Cambridge University Press, 1958.

Campbell, A., Converse, P. E., Miller, W. E., and Stokes, D. E. *The American Voter*. New York: Wiley, 1960.

Chapman, D. E. Models of the Working of a Two-Party Electoral System —Parts I and II. Part I in *Papers on Non-Market Decision Making*, Fall 1967; Part II in *Public Choice* (formerly *Papers on Non-Market Decision Making*), Fall 1968.

Coleman, J. S. Foundations for a Theory of Collective Decisions. *American Journal of Sociology*, May 1966.

Downs, A. *An Economic Theory of Democracy*. New York: Harper, 1957.

Leibenstein, H. Notes on Welfare Economics and the Theory of Democracy. *Economic Journal*, June 1962.

Musgrave, R. A. *The Theory of Public Finance*, New York: McGraw-Hill, 1959.

Shubik, M. *Notes on the Taxonomy of Problems concerning Public Goods*, Discussion Paper No. 208. Cowles Foundation, Yale University, New Haven, 1966.

Ward, B. Majority Rule and Allocation. *Journal of Conflict Resolution*, December, 1961.

AN ESTIMATE FOR THE DECISIVENESS
OF ELECTION OUTCOMES

DOUGLAS W. RAE

Yale University

No one should write another paper about inter-party competition withou
some very good excuse, but I think I have found two related difficulties
which together justify another paper on the subject. The first and most
important of these follows from the very special place given to party competition in contemporary democratic theory, and from an ambiguity which
arises from it. We no longer pretend that the citizens of a democratic state
literally choose the policies with which they must live: rather, we now say,
they choose the political parties which make these policies. This view,
which emerged as a substitute for the naivetes of earlier positions,[1] presumes
that election outcomes decide which party or coalition of parties will make
policy during an inter-election period. Anthony Downs, for example,
suggests that the following condition is met in practice by all those regimes
which we think of as 'democratic':[2] *A single party (or coalition of parties)
is chosen by popular election to run the governing apparatus.*

Those who have examined elections outside the English–speaking world
know quite well that this is often not the case. Election outcomes merely
limit the set of parties and coalitions which can govern, the eventual decision
within this set being taken by elite bargaining. This is a discrepancy of the
greatest moment to democratic theory in general and to Downs' model in
particular. It implies, after all, that voters make an even more limited
choice—leave more to elites—than the new democratic theory suggests. It
might, accordingly, be helpful to measure degrees of deviation from the
normative presumption that elections determine *the* governing party or

379

coalition. No existing analysis of party competition performs this task, and the one presented here is specifically intended to do so.

A second difficulty arises from the growing importance of cross-national comparisons in political analysis. Explanatory theory, even the most rudimentary theory, can be disciplined by experience only if truly generic categories of analysis are available. The minimum requirement for a generic conception of party competition is that it be general to what we may call "*n*-party systems." Our analysis must speak with equal theoretical cogency to systems where two or three or ten parties compete. Most of the existing measures of party competition are, quite understandably, predicated upon the assumption of two-party competition.[3] The two measures which are general to *n*-parties are, on the other hand, quite insensitive to the question of "decisiveness" in democratic elections.[4] The present analysis is meant to represent degrees of decisiveness (and indecisiveness) for *n*-party systems.

The object, then, is to estimate degrees to which actual elections approximate Downs' condition—uniquely decisive election outcomes—without presuming any fixed number of parties. We may proceed by establishing a simple model of legislative decision-making, assigning to each party a score corresponding to the opportunity which the election outcome gives it to govern, and then aggregating these scores for *n* parties to represent electoral decisiveness.

1 A SIMPLIFIED MODEL OF LEGISLATIVE POLITICS

We are interested in estimating the way in which the authority to govern is distributed amongst political parties by election outcomes. For this purpose, a simple (and unrealistic) model may be useful. We begin, accordingly, with the following definitions and assumptions.[5]

Definitions

a) A *legislative party* is a group of legislators elected under the same label.[6]

(Let *P* represent a party, and let *p* represent the number of seats it holds.)
b) A *policy* is an action taken in the name of the legislature, whether the action be positive (i.e. enacting a law) or negative (rejecting a bill). Policies also include the act of investing, supporting, or rejecting parliamentary governments.

c) A *potential governing coalition* is any set of parties large enough to successfully make a policy.

(Let *G* represent a governing coalition and let *g* represent the number of seats its constituent parties control.)

NOTE: Such a set may include only one party, in which case we will see that Downs' condition holds.

d) A *decision-rule* stipulates the number of votes required to make a policy-*viz.*, to form a governing coalition.

(Let *k* represent a decision-rule.)

e) A "*bargain*" accrues to a party when it is a member of a potential coalition which would no longer be governing without that party:[7]

$$Pi \in G$$

$$g \geq k$$

$$g - Pi < k$$

f) A party's *a priori opportunity to govern* (APOG) is defined as the proportion of all bargains which accrue to it:

$$APOG = \frac{\text{number of bargains for } i \text{ th party}}{\text{total number bargains for all parties}}$$

Assumptions

1 Parties vote as units.[8]
2 The decision–rule followed by legislatures is simple majority–rule.

$$k = \frac{n + 1}{2} \quad (n \text{ odd}) \quad \text{or} \quad \frac{n}{2} + 1 \quad (n \text{ even})$$

(Letting *n* be the number of seats in a legislature.)
3 All potential governing coalitions are possible and equally probable.

NOTE: This assumption may be altered to fit specific situations, see below.

This is a skeletal account of legislative politics—the bare bones of a complete organism. Parties differ in their electoral success, but do not necessarily differ in their ideologies or even in their policy positions (implied by Assumption 3). Parties are perfectly cohesive—an assumption which is preposterous in the American context, though quite reasonable in most European settings (Assumption 1). Committees do not make sub-majority vetoes possible (implied by Assumption 2). However unrealistic the model may seem, it provides a flexible and very simple point of departure. And it leaves open the opportunity to add specifications which will enable us to give more realistic accounts at the price of generality. Leaving these alterations aside for the moment, let us proceed with an example.

Consider the case of three parties, P_a, P_b, and P_c. Suppose, for the moment, that no one of them holds a majority but that any two of them do hold a majority:

$$p_a < k$$
$$p_b < k$$
$$p_c < k$$

but,

$$p_a + p_b \geq k$$
$$p_a + p_c \geq k$$
$$p_b + p_c \geq k$$

It follows that no party is itself a governing coalition, and that exactly four such coalitions are possible (and, under our model, equally probable):

1) P_a, P_b

2) P_a, P_c

3) P_b, P_c

4) P_a, P_b, P_c

Each member of coalitions 1, 2, and 3 is essential and therefore holds a "bargain." No one member of coalition 4 is essential to it and accordingly no party holds a "bargain."

There are, accordingly, six "bargains" divided equally amongst the three parties. The a priori opportunity to govern (APOG) for each is, then, two-sixths, or 0.33. This indecisive election outcome corresponds to a variety of actual seat distributions, including several in which the seats are much less evenly divided than are the opportunities to govern. One such case is offered by the returns of the 1962 Austrian election, which divided 165 seats 81, 76, and 8 among the People's, Socialist, and Freedom Parties. Since all governing coalitions must contain an 83-seat majority, and since no one but any two of these parties meet that requirement, it is seen that this case corresponds to our example, and that the APOG for each party is 0.33.[9]

This example illustrates the naivete of measuring decisiveness solely on the basis of seat distributions, for there is no linear correspondence between the number of seats won by a party and its a priori share in the policy-making process. A party with more votes than one of its competitors may enjoy a greater opportunity to govern, and it cannot have less opportunity. But it need not *necessarily* enjoy more opportunity, and it certainly does not enjoy added opportunity in direct proportion to its numerical advantage. This is analogous to the observation made by L. S. Shapley with respect to the value of n-party games, and by him and Martin Shubik with respect to their conception of "power."[10] In what they call a "weighted majority game," more weight cannot mean less value or less power, but it need not mean more, and the increment, if any, is not a linear function of the added weight.

Our scheme estimates a party's opportunity to govern by counting the number of governing coalitions in which it is an essential member. The presumption is that these "bargains" give the party an effective claim to a voice in policy-making. This is because the governing coalition's other members must depend on the party at hand if they are to continue as a governing coalition. All essential members of a governing coalition are mutually dependent, and inessential members, if any, are simply dependent upon each essential member.[11]

This implies that the values are computed from all possible "winning" combinations of parties, rather than all possible permutations, as with Shapley values. A bargain occurs when a party is *an* essential member, rather than *the* pivot which pushes the coalition to winning size. This conception of mutual dependence seems more plausible than the concept of unilateral control if we are interested in legislative policy-making—be it the formation of a bill-passing (or rejecting) majority, or the formation of a parliamentary government. For this reason, and because of the much less laborious computing routine, the APOG score seems preferable to the Shapley value for present purposes. Since the APOG lacks the useful formal properties associated with the Shapley value, however, it is proposed only for the specific purposes of this analysis. Those who are interested in comparing the results produced by the two indices will find that Shapley values are given beside APOG scores throughout our tables (see Appendix).

Actual variations in the distribution of the a priori opportunity to govern are illustrated by the sixteen election outcomes analyzed for this paper. These elections were selected arbitrarily—the first lower-house general election for each country in the present decade—and constitute an accidental sample. For that reason, I will resist any sweeping generalizations, but it is worth noting here that four broad qualitative patterns emerge from the data.

One-party monopoly

In these cases, which conform exactly to Downs's condition, one party alone enjoys at least a formal monopoly over legislative policy-making. The four examples, all English-speaking nations, are the U.S., Australia, Great Britain, and New Zealand.

Symmetrical three-sided dispersion

In these two cases, three parties enjoy an equal a priori opportunity to govern after the election. The two examples are Bonn Germany[12] and Austria.

Radial dispersion

In these cases, one party enjoys a substantial advantage over several other parties which have coequal APOG scores. Canada, France, and Iceland example this pattern.

Step-wise dispersion

In these cases, several parties share the a priori opportunity to govern, each enjoying some advantage over the next. In three instances—Belgium, Denmark, and Luxembourg—the downward progression is fairly regular. In two others—Israeli and Irish—the strongest party stands well above its competitors, yet the step-wise decline persists amongst the latter.

The emergence of only these four patterns may seem surprising. Conspicuous by its absence is any simple bi-polar distribution: if there are as many as two sharers of the opportunity to govern, there are also at least three. This is, of course, because the second party—say, the German SPD—requires the intercession of a third—say, the German FPD—for its leverage against the first party. The interested reader may examine the tables given in the Appendix to see this and other peculiarities of the data. He will notice, incidentally, that there is a very strong correlation between APOG and Shapley scores for the cases analyzed.

But if we are to proceed with the development of a measure for the decisiveness of elections for n-party systems, these variations must be ordered over some single continuum. The a priori opportunity to govern is, as we have said, the relevant datum for each party, and its raw seat proportion is not. But a useful measure of decisiveness for the system at large must be based on the dispersion of these values amongst competing parties. We must, therefore, proceed with one additional leap of abstraction from the raw election returns. This is explained in the paper's next section.

2   A MEASURE FOR THE DECISIVENESS OF ELECTION OUTCOMES IN *n*-PARTY SYSTEMS

We may think of an election's decisiveness as the degree to which it concentrates the a priori opportunity to govern in the hands of one or a few parties. Its indecisiveness can, accordingly, be conceived as the degree to which it disperses the APOG among several parties. *The more an election outcome concentrates the a priori opportunity to govern, the more decisive it becomes.* This definition relies for its interpretation upon a simple measure for "concentration" which may be applied to APOG distributions.

A "sum of the squares" measure seems appropriate. This procedure, used recently by the economists to represent the concentration of market shares and production in industry, is simple and readily interpreted.[13] It approaches unity when Downs' condition prevails and a single party monopolizes the APOG. This is complete (and decisive) concentration. It approaches zero as a very large (and in the end infinite) number of parties share more or less equally in the a priori opportunity to govern. This is complete (and completely indecisive) dispersion.

Formally, let us define the decisiveness of an election outcome as the sum of the squares of the APOG scores for all parties:

$$D = \sum_{i=1}^{n} (\text{APOG})_i^2$$

Where: D = decisiveness

n = the number of parties

APOG = a priori opportunity to govern, as previously defined.

Consider an example: $p_a \geq k$, $p_b \dots n < k$. P_a alone has an APOG score and the calculation becomes:

$$D = 1^2 + 0^2 + \cdots + 0^2$$
$$= 1 + 0 + \cdots + 0$$
$$= 1$$

This then is a fully decisive outcome. Consider a much less decisive outcome: $p_a = 0.4$, $p_b = 0.3$, $p_c = 0.15$, $p_d = 0.15$. The APOG scores are then $1/2$, $1/6$, $1/6$, $1/6$ respectively and the calculation becomes:

$$D = 1/2^2 + 3 \cdot 1/6^2$$
$$= 1/4 \ + 3 \cdot 1/36$$
$$= 1/3, \quad \text{or} \quad 0.333$$

This, then, is a much less decisive outcome. The lower limit of decisiveness occurs in the case where each party's APOG share is infinitely small, so that we arrive at D equal to the sum of an infinity of zeros. Actual distributions will, of course, never approach this limit.

Table 1　Decisiveness of outcome

Country, Year	$D = \Sigma(APOG)^2$	$\Sigma\phi^2$
Australia, 1961	1.0000	1.0000
Austria, 1962	0.3333	0.3333
Belgium, 1961	0.2685	0.2772
Canada, 1962	0.3333	0.3333
Denmark, 1960	0.3210	0.3050
France, 1962	0.5750	NA
Germany, 1961	0.3333	0.3333
Great Britain, 1964	1.0000	1.0000
Iceland, 1963	0.3333	0.3333
Ireland, 1961	0.4739	NA
Israel, 1961	0.2903	NA
Luxembourg, 1964	0.2368	0.2473
New Zealand, 1960	1.0000	1.0000
Norway, 1961	0.5750	0.4714
Sweden, 1960	0.4420	0.4000
United States, 1960	1.0000	1.0000

Table 1 provides D values for the sixteen actual cases analyzed in the Appendix, and these are compared with the very similar results which emerge when Shapley values are subjected to the sum of squares concentration measure.

The striking feature of these fragmentary data is the very great variation. Four English–speaking nations are clustered at the top—D equals one. And three other nations—Belgium, Luxembourg, Israel—hover around the lower limit of the range, where D equals about one-fourth. The rest are strewn along the path between these extremes. Elections vary greatly in their decisiveness.

3 DISCUSSION

We began with the normative presumption that elections give direct and unique answers to the question, "Who governs?" Our measure defines this condition as its upper limit and allows actual cases to diverge progressively toward total indecision.

Our application of the measure to a sample of actual election outcomes demonstrates at the very least that this normative criterion is an idealization often violated by experience. All elections eliminate *some* possible bargains to govern but only a few eliminate all but one. Consequently, the a priori opportunity to govern is often widely dispersed among the competing parties. And this in turn suggests the necessity of a further retreat from unguarded populism in democratic theory.

We cannot permit ourselves the bald statement that elections determine governing parties or coalitions of parties. It is not enough to say that specific policies are left to elites; we must say, further, that the choice of governing elites is often, in varied degree, the province of elite bargaining and not of mass choice. In so far as this is so—and the present measure lets us specify the degree—our operative view of political democracy requires revision.

In Chapter 9 of his *Economic Theory*, Anthony Downs recognizes this difficulty. Where indecisive outcomes must be anticipated (i.e. $D < 1$), Downs notes that voting for a party becomes a complex decision whose meaning "depends upon what coalitions it is likely to enter, which in turn depends upon how other voters will vote."[14] Noting the difficulty of such decisions, Downs goes on to the proposition that "... most citizens do not vote as though elections were government-selection mechanisms."[15] This is inconsistent with the descriptive generalization with which Downs began, and it demonstrates the very substantial consequences of indecisive election outcomes for democratic theory.

This is a problem well worth analyzing in detail. One interesting hypothesis might be that publicly understood incompatibilities between specific parties so greatly constrict the set of possible governing coalitions that we can substantially raise our D values by building these incompatibilities into

25*

our skeletal model. We could, according to this conjecture, assume that certain governing coalitions—say those including both Communists and Agrarians are ruled out *regardless* of election outcomes. Or, we could assign specific probabilities to all possible governing coalitions, making those joining hostile parties less probable than those joining vriendly ones.

These restrictions might take any of several forms, of which these are examples:

1)   No governing coalition may contain X...
in any event
if it also contains Y
unless it contains Y... etc.

2   Any governing coalition must contain X...
in any event
if it does not include Y... etc.

3)   Governing coalitions must be of minimum winning size.

The X and Y terms may be given a variety of interpretations. Specific parties or whole classes of parties may be designated. So, for example, "X" might mean "middle-class parties" or it might simply mean same single middle-class party, say "the Conservatives". Alternatively, the terms may be filled with specifications general to all parties—"the party which gained the largest number of new seats in the last election," for example.

These restrictions will produce new APOG distributions and will increase our estimate of decisiveness by concentrating these socres. Consider, for example, the Canadian case, which produces the following computations under the a priori model.

Party	# Seats	Pos	# Pivots	∅	$Kn = 133$ # Barg's	APOG
Progressive Conservative [Pa]	116	0.437	12	0.50	6	0.50
Liberals [Pb]	100	0.377	4	0.167	2	0.167
Social Credit [Pc]	30	0.113	4	0.167	2	0.167
New Democrats [Pd]	19	0.071	4	0.163	2	0.167

The decisiveness of this election is estimated at 0.333. But suppose that we add restriction to our model as follows:

1) P_a and P_d must not be in the same governing coalition.

Decisiveness = 0.437.

2) P_a must be in any giverning coalition.

Decisiveness = 0.481

3) P_a and P_c must be in any governing coalition.

Decisiveness = 0.625.

Clearly enough, these restrictions produce an upward revision in our estimate of electoral decisiveness.

An interesting prospect for democratic theory is raised by the possibility that joint application of the a priori model along with a restricted model will allow us to factor decisivness into two components: 1. that which is produced by the outcome itself, and 2. that which is produced by the joint effect of outcomes and restrictions within the elite bargaining system. The former would be estimated by the dispersion of the a priori scores, and the latter by the dispersion of scores under restrictions representing incompatibilities and norms found amongst the party elites. The difference between the two estimates for decisiveness could then be attributed to the influence of these elite patterns. We would thus obtain three estimates: 1. the a priori decisiveness of the outcome, 2. the effective decisiveness of the outcome given the elite culture, and 3. the increment in decisiveness which may be attributed to the culture of the political elite. The first would be given as our simple decisiveness score; the second as the restricted decisiveness score; and the third as the difference between them.

This sort of analysis would obviously require careful empirical investigations of elite patterns in every system to which it were applied. But this might be a price worth paying, for it would help us to establish another bridge—however, narrow, however swaybacked—between the distant continents of prescriptive democratic theory and empirical political science.

APPENDIX

Australia 1961

Party	# Seats	POS	# Pivots	Ø	K = 112 # Barg's	APOG
Liberal & Country	62	0.508	1	1.00	2	1.00
Labour	60	0.492	0	0	0	0

Austria 1962

Party	# Seats	POS	# Pivots	∅	# Barg's	APOG
				$K = 83$		
People's	81	0.490	2	0.333	2	0.333
Socialist	76	0.460	2	0.333	2	0.333
Freedom	8	0.048	2	0.333	2	0.333

Belgium 1961

Party	# Seats	POS	# Pivots	∅	# Barg's	APOG
				$K = 107$		
Christian Socials	96	0.452	276	0.383	18	0.383
Socialists	84	0.396	186	0.258	13	0.277
Liberals	20	0.094	174	0.242	9	0.191
Communists	5	0.023	36	0.050	3	0.064
Flemish Nationalists	5	0.023	36	0.050	3	0.064
Independents	2	0.009	12	0.017	1	0.021

POS = Proportion of Seats
∅ = Shapley Value
APOG = A Priori Opportunity to Govern
# Barg's = Number of Bargains

France 1962

Party	# Seats	POS	# Pivots	∅	# Barg's	APOG
				$K = 233$		
UNR-UDT	229	0.493	N.A.	N.A.	60	0.75
Socialists	65	0.140	N.A.	N.A.	4	0.05
Conservatives	49	0.106	N.A.	N.A.	4	0.05
Radicals	43	0.092	N.A.	N.A.	4	0.05
Communists	41	0.088	N.A.	N.A.	4	0.05
MRP	36	0.077	N.A.	N.A.	4	0.05
New Left	2	0.004	N.A.	N.A.	0	0

Iceland 1963

Party	# Seats	POS	# Pivots	∅	# Barg's	APOG
				$K = 31$		
Independence	24	0.400	12	0.50	6	0.50
Progressive (People's)	19	0.317	4	0.167	2	0.167
Communists	9	0.150	4	0.167	2	0.167
Social Democrats	8	0.133	4	0.167	2	0.167

Israel 1961

Party	# Seats	POS	# Pivots	∅	# Barg's	APOG
				$K = 61$		
Mapai	42	0.350	N.A.	N.A.	418	0.504
Herut	17	0.141	N.A.	N.A.	87	0.105
Liberals	17	0.141	N.A.	N.A.	87	0.105
Nat'l Religious	12	0.100	N.A.	N.A.	68	0.082
Mapam	9	0.075	N.A.	N.A.	43	0.052
Ahdut Avoda	8	0.066	N.A.	N.A.	35	0.042
Communists	5	0.041	N.A.	N.A.	28	0.034
Agudat Israel	4	0.033	N.A.	N.A.	22	0.027
Arab Mapai	4	0.033	N.A.	N.A.	22	0.027
Poalei Agudat Israel	2	0.016	N.A.	N.A.	19	0.023

United States 1960

Party	# Seats	POS	# Pivots	∅	# Barg's	APOG
				$K = 229$		
Democratic	263	0.601	1	1.00	1	1.00
Republican	174	0.398	0	0	0	0

NOTES

1 See, for example, Joseph Schumpeter, *Capitalism, Socialism, and Democracy*, 1942, especially Chapter 22.

2 Anthony Downs, *An Economic Theory of Democracy*, 1957, p. 23.

3 Edward F. Cox, "The Measurement of Party Strength," *Western Political Quarterly*, 13, 1960, 1022–42; Robert T. Golembiewski, "A Taxonomic Approach to State Political Party Strength," *Western Political Quarterly*, 11, 1958, 494–513; Malcolm Jewell, *The State Legislature*, 1962; Richard I. Hofferbert, "Classification of American State Party Systems," *Journal of Politics*, 26, 1964, 550–67; David G. Pfeiffer, "The Measurement of Inter-Party Competition and Systemic Stability," *American Political Science Review*, 61, 1967, 457–67; Austin Ranney and Willmoore Kendall, "The American Party System," *American Political Science Review*, 48, 1954, 477–85; Austin Ranney, "Parties in State Politics," *Politics in the American States*, Herbert Jacob and Kenneth N. Vines, eds., 1965, see especially pp. 63–70; Joseph A. Schlesinger, "A Two-Dimensional Scheme for Classifying the States According to Degree of Inter-Party Competition," *American Political Science Review*, 49, 1955, 1120–28; *American State Legislatures: Report of the Committee on American Legislatures*, American Political Science Association, Belle Zeller, ed., 1954, Chapter 12.

4 Mark Kesselman, "French Local Politics: A Statistical Examination Grass Roots Consensus," *American Political Science Review*, 60, 1966, 963–73; Douglas W. Rae, "A Note on the Fractionalization of Some European Party Systems," *Comparative Political Studies*, 1, 1968.

5 This model is not of course meant as an explanation of a set of events, but as a definitional basis for the measure proposed below.

6 This definition was suggested by Leon Epstein's *Political Parties in the Western Democracies*, 1968.

7 This corresponds to what may be called the "loose" definition of a "minimum winning coalition." Note that it does not require that *every* party be essential, but only that this one party be essential.

8 This corresponds to Downs' assumption that parties are teams. *Ibid.* 25–27.

9 This, of course, ignores the possibility of a minority government, but it will be apparent that such governments require outside support for individual policies: they are therefore "shifting" majority coalitions.

10 L. S. Shapley, "A Value for *n*-Person Games," *Annals of Mathematical Studies*, 28, 1953, 307–1; L. S. Shapley and M. Shubik, "A Method for Evaluating the Distribution of Power in a Committee System," *American Political Science Review*, 48, 1954, 787–92.

11 The intuitive assumption is that something analogous to log-rolling occurs in governing coalitions and that only essential members can expect to be full partners in all trades. This is not to say that inessential members are altogether impotent. Suppose, for example, that a governing coalition contains one essential member and two or more inessential ones. By forming a sub-coalition—becoming a single essential member—these inessential partners may exert a full claim on government decisions. The present measure does not take this possibility into account, and this must be considered a shortcoming. On the other hand, any effort to consider potential sub-coalitions would enormously complicate our estimates. It is worth noting that Shapley values are equally insensitive to the potentiality for sub-coalition formation.

12 This holds for Germany only on the reasonable presumption that the CDU and CSU are a single party.

13 See Marshall Hall and Nicolaus Tideman, "Measures of Concentration," *Journal of the American Statistical Association*, 62, March, 1967, 162–68.

14 Downs, *op. cit.*, pp. 112–13.

15 Downs, *op. cit.*, Proposition Twenty-Five, p. 300.

A GAME-THEORETIC ANALYSIS
OF SOCIAL CHOICE[1]

ROBERT WILSON[2]

Stanford University

---

1 INTRODUCTION

The major theme in social-choice theory has been the possibility of including social choices within the realm of maximizing processes, as was done successfully with individual-choice theory. That is, it is desired to know whether social choices can be construed as maximizing a social welfare function which aggregates individuals' preferences in some fashion. Originally, Abram Bergson (1938) held that the elements of welfare economics could be derived from postulated properties of a social welfare function, or some variant such as the Compensation Principle, where admittedly in any particular application the aggregation of individuals' preferences would be based upon ethical judgments. Bergson's proposition amounts to defining welfare economics as the implications of Pareto optimality, since to each ethical judgment there corresponds a Pareto-optimal choice, and conversely.

Kenneth Arrow (1963), however, refuted Bergson's contention on the grounds, essentially, that ethical judgments are not consistent with any process of maximizing social welfare; indeed, that the set of postulates Arrow offered were inconsistent among themselves. Arrow showed that in general, given the other assumed properties of social preferences, an ethical judgment must either violate the Independence of Irrelevant Alternatives, in which case social preferences are not well-defined, or lead to an intransitive ordering of alternatives, in which case maximization is not always possible. Special cases have been found in which Bergson's approach is tenable (e.g. Arrow (1963), Chapter VII), but these require restrictions on the, individuals' preferences which are rarely evident in practice.

In the ensuing debate there have been few attempts, following from an acceptance of Arrow's conclusions, to examine their content and ramifications in the study of the actual processes of social choice which are found in practice and which provide the empirically-given subject matter of welfare theory.[3] In reality, major decisions in a society are rarely made by individuals exercising their ethical judgments (although often they are made by individuals of expert competence), but more often by a variety of institutionalized legislative bodies and other multi-person mechanisms; e.g. representative assemblies and market processes. The procedures of these institutions define social decision processes which deserve detailed study.

It is at least clear, for example, that the legislative process of majority rule, and the market process of unanimous consent among the parties to an exchange, severely limit the set of Pareto-optimal outcomes that may obtain. Therefore, they constitute implicit ethical judgments sanctioned by the law whose consequences should be examined.

The existence and importance of institutionalized processes, moreover, derive from a fact which denies a corresponding role for the ethically–motivated decision maker in Bergson's paradigm. Not only does such a person face a conflict of interest which can be resolved in a wide variety of ways, even if there is a uniform ethical standard, but when a citizen's welfare is decided by another there is every incentive for him to misrepresent his preferences in order to bias the ultimate decision in his favor. It is only by engaging each citizen in a process (e.g. voting) that requires him to commit his resources (e.g. votes) to affect the social choice that one is assured of unbiased representations of preferences.

2 MAJORITY-RULE VOTING IN A LEGISLATIVE BODY

The purpose of this paper is to provide an introductory analysis of one of the most important mechanism of social choice; namely, the process in a legislature of choosing among several proposed bills by majority rule.[4] By applying the methods of game theory to an example, the solution to which is shown to be a member of a general class, we shall illustrate several of the features of legislative processes. In addition, the game–theoretic analysis will be used to examine Arrow's construction with the aim of elucidating the nature of the phenomenon of intransitivity among social choices which he demonstrated by other means.[5]

The example is constructed to address also a topic of current interest in social-choice theory; viz., the effects of vote trading or "logrolling" among the members of a legislature. The example provides strong evidence that no straightforward application of the economic theory of exchange to the process of vote trading will suffice to model voting processes, in contrast to the recent proposals of James Buchanan and Gordon Tullock (1962) and James Coleman (1966). These authors have argued that since votes are private goods to the legislators (even though they affect the disposition of bills which are public goods), an exchange economy for vote trading should share some of the merits usually accorded to market mechanisms. In contrast, our analysis shows that in general a game-theoretic solution may require randomized strategies, a result which can not be achieved by vote trading (unless, of course, one introduces contingent contracts). This conclusion has been anticipated obliquely by R. E. Park (1967); also, Arrow [1963, p. 109] has remarked that vote trading in no way escapes the consequences of his argument.[6]

3 FORMULATION

We shall consider a legislature composed of m voters indexed by $i = 1, \ldots, m$ and comprising a set $I = \{i | 1 \leq i \leq m\}$. Before the legislature are n bills indexed by $j = 1, \ldots, n$ and comprising a set $J = \{j | 1 \leq j \leq n\}$. Each bill is to be passed or failed by majority rule, in the sense that a bill passes if and only if the number of voters casting their votes affirmatively exceeds the number casting theirs negatively. It will suffice to suppose that there are an odd number of voters in total, and that each voter is endowed with one vote on each bill.

The outcome of the legislative process will be a set of bills passed; hence, the set of social states that may obtain is the set of subsets of J; viz., $S = \{s | \phi \subseteq s \subseteq J\}$, where the status quo is identified with the empty set ϕ. Each voter is assumed to have a complete and transitive preference ordering among the social states; say, xR_iy means that the ith voter prefers x to y or is indifferent, and P_i is the relation of strict preference. Let $u_i(\cdot)$ be a utility function defined on S which represents the preference ordering of the ith voter, and assume $u_i(\phi) = 0$ without any loss of generality. When a voter makes decisions under uncertainty, as in the case of randomized voting strategies, we shall suppose further that he adheres to the Savage axioms, and, therefore, that each utility function u_i is unique up to a positive linear transformation. In this case, u_i is extended to the set S^* of probability distributions on S by the relation

$$u_i(z) = \sum_{s \varepsilon S} z(s)\, u_i(s), \quad z \varepsilon S^*,$$

according to the rules of expected utility.

4 THE VOTING PROCESS AS A COOPERATIVE GAME

The voting process in the legislature can be modeled as a cooperative game if three assumptions are made, although alternative game-theoretic analyses could be made with weaker assumptions. We shall assume first that there is perfect information among the legislators about each other's preferences, and second that all contractual agreements (or "coalitions") among them are possible. [These assumptions are in distinct contrast to the assumptions of (1) uncertainty or ignorance, and (2) individualistic behavior in a price-mediated exchange economy, employed in the recent discussions of vote trading.[7]] Third, we shall suppose that there are no legitimate means for side payments (e.g., money) among the legislators (or their constituencies); that is, any transfers must be included among the provisions of the bills, which are pure public goods not susceptible to divisions. This assumption corresponds well to the actual facts of legislative procedures in government.[8] These assumptions suffice to define the voting process as a cooperative game without side payments. An extension of the von Neumann–Morgenstern theory to such games has been developed by Robert Aumann and Bezalel Peleg (1967, 1960) and it is this theory that we shall employ henceforth.[9]

The chief instrument of the theory is the characteristic function, which specifies for each coalition of voters the outcomes, measured in the voters' utilities, that it can ensure. In the present case of majority rule, and majority coalition of the voters can ensure any social state, whereas a smaller coalition is powerless to ensure more than the respective worst social states for its members.[10] Hence, if randomized voting strategies are allowed, then the set of social states is

$$H = \{u \mid u \varepsilon E^I,\ u^i = u_i(z),\ z \varepsilon S^*\}$$

measured in the voters' utilities, and the characteristic function $v(c)$ for a coalition c, $\phi \subset c \subseteq I$, with $|c|$ members is

$$v(c) = \begin{cases} \{u | u \varepsilon E^c, \ u^i \leq x^i \ \text{for all } i \varepsilon c \text{ for } \textit{some } x \varepsilon H\} \text{ if } \ |c| > m/2 \\ \{u | u \varepsilon E^c, \ u^i \leq x^i \ \text{for all } i \varepsilon c \text{ for } \textit{all } x \varepsilon H\} \quad \text{if } \ |c| < m/2 \end{cases},$$

where E^c is the $|c|$-dimensional Euclidean space with coordinates indexed by the members of the coalition c.[11] Hereafter, for $u \varepsilon E^I$ we shall denote the projection of u on E^c by u^c and employ the vector inequality $u^c \leq x^c$ to mean $u^i \leq x^i$ for all $i \varepsilon c$.

5 SOLUTION CONCEPTS

If in a collection c of voters each one prefers an outcome x to another y, and as a coalition they are sufficiently powerful to ensure x, then there is a potential incentive for them to organize to obtain x if y would result otherwise. In this case, we say that the coalition c is effective for x and that x dominates y via the coalition c. In the present case, a coalition is effective for an outcome $x \varepsilon H$ only if it constitutes a majority. Now, if some one outcome dominates all others, and therefore no other dominates it under majority rule, we can readily suppose that that distinguished outcome will result. This is the familiar Condorcet criterion that has played a central role in the study of voting processes; namely, the social choice will be the outcome that commands majority support against every alternative. Unfortunately, it is well known that often an outcome satisfying the Condorcet criterion will not exist, as evidenced for example by the instance of cyclical majorities [Arrow (1963), p. 3]. Indeed, even the weaker criterion that the social choice will be among the set of undominated outcomes is often vacuous, sincethere need not be any undominated outcomes.[12] These features describeessentially the difficulty characterized by Arrow. Game theory, therefore, seeks a weaker characterization of the social choice, called a solution by von Neumann and Morgenstern.

A solution is a subset of the possible outcomes which among them dominate all alternatives, but not each other. That is, any alternative that a coalition can seek in preference to one in the solution is in turn dominated by another in the solution. If we identify the outcomes in a solution with proposals by the various majority coalitions that may form, then a solution possesses stability in the sense that to every proposal against one in the solution there is a counterproposal in the solution. The solution concept recognizes the multiplicity of majority coalitions that might form, leaving unresolved which one will form in any specific situation—a subject best analyzed in terms of historical and behavioral factors, party affiliations, and the other data of political science—but requiring in any case that the various coalitions' proposals be stable in relation to each other so as to thwart alternative proposals by other coalitions that might form in response. The applicability of this approach should be evident in the case of cyclical majorities, and we shall illustrate it further in the example in Section 6 below. In sum, stability is the essential requirement of a solution in the game-theoretic analysis.

The formalization of the solution concept runs as follows. For any two outcomes x and y in E^I, x dominates y via the nonempty coalition c if $x^c > y^c$ and $x^c \varepsilon v(c)$, and this relation is denoted by $xD_c y$. Also x dominates y, denoted xDy, if $xD_c y$ for some nonempty coalition c. Correspondingly, define the dominion $D(x) = \{y | xDy\}$ of outcomes dominated by x, and for any set of outcomes X let $D(X) = \bigcup_{x \varepsilon X} D(x)$. Hence, for any set A of attainable outcomes, a solution V or $V(A)$ is a subset of A (1) which dominates all alternatives, expressed by the condition $V \cup D(V) \supseteq A$, and (2) no element of which dominates another, expressed by the condition $V \cap D(V) = \phi$. Condition (1) is called external stability and condition (2) is called internal stability. Together they yield the equivalent condition $V = A - D(V)$ of total stability. The weak form of the Condorcet criterion is represented by the core, $C(A) = A - D(A)$, consisting of the undominated outcomes in A (if any). Since $V \subseteq A$ implies $D(A) \supseteq D(V)$ it follows that the core is contained in every solution, $C(A) \subseteq V$, although possibly the core may be empty. In the present discussion we shall be concerned only with finding solutions for $A = H$.[14]

6   AN EXAMPLE

An illustration of the application of the game-theoretic analysis will clarify the solution concept and convey some of the interesting properties of solutions. As an example, consider an assembly consisting of three voters which will choose among three proposed bills by majority rule. We will assume that the bills are independent in the sense that for each voter the utility assigned to the passage of any set of bills is independent of the disposition of the other bills; cf. Wilson (1969) for an axiomatic formulation of this property. In this case, for any $i \varepsilon I$, $s \varepsilon S$, we have $u_i(s) = \sum_{j \varepsilon s} u_{ij}$ for some set $\{u_{ij}\}$ of utilities assigned to the individual bills. The data of the example are displayed in Table 1.[15] The set H of possible utility outcomes using randomized strategies, and the characteristic function v, are computed from this data as indicated in Section 4. Figure 1 displays the characteristic

Table 1 Data of the Example ($m = 3, n = 3$)

Voter (i)	Bill (j):	u_{ij}		
		1	2	3
1		-1	3	-8
2		-3	-8	1
3		8	1	3

function $v(c)$ for the minimal winning coalitions; i.e. those with precisely two members. (See Figure 1 on page 400.)

In Figure 1 there is also a solution $V_0(H) = \{x_1, x_2, x_3\}$ which is indicated in each characteristic function.[16] The outcomes in this solution are the randomized strategies exhibited in Table 2, where $z_k \varepsilon S^*$ denotes the randomized strategy yielding x_k. Figure 1 also indicates portions of the dominions $D(x_k)$ of the outcomes in the solution.

The verification that $V_0(H)$ is a solution consists of checking that external and internal stability are attained. External stability is achieved since the dominion of the solution includes all of H except the solution. This can be checked in Figure 1; e.g. a randomization between the status quo and the passage of bill 2, denoted by ϕ and $\{2\}$ respectively, is not dominated by x_1 but is dominated by x_2 if the probability assigned to the passage of bill 2 exceeds $2/11$ and by x_3 if the probability is less than $2/11$, as can be seen in Figures 1a, 1b, and 1c respectively. Internal stability follows from the observation that some voter is indifferent between any two outcomes in the solution.

There exist other solutions than $V_0(H)$, but these are all of the kind called discriminatory and might well be judged extraneous in most practical contexts; that is, each discriminatory solution consists of all outcomes in H for which $x^i = k$ for some voter i and some feasible k. An example is $i = 2, k = -3$: observe that every outcome which dominates an outcome in this discriminatory solution via $c = \{1, 2\}$ or $c = \{2, 3\}$ is in turn dominated by an outcome in the solution via $c = \{1, 3\}$, and conversely one that dominates via $\{1, 3\}$ is dominated via $\{1, 2\}$ or $\{2, 3\}$. The situation therefore reduces to a two person game between voters 1 and 3.

In this example the core is empty, as one readily verifies from the property $C(H) \subseteq V_0(H)$ and the observation that $V_0(H) \subset D(H)$; that is, none of x_1, x_2, x_3 is undominated. Hence, the Condorect criterion is vacuous in this example.

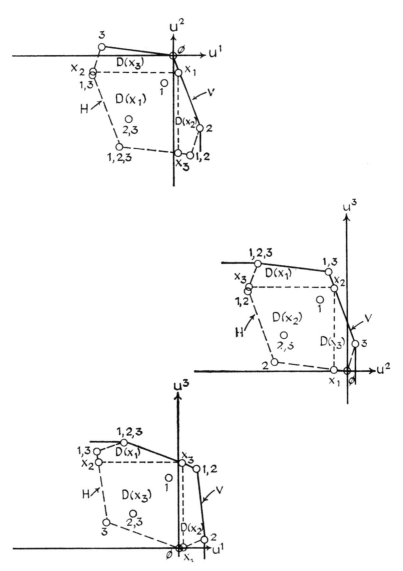

Figure 1   The characteristic function for the minimal winning coalitions and the solution x_1, x_2, x_3.

Table 2   The solution $V_0(H) = \{x_1, x_2, x_3\}$

k	x_k			$z_k(s)$							
	x_k^1	x_k^2	x_k^3	$s \varepsilon S$: ϕ	1	2	3	$1, 2$	$1, 3$	$2, 3$	$1, 2, 3$
1	6/11	−16/11	2/11	9/11	0	2/11	0	0	0	0	0
2	−97/11	−16/11	105/11	0	0	0	2/11	0	9/11	0	0
3	6/11	−119/11	105/11	0	0	0	0	9/11	0	0	2/11

It is natural to consider the role of the randomized strategies in the solution. Consider, therefore, replacing S^* by S in the definition of H so that randomized strategies are not allowed. One readily verifies that in this case there exists no solution for H; e.g. a systematic procedure consists of defining $D^{-1}(x) = \{y | yDx\}$ and checking that $D^{-1}(x)_\cap H \neq \phi$ and $\{x\}_\cup D(x)_\cup D^{-1}(x) \supseteq H$ for all $x\varepsilon H$, indicating that internal and external stability cannot both be satisfied. Also, the core is empty. In general, therefore, stability may require the admissibility of randomized strategies. In the present example, the necessity of randomized strategies to ensure the existence of a solution, and the fact that the unique nondiscriminatory solution $V_0(H)$ employs only randomized strategies, demonstrate that vote trading will not lead to any outcome in the nondiscriminatory solution.[17, 18]

The structural features of the nondiscriminatory solution are of considerable interest. The striking features are that (1) for each minimal winning coalition there is associated an outcome in the solution which is Pareto optimal for that coalition, and (2) a voter common to two minimal winning coalitions is indifferent as to which one he joins but prefers that one or the other form rather than to be excluded.[19] The first property allows us to identify outcomes in the solution with proposals by the various minimal winning coalitions that might form, while the second ensures internal stability. Evidently, given the requirement of internal stability in the form of (2), (1) provides a guarantee of external stability. Clearly, it would be fruitless to suppose that a coalition would propose a non-Pareto-optimal outcome. In the next Section we shall see that these features are in fact quite general; or, the reader can skip to Section 8 without loss of continuity.[20]

7   GENERALIZATION

The features of the nondiscriminatory solution in the example can be generalized as follows. Let K be a set of indices for the minimal winning coalitions, those with $|c| = (m + 1)/2$ members, and let $V_0 = \{x_k | x_k \varepsilon H,$ $k\varepsilon K\}$ be a set of outcomes in H proposed by the various coalitions in K. If there are several outcomes in H yielding any $x_k^{c_k}$ then extend V_0 to include all such outcomes. We shall assume that V_0 possesses the two properties noted above: for all $k\varepsilon K$,

1   x_k is Pareto optimal for coalition c_k; viz., there exists no $y\varepsilon H$, $y^{c_k} \neq x^{c_k}$, for which $y^{c_k} \geq x^{c_k}$;

2   $x_k^{c_k} \geq x_\ell^{c_k}$ for all $\ell \varepsilon K$.

Note that (2) requires $x_k^e = x_\ell^e$ for $e = c_k \cap c_\ell$, so that a voter common to coalitions c_k and c_ℓ is indifferent between x_k and x_ℓ.

Our theorem is that V_0 must be a solution for H. To show this, consider first the question of internal stability. Suppose that $x_\ell D_c x_k$ for some k and ℓ in K and some nonempty coalition c; i.e., $x_\ell^c > x_k^c$ and $x_\ell^c \varepsilon v(c)$. Now (2) requires that $x_k^{c_k} \geq x_\ell^{c_k}$ so $c_\cap c_k = \phi$ and therefore $|c| < m/2$. But in this case, $x_\ell^c \varepsilon v(c)$ requires $x_\ell^c \leq x_k^c$ since $x_k \varepsilon H$, a contradiction. Thus V_0 must be internally stable. External stability, on the other hand, is demonstrated by showing that any outcome $x \varepsilon H$ is either in V_0 or is dominated by some coalition proposal in V_0. We shall show this constructively by actually finding such a coalition proposal. For each $\ell \varepsilon K$ let $d_\ell = \{i | i \varepsilon c_\ell, x^i \geq x_\ell^i\}$ be the subset of members of the coalition who do not prefer x_ℓ to x, and assume that the choice $\ell = k$ maximizes $|d_\ell|$. If $d_k = c_k$ then $x^{c_k} = x_k^{c_k}$ and $x \varepsilon V_0$, since otherwise x_k is not Pareto optimal for coalition c_k; also, if $d_k = \phi$ then x_k dominates x via c_k. Hence, assume $0 < |d_k| < m/2$.[21] Now, for any $\ell \varepsilon K$ for which $c_{k \cap} c_\ell = d_k$ we have from (2) that $x_\ell^i = x_k^i \leq x^i$ for all $i \varepsilon d_k$ and therefore $d_\ell \supseteq d_k$; but $|d_k|$ is maximal, so $d_\ell = d_k$ and $x_\ell^i > x^i$ for all $i \varepsilon c_\ell - d_k$. As ℓ varies, each $i \notin d_k$ is included in some such c_ℓ; consequently, for each $i \notin d_k$ there exists $\ell(i) \varepsilon K$ such that $x_{\ell(i)}^i > x^i$. Choose any $\ell \varepsilon K$ for which $c_{\ell \cap} d_k = \phi$; then using (2) again, $x_\ell^i \geq x_{\ell(i)}^i > x^i$ for all $i \varepsilon c_\ell$. Thus, x_ℓ dominates x via c_ℓ, which completes the demonstration of external stability as well as the proof that V_0 is a solution.[22]

8   A GAME-THEORETIC ANALYSIS OF ARROW'S CONSTRUCTION

The game-theoretic concept of a solution differs from the usual formulations of social choice chiefly in its recognition of the multiplicity of coalitions that might form. In contrast, traditional constructions of the problem of social choice have attempted to determine a definite outcome without imposing further assumptions about coalition formations. Most of these approaches follow the lines of Arrow's axiomatic development.

In the instance of majority-rule voting, Arrow (1963) [p. 76], defines the relation R of social preference by the condition that xRy if and only if $N(x, y) \geq N(y, x)$, where $N(x, y)$ is the number of voters who prefer x to y or are indifferent. Similarly, the relation P of strict social preference means $N(x, y) > N(y, x)$. The latter is closely related to the relation of dominance

26*

in game theory. For example, if xDy for some outcomes x and y in H, then a majority of the voters prefer x to y and we can conclude that xPy. The converse is not generally valid, however, since xPy may hold even when xDy does not if some of the voters are indifferent between x and y.[23]

Arrow also defines the choice set $\Gamma(H) = \{x|x\varepsilon H, \ xRy \text{ for all } y\varepsilon H\}$ as the set of socially preferred outcomes in H(Arrow, 1963), [p. 15]. Clearly, the choice set is always a subset of the core, and therefore is contained in every solution. The choice set, however, may be empty, as the absence of a core in the example of Section 6 demonstrates. Arrow's General Possibility Theorem can be constructed as a proof that the choice set may be empty. Essentially, this result derives from requiring an excessively strong form of external stability in the definition of the choice set. If one instead were to define the choice set as a game-theoretic solution then Arrow's negative conclusion would no longer be true.[24]

9   THE BARGAINING SET

Besides the one of von Neumann and Morgenstern, a variety of other solution concepts have been proposed in the literature of game theory. One of them, the bargaining set introduced by Aumann and Maschler (1964), is especially worth mentioning here because of its intuitive appeal in the analysis of actual voting behavior. Also, the "solution" it offers is a unique set, in contrast to von Neumann and Morgenstern's. Our treatment is specialized to majority-rule voting games with an odd number of voters.

Let us consider an outcome to be a pair (x, c) in which $x\varepsilon H$ and c is a majority coalition. Consider two disjoint subsets d and e of c, either of which may be empty. An objection to (x, c) by d against e is defined to be an alternative outcome (y, c') such that $c' \supseteq d$ and $c' \cap e = \phi, y^d > x^d$, and $y^{c'} \geq x^{c'}$. That is, an objection is an argument by d that it could do better in another majority coalition without e. A counterobjection to (y, c') by e against d, provided $e \neq \phi$, is another outcome (z, c'') such that $c'' \supseteq e, \ c'' \not\supseteq d$, $z^{c''} \geq x^{c''}$, and $z^{c' \cap c''} \geq y^{c' \cap c''}$. That is, e counters that compared to both x and y it can do as well in another coalition without all d. An outcome is said to be stable if to every objection there is a counterobjection, and the set of all stable outcomes is called the bargaining set. In the example of Section 6, the bargaining set is precisely the nondiscriminatory solution.[25]

NOTES

1 Presented at the Social Choice Conference, University of Pittsburgh, September 9–12, 1968. This study was prepared in part during the tenure of a Ford Foundation Faculty Research Fellowship, and in part with the support of the Atomic Energy Commission, Grant AT(04-3) 326-PA #18. It appeared originally as Working Paper 145 of the Graduate School of Business, Stanford University, August 1968.

2 Graduate School of Business, Stanford University.

3 For Arrow's review of the debate, and references, cf. Arrow (1963), [Chapter VIII].

4 Of course the formal analysis applies equally to referenda, elections, and the deliberations of a corporation's Board of Directors.

5 The present results were anticipated by Arrow: "The negative outcome expressed in this theorem (the General Possibility Theorem) is strongly reminiscent of the intransitivity of . . . domination in the theory of games" [Arrow (1963) p. 59, fn. 1].

6 For an alternative axiomatic analysis of vote trading, cf. Wilson (1969).

7 Here we would rather follow the excellent dictum of John von Neumann and Oskar Morgenstern (1947, pp. 14–15) that an adequate understanding of multi-person problems must begin with an understanding for few participants. Our present assumptions are the more tenable ones in the case of a small number of participants, and surely the second has the advantage of not prejudging the outcome.

8 One possibility we shall not analyze explicitly is the process of forming a compromise among several bills by the introduction of amendments or new bills. Here, the set of bills is a fixed datum.

9 Earlier suggestions of such an extension were proposed by Lloyd Shapley and Martin Shubik (1953) and by R. Duncan Luce and Howard Raiffa (1954). The theory of the bargaining set will be introduced in Section 9 also.

10 If the number of voters were even, then a coalition with $m/2$ voters could also ensure the status quo ϕ by blocking all bills.

11 If randomized strategies are excluded, then one could use S instead of S* in the definition of H.

12 Nor is ignoring the unpleasant an acceptable criterion since under most reasonable assumptions cyclical majorities occur with increasing frequency as the number of bills increases.

13 Generally it is the requisite property of stability that removes social choices from the realm of maximizing processes, and it is the feature that precludes a social welfare function as sought by Bergson and refuted by Arrow.

14 A solution for H is both individually and collectively rational in the case of majority rule; cf. Aumann (1967).

15 This example is drawn from Wilson (1969), with which the results obtained here can be compared.

16 A means of computing solutions to majority-rule voting games is given in Wilson (1968).

17 Unless of course contingent contracts are employed. For example, x_1 could result from an agreement between voters 1 and 2 that 2 would vote against bill 3 provided 1 voted against bill 2 with probability 9/11, and neither would strike any agreement with 3. Alternatively, the effects of randomization could be achieved by allowing a sufficiently rich set of compromises among the bills.

18 In Wilson (1969) it is shown that under certain conditions the passage of precisely bill 1 is the outcome predicted in the case of vote trading. Note that bill 1 alone is Pareto optimal only for the coalition of the whole.

19 Briefly, an outcome x is Pareto optimal for a coalition c if there is no other outcome y for which $y^c \varepsilon v(c)$ and $y^c \geqq x^c$. That is, any feasible alternative which one member prefers another will reject.

20 An expanded exposition of the subject of Section 7 is given in [Wilson (1968, 1969b)], which includes a demonstration that an arbitrary solution satisfying property (2) sa-satisfies property (1) and a presentation of procedures for calculating such solutions by solving a set of linear and bilinear inequalities.

21 It is only here that the proof depends upon the number of voters, m, being odd.

22 The general question of the existence of solutions having the properties (1) and (2) has not been resolved to date.

23 The role of indifferent voters is the source of randomized strategies in game-theoretic solutions. For example, if randomized strategies are not available, and no voter is indifferent between any two social states, then there need not exist a solution to a majority-rule voting game: (1) there cannot be more than one outcome in a solution since for any two outcomes in a solution there must be some voters who are indifferent in order to preserve internal stability; (2) if there exists a solution consisting of a single outcome then it must also be the core and satisfy the Condorcet criterion, since external stability ensures that it dominates all alternatives.

24 A game-theoretic solution satisfies Arrow's postulates of admissibility of voters' preferences, Pareto optimality, independence of irrelevant alternatives, and nondictatorship [Arrow (1963), p. 96]. Presumably one would forego transitivity of social preference in favor of requiring that the choice set be nonempty, since in Arrow's construction intransitivity is of consequence only when it yields an empty choice set.

25 In Wilson (1969 b) this result is generalized to demonstrate that a member of the class of solutions established in Section 7 is precisely the unique maximal subset of the bargaining set such that for every objection to an element of the subset there exists a counter-objection in the subset.

REFERENCES

Arrow, K. J. *Social Choice and Individual Values.* (2nd Ed.) Wiley, New York, 1963.
Aumann, R. J. A Survey of Cooperative Games Without Side Payments. M. Shubik (Ed.), *Essays in Mathematical Economics,* Princeton University Press, 1967. Pp. 3–27.
Aumann, R. J. and Maschler, M. The Bargaining Set for Cooperative Games, M. Dresher *et al.* (Eds.), *Advances in Game Theory*, Princeton University Press, 1964. Pp. 443–476.

Aumann, R. J. and Peleg, B. Von Neumann-Morgenstern Solutions to Cooperative Games Without Side Payments, *Bulletin Amer. Math. Soc.*, 1960, Vol. **66**, 173–179.

Bergson, A. A Reformulation of Certain Aspects of Welfare Economics, *Q. J. Economics*, 1938, Vol. **52**, 310–334.

Buchanan, J. and Tullock, G. *The Calculus of Consent.* University of Michigan Press, 1962.

Coleman, J. The Possibility of a Social Welfare Function. *Amer. Econ. Rev.*, 1966, Vol. **LVI**, 1105–1122.

Luce, R. D. and Raiffa, H. *Games and Decisions.* Wiley, New York, 1957.

Von Neumann, J. and Morgenstern, O. *Theory of Games and Economic Behavior.* (2nd ed.) Princeton University Press, 1947.

Park, R. E. "Comment" on Coleman (1966), *Amer. Econ. Rev.*, 1967, Vol. **LVII** 1300–1304.

Shapley, L. and Shubik, M. "Solutions of *n*-Person Games with Ordinal Utilities" (Abstract), *Econometrica*, 1953, Vol. 21, p. 348.

Wilson, R. An Axiomatic Model of Logrolling, *Amer. Econ. Rev.*, 1969, **LIX**, 331–341.

Wilson, R. A Class of Solutions for Voting Games, Paper 156, Graduate School of Business, Stanford University, October 1968.

Wilson, R. Coalition Formation in Majority-Rule Voting, Paper 167, Graduate School of Business, Stanford University, November 1969.

A GAME-THEORETIC ANALYSIS OF
PARTY PLATFORM SELECTION[1]

JOHN CHAMBERLIN

Stanford University

Party platforms play an important part in the democratic process as expressions of what the parties will do if elected to office. This work examines several aspects of the platform selection process and seeks to find equilibrium conditions for the process in the context of a two party system operating with majority rule. The frequently expressed doubts concerning the truthfulness and usefulness of party platforms will be avoided in this paper by the assumption that the party elected will have dictatorial powers, and thus will be able to (and will) implement its platform as announced to the voters.

A basic model of the platform selection process has been given by Shubik (1968). The present work will begin with Shubik's model, show that Shubik's results concerning equilibrium strategies are insufficient, and attempt to characterize the correct equilibrium conditions. While a complete characterization of the equilibrium strategy set is not obtained, a nearly exhaustive list of those strategies which cannot be equilibrium strategies is derived, and the problem whose solution gives the equilibrium strategy (if it exists) is formulated. In fairness to Shubik, it should be mentioned that he explicitly made no claim concerning the completeness of his model with respect to the platform selection process or its similarity to the real world of politics, but instead intended it to be a basic model with which to begin the study of a broader problem than platform selection.

The platform selection process can be studied as a $(2 + n)$–person compound game. In the first subgame, the two parties choose and announce platforms. In the second subgame, the voters select one of the parties, after which the payoffs occur—the resulting social state being the payoff to the voters, and election being the payoff to the winning party (it is assumed that parties attach a value to being elected). The process is thus composed of two decisions, the party decision on a platform (made with the knowledge of voter preferences), and the voters' decision of a party to elect. This work focuses on the party decision, as the voters' decision is determined easily from basic assumptions concerning individual preference functions.

Casual reference to real political situations points out several characteristics which are desirable attributes of an equilibrium strategy for the platform selection process. In general, these lead to a preference for pure strategies over mixed strategies. Pure strategies have two significant advantages: (1) they do not require simultaneous announcement of platforms by the two parties since this necessary only in the case of mixed strategies, where secrecy is important, and (2) they allow ideology to play a greater part in the choice of a platform. Mixed strategies require the two parties to "jump around" the political spectrum, and thus make no allowance for the preferences and constraints imposed by ideology.

In the 2-person game played by the parties, the existence of an equilibrium pure strategy requires the existence of a core for the game played by the voters, and it is well known that the special case of the game to be examined later (that of cyclical majorities) has no core. Thus the equilibrium strategy cannot exhibit the desirable properties of a pure strategy, and a Nash equilibrium strategy must be sought. However, in anticipation of the final result of this paper that equilibrium strategy may not exist, we shall consider several pure strategy spaces and examine their properties in relation to several mixed strategy spaces.

SHUBIK'S MODEL

The main assumptions of Shubik's model are:

1) The political contest can be represented as a game of strict opposition.

2) Each voter has a single vote, which is not salable, and which he casts passively (i.e. no coalitions are formed).

3) There are two parties, each of which presents to the voters a single alternative as its platform.

4) A platform is characterized by a social state which, if elected, the party will bring about.

5) Each voter has a known and fixed preference ordering over the possible social states.

The voters' decision in this case is trivial. Each voter casts his vote for the party whose platform ranks highest in his ordering. The party whose platform ranks higher with a majority of the voters is thus elected. Shubik derives the following results for the party decision:

1) The presence of two parties each presenting a single alternative to the electorate guarantees that the resulting social state will be Pareto optimal.

2)(a) If there is a unique preferred social state both parties will offer it as their platform.

(b) If there is a set of social states which are preferred over all others (i.e. each element of the set is preferred to all elements not in the set) but are indifferent among themselves, then any one will do as a party platform.

(c) If there is a set of social states which are intransitive among themselves but are preferred to all others the resulting game of strict opposition between the two parties will call for a mixed strategy over the set of alternative which display the intransitivity.[2]

Shubik has studied the three cases with the help of a matrix describing the game played by the parties. The set of possible platforms is identical to the set of social states. Each party must select a social state to present to the voters as its platform. Platforms may be chosen with pure strategies (a single social state) or mixed strategies (a randomization over several social states). Each party seeks a platform which maximizes its probability of election. The matrix entries indicate which party is elected if Party I chooses the platform (social state) corresponding to the row index and Party II chooses that corresponding to the column index.

Case a) of a Condorcet winner corresponds to a voters' game which has a core consisting of a single social state. The symmetry of the game implies that both parties will choose the same social state as their platform, as Shubik has observed. This situation corresponds to a matrix which has only a single row (column) with no negative (positive) entries.

Case b) is a voters' game with a core containing several social states. It corresponds to a matrix with several rows (columns) having no negative (positive) entries. A submatrix formed from these rows and columns will have all zero entries (i.e. the states are socially indifferent). This case has one very appealing political characteristic—it makes total allowance for ideology in the selection of a platform strategy. Both parties will be led to choose from the same set of social states, but the social state (or randomization) chosen may be different, corresponding to differences in party ideology.

27*

Party II

| | S_1 | S_J | S_k |

Party I S_i		$U(S_i, S_j)$	

where:

$$
U(S_1, S_2) = \begin{cases}
1 & \text{if Parties I and II choose platforms } S_1 \text{ and } S_2 \text{ and } S_1 \text{ is} \\
& \text{socially preferred to } S_2 \\
0 & \text{if Parties I and II choose platforms } S_1 \text{ and } S_2 \text{ and } S_1 \text{ is} \\
& \text{socially indifferent to } S_2 \\
-1 & \text{if Parties I and II choose platforms } S_1 \text{ and } S_2 \text{ and } S_2 \text{ is} \\
& \text{socially preferred to } S_1
\end{cases}
$$

Case c), which involves cyclical majorities, corresponds to a voters' game with no core, whose solution is a mixed strategy, the components of which are socially intransitive. It is this case which will be studied in detail in the remainder of this paper. An example of case c) (to be used throughout the paper) is as follows (three voters and four social states A, B, C, D):

Voter Preference Orderings

Voter 1	Voter 2	Voter 3
A	C	D
B	A	B
C	D	C
D	B	A

Matrix of Game Played by Parties

Party II

		A	B	C	D
	A	0	1	−1	1
Party I	B	−1	0	1	−1
	C	1	−1	0	1
	D	−1	1	−1	0

Inspection of the matrix shows that majority rule yields an intransitive result: A defeats D, D defeats B, B defeats C, and C defeats A. Solving, as Shubik suggests, for a mixed strategy yields the result that each party should announce social states A, B, and D with probability 1/3 each. Note that D is defeated by A and C.

THE PLATFORM SELECTION MODEL

In contrast to Shubik's model, in which social states are defined directly, this model will define social states indirectly as outcomes of decisions on a set of bills $B = \{b_j | 1 \leq j \leq J\}$. A social state is defined as a J-vector, $S_i = (s_{i1}, \ldots, s_{ij}, \ldots, s_{iJ})$ of zeroes and ones, where $s_{ij} = 1$ if b_j passes in S_i, and $s_{ij} = 0$ if b_j fails. The set of possible social states is $S = \{S_i | 1 \leq i \leq 2^J\}$. Social states are represented by the vertices of a J-dimensional unit cube. Moreover, we shall suppose that a *platform* is characterized by a J-vector $X_k = (x_{k1}, \ldots, x_{kj}, \ldots, x_{kJ})$ with $0 \leq x_{kj} \leq 1$, where x_{kj} is the probability that party k, if elected, will pass b_j. The x_{kj} will be assumed to be independent probabilities of passage (i.e. the probability of party k passing a set of bills $B'(B' \subset B)$ is $\prod_{b_j \in B'} x_{kj}$). This assumption will be relaxed later, but throughout the paper the x_{kj} will be treated as independent probabilities. A platform is thus a point in a J-dimensional unit cube. With this characterization (as opposed to that of Shubik), a platform is more closely related to its counterpart in the actual political world in two ways: 1), it consists of statements about a number of particular issues (represented by bills) rather than about an abstract social state, and 2), it permits uncertainty as to what action would take place if the party were elected, a phenomenon often observed in political party platforms.

A final assumption, adopted for simplicity in the present discussion, concerns the voters' preference functions. Each voter is assumed to have a known and fixed additive utility function on the set of bills U_i $= (u_{i1}, \ldots, u_{ij}, \ldots, u_{iJ})$ where u_{ij} is the utility which voter i derives from the passage of b_j. Each voter casts his vote for the party which offers him the greatest expected utility (i.e. voter i votes for Party I if and only if $\sum_j u_{ij}x_{Ij} \geqq \sum_j u_{ij}x_{IIj}$, where X_I and X_{II} are the platforms of Parties I and II respectively). Indifferent voters are assumed to abstain. As before, that party offering the platform which ranks higher with a majority of the voters is elected. In the case of a tie vote, each party is elected with probability 1/2.

The use of cardinal utility might be objected to because of the increased amount of information which is required for the analysis of the model. While this objection is recognized, cardinal utility functions are included in the analysis for the following reasons: (1) they permit the voters to make their decisions under conditions of uncertainty, (2) they allow a much richer (and more realistic) strategy space from which to choose platforms, and (3) the results of the platform selection process under conditions of complete information (i.e. cardinal utility functions) may be compared with those derived under conditions with less information, providing some insight into the effects upon and costs to society of the lack of complete information. And surely, if a party can do better by employing a platform involving uncertainty, such a platform should be included in the model for completeness.

The fact that individual voters have additive utility functions allows platforms containing conditional probabilities to be decomposed into equivalent platforms containing independent probabilities. This possibility, which is demonstrated in Appendix A for the case of two bills, allows the analysis in this paper to be carried out in terms of independent probabilities only without precluding the use of conditional probability platforms by the parties. It does, however, render ineffectual any attempts by a party to gain votes through the use of a conditional probability platform, since the voters can easily find and evaluate the equivalent platform containing independent probabilities.

The analysis to follow will consider only a special case of the platform selection problem—that of three voters deciding between parties whose platforms deal with two bills. For this case, the platform space is a square, as shown in Figure 1. The corners of the square correspond to the possible social states.

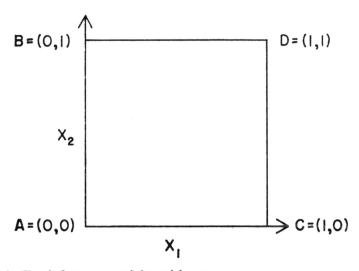

Figure 1 The platform space and the social states

The example used previously in relation to Shubik's model can now be restated in terms of the new assumptions. Figure 1 shows the platform space and the social states.

Social States

$A = (0, 0)$: the passage of neither bill
$B = (0, 1)$: the passage of b_2
$C = (1, 0)$: the passage of b_1
$D = (1, 1)$: the passage of b_1 and b_2

Voter Utility Functions
Utility from passage of

Voter	b_1	b_2
1	-2	-1
2	1	-2
3	1	4

Voter Preference Orderings
(utilities in parentheses)

Voter 1	Voter 2	Voter 3
A (0)	C (1)	D (5)
B (−1)	A (0)	B (4)
C (−2)	D (−1)	C (1)
D (−3)	B (−2)	A (0)

The preference orderings of the voters are unchanged and thus the Shubik-type randomization strategy would be to announce states A, B, and C each with probability 1/3. The problem for the parties remains the same, to choose a platform strategy (pure or mixed) which maximizes its probability of election.

The choice of the utility functions for this example has been made for a particular reason. These utility functions guarantee the existence of a strategy space (h_3 below) which has a unique property and is of special interest. In addition, the analysis of strategy space h_2 requires that no voter be indifferent about the outcome of a bill. Otherwise, the analysis below is true for any set of utility functions yielding cyclical majorities.

In Shubik's model, strategies may be drawn from either of two strategy spaces—the pure strategy space containing the social states as single elements, or the mixed strategy space containing randomizations over the social states. With social states defined as outcomes of decisions on two bills, the list of possible strategy spaces can be expanded. Let H be the expanded collection of strategy spaces. It includes, among others (each space is identified below by the strategies it contains):

h_0: the pure strategies consisting of a single social state (A, B, C, or D)

h_1: the randomizations over the social states A, B, C, and D

h_2: the pure strategies consisting of a single point in the platform space $X = (x_1, x_2)$ where $0 \leq x_j \leq 1$

h_3: the pure and mixed strategies on a set of points in the platform space which dominate all strategies in h_0 and h_1

h_4: the pure and mixed strategies on the straight lines in the platform space which connect opposite sides of the square and are parallel to an indifference line of one of the voters.

h_5: the randomizations over the points in the platform space. [More will be said later about h_3 and h_4 and the reasons for their inclusion.]

At this point it may be helpful to discuss the two types of randomization that gave been introduced into the analysis. The first is that introduced by Shubik and is the randomization involved in the use of a mixed strategy. This randomization over a set of pure strategies is carried out by the party leaders unbeknown to the voters. Its purpose is to provide secrecy, insuring that the opposing party will not be able to deduce its platform beforehand and profit from this knowledge. The second type of randomization is that explicity contained in a platform containing uncertainty about the outcomes of the bills (i.e. any platform not corresponding to a corner of the strategy space). The purpose of this type of randomization, which is considered by the voters in their voting decisions, is to take advantage of the different strengths of preference of the voters for the passage of the bills. In the following analysis either or both types of randomizations will occur in the different strategy spaces under consideration, and the above distinctions between them may be an aid in understanding exactly what types of platforms are contained in the various strategy spaces.

Shubik has shown that, for the case of cyclical majorities, an equilibrium strategy in h_0 cannot be found. The analysis below will show that, for the example chosen for this paper, an equilibrium strategy cannot be found in any of the next four strategy spaces h_1 through h_4. The fact that the first five strategy spaces do not contain an equilibrium strategy strongly suggests that the equilibrium strategy (if one exists) must be an element of h_5. That h_5 must contain the equilibrium strategy if it exists follows from the fact that h_5 is the most complete strategy space possible for this problem (it contains all other strategy spaces as subsets). The problem whose solution provides the equilibrium strategy in h_5 if one exists will be formulated.

STRATEGY SPACES h_1 AND h_2

For a given problem involving cyclical majorities, consider the solution in h_1 which is derived as Shubik has suggested. Let S' be the set of social states over which the randomization is to take place. For a point Y in h_2, let the set $D(Y)$ contain those elements of S' to which Y is strictly preferred by a majority of the voters. These states may be identified with the use of Figure 2, the shaded area of which shows those points which are dominated by an arbitrary point Z. (The lines in Figure 2 are the voter indifference lines from the example.)

Let $P(Y)$ be the sum of the probabilities assigned by the randomization over S' to the elements of $D(Y)$. Then any point Y for which $P(Y) > \frac{1}{2}$ will dominate the randomization over the elements of S'. In the example, any point preferred to A and B, or A and C, or B and C fulfills the above requirement. The set of such points is shown in Figure 3 E by the intersection of the areas dominating A, B, and C, where the areas have been constructed using the voter indifference curves. It will be noted that these areas (Figure 3 A–D) are cones, and that they are generated from three different

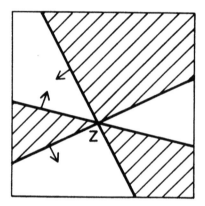

Figure 2   Areas dominated by an arbitrary point in a set of social states

vertices. The latter fact is due to the intransitivity among the social states, with no two voters preferring the same social state. A sufficient condition for the cones to have at least one non-empty intersection, when the cones are intersected pairwise, is that there be no voter who is indifferent about the outcome of one of the bills. This is the only condition which must be placed on the utility functions. This condition is sufficient to guarantee that all of the cones will have positive area; and three cones, each with positive area and generated by different vertices of a square, must have at least one non-empty pairwise intersection. If this condition is met, there will be a set of points in h_2, any of which will, as a pure strategy, dominate the randomization in h_1. Thus the latter cannot be an equilibrium strategy. For the example, it is interesting to note that while Shubik's strategy from h_1 yields no probability of D occurring, all of the points in h_2 that are shaded in Figure 3 E dominate Shubik's strategy and yield D with positive probability, and some (those in the northeast quadrant) yield D with higher probability than either A, B, or C.

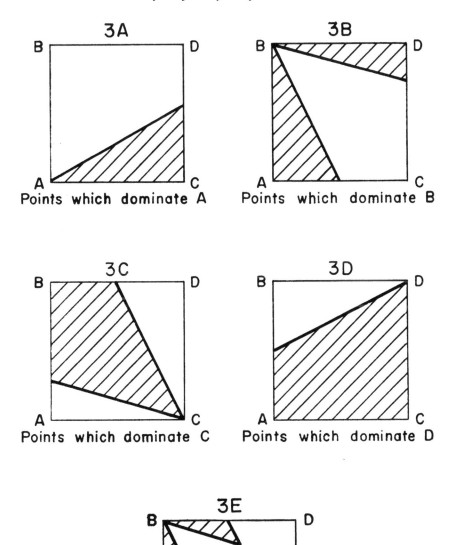

Figure 3 Examples of dominated points

It is also true that none of the points in h_2, including those shown shaded in Figure 3E, can be a pure equilibrium strategy. Reflection on Figure 2 will show that every point in the square is dominated by at least one other; therefore the first point cannot be an equilibrium strategy.

STRATEGY SPACE h_3

There is a particular set of points of special interest which might be consider-ed as a possible equilibrium strategy set. These are the points in the platform space which are socially preferred (as platforms) to all four social states (as platforms). As such, they dominate *any* strategy in spaces h_0 and h_1 for the case of cyclical majorities. This set of points is shown in black in Fi-gure 3E, as the intersection of the areas dominating social states A, B, C, and D. The existence of this set depends very critically upon the specific utility functions and it is therefore not of great value in a theory of platform selection, but its appeal as a set to be considered, if it exists, is strong. However, a pure strategy drawn from h_3 cannot be an equilibrium strategy since all points in the set are dominated by point V in Figure 3E, a fact which means that V is also socially preferred to any randomization over points in the set.

STRATEGY SPACE h_4

A line, connecting opposite sides of the platform space, and parallel to one of the voter indifference lines, contains strategies having interesting pro-perties—they are socially indifferent and collectively they dominate all other pure strategies available. For the example, consider Figure 2. If Z is moved along any of the three indifference curves, all of the area in the square will eventually be dominated by at least one point on the line. It was stated in the introduction that if the equilibrium strategy is a pure strategy, si-multaneous announcement of platforms by the parties is unnecessary. The strategies in h_4 cannot therefore be equilibrium strategies because simulta-neity is necessary if the party to announce first is not always to lose. That simultaneity is necessary can be seen from consideration of Figure 2 which shows that any point in the space is dominated by a set of points in the space, and there is thus no pure strategy which cannot be defeated. Strategy space h_4 also contains randomizations over these lines, but these strategies also cannot be equilibrium strategies. In Figure 4, let the chosen strategy be a randomization on the line PQ which is parallel to voter three's in-difference line. Consider point R an ε-distance above the line PQ, and point

S, below *PQ* and directly under *R.* As a pure strategy, *R* dominates all of *PQ* except the very small segment below *R. R* thus defeats any randomization on *PQ* which assigns probability greater than 1/2 to the part of *PQ* dominated by *R. S,* on the other hand, dominates that segment of *PQ* which is not dominated by *R.* So *S* defeats any randomization not defeated by *R,*

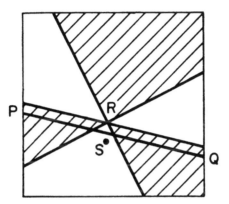

Figure 4 Strategies on a line parallel to a voter's indifference line

and therefore no randomization on *PQ* can be an equilibrium strategy. Similar constructions yield the same result for lines parallel to the indifference lines of the other two voters.

STRATEGY SPACE h_5

The above analysis has failed to locate an equilibrium strategy for the example under consideration. Strategy space h_5 will contain the equilibrium strategy if it exists because h_5 is the most general strategy space possible for the example, and the equilibrium strategy will be obtained by solving the following problem: Let $X = (x_1, x_2)$ be the platform space, where x_j is the probability of passing b_j. Let X_I and X_{II} be the platforms chosen by Parties I and II respectively. Let $\mu_i(X)$ be a measure on X for Party i such that (1) $\mu_i(X) \geqq 0$ for all X and (2) $\int_X \mu_i(X) = 1$. Furthermore, let

$$U(X_I, X_{II}) = \begin{cases} 1 & \text{if Parties I and II choose } X_I \text{ and } X_{II} \text{ and } X_I \text{ is socially} \\ & \text{preferred to } X_{II} \\ 0 & \text{if Parties I and II choose } X_I \text{ and } X_{II} \text{ and } X_I \text{ is socially} \\ & \text{indifferent to } X_{II} \\ -1 & \text{if Parties I and II choose } X_I \text{ and } X_{II} \text{ and } X_{II} \text{ is socially} \\ & \text{preferred to } X_I \end{cases}$$

Then Party I seeks that $\mu_I(X)$ which maximizes

$$\underset{\mu_{II}(X)}{\text{minimum}} \iint_X U(X_I, X_{II}) \, d_I(X) \, d_{II}(X)$$

for $\mu_I(X)$ in h_5. Party II seeks that $\mu_{II}(X)$ which minimizes

$$\underset{\mu_I(X)}{\text{maximum}} \iint_X U(X_I, X_{II}) \, d_I(X) \, d_{II}(X)$$

for $\mu_{II}(X)$ in h_5. The facts that the choice spaces h_5 for $\mu_I(X)$ and $\mu_{II}(X)$ are identical, and that the payoff function $U(X_I, X_{II})$ is skew-symmetric, imply that $\mu_I(X) = \mu_{II}(X)$, at equilibrium.

The author has been unable to prove or disprove the existence of an equilibrium strategy for this game. Appendix B discusses further the properties of the game in relation to the existing theory. In the event that no equilibrium strategy exists, the strategy spaces h_0 through h_4 assume new relevance, since they might then contain an "acceptable" (though not optimal) strategy. Since game theory cannot be of great assistance in choosing such an "acceptable" strategy, no more will be said concerning this choice process other than to point out two criteria which might be useful in the decision. These are (1) internal consistency in the strategy corresponding to the concept of ideology, and (2) a property similar to that of external stability in the Von Neumann–Morgenstern solution concept which insures that an "acceptable" strategy can with positive probability defeat any pure strategy chosen by an opponent (density functions in space h_4 have this property, for instance).

APPENDIX A

Let $X'_k = (x'_{k1}, x'_{k2}, x''_{k2})$ be the platform of Party k, where x'_{k1} is the probability of passage of b_1 (which be decided upon first), x_{k2} is the probability of passage of b_2 conditional upon b_1 passing, and x_{k2} is the probability of passage of b_2 conditional upon b_1 failing. Then

Proposition

X'_k is equivalent to a platform containing independent probabilities $X_k = (x_{k1}, x_{k2})$, where $x_{k1} = x'_{k1}$ and $x_{k2} = x'_{k1}x'_{k2} + (1 - x'_{k1}) x''_{k2}$.

Proof: The expected utility of voter i for X'_k is

$$E(U_i(X'_k)) = (u_{i1} + u_{i2}) x'_{k1}x'_{k2} + u_{i1}x'_{k1}(1 - x'_{k2}) + u_{i2}(1 - x'_{k1}) x''_{k2}$$
$$+ (0)(1 - x'_{k1})(1 - x''_{k2})$$
$$= u_{i1}(x'_{k1}x'_{k2} + x'_{k1} - x'_{k1}x'_{k2}) + u_{i2}(x'_{k1}x'_{k2} + (1 - x'_{k1}) x''_{k2})$$
$$= u_{i1}x'_{k1} + u_{i2}(x'_{k1}x'_{k2} + (1 - x'_{k1}) x''_{k2})$$

The expected utility of voter i for X_k is

$$E(U_i(X_k)) = u_{i1}x_{k1} + u_{i2}x_{k2}$$

Letting $x_{k1} = x'_{k1}$ and $x_{k2} = x'_{k1}x'_{k2} + (1 - x_{k1})x_{k2}$ in the above equation shows the desired equivalence. In his voting decision, voter i can treat the platform X'_k exactly as he would the platform X_k.

APPENDIX B

The 2-person game played by the parties has an infinite number of pure strategies for each player. Karlin (1959) has shown that 2-person games with infinitely many pure strategies have equilibrium solutions if:

1) the strategy spaces of two players are convex
2) the payoff function $U(X_I, X_{II})$ is a real-valued function that is convex in X_{II} and concave in X_I.

Subsequent generalizations have relaxed the conditions imposed on the payoff function, but the generalizations have not been so broad as to include the type of payoff function exhibited by the game discussed in this paper. The strategy sets of this game are convex, but the payoff function is not convex/concave in pure strategies as is required. Figure 5B below shows the shape of the payoff function for Party I when Party I uses pure strategy A and Party II uses a pure strategy on the line BC. The payoff function obviously has none of the convexity properties required by the theory. The payoff function is convex/concave (it is bilinear) in mixed strategies, however. Figure 5C shows the payoff function for Party I when it uses pure strategy A and Party II uses a mixed strategy between pure strategies B and C, playing B with probability p. In addition to this property, the game has two other regularity properties which are not required by the theory, but which might be helpful in constructing proofs concerning the game. These are the facts that the payoff function is zero-sum and skew-symmetric. The author, however, has been unable to prove or disprove the existence of an equilibrium solution using these facts.

The general difficulty in proving that no equilibrium solution exists is due to the intractability of the payoff function when strategies consisting of density functions or mass functions on a denumerable number of points are under consideration. These difficulties were sufficient to force the author to abandon his search for a definite answer concerning the existence of an equilibrium solution.

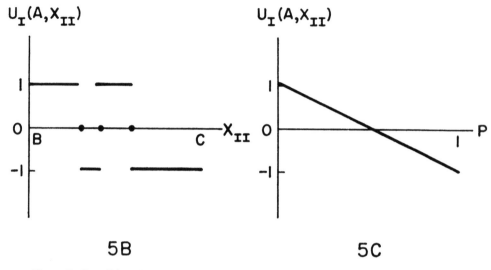

Figure 5 Payoff functions

NOTES

1 Prepared for presentation at the Social Choice Conference University of Pittsburgh, September 9–12, 1968.
2 Shubik (1968), p. 9–10.

REFERENCES

Karlin, S. *Mathematical Methods and Theory in Games, Programming and Economics.* Vol. 2. Massachusetts: Addison-Weslay, 1959.
Shubik, M. A Two-Party System, General Equilibrium and the Voters' Paradox. Research Memorandum No. 16, Institute for Advanced Study, Vienna, Austria, 1968.

PARTICIPANTS AND ATTENDANTS
OF THE CONFERENCE

The Conference on the Descriptive and Normative Aspects of Social Choice was held at the University of Pittsburgh from September 9 through 13, 1968. The following people participated in, or attended, one or more sessions of the conference. The institutions listed below are the institutions the participants were affiliated with at the time of the conference:

Bernhardt Lieberman	University of Pittsburgh
R. Duncan Luce	University of Pennsylvania
Jacob G. Birnberg	University of Pittsburgh
Bliss Cartwright	University of Chicago
Dorwin Cartwright	University of Michigan
John Chamberlin	Stanford University
David Chapman	University of Lancaster
James S. Coleman	Johns Hopkins University
L. L. Cummings	University of Wisconsin
Otto A. Davis	Carnegie-Mellon University
Lawrence Fouraker	Harvard University
D. L. Harnett	Indiana University
Charles Harsch	Office of Naval Research
Melvin J. Hinich	Carnegie-Mellon University
Lawrence A. Messe	Michigan State University
Charles Plott	Purdue University
Louis R. Pondy	Duke University
Douglas W. Rae	Yale University
Howard Raiffa	Harvard University
William H. Riker	University of Rochester
Jerome Rothenberg	Massachusetts Institute of Technology
Sam Rothman	Department of the Navy
Jack Sawyer	University of Chicago
Maynard Shelley	University of Kansas
Lorraine Torres	National Institute of Mental Health
W. Edgar Vinacke	State University of New York at Buffalo
Richard H. Willis	University of Pittsburgh
Robert Wilson	Stanford University

For Product Safety Concerns and Information please contact our EU
representative GPSR@taylorandfrancis.com
Taylor & Francis Verlag GmbH, Kaufingerstraße 24, 80331 München, Germany

www.ingramcontent.com/pod-product-compliance
Ingram Content Group UK Ltd.
Pitfield, Milton Keynes, MK11 3LW, UK
UKHW021836240425
457818UK00006B/208